About the Authors

ARTHUR C. KLEIN & DAVA SOBEL are the authors of *Arthritis: What* Really *Works* (Robinson, 1994), an evaluation of treatments that really help, based on an unprecedented and extensive survey of more than 1,000 people in the USA with osteo- or rheumatoid arthritis. The result was described in the *Sunday Telegraph* as "a truly excellent book" and sold nearly half a million copies in the USA alone. Their finding that exercise was the most powerful treatment for many forms of arthritis led to a follow-up book, *Arthritis: What Exercises* Really *Work*, which was published in the UK in 1996. The two books were issued in a combined edition, *Arthritis: The Complete Guide to Relief* (Robinson, 1998).

Dava Sobel has spent most of her professional life as a science writer, and is the author of the bestseller, *Longitude*. Arthur C. Klein is a member of the American Society of Journalists and Authors, and the American Medical Writers Association.

D1149610

Note

This book is intended as a reference volume only, not a manual for self-treatment.

Every effort has been made to ensure the contents of this book are accurate and current. Medical and pharmaceutical knowledge is constantly changing and the application of it to particular circumstances depends on many factors. Therefore readers are urged always to consult a qualified medical specialist for individual advice. The writers, researchers and publishers of this book cannot be held liable for any errors or omissions, or action that may be taken as a consequence of using it.

A list of useful names and addresses for those with back problems is included at the end of the book.

The Daily Telegraph
BACKACHE
The Complete Guide to Relief

comprising

BACKACHE RELIEF
&
BACKACHE
WHAT EXERCISES *REALLY* WORK

Arthur C. Klein and Dava Sobel

ROBINSON
London

Robinson Publishing Ltd
7 Kensington Church Court
London W8 4SP

This combined edition first published
in the UK by Robinson Publishing Ltd 1999

Backache Relief first published in the USA by St Martin's Press 1985.
Backache: What Exercises Really *Work* first published in the UK
by Robinson Publishing Ltd 1996; first published in the USA
by St Martin's Press 1994.

A copy of the British Library Cataloguing in Publication data
is available from the British Library.

ISBN 1–84119–087–X

Printed and bound in the EC

10 9 8 7 6 5 4 3 2 1

Introduction

For virtually everyone the chances that at some time in their lives "something will go wrong" with their backs are considerable. There are, after all, more muscles, joints, bones, nerves and ligaments running up and down the vertebrae in close proximity to each other than in any other part of the body. The subtle complexity of the interaction of these spinal structures, as back pain sufferers know only too well, can make it difficult for even the best trained doctors with the most sophisticated diagnostic techniques to determine precisely what is amiss.

Hence the impasse. Tens of thousands of people are laid low with back pain — whether acute or chronic — every year. For some, the lucky ones, it resolves within a few weeks with the judicious combination of rest and exercises supplemented by painkillers and anti-inflammatory drugs. But what of the rest? There are, as Arthur Klein and Dava Sobel point out, a myriad of different specialists involved in the treatment of back pain, each with their own opinion as to the likely explanation and the best way of putting it right. Amidst this babble of competing views, the back pain sufferer can understandably find it difficult to know where to turn or how to evaluate their claims of efficacy. One vital source of information, much neglected but of great importance, is the judgment of the real experts, back pain sufferers themselves.

It was a most ingenious idea to invite the jury, namely 500 people with back pain, to deliver their verdict based on their own personal experience of the relative efficacy of the various treatments on offer. There are, of course, several different types of back pain, even though in any individual the precise pathology that gives rise to their symptoms may not be easy to pin down. These subdivide into a few main groups — slipped (or ruptured) disc, arthritis, sciatica and spondylosis and the authors invited the participants in their survey to assess which of the several options — manipulation, physiotherapy, cortisone injections or an operation proved most effective and in what situation.

The overall impression is of "horses for courses" where the efficacy of the various approaches varies widely. There are several surprises with chiropractic rating less well than might be expected, while the apparently definitive method of curing back pain — surgery — proved, in the experience of the respondents to the survey, to be particularly disappointing.

There are obvious limitations to this personal and anecdotal assessment of therapy but this is far outweighed by its virtues. First, it conveys very well the scope of possible treatments, both orthodox and otherwise, along with their drawbacks. Further, it emphasizes how, for many of those with chronic back pain the best solution lies in going beyond expert opinion to take control of their condition by deploying judicious forms of self-treatment. Much the most important of these are the exercises deemed safe and effective by specialists at Cornell University in New York that increase the suppleness of the spinal column and strengthen the muscles that sustain it. These are described in detail in the second half of this book.

Like all family doctors I see at least a couple of patients with back pain every week and am delighted that in addition to other appropriate advice and specialist referral I can now recommend a book that offers the best hope of long-term relief of their symptoms for many of them.

Dr James Le Fanu

Backache Relief

For Zoë Rachel Klein

A Note for the UK Edition

Throughout the book, some terms common to the US rather than the UK are used. Your physical therapist means your physiotherapist, and orthopedist is an orthopaedic surgeon, for example. The term physiatrist does not have an exact equivalent in the UK, the closest probably being a physician who specializes in rehabilitation. In addition, the symbol "#" is sometimes used to indicate "number". There are also references to private healthcare costs which do not apply to the UK in the same way.

Many of the drugs mentioned in this book are known under different brand names in the UK and the USA. A few are not available in the UK, and in addition new drugs, not mentioned here, have become available since this book was first written. The following list covers the different names under which the principal drugs mentioned in the text are known in the two countries:

Name in USA	UK
acetaminophen	paracetamol, Panadol
Ascriptin	aspirin
Ben-Gay	Deep Heat
chymopapain	not available in UK
Clinoril	available in UK
Darvocet	paracetamol
Darvon	paracetamol
Demerol	morphine
DMSO	not available in UK
Equagesic	available in UK
Indocin	Indomethacin
Mobisyl	Deep Heat
Motrin	available in UK
Naprosyn	Naproxen
Pantopaque	not available in UK
Parafon Forte	not available in UK
Percodan	Oxycodone (available in UK as suppository)
Robaxin	available in UK
Salon Pas	paracetamol
Soma	Carisoma (not available in UK)
Tylenol	Tylex (prescription only)
Valium	available in UK

Acknowledgements

Our thanks to Donna Danyluk, Millie Mascia, Page McBrier, and especially Evelyn Poitras for their help with the research on which this book is based and the preparation of the manuscript;

To our literary agent, Max Gartenberg, who helped define the scope and structure of the book;

To Miriam Fisher, our first survey participant, for her many contributions to the background research;

To Frank Anello for his support and inspiration;

And to Jonathan B. Segal of Times Books for his advice, encouragement, and enthusiasm.

Foreword

This updated edition provides important new information about diagnosing and treating back pain. It also contains the landmark research that makes *Backache: The Complete Guide to Relief* the definitive guide to what works, and what doesn't work, in relieving different kinds of back pain.

The major questions on back sufferers' minds are answered in this book.

For example, what steps can you take right now to stop pain? Which kinds of health-care practitioners are most likely to help you . . . or waste your time . . . or make you worse? Which new treatments should you know about? What are the best exercises for your back? Which methods work best for specific kinds of back pain? Are there unorthodox healing approaches that get proven results?

Backache: The Complete Guide to Relief brings you solutions based on an unprecedented survey of the ultimate experts on back pain—*sufferers themselves*.

These are the individuals who have found ways out of seemingly incurable back pain. They are the people who have been through it all, heard it all, tried it all, yet managed to emerge on the other side with life-changing answers.

I am one of these people, although, ironically, there was a time in my own life when I would have looked down my nose at anyone who couldn't manage back pain.

Low back pain ran in my family and I had my first acute episode of muscle spasms at 18. For more than 20 years, I held back pain at bay. I bought a bed board and a firm mattress. I found a good "writer's chair"—one that supported my lower back and raised my knees higher than my hips. I worked out three times a week at a gym. I did daily stretching and strengthening exercises for my back. I swam. I ran six miles a day. Incapacitating back pain? Bed rest? Lost work days? Ha! No way. Not me. That was for other people.

Then one day my right Achilles tendon swelled up and my ankle all but locked in place. I had to walk with crutches. I got to the gym pool every day, but, generally, I had to sit more and exercise less. My legs, hips and buttocks began to spasm day and night. The backs of my things ached intensely. Still, I felt relatively fortunate. I finally had a diagnosis for my ankle problem. I was sure I could find a treatment for it. I eagerly envisioned the day when I could walk normally again and get my back into better shape.

That didn't happen for a while. One evening, after dinner at a restaurant with my wife, I felt a horrid vice-like aching in my back and legs. The tightening soon became unendurable and I lowered myself to the floor before I fell. It was hours before I could crawl to my bed.

A year later, I still wasn't on top of the world, in spite of having seen an internist, two orthopedists, a sports podiatrist, a neurologist, a Chinese herbal specialist, a doctor of physical medicine, an acupuncturist, a chiropractor and a physical therapist.

Eventually, I found the help I needed. Had I known then what I know now, however, I would have saved myself an awful lot of anguish, including the almost unbearable emotional pain of not being able to pick up, hold, and cuddle my newborn daughter.

I don't mention all this because the answers I found for myself will solve your problems. I needed ankle surgery and treatment of a neuromuscular disorder to correct the underlying cause of my back pain.

I mention my own experience because they motivated me to carry out the research for this book.

I simply couldn't get the same answer twice about back pain. And, many times, I couldn't get *any* answers. Small wonder. Owing to the thinness of research in the field, even back practitioners themselves often don't know how well or poorly most treatments work. The common cold is taken more seriously. However, I believe that the research in this book—including a new Appendix updating treatments and diagnostic procedures—will help change that. For certain, I expect, hope, and pray that this book will be the start of the end of *your* back misery.

Arthur C. Klein
January 1999

A Note About the Research

The information, ratings, and advice in this book are based on the results of the most extensive survey of back sufferers ever undertaken. Individuals volunteered to participate in the survey by responding to public notices and advertisements in the following publications: *American Business, Columbia Journalism Review, East-West, Family Weekly, In These Times, Moneysworth, Mother Jones, New Era, New York* magazine, *The New York Times, Prevention,* and *Saturday Review.* In addition, some participants referred us to other back sufferers, who became participants.

Ninety-three of the total 492 participants responded by telephone. We interviewed each of these for an average of fifty-five minutes. The remaining participants inquired by mail and were sent a questionnaire. When we received a completed questionnaire, we followed up by telephone whenever necessary to expand or clarify a particular point of information.

Nearly 40 percent of individuals surveyed were readers of *Family Weekly.* This magazine is distributed in more than 200 medium-sized American cities, and the demographics of its readers closely match those of the general public.

Survey participants represent every stratum of American society, from the wealthy and famous to those who can no longer afford medical treatment. Arthur Ochs Sulzberger, publisher of *The New York Times,* filled out a questionnaire. John Davidson, goalie for the New York Rangers, phoned in his response after a chymopapain injection for a herniated disc. A weight-lifting champion and a Pulitzer Prize-winning author also told us about their back problems. Health-care specialists—including medical technicians, dentists, chiropractic students, nurses, psychotherapists, massage therapists, marriage counselors, and alcoholism counselors—told about their ups and downs with back pain. Farmers and forest rangers, teachers and students shared their experiences. So did a federal labor arbitrator, a concert pianist, housewives, truck drivers, secretaries, professors, marathon runners, construction workers, salespeople, entrepreneurs, and prisoners. The youngest participant was a 10-year-old girl whose mother helped her fill out the questionnaire. The oldest participant was a 90-year-old woman who had just encountered back pain for the first time and who rid herself of her pain by taking her doctor's advice to walk one mile every day.

At least 55 percent of the participants were female and 44 percent were male; one percent chose not to answer the question about sex. The vast majority of individuals were under age 50. Persons 18 and younger constituted one percent of the sample; 19 to 29, 28 percent; 30 to 49, 44 percent; 50 to 64, 18 percent; and 65 and older, 7 percent. These findings concur with available research about the sex and age of back sufferers.

All participants, whether orally or in writing, answered questions contained in a two-page questionnaire. Topics included types of practitioners seen, diagnosis from each practitioner, treatments and advice received, evaluation of each practitioner and treatment, exercise (frequency and source of instruction), emotional stress (its role in back pain and the practitioner's approach to it), tips for back sufferers, and personal data (optional).

Two years passed from the time the first public notice appeared until the results of this survey were tabulated. When the number of participants reached 100, significant trends were already apparent for the most widely seen practitioners—orthopedists, chiropractors, general practitioners, physical therapists, and osteopaths. At 200, the reasons behind these trends were clear, and more than twenty-five different kinds of health-care specialists and thirty-five different kinds of treatments had been reported. However, these could not be adequately evaluated. At 400, we had enough data to appraise virtually every kind of practitioner and treatment available to back sufferers.

Why, then, was the final count 492? Because the authors had a whim to have participants from every one of the fifty states.

So, thank you Laura L. of Alaska for allowing us to conclude this research on a happy note.

CONTENTS

position for lying in bed, how to ease pain, techniques for stress reduction, diet, preparation for exercise, posture, avoiding reinjury) . . . Summary and evaluation of treatments and practitioners for acute, severe low back pain

Two exemplary case histories . . . Attitude: taking charge of the problem and changing your life accordingly . . . How to lift and carry (from groceries to children) . . . Sitting (how to select a good chair for relaxation or desk work, how to make a car seat more comfortable) . . . Exercise (how to structure an individualized exercise regimen; complete instructions for a safe, eleven-step exercise program based on survey participants' experiences) . . . Summary and evaluation of treatments and practitioners for chronic low back pain

Acute pain: bed rest . . . Home vs. hospital . . . Risks of traction . . . Advisability of surgery—laminectomy, diskectomy . . . Outcomes of surgery . . . Outcomes of nonsurgical treatments . . . Danger of chiropractic treatment for acute disc pain . . . Summary and evaluation of treatments and practitioners for acute disc pain . . . Chronic disc pain: special exercise advice . . . Individualized exercise therapy . . . Walking and swimming as alternatives to back exercises . . . Gravity inversion . . . Spinal fusion . . . Summary and evaluation of treatments and practitioners for chronic disc pain

Differences between neck pain and other kinds of back pain . . . Onset . . . Diagnosis . . . Acute, severe neck pain: staying active . . . Best sleep positions . . . Risks of traction . . . Ice . . . Self-massage techniques . . . Prescription drug pitfalls . . . Manipulation . . . Cervical collars . . . Practitioners to see for neck pain . . . Summary and evaluation of treatments and practitioners for acute, severe neck pain . . . Chronic neck pain: physical, emotional, and attitudinal changes . . . Stress management . . . Neck posture . . . Neck exercises . . . Integrating neck and shoulder exercises into basic back regimen . . . Tips on avoiding neck pain while talking on telephone, reading, watching television, driving . . . Summary and evaluation of treatments and practitioners for chronic neck pain

Arthritis Foundation vs. the medical profession . . . Diagnostic terms . . . Medical specialists who can help . . . Medical practitioners with less to offer . . . Guidelines for getting

Chapter 16
Helping Your Back: Tips for Performing Twenty-Five Common Activities

Making love . . . Making the bed . . . Staying warm . . . Getting enough rest . . . Reading at bedtime . . . Organizing closets for easy dressing . . . Using the toilet . . . Bathing . . . Cleaning the bathroom . . . Washing dishes . . . Dining . . . Washing floors . . . Sweeping . . . Reaching high shelves . . . Sitting . . . Vacuuming . . . Dusting and window washing . . . Moving furniture . . . Painting . . . Raking leaves . . . Shoveling snow . . . Splitting and carrying firewood . . . Lifting and hauling debris . . . Gardening . . . Sitting at stadium, beach, or picnic

Appendix
Update of Treatments and Diagnostic Procedures

Part One
An Introduction

"Given the ubiquity of [back pain], its importance to society, and its impact on the delivery of medical services, both the quantity and quality of therapeutic research in this area are disappointing."

—Richard A. Deyo, MD, MPH,
writing in the *Journal of the
American Medical Association
(JAMA)*
August 26, 1983

"I believe that back sufferers could help one another a lot by sharing their experiences."

—A survey participant

Chapter 1

Relief Is in Sight

Americans suffer more pain and disability from back problems than from any other ailment. To add to their woes, they also suffer the frustration of having to figure out for themselves which of the many kinds of practitioners, all of whom claim high degrees of success, can help them—and which of the numerous, highly touted treatments and self-help approaches may offer relief.

Suppose you have recurring and incapacitating muscle spasms with accompanying low back pain. Do you simply start making the rounds and hope for the best? Is self-treatment the best answer? Do you listen to your neighbor when she suggests acupuncture? If the meter reader was helped by triggerpoint injections, does that mean they will work for you? Is your mother-in-law right about the value of manipulation? Which kinds of exercises help most? Does gravity inversion help at all? Are chymopapain, TENS, biofeedback, and yoga effective?

What about medical doctors versus other practitioners? Do doctors know best? If so, which kinds of doctors? The orthopedist, the doctor of physical medicine, the sports medicine specialist, the neurologist, the psychiatrist who administers biofeedback, the rheumatologist, the MD acupuncturist? Will your general practitioner do just as well?

How about the sometimes maligned but increasingly popular practitioners like chiropractors, physical therapists, holistic massage therapists, kinesiologists, Rolfers, posture therapists, and yoga instructors? What do their track records look like for various back problems? And why do a *majority* of back sufferers eventually get around to seeing one or more of them?

The questions are almost endless. Answers, at least unbiased and documented ones, scarcely exist. Indeed, "Research on back ailments has lagged far behind the study of other disorders," according to *The New York Times*. "Controlled trials for backache treatments are all but non-existent," proclaims Dr. Murray Goldstein, director of the National Institute for Neurological and Communicative Disorders and Stroke. And a physician writing recently in the *Journal of the American Medical Association* concludes that even the few existing studies were conducted so poorly that their findings are of virtually no use to practitioners.

Backache Relief was written to fill this void—to provide answers that can save you literally months and years of needless pain and incapacitation. No matter how long you've suffered back pain, no matter how many practitioners, treatments, and self-help approaches you've tried, you'll find answers here that will help you.

Backache Relief is the only resource that actually documents the effectiveness and ineffectiveness of *more than 100 different practitioners, treatments, and self-help therapies*. Its findings are based on an extensive survey that took two years to complete—correspondence and interviews with nearly 500 back sufferers from every state in the nation.

These people have a great deal to offer you. They understand the time- and money-saving truths about a chaotic and fragmented area of health care. They know when self-care should include professional care—and when you're better off treating yourself. They can tell you what works and what doesn't in treating the following kinds of back pain: low back syndrome, sciatica, herniated discs, osteoarthritis-based back pain, neck pain, scoliosis, and spondylolisthesis. They know because, collectively, they have tried everything.

They can also help you steer clear of inept and worthless practitioners and treatments that account for a significant chunk of the roughly $20 billion spent every year on back care. They can tell you which therapies are often injurious. To cite just one example, 29 percent of individuals with herniated discs were injured by one widely used treatment, and another 23 percent were injured by a second common treatment approach. And nonmedical practitioners are not the only villains. Practitioner-related injuries are spread throughout the field of back care.

Here are some specific highlights of how you will benefit from the unique information in this self-care guide:

- You will discover how to put together an *individualized* back exercise program that is likely to be far more effective than others you may have tried.

- You will learn about the virtually unknown medical specialist who is *300 percent* more effective than his orthopedist colleague.

- You will learn the truth, once and for all, about chiropractic medicine—why manipulation is *not* the most useful treatment in the chiropractor's arsenal, what percentage of patients were helped or hindered in the short and long run by 422 chiropractors mentioned in the survey, and which chiropractors are achieving far and away the best results with their patients.

- You will learn who is more effective, the orthopedist or the chiropractor. Overall, the chiropractor has a slight edge. But there are more than a dozen practitioners—doctors and non-doctors alike—who achieve results that are superior to those of either the orthopedist or the chiropractor.

- You will receive documented results about the use of new or controversial techniques such as anti-gravity devices, chymopapain, sclerotherapy, acupuncture, nerve blocks, nutritional supplements, and many others.

- You will find out why the emergency room of a hospital is one of the most dangerous places to go when you have a back problem.

- You will learn the twenty-five most popular and proven-effective tips from back sufferers all over the country as well as suggestions on safely carrying out twenty-five common activities, from making love to raking leaves and shoveling snow.

- You will receive information about "home remedies," from liniments to hot soaks to facts and figures about the illegal substances DMSO and marijuana.

- You will learn to identify, and avoid, the many widely prescribed back treatments (about *half* of all those available) that have no more value than a placebo.

- And women readers will discover why it is almost always a mistake to mention back pain to an obstetrician.

Backache Relief fills the void between what practitioners *claim* is true and what back sufferers *know* is true. And this void is largely responsible for perpetuating an ignored epidemic in this country.

The numbers tell the story. Some 80 million Americans have back pain at some point in their lives. And this figure continues to grow, in spite of the burgeoning number of books, magazine articles, and TV shows on the subject. Moreover, according to a finding recently reported in *The New York Times* by personal health columnist Jane Brody and confirmed by our research: "For about half of its victims backache becomes a recurring affliction that repeatedly disrupts normal habits of work and play."

The myths also tell the story. The most widely seen practitioners—orthopedists and chiropractors—are among the *least* effective (although this book tells you how to select members of both professions who are highly successful). The most helpful practitioners are seldom heard about, and many are not even thought of as back practitioners. A majority of routinely administered treatments are all but worthless, while less expensive, less publicized, and more beneficial approaches are seldom brought to the public's attention.

All in all, and certainly through no fault of their own, back sufferers are misinformed and uninformed. Hence, we have the unmerry-go-round effect in which the average, long-term back sufferer has seen five practitioners and has incurred untold expense and pain for twelve years before getting the problem under control. *Backache Relief* gives you the information you need to minimize or eliminate pain—not just in the short run, but for a lifetime. In effect, it puts you in touch with dozens or hundreds of people with back pain similar to yours—people who have "been through it all," but, more important, people who have put their problems behind them.

Most of the information in this book takes the form of immediately usable, pain-preventing advice. The remaining information is more subtle but no less valuable. It includes knowing what questions to ask; being knowledgeable enough not to be taken in by meaningless or irrelevant diagnoses; understanding the odds that certain therapies have of working; knowing if you are on a dead-end course, and if so, what to do about it; taking comfort that you are not the only person who has been blamed for having a chronic back problem; realizing that a thirty-minute daily regimen of back exercises does not prevent or solve everyone's problems—but that there are alternatives.

This book amounts to a nationwide self-help group in print. It is filled with real people who had or still have problems like yours, who made the rounds without the benefit of guidelines. The average participant in our survey was given a half-dozen different kinds of treatments and relieved of untold amounts of time and money in the process.

It doesn't have to be that way for you. This book lets back sufferers speak for themselves, and to each other, *to help one another.*

Chapter 2

These People Can Help You

At age 45 Tony was a superb physical specimen. He ran ten miles every day. His abdominal muscles were so highly developed that fifty bent-knee sit-ups felt like child's play. He was also remarkably limber. The yoga Plough was a comfortable exercise for him. So was bending over with his knees locked and touching his palms to the floor.

This was Tony's physical condition when he first experienced back pain—"twisting his back," as he put it—while playing basketball with his 16-year-old son.

More than four years passed before Tony found a way to treat and solve increasingly incapacitating muscle spasms. For four years, he somehow coped well enough with the pain to make a living as a top executive for a computer company. He saw some of the most illustrious back specialists in the country, including a sports orthopedist for a professional football team, the chief neurologist of a major rehabilitation center, and a doctor of physical medicine who is a well-known author. He tried a wide array of treatments, from triggerpoint injections to biofeedback, from manipulation to acupuncture to a prescribed exercise program.

Tony finally did find a solution. But the trial-and-error course he had to trace through a maze of practitioners and therapies cost him dearly in dollars, time, and suffering.

It doesn't have to be that way.

For thirteen years Teresa worked as a teacher, spending most days on her feet, stooping to look at children's work, bending to help tie shoes, and stretching to write on the blackboard. Throughout these years, although she never did any kind of regular exercise, Teresa was free of back pain until she painted her house during a summer recess. Then she felt aching in her legs, and a week later, she recalled, "I couldn't move, couldn't get dressed or get to the bathroom, and I was admitted to the hospital." The orthopedist in charge of her case prescribed muscle relaxants, painkillers, traction, and a month of bed rest. By the end of the summer, Teresa had improved enough to return to work.

A few months later, though, the pain returned. This time it was even worse. "It was decision time," Teresa said. "My family doctor was finished with me. Should I try another orthopedist, an osteopath, a chiropractor, a neurosurgeon? My husband and I discussed it at length and we decided to try a chiropractor."

After fifteen months of chiropractic care, Teresa was hanging on, but just barely. Something else had to be done. "It looked like I was going to be tied to this chiropractor for life . . . never mind the monthly expense. I really couldn't figure out where to turn."

Eventually Teresa stumbled on to an alternative plan that worked. But the misery she suffered probably could have been avoided *if* the information she needed had been available.

Ann could always put up with the minor low back pain she felt for a few days every month before her menstrual period. But the pain flared up during her first pregnancy and then continued to grow considerably worse.

"That's the price we pay for walking upright," a gynecologist told her, adding, "No one ever died of low back pain." He also told her that she would be fine once she had given birth.

When Ann's pain worsened during her child's infancy, she went to an orthopedist. He found nothing wrong and suggested sit-ups and double leg raises (lying on her back and simultaneously raising both legs). The pain increased until she had to rule out exercise of any kind.

As her child became heavier, Ann suffered every time she picked him up. About every three months she had an episode of back spasms that made it impossible for her to get out of bed without her husband's help. Five years and numerous practitioners later, Ann finally brought her problem under control.

"But my back problem should never have gotten out of control in the first place," Ann concluded. "I listened to the usual medical advice and wound up with the usual outcome—more back pain. Back sufferers deserve to know some hard facts and truths. And this kind of 'consumer guide' information simply hasn't been available."

Bob is the kind of back sufferer no back specialist likes to talk about. He has been examined and treated by orthopedists and chiropractors, osteopaths and naturopaths, and other conventional and alternative health-care practitioners. He doesn't know what is wrong with his back. No two of his twelve diagnoses are the same—and none makes sense to him. He has read widely about back pain, been everywhere, tried everything.

There are at least 1.5 million—and maybe as many as 5 million—severely disabled back sufferers like Bob.

"Some doctors who know about the chronicity of my problem," Bob said, "won't even allow me to make an appointment to see them. If they do agree to examine me, they're all but itching to get me out the door. It is assumed that I have workmen's compensation or some other kind of insurance, which I don't, or that I am a neurotic who enjoys the attention. Actually I live alone and nobody pays me any attention unless I'm up and about. Some obviously think I'm a malingerer, even though I worked from age 14 to 40. It's just been the past five years that I've not been able to be on my feet long enough to hold down a job. I am living off my savings, which are about depleted."

After filling out his survey questionnaire, Bob wrote in a postscript, "I hope that your book won't leave out people like me. I hope it won't be another simplistic Six Minutes a Day to Relief, full of 'guaranteed safe' exercises I can't even do."

In our own postscript, we are happy to add that Bob has started to find a way out of his prolonged nightmare of disability. His prognosis for normal functioning is good.

Teresa, Tony, Ann, and Bob—and the 488 other people in this survey—give you information, insights, and practical advice that have never before been available, *and that often run counter to so-called common wisdom.*

The experts have had their say about relieving back pain. Now listen to the people who know which prescriptions work.

Part Two

Back Practitioners

"Health, like excellence in any form, comes from the individual's own efforts. The doctor who doctors best is a thoughtful spectator to this process."

—George A. Sheehan, MD,
from *Dr. Sheehan on Running*

"The goal of every back sufferer should be self-care. The question is who can best help us to reach that goal."

—A survey participant

Chapter 3

Medical Doctors: The Best Are the Least Known

Whether you swear by doctors, swear at doctors, or aren't sure what to think about their role in treating back sufferers, the information that follows will provide you with useful guidelines.

Myths and misconceptions about back doctors abound, for two major reasons. First, little information is available about the success or failure of doctors who treat backs. Second, the public usually hears only one side of the story—the doctors'. Doctors pen the best-selling back books, regularly offer advice to magazine and newspaper readers, and most often appear on TV and radio shows to talk about relieving back pain.

Not surprisingly, then, the most commonly held myth about back care is that most people will find an answer to their back problems by seeing a medical doctor.

The facts say otherwise. It is true that nine out of ten people in this survey started their treatments by seeing a medical doctor, but only 38 percent concluded their treatments under a medical doctor's care. The rest resolved their problems by seeing a practitioner who was neither a medical doctor nor an individual working under the supervision of a medical doctor, such as a physical therapist.

Other unexpected facts and helpful insights about medical doctors that emerged from the survey can help you pursue the proper treatment for your back now and help you care for it yourself in the long run. Here are some highlights that will be explored further in this chapter.

- Physiatrists (doctors of physical and rehabilitative medicine) don't get much publicity, but they have the best record of any practitioner for treating all kinds of back problems, including low back pain and herniated discs.

- Doctors who catch your attention in the mass media are *not* representative of their colleagues. For example, the orthopedist who talks about his new book on the *Phil Donahue* show may indicate a great interest in working with most back sufferers—not just the few who require surgery—but this interest is atypical. And unless you learn how to select the right kind of doctor, the search can take years of hit-and-miss appointments.

- Despite the positive attitude of the American Medical Association toward back exercise, and the advice about exercise published in its own consumer back book, our survey found that only 15 percent of medical doctors prescribe (or even mention) exercise. By knowing which kinds of doctors to see, however, you can practically guarantee yourself a corrective exercise regimen if a self-help program isn't helping you maximize your progress.

- Prominent back specialists have popularized the idea that stress contributes to back pain. Yet only 29 percent of doctors mentioned stress to their back patients, and half these doctors talked about it in a "hostile and unconstructive way," as though the patient were beyond help, according to survey participants. Nearly all negative comments about stress came from medical doctors.

- Unless you need surgery, only one out of nine orthopedists is willing or *able* to help you.

- Almost half the survey participants who saw doctors volunteered the comment that their doctors had a negative attitude about back pain. "There is nothing really wrong with you," "Just wait it out—back problems take care of themselves," "It's the price we pay for walking upright," and "Old age is catching up with you" typify this negativism and, in effect, tell back sufferers to seek help elsewhere.

• Even if you decide not to see a medical doctor for *treatment*, you still should have a thorough medical examination to rule out illness, disease, neurological impairment, or structural abnormality as a cause of your back problem.

The following doctors are listed according to frequency seen, *not* according to their effectiveness in helping back patients.

ORTHOPEDIST

(Also known as Orthopedic Surgeon)

• According to common wisdom, you should see an orthopedist if you have persistent back pain. According to this survey, however, you should usually seek help elsewhere.

• Orthopedists tend to send you packing if a reason for your pain can't be seen on X rays.

• Only one in nine orthopedists is effective in nonsurgical cases, and you can learn to tell which one.

Number of orthopedists in this survey:	429
Provided dramatic long-term help:	13%
Provided moderate long-term help:	10%
Provided temporary help:	9%
Ineffective:	61%
Made patient feel worse:	7%

More people see orthopedists than any other kind of practitioner (chiropractors are a close second). More people find them ineffective and comment negatively about them.

Orthopedists are specialists in diagnosing and treating injuries and diseases of bones and muscles, as well as joints, tendons, and ligaments. Hence, one would expect them to provide at least some relief to most back sufferers or, minimally, to refer patients to someone who could help—a specialist in such areas as rheumatology, neurology, or urology. But this is not the case.

Don't despair, however, if you live in an area where orthopedists are the only "back specialists" available to you. It is relatively easy to find an orthopedist who can give you the advice or treatment you need if you know the criteria that distinguish him from the rest.

Here is what survey participants say about finding a competent orthopedist:

Effective orthopedists spend more time listening than examining. If you sense a lack of interest during your initial consultation, the orthopedist is unlikely to help you. Survey participants who found orthopedists to be disinterested and difficult to talk to were invariably disappointed in the course of treatment they received.

A construction worker with a low back problem said, "My orthopedist seemed not to even care about my problem."

A backcountry ranger added, "I went to an orthopedist who did a rough-and-hurried and painful examination. He dismissed me by saying, 'I'm not interested in your life history, I just want to know how you feel today.' "

A young housewife explained, "Orthopedists don't have time for patients and don't try to find out what the real problem is. Just because you can't see anything specific does not mean there isn't anything wrong."

Orthopedists who spend most of their time in the operating room are least likely to be helpful. If most of their practice involves surgery, orthopedists may make terrific surgeons. But unless you need surgery, and chances are at least 95 percent that you don't, your back problem is likely to receive a back-of-the-hand approach from surgically oriented orthopedists.

Back patients are emphatic about this point:

"Two orthopedists showed little interest when no surgery was indicated," reported a teacher. "One spent exactly twenty seconds on the follow-up examination."

A photographer who was ultimately helped by acupuncture and biofeedback said, "My X rays yielded no sign of injury. Therefore, from the viewpoint of the orthopedist, there *was* no injury. The orthopedist could not or would not look beyond his professional tunnel. None was helpful or even sympathetic, once surgery wasn't indicated."

A nurse with low back pain: "The orthopedist appears to care less when a set of X rays shows no need for surgery."

An attorney with recurring muscle spasms: "I am not impressed with orthopedists, who I do not believe can help unless he or she can find a surgical problem through X rays."

Some doctors agree with this conclusion. Dr. Mike Oppenheim, writing in the mass-circulation *Family Circle* magazine, is one of them: "Consult a doctor who is not a surgeon. Your family doctor may be able to recommend an orthopedist or neurosurgeon who has a special interest in back problems and does not operate often."

Dr. Hamilton Hall, an orthopedic surgeon and author of the popular book *The Back Doctor*, adds another dimension to this viewpoint. "To the surgeon whose life revolves around the operating table," he writes, "back patients are chronic complainers whose conditions neither appeal to his mentality nor challenge his well-honed skills. . . . All in all, a doctor who is dedicated exclusively to surgery sees back treatment as a thankless and unrewarding task."

And a sporting-goods store owner added: "I had muscle strain in the low back and my family doctor sent me to an orthopedist who said, 'You don't need surgery; it's just the price you pay for walking upright!' Well, I wasn't walking upright. I was bent over from the pain. So I called orthopedists in the yellow pages and asked the receptionists if the doctor treated a lot of back patients who didn't require surgery. Three seemed put off by my question. The fourth was very positive, gave me an appointment, and that was the beginning of the end of my back problem."

Orthopedists willing to treat soft-tissue problems are most helpful to back sufferers. Soft-tissue problems are what most back sufferers have. They usually involve a strain (torn fibers caused by overstretching), spasms, or inflammation of back muscles—or all of the above. Soft-tissue problems can also involve damage to ligaments, tendons, or connective tissue. Although orthopedists who effectively treat soft-tissue injuries use a variety of procedures, all these doctors have certain approaches and attitudes in common.

For starters, the effective orthopedist realizes that prescription drugs will play a minuscule role in your recovery program. He may prescribe pills, but he keeps the role of drugs in perspective and does not end your treatment with them.

Also, the effective orthopedist will insist that you keep in touch with him (or his physical therapist) on a regular basis until you're fully recovered. He knows that *personal interaction* is the only way to keep tabs on how you feel and what new steps you're ready to take.

GENERAL PRACTITIONER

(GP, Family Practitioner, Internist)

- The notion that orthopedists are more effective than GP's for common back ailments is untrue. Stick with your own doctor if he is willing to work with you.

- Beware of GP's who limit treatment to writing a prescription. It's not a long-run answer. And it often doesn't even help in the short run.

- Most referrals by GP's are *not* effective.

Number of general practitioners in this survey:	266
Provided dramatic long-term help:*	8%
Provided moderate long-term help:*	12%
Provided temporary help only:	14%
Ineffective:	54%
Made patient feel worse:	12%**

General practitioners are the starting point for almost everyone with back pain. But the doctor-patient relationship has a shorter life than a bad back, with most back sufferers quickly moving on to other kinds of practitioners. The reason for this is best summed up by one patient's comment: "All that GP's do for back pain is push pills."

On the other hand, general practitioners know their patients better than specialists do. With this advantage, and with appropriate interest and skill, they could be the ones to do more than any other type of doctor to eliminate back problems or prevent them from happening in the first place. Although this is not the case today, it may be true in the future. Some medical schools have begun training their students to be "compassionate healers" by empha-

---

*Includes help that eventually came from appropriate referrals.
**This high figure is due primarily to adverse reactions from prescribed drugs.

sizing the promotion of health and prevention of degenerative ailments, including back pain.

If your family doctor is determined to help you all the way through a back problem, count your blessings. Running around to see this or that specialist just because "common wisdom" says that you should will usually cause you needless trouble.

One young woman, a recreational counselor, was making slow progress under the care of her general practitioner, whom she described as "very gentle, thorough, concerned about lifestyle, habits, exercise, and activity." The GP diagnosed the patient's problem as spinal stenosis (a narrowing of the spine, which puts pressure on nerve roots). This diagnosis was confirmed at the doctor's request by an orthopedic colleague. Fine so far. But the young woman was berated repeatedly by well-meaning friends for taking the word of "just a GP," so she went to an orthopedist, paid a handsome fee, and got nothing more for her efforts than "a rushed examination and a sheet of do's and don'ts."

In contrast, her GP "provided a rocking chair in the waiting room, a relaxed and inquiring examination, and concern for long-run progress." Also, as the patient explained, "My GP treated acute pain with drugs to relax muscle spasms and reduce inflammation. Then after bed rest for several weeks, the doctor provided me with an extensive exercise program, with notes and suggestions for exercise to start with and a progression to build into as pain subsided and strength increased. She also provided pointers about posture and mattress."

What to do if your general practitioner makes a referral. If a specialist is needed, a competent general practitioner will make a referral. In the best of circumstances, the doctor makes the referral to call in more expertise, not to get rid of you and your backache by sending you elsewhere. For example, 5 percent of the general practitioners in this survey referred their patients to a physical therapist and achieved outstanding results. These doctors wanted to stay involved, to be ultimately responsible for their patients' care, and appreciated the value of having someone work closely with the patients in a comprehensive rehabilitation program.

But what happens when you're referred to another medical doctor such as an orthopedist, neurologist, or neurosurgeon? Are you getting the brush-off? Should you simply accept the referral? Or should you try to discuss it with your doctor?

Most people in this survey found it hard to discuss referrals because they were afraid their GP would not want to treat them for other problems in the future. Some of them learned, however, that a few key questions were essential:

(1) What will be the next step if the diagnostic procedure conducted by the specialist does not reveal a tangible reason for my problem?

(2) Will you or the specialist still try to help me even if there is no disease or serious malformation?

(3) What will be done about my soft-tissue (muscular) problems? (Even if you are a candidate for surgery, your musculature will still need postoperative rehabilitation.)

If the answer to any of these questions is unsatisfactory to you, you'll be better off, no matter how unsettling it may feel, to find a good back practitioner on your own.

If, on the other hand, you learn that your general practitioner will act as coordinator for all forms of treatment involving your back, you can relax. Having a doctor pave the way for you with other health-care practitioners often guarantees a more positive reception, especially if you are a chronic back sufferer. As a retired teacher suffering through years of sciatica pain remarked, "My GP's involvement with my problem has made a big difference. Even when nothing significant can be done for my pain, he confers with other doctors and talks with me about ways to lower the stress from my pain."

OSTEOPATH

(Also called Osteopathic Physician and Doctor of Osteopathy)

- Osteopaths seldom accomplish more than temporary relief of acute pain.

- Osteopaths will take on severe and chronic problems other practitioners have given up on, but achieve only moderate success.

Number of osteopaths in this survey: 71
Provided dramatic long-term help: 7%

Provided moderate long-term help:	21%
Provided temporary help:	15%
Ineffective:	46%
Made patient feel worse:	11%

Technically, osteopaths are not medical doctors, but they are included in this section because they are trained to practice conventional medicine. They can write prescriptions and perform surgery. Osteopaths are also trained in spinal manipulation. They believe manipulation can correct "structural derangements" that cause diseases and ailments, and here they part company with most members of the medical establishment.

On paper, then, osteopaths offer you and your back problem whatever is required—orthodox medicine or natural means of healing. In practice, however, when it comes to helping patients achieve dramatic *long-term* relief, osteopaths have the poorest record of any widely seen practitioner: they do 50 percent *worse* than orthopedists and chiropractors. The major reason for this is their almost exclusive reliance on manipulation or drugs, neither of which promotes long-run improvement, without competent advice about daily living habits and exercise.

On the other hand, the small amount of help provided by osteopaths gives them a good "provided moderate long-term help" record and enables chronic patients to function better, albeit with significant pain and limitations. But most people who see osteopaths move on to other kinds of practitioners.

Osteopaths also have a relatively high "made patient feel worse" rate of 11 percent, due mostly to injuries from manipulation. In fact, osteopaths are not as effective as chiropractors in using manipulation to alleviate most kinds of back pain.

"The treatment from my osteopath helped a bit" and "My osteopath helps keep me functioning" were the most enthusiastic statements by survey participants. Osteopathy is one mode of treatment that fails to live up to its promises, at least as far as back problems are concerned.

NEUROSURGEON

- The average back sufferer will get no help here.

- Neurosurgeons overprescribe drugs, including anti-depressants.

- They are relatively successful with patients whose only alternative is surgery.

Number of neurosurgeons in this survey:	53
Provided dramatic long-term help:	13%
Provided moderate long-term help:	13%
Provided temporary help:	8%
Ineffective:	51%
Made patient feel worse:	15%

Having your back pain treated by a neurosurgeon is usually a make or break proposition. Either you'll be eternally grateful for the wonders of modern surgery or you'll rue the day that the word "neurosurgeon" was mentioned to you.

The neurosurgeon doesn't do quite as well as the orthopedist in bringing about long-run results through surgery. And the neurosurgeon's almost exclusive reliance on surgery and drugs makes him the most hazardous of all widely seen practitioners. Fifteen percent of patients who saw neurosurgeons wound up in worse shape, compared with 7 percent of patients who saw orthopedists. The inevitable risks of surgery speak for themselves. In addition, neurosurgeons prescribe more drugs per patient than any other kind of doctor except their neurologist colleagues. Some of these medications are not just painkillers, but psychoactive drugs such as anti-depressants.

Neurosurgeons are *surgeons* who specialize in operations involving the nervous system. They hardly ever treat backs in general; they treat them surgically. Survey participants make it clear that the neurosurgeon is not only disinterested in nonsurgical problems but also unlikely to be well-versed in a long-run recovery program. If you want personal, pre- or postoperative care for your back, know that the neurosurgeon is not inclined to provide it.

What neurosurgeons can provide, 13 percent of the time, is the skill to achieve results that patients in severe pain rightly consider to be miraculous.

Consider the testimony of this Indiana truck driver: "I saw a GP and a chiropractor for three years. They never relieved my pain from osteoarthritis, bone spurs and a ruptured disc, and I never received a referral until I was totally incapacitated. The neurosurgeon was my salvation. His corrective surgery to remove a large bone spur and a disc provided me with the first relief from years of agonizing and sometimes paralyzing pain." The patient was able to resume his truck driving and loading activities after a few months of instruction and care from a physical therapist recommended by the neurosurgeon.

More typical is the comment of a research sociologist who had a disc removed by a neurosurgeon: "Back surgery worked well for my acute pain. However, the neurosurgeon was not helpful for anything except surgery. He did not mention stress, exercise, or anything else for that matter." This patient's greatest progress came from a physical fitness instructor at a local health spa, but the surgery *did* relieve her pain enough for her to take up the exercise.

Another example tells more of the story. A teacher from Virginia had struggled through two years of pain from a ruptured disc. She tried rest and analgesics under the care of her family doctor. She also received twice-a-week chiropractic adjustments for a year. When her pain grew unbearable, the chiropractor referred her to a neurosurgeon. But it was the neurosurgeon's associate who examined her, and technicians who performed a CAT scan and myelogram to confirm the preliminary diagnosis of a herniated disc, so that even though the neurosurgeon performed a successful operation, the teacher never met him—except on videotape in her room after surgery. She found his instructions on the tape about how to care for herself in the weeks and years ahead to be most useful. She has been completely pain-free for three years now and is grateful to the stranger who restored her to an active life. Still, this participant said: "If there had been problems after the surgery, I doubt that I would have been able to talk to the surgeon."

Perhaps only one percent of all back sufferers need surgery. But if you see a surgeon and are advised to have an operation, participants in this survey suggest the following:

(1) Get additional opinions from at least one other surgeon and one practitioner who is not a surgeon. Explore the potential benefits

of rest and physical therapy as well as chymopapain (see Chapter 7) if you have a ruptured disc.

(2) Ask about your chances of success. Specific figures should be available at every medical center. Go elsewhere if you get an evasive answer.

(3) Ask about postoperative care. According to the neurosurgeon-on-videotape in the case history cited above, "Successful surgery is only 10 percent of the process of making you well." If your surgeon isn't interested in the remaining 90 percent of treatment needed to restore you to full activity, either change doctors or make other arrangements for postoperative care.

NEUROLOGIST

- Neurologists prescribe more drugs, with more adverse effects, than any other practitioner.

- They offer useful advice when giving a second opinion about neurological impairment or the need for surgery.

- They do nothing to help the average back sufferer.

Number of neurologists in this survey:	44
Provided dramatic long-term help:	2%
Provided moderate long-term help:	2%
Provided temporary relief:	4%
Ineffective:	76%
Made patient feel worse:	16%

Neurologists are less effective in aiding back sufferers than any other kind of medical doctor in this survey. They also prescribe more drugs per patient than any other back practitioner, with the most harmful results. Only two of the forty-four neurologists in this survey suggested any treatment other than prescription drugs. Their value to back sufferers, when there is any, lies in diagnosing and treating uncommon diseases of the nervous system. In short, the average back sufferer has no use for a neurologist.

If you are referred to a neurologist, be aware that one out of five mentioned in this survey prescribed anti-depressant drugs, on the grounds that chronic back sufferers are, by definition, depressed. Whether this is true isn't established. But it is known that these drugs, some of which fall into the anti-psychotic category of medications, have enough potential for harm to warrant a second opinion about taking them.

PHYSIATRIST

(Also called Doctor of Physical Medicine, Doctor of Rehabilitative Medicine, or Physiatrician)

- This exceptional healer is your best bet among all practitioners—medical or nonmedical—for both acute and chronic back problems.
- The only major problem you'll face is the limited number of practitioners.

Number of physiatrists in this survey:	30
Provided dramatic long-term help:	33%
Provided moderate long-term help:	53%
Provided temporary relief:	0%
Ineffective:	7%
Made patient feel worse:	7%

The physiatrist (pronounced fizz-EYE-uh-trist) has the best record of any practitioner—doctor or non-doctor—who treats a broad spectrum of back problems. The reasons for this success are both tangible and attitudinal.

Most important, rehabilitating the body through natural means—movement, water, heat, cold, and specific exercises—is the physiatrist's specialty. After his regular training as a medical doctor, he concentrates on all aspects of the rehabilitation process.

Soft-tissue injuries that are not revealed by neurological tests or on X rays are accepted by the physiatrist as ailments to be treated. Indeed, *any* problem in moving normally falls into the physiatrist's domain. He works with patients who have many kinds of functional disabilities, from strokes, paralysis, burns, and amputations to back pain of every description. Chronic back sufferers offer a routine challenge to the physiatrist, who is used to spending months and even years trying to help stroke victims regain partial movement of a limb.

A newspaper editor talked about his physiatrist this way: "By the time I saw a physiatrist, I had been fighting back pain for years. I had seen every practitioner under the sun and tried every treatment imaginable. The physiatrist did what no one else did. He took his time learning about my problem and my lifestyle. He totally ignored all the dire warnings from surgeons that I would soon become an invalid without disc surgery. He took the time to explain the mechanism of my pain, prescribed an individualized exercise program, and assigned a physical therapist to work with me on all daily activities that affected my back."

Physiatrists aren't surgeons. What's more, remarkably, none in this survey "lost" a back patient to surgery. All of them tend to prescribe drugs only when absolutely necessary. Aspirin was their drug of choice, although a few prescribed analgesics and anti-inflammatory medications in extreme cases, and then only for short periods of time.

The one difficulty about seeing a physiatrist is finding one. Medical students apparently do not consider physiatrics to be especially glamorous or lucrative. There are fewer than 1,500 physiatrists in the country, and virtually all of them are in major metropolitan areas. The specialty is rarely listed in the yellow pages, but you may be able to locate a physiatrist by calling hospitals within traveling distance of your home or checking with your county medical association.

ACUPUNCTURIST

- Acupuncturists are definitely worth a try, with virtually no risk of adverse effects.

- All kinds of back pain can respond favorably to acupuncture, even chronic pain that has worsened over the years.

- The most successful acupuncturists combine acupuncture with exercise and lifestyle counsel.

Number of acupuncturists in this survey:	25
Provided dramatic long-term help:	16%
Provided moderate long-term help:	20%

Provided temporary relief:	32%
Ineffective:	28%
Made patient feel worse:	4%

Most acupuncturists in this survey are medical doctors, a phenomenon that underscores the growing acceptance of acupuncture as a bona fide medical procedure. Nevertheless, acupuncturists are usually practitioners of last resort for chronic back sufferers, and most people with any kind of ongoing pain remain leery about trying them.

As the results above show, being treated by an acupuncturist *is* worth a try and has far more healing value than a placebo. Sixty-eight percent of the acupuncturists in this survey helped their patients find relief. This figure is even more encouraging than it appears, because some of the patients in the "temporary relief only" group were pain-free for up to two years. By comparison, the temporary relief gained from most other forms of treatment, including all prescription medications, usually lasts a few hours at best.

Acupuncturists in this survey who were medical doctors were neither more nor less successful than non-physician practitioners. The important variables were the number of years' experience with acupuncture and the time invested in advising patients about exercise, stress, and day-to-day living habits.

RHEUMATOLOGIST

- Their good interpersonal dynamics are an important plus for arthritis sufferers.

- Rheumatologists are also worth seeing for other kinds of chronic back problems.

Number of rheumatologists in this survey:	15*
Provided dramatic long-term help:	7%
Provided moderate long-term help:	33%
Provided temporary relief:	20%

*Forty-six rheumatologists were cited in the survey data, but only those who treated patients with osteoarthritis were included in the statistics for the final report. Other forms of arthritis, although they do cause back problems, are beyond the scope of this project.

Ineffective: 40%
Made patient feel worse: 0%

Rheumatologists are medical doctors who specialize in diagnosing and treating the more than a hundred forms of arthritis and related diseases. Certainly, if you have reason to believe that arthritis plays a role in your back condition, you should consult with this specialist. But people with chronic and serious back problems *not* primarily due to arthritis can also benefit from a rheumatologist's care. They frequently find him both interested and experienced in working with long-term, soft-tissue problems.

The following comments are typical:

"I was lucky that the rheumatologist I consulted recognized my problem and believed as I do in moderate treatment," said an editorial researcher, who received nonprescription pills for pain and inflammation. He also got needed advice about changing his work routine and sticking to a sensible exercise plan.

"So far, the rheumatologist has proved the most useful of all doctors," reported a speech pathologist who had been assured by her family doctor that her pain would vanish on its own. When she could no longer sit without severe pain, she sought help from a specialist. "The rheumatologist was very supportive about my joining a YMCA exercise program. He also talked constructively about stress, not as a single cause, but as a contributing factor to back pain."

OTHER MEDICAL DOCTORS

Reports of other medical doctors seen by survey participants were too few to yield significant statistics. Nevertheless, some comments are included here because they offer valuable firsthand experience.

EMERGENCY ROOM MEDICAL DOCTORS

- Avoid them if you possibly can. They make back sufferers wish they had stayed in bed.

Stay out of emergency rooms if at all possible. Of the nine patients in this survey who were treated in emergency units, all were the worse for having made the trip. None received even temporary relief. All found that their pain grew worse during the wait for examination and treatment (the average wait was two hours). Two of the patients wound up back in the hospital within a few days of leaving the emergency room because of vertebrae fractures that had been overlooked.

A construction worker whose fractured spine was misdiagnosed by an emergency room physician had this to say: "I swear you'd think I was interested in workmen's compensation. I lay on the floor, because I couldn't stand or sit. They didn't seem concerned with me—annoyed would be more like it."

Of course, if you are in an accident and sustain a serious injury, you have no alternative but to seek emergency care. On the other hand, if you reach for a tissue and your back "goes out," resulting in severe pain, you probably do have a choice, including trying to convince a doctor to see you at home. Making a trip anywhere is likely to increase your pain. If you must travel, make every effort to go to a private doctor's office instead of an emergency room.

"The second time my back went into spasm, I used one of those visit-your-home medical services," said a retail executive. "I got a shot of novocaine and the assurance that there seemed to be no need to go to the hospital. I had been to an emergency room the first time and just seeing all the terrible cases there convinced me not to go back unless it were a life-threatening situation."

OBSTETRICIAN/GYNECOLOGIST

- His advice about back pain is unconstructive and unsympathetic.

"I explained the problem of my back pain to my gynecologist," a librarian said. "But he has never referred me to a back specialist or done anything about it. He said it was common for women to have back pain, especially when they reach my age." This patient is 32 years old and performs her job in spite of nearly intolerable pain.

A 28-year-old receptionist and mother of four voiced a similar complaint: "My gynecologist did not even look at my back, and he said that back pain was normal for women. I think that he was not qualified to treat me or that he did not care enough to refer me. I will just endure my pain until it subsides or reaches the excruciating point."

These kinds of attitudes about women's back problems are representative of all eight obstetricians and gynecologists mentioned by survey participants. So, unless you are certain your back pain has a gynecological basis, don't look for help from these specialists. The attitude that women, including pregnant women and mothers, can do nothing about back pain is incorrect and potentially destructive.

SPORTS MEDICINE SPECIALIST

- If you can get an appointment, you probably will get the help you're looking for.

Sports medicine is a relatively new and underpopulated specialty. Only five sports medicine doctors treated participants in this survey.* Of the five, four helped their patients achieve dramatic long-term help; the other provided moderate long-term help. The physical-medicine orientation of these doctors makes them a good choice for a wide range of back problems.

A Kentucky journalist who had suffered debilitating back pain for six years before he saw one of these practitioners said: "Stretching exercises prepared specifically for me by a sports medicine specialist solved my problem in the long run. Since I started my program, except for two occasions when I was lax in performing my required exercises, I have had little pain and no major problems."

---

*Another ten survey participants tried unsuccessfully to make appointments with sports medicine doctors, many of whom were physicians for professional sports teams and unable to see "ordinary" back sufferers within a month of their call.

Chapter 4

Non-MD Practitioners: Which Ones Can Help *Your* Problem?

Most back sufferers get the help they need from the non-physician practitioners described and rated in this chapter. Some of the practitioners, like chiropractors and massage therapists, are well known, but documentation about their relative effectiveness or ineffectiveness has been generally unavailable until now. Others, like Tai Chi instructors and Feldenkrais therapists, are unknown to most back sufferers. Still others, like physical therapists, usually need a doctor's authorization to treat you. And a few, like podiatrists and dentists, who seem far removed from back care, can be surprisingly helpful with certain back problems.

Collectively, these practitioners are enormously popular, with chiropractors alone receiving some 55 million back-patient visits a year—or about three times as many as the entire medical profession.*

Twenty-one kinds of practitioners are evaluated in this chapter. But as

---

*Based on a membership survey, the American Chiropractic Association estimates that 118.86 million patient visits were made to chiropractors during 1981, "with approximately 45 percent of initial complaints being low back related," and an additional 10 percent involving other back problems. According to *The New York Times* (January 12, 1982), there are more than 19 million back-patient visits to medical doctors each year.

you'll see, only about one-third of them can benefit most back sufferers in a major way. The rest are included because knowing the truth about them enables you to avoid wasting your time and money as so many other back sufferers have. It also gives you greater peace of mind when well-meaning friends ask you whether you have seen this or that kind of health-care specialist.

The following practitioners are listed according to frequency seen, *not* according to their effectiveness in helping back patients.

CHIROPRACTOR

- Chiropractors can help you get temporary relief from minor or moderate low back or neck pain. But for severe, chronic low back pain, don't expect miracles.

- The most effective chiropractors use gentler forms of manipulation and consider advice about lifestyle, stress, and exercise as important as manipulation in the long run.

- Beware of seeing a chiropractor for treatment of a herniated disc, severe sciatica and arthritis pain, or for attempts to "correct" scoliosis.

Number of chiropractors in this survey:	422
Provided dramatic long-term help:	14%
Provided moderate long-term help:	14%
Provided temporary help:	28%
Ineffective:	33%
Made patient feel worse:	11%

Yes, manipulation helps. No, chiropractors are not quacks. In fact, in this survey chiropractors were considered more effective than most medical doctors. On the other hand, chiropractic care does carry a risk of pain or injury or both, depending on the techniques of the practitioner and on the specific nature of the back problem.

Before we look at just how well chiropractors handle back problems, let's briefly explore who they are, what they're trained to do, and what philosophy underlies this specialty that is now the second largest system of health care in the world. (Allopathic, or medical, is first; osteopathic is third.)

There are some 23,000 chiropractors in the United States today, and they outnumber orthopedists by almost two to one. Chiropractors are accredited in all fifty states. Federal health-insurance programs such as Medicare cover their services. So do most private health-insurance plans, the major exception being Blue Cross/Blue Shield, an organization run by medical doctors.

Newly licensed chiropractors have at least six years of college study and internship. They have extensive training in manipulation and X-ray technology and interpretation, as well as some background in nutrition, pathology, pediatrics, physical therapeutics, and geriatrics. They see their role as helping to maintain patients' health, as opposed to simply curing their ills.

The chiropractic profession was born in America nearly a century ago. From 1868 to 1953 the American Chiropractic Association believed that the interruption of psychic energy from the brain was the cause of many ailments and diseases. The current theory holds that irritated nerve roots, or interruptions of nerve impulses, cause most problems. Manipulation, which is said to restore the body to its natural state of well-being, is the predominant form of treatment.

Of course, back pain cares nothing for theory. So here are facts and figures, and unprecedented opportunities to learn from the experiences of other back sufferers.

Manipulation alone:
unsuccessful long-term results

Survey results show conclusively that manipulation does *not* relieve back pain in the long run. To see this point more clearly, look at the way back sufferers compare the effectiveness of manipulation *alone* with the success of *total* chiropractic care:

	Manipulation only	Total chiropractic care
Number of chiropractors:	333	422
Provided dramatic long-term help:	5%	14%
Provided moderate long-term help:	7%	14%
Provided temporary help:	44%	28%
Ineffective:	34%	33%
Made patient feel worse:	10%	11%

Contrary to popular belief, manipulation alone is seldom the key to long-run success under chiropractic care. This means that if you see a chiropractor who relies exclusively on manipulation, you are likely to be helped for just a few days or weeks at a time, no matter how many months or years you continue treatment.

"The only thing about receiving manipulation treatments is that you have to keep seeing the chiropractor to keep from getting worse, but not necessarily better," wrote a housewife who had been receiving adjustments of specific areas of her spine for twelve years.

An assembly line worker said, "I feel great when I leave the chiropractor's table, but then bones apparently slip back out of place in a matter of days."

A retail store owner related, "Manipulation just works for a while. It's not a cure-all by any means."

What, then, accounts for the relative success of chiropractic care?

"Holistic" is the word that came up repeatedly when back sufferers who favored chiropractic care tried to explain why it was effective. In short, these survey participants felt that *they*, and not just their back problems, were being treated.

Some typical comments illustrate this point.

A bricklayer with low back pain: "My chiropractor offered nutritional advice, rather than drugs, and put me on an excellent yoga program to strengthen my muscles. He also encouraged relaxation exercises and the use of a B vitamin for stress, as well as regular exercise such as swimming."

A New York truck driver: "Regular chiropractic adjustments offer steady improvement if used regularly and if combined with the kind of program that I received—stretching and strengthening exercises and advice about nutrition."

A bartender who suffered nearly incapacitating neck and lower back pain: "I saw one chiropractor who adjusted my spine, but without constructive results. I saw another chiropractor who manipulated my spine without promoting the help I needed so much. The third chiropractor put me on a complete mineral and vitamin regimen (through hair analysis) to correct the metabolic imbalances which cause biochemical stress. He provided me with a program of walking exercises to relieve back stress, a firm cushion to sit against, and squatting exercises to unlock spinal tension. This was all carefully monitored by one to three visits a week for gentle adjustments, consultation, and any special treatment I needed. I now feel like I have triple the energy I once had. More important, I very seldom experience the chronic discomfort that plagued me for years."

Chiropractor-patient rapport

The chiropractor's relationship with his patients also explains the relative success of the profession in helping back sufferers. Hundreds of unsolicited comments from survey participants show, unquestionably, that patients relate more comfortably to chiropractors than to doctors. They tend to like chiropractors as individuals and can talk to them about their feelings and their lives. A good practitioner-patient relationship apparently helps the back sufferer because the most effective "treatment" for back pain takes the form of talking and listening, of advice rather than procedures.

Advice about daily living habits, stress, and exercise is considered vital by back sufferers. This advice takes time for a practitioner to dispense. And chiropractors are more willing than doctors to spend this time with their patients. Survey participants were emphatic about this point.

A health educator said, "My chiropractor has always been very concerned and helpful to me regardless of what my problem is. I would pay his fee just for an opportunity to talk to him."

A librarian: "I felt for the first time in my life, in terms of medical treatment, that I was in competent and nonantagonistic hands."

A housewife: "I would always recommend a chiropractor before an MD, because the chiropractors I have seen are interested in all functions of the mind and body."

A musician: "The chiropractor I see genuinely cares about me and my problems."

A caterer: "Chiropractors tell you all kinds of things, whereas MD's tell you very little."

Chiropractors "know" what's wrong with you.

When you're in pain, it is natural to want an answer to the question, "Exactly what's wrong with me and what can be done about it?" The more severe the pain, or the longer it lasts, the greater the need for answers. Whether it helps and is medically legitimate, chiropractors almost always offer their patients specific descriptions of what is wrong and how the problem can be corrected. By comparison, medical doctors usually give a generalized diagnosis such as low back syndrome. (As the results of this survey show, doctors almost never believe in the validity of the misalignment diagnosis given by chiropractors. Show the same X ray to a doctor and a chiropractor, and their interpretations will almost always be different. In short, a chiropractor will look at an X ray and say, "Your spine is misaligned." A doctor will look and say, "Your spine is normal.")

If you believe in basic chiropractic concepts, the chiropractor's specificity in diagnosis is comforting. It builds your confidence. It removes the disquieting feeling of not knowing what's wrong. For some people, a specific diagnosis lowers stress and anxiety about back pain.

For example, a farmer who regularly put in long, physically demanding hours suffered pain in his hips and lower back. When doctor after doctor failed to come up with a specific diagnosis, he rejected all their advice (which may have been sound and helpful) and sought the help of a chiropractor. The chiropractor explained the origin of the problem as "a malformed hip due to premature birth," and the patient accepted this diagnosis. More to the point, the patient accepted an exercise program (which had also been proposed by a medical doctor) that put him on the path to good health.

Another survey participant, a potter, went to an orthopedist to seek help for pain in her neck. The orthopedist called the problem a "pinched nerve." The patient, dissatisfied with what she felt was a vague and rushed diagnosis, went to a chiropractor. The chiropractor's diagnosis of "misalignment of neck and spine" was termed "valid" by the patient, because, as she put it, "He took the time to show me the X rays, and I could see it for myself."

"The chiropractor was the only one who seemed confident about his diagnosis," said a computer programmer, who stopped worrying about his low back pain after a chiropractor diagnosed his problem as a "bilateral sprain of the sacrolumbar." Before this, each of three medical doctors had diagnosed the problem in a different way—kidney infection, hypertension, and low back strain—leaving the patient increasingly concerned and distressed.

Finally, and not atypically, is the case of a young mother who was unhappy about being told by medical doctors that she simply had a "bad back." Although she still reported having "a lot of discomfort" after chiropractic care, she was less worried in part because she finally had a name for her ailment: "Subluxation T11, T12, C3 and 4, manifesting as myospasm, radiculitis associated with curvature and complicated by loss of cervical curve."

Other things to know about chiropractic care

The statistics at the beginning of this chapter show that 56 percent of back sufferers who see chiropractors receive some help. This is a success story, since only 32 percent could say the same for orthopedists and 34 percent for general practitioners.

Still, the "dramatic long-term help" figure for chiropractors, 14 percent, is almost as low as that for orthopedists (13 percent), and it is less than half that of practitioners such as physiatrists and physical therapists.

Chiropractors can also make patients worse. The 11 percent "made patient feel worse" figure associated with chiropractic treatment is based on reports of a temporary but substantial increase in pain from manipulation, without any improvement in the condition after the pain subsided.

This 11 percent statistic, however, is based on the whole group of survey participants. When we consider just the average back sufferer with muscular low back discomfort, the "made patient feel worse" rate is only 3 percent. But it climbs as high as 50 percent for the acute phase of herniated disc pain. See Chapters 9–14 for details on the usefulness and risks of chiropractic care for specific kinds of back problems.

High cost and contracts. Ironically, given the national uproar over medical doctors' fees, it was the high cost of chiropractic care that bothered survey participants most—not the cost per visit but the long-range nature of the treatment.

It is not unusual for a chiropractor to schedule regular "maintenance" visits to ensure that problems don't recur. A few chiropractors even ask the patient to sign a contract agreeing to regular treatments for one or two years. Most survey participants who mentioned contracts objected strenuously to them. "The chiropractor's greed put me off," a factory worker commented, "especially when I was told I had to sign a contract for two years of treatment."

Unorthodox procedures and advice. About 5 percent of chiropractic patients in this survey reported what they believed to be unusual, even bizarre, advice or treatments. To illustrate:

- "The chiropractor told me that I must have headaches because of my spinal curvature. I almost never have a headache. But I felt that with repeated suggestions I would, so I stopped the treatments."

- "I was told that my low back pain was caused, in part, by the locking of one of the pumping mechanisms affecting my cerebrospinal fluid."

- "My chiropractor prescribed nonprescription pills for 'liver flushes.' I still don't know why my liver needed flushing."

- "Once, when I had acute pain, I had my tailbone manipulated through my rectum by a chiropractor. The relief was amazing."

In summary, chiropractors are neither miracle workers nor quacks. They are legitimate, professional dispensers of back care. And, on average, they treat back pain more successfully than most kinds of medical doctors.

PHYSICAL THERAPIST
(Also called Physiotherapist)

- Physical therapists are, by far, the most successful non-MD practitioner for helping patients with almost any kind of back ailment.

- In some countries, many physical therapists, even those in private practice, cannot treat you without the consent of a medical doctor.

Number of physical therapists in this survey:	140
Provided dramatic long-term help:	34%
Provided moderate long-term help:	31%
Provided temporary help:	8%
Ineffective:	17%
Made patient feel worse:	10%

Physical therapists cannot prescribe pills or perform surgery. Most are not trained in manipulation. Yet they are extremely helpful to back sufferers, especially those with low back pain as well as ruptured discs and osteoarthritis.

One key factor is that physical therapists try to learn a lot about you. "A good physical therapist gives you all the individualized input that you need to take care of your back for the rest of your life," said one survey participant, a writer who managed to control back pain for twenty years before she ran into incapacitating problems that she couldn't solve by herself. "Even if you take full responsibility for solving your back problem yourself," she continued, "and I believe that everyone should have this attitude, you still have to know *how* to accomplish this. The road to recovery isn't always an obvious one. You can read all the books in the world and still not know what to do because books talk about the average back sufferer, and there is no such person."

Once a physical therapist gets to know *you*, not just your back pain, he or she can use a wide variety of natural corrective techniques, such as heat, cold, postural instruction, relaxation therapy, and exercise therapy.

Physical therapists are also trained to apply modern technology to back problems, including ultrasound, electric muscle stimulation, diathermy, and transcutaneous electric nerve stimulation (TENS). But the value of these techniques is slight compared with what the physical therapist can do for you by looking, listening, and talking.

If you have weak or overly tight muscles, a physical therapist's special training will usually help you correct these conditions. Is your posture bad? Do you sit properly? Are your chairs and mattress providing you with optimal support? Is your average day so stressful that you believe it to be aggravating your back pain? All these aspects of back care, and more, come under the physical therapist's domain.

If you're seriously disabled, having a physical therapist come to your home is often more helpful than making the trip to see one at a medical center. At your home, the therapist isn't as rushed. He or she can check out virtually all the day-to-day routines and activities that can affect your back. (The only catch here is cost: home visits cost more and your insurance may not provide full coverage.)

Many back sufferers in the survey lavished praise on physical therapists. An actress: "My back problems of many years were solved by a physical therapist through a combination of massage, foot reflexology, exercises, and advice about stress."

A professional tennis player: "My suggestion is that you find a physical therapist and stick to exercises they recommend. My physical therapist was top notch and helped me tremendously."

A reading specialist: "If any practitioner deserves to be called a back specialist, it's the physical therapist. They have more training in musculoskeletal problems than do doctors."

Keep in mind that you usually need a doctor's "permission" to be treated by a physical therapist. Just a few words scrawled on a prescription pad will do. The doctor need not select the therapist or provide detailed instructions. And, importantly, not many doctors will turn down a politely stated request for treatment by a physical therapist. "'I asked my GP to write a prescription for physical therapy when no relief was forthcoming from pills," said an X-ray technician. "He wrote the prescription and there were excellent results within two weeks. Even the breathing exercises I learned from the physical therapist relieve stress in general."

Sources outside our survey also indicate that more physicians are becoming aware of the value of physical therapy for back patients. In a recent issue of *Internal Medicine News*, one medical doctor observed from his research that physical therapists appear to be more effective than doctors in helping disabled back sufferers.

A note of caution about physical therapists: their "made patient feel worse" rate of 10 percent was caused almost entirely by pushing patients too fast in the exercise rehabilitation process, and ignoring patients' complaints about pain. It is crucial that *you* judge whether the pace of prescribed exercise is helping or hurting you. You must also realize that physical therapists routinely work with such patients as quadriplegics and stroke victims, where "no pain, no gain" is a reality. This qualification aside, you can expect the care you get from a physical therapist to help you for the rest of your life.

YOGA INSTRUCTOR

- Here is the *most successful* of all approaches to backache relief for *non-incapacitated* backache sufferers—with twenty-three out of twenty-four survey participants reporting significant long-run improvement.

- Most yoga positions are dangerous to do *while* you are experiencing back pain.

Number of yoga instructors in this survey:	24
Provided dramatic long-term help:	50%
Provided moderate long-term help:	46%
Provided temporary help:	4%
Ineffective:	0%
Made patient feel worse:	0%

To the extent that stretching and strengthening your body is helpful—and most survey participants agreed that it is—yoga instruction can be an excellent way to rid yourself of back pain. To the extent that stress contributes to back pain—and most survey participants felt that it does—yoga instruction scores again. The yoga philosophy of never forcing or straining, and of moving in a meditative manner, has obvious value. But yoga philosophy also encompasses the harmony of mind, body, and spirit—a concept that is foreign, even laughable, to many people.

Yoga instructors achieve the best results with back sufferers who are not incapacitated by pain and who are receptive to yoga's spiritual message. People in the survey who tried to avoid philosophical concepts by studying yoga through books, articles, and tapes got some help—but *not nearly as much as those who worked with a yoga instructor.*

A word of caution: most yoga exercise positions are too difficult (and far too risky) for back sufferers who are not fully up and around and functioning reasonably well. Once you are able to perform normal day-to-day activities, however, yoga offers day-to-day help for the rest of your life.

Try this simple form of yoga therapy suggested by several survey participants. It involves nothing more than deep abdominal breathing that has helped many back sufferers to relax and tone up abdominal muscles. Try it during your peak work hours. Five minutes is optimal; even a few breaths are useful. Start by taking a deep breath from your abdomen (put your fingers on it at first to make sure that it, and not your chest, is expanding). Now inhale through your nose for six seconds . . . hold your breath for three seconds . . . then exhale through your mouth for seven seconds. When you exhale let yourself go limp. After a few minutes see if you feel both invigorated and relaxed.

MASSAGE THERAPIST

(Acupressure and holistic massage therapists are described next in this chapter.)

- Strictly a luxury, albeit a very comforting one, for temporary relief of minor back pain.

- Swedish massage therapists almost never provide information needed for long-run improvement.

- Massage is worth trying with a friend or mate.

Number of Swedish massage therapists in this survey:	22
Provided dramatic long-term help:	5%
Provided moderate long-term help:	5%
Provided temporary help:	63%
Ineffective:	27%
Made patient feel worse:	0%

As a rule, individuals trained in Swedish massage provide neither the self-care advice nor the treatment needed for significant improvement of back problems. Yet there is no denying that a good massage is a relaxing pleasure—one that can take the edge off low-grade pain caused by tight or tired muscles.

The best way to find a good massage therapist is through a recommendation. Short of this, consult your local yellow pages, looking for small ads that emphasize "medical massage." Newspaper advertisements that proclaim the attractiveness of massage personnel—or that use phrases like "total discretion" and "assured privacy"—are offering sexual stimulation, not backache relief.

Several survey participants had friends or mates who were willing to play the role of amateur massage therapist, getting instruction from one of the many books on this subject. If you're interested in getting started, the following steps, based on discussions with survey participants, will point you in the right direction:

(1) Create a relaxing environment. Lower the lights; play soft, pleasing music; and make sure the room is warm and as draft-free as possible.

(2) Have the attitude that touch alone can make you feel better. Relax as much as possible.

(3) Use a lotion or oil. Otherwise, massage can irritate your skin.

(4) Have your partner work up from the feet to the waist, using smooth, fluid motions. Then massage from the waist to the neck.

(5) A massage of your feet and head, including scalp, can complete the procedure. Thirty minutes to one hour of this kind of pampering is bound to make you feel better.

SHIATSU THERAPIST

(Also called Acupressure Massage Therapist)

- You'll often find the interest, skill, and health approaches that help minor to moderate low back pain.

- Survey participants report surprising success with do-it-yourself techniques for "pushing away" pain.

Number of Shiatsu therapists in this survey:	20
Provided dramatic long-term help:	35%
Provided moderate long-term help:	15%

Provided temporary help:	40%
Ineffective:	0%
Made patient feel worse:	10%

The massage technique of Shiatsu massage therapists is often referred to as acupuncture without needles, because the same meridian lines, or "channels of energy," used in acupuncture are the focus—but thumbs are used instead of needles.

Depending on how tight your muscles are, and on how vigorous your Shiatsu therapist is, you can expect acupressure to create mild discomfort during treatment. Pressure is usually applied with the balls of the thumbs. The procedure works you over from head to foot, without necessarily concentrating on the afflicted area. For example, if you have low back pain, the therapist may emphasize working on points in your legs and feet in order to help your back.

Contrary to popular belief, Shiatsu is not an ancient practice but a twentieth-century Japanese innovation. And it does not necessarily involve the therapist's walking on your back. Indeed, judging from survey participants' comments, individuals with major back pain should definitely *not* allow anyone to walk on their backs.

How you can treat yourself. Shiatsu is far too complex a skill and an art form to be mastered from a book. However, many survey participants found it easy to learn how to use pressure to relieve pain themselves in small areas of muscle tissue that feel "knotted." Here is some of their advice:

(1) For minor to moderate pain from muscle spasms in areas that you can reach comfortably yourself—neck, lower back, buttocks, hips, thighs—push gently with the ball of your thumb for about twenty seconds all around the knotted area. Then apply pressure on the knot itself for seven seconds. There will be some pain. If it's more than the slight wincing variety, use less pressure or stop. If the pain is not intense, you can use this procedure twice a day.

(2) For major muscle spasm that all but prevents you from moving, have someone else "press out" the affected area for seven seconds in each spot. At times, this can be as effective as a muscle-relaxant injection. And according to survey participants,

it is almost always more effective than muscle-relaxant pills when you have specific areas of tightness.

Five Shiatsu therapists in this survey referred to themselves as *holistic massage practitioners*, meaning that their training included more than Shiatsu or Swedish massage. These practitioners were skilled in at least one other kind of deep massage therapy—connective-tissue massage or polarity massage, for example—as well as in stress-reduction techniques. If you get a strong recommendation from a friend about a holistic massage practitioner, you probably will benefit considerably by seeing this specialist.

PHYSICAL FITNESS INSTRUCTOR

- If you're functioning well but have a nuisance level of chronic backache, or episodes of pain a few times a year, successful results are more than likely.

- Some physical fitness experts are exercise physiologists with expertise in treating back conditions; others have no such training.

Number of instructors in this survey:	17
Provided dramatic long-term help:	58%
Provided moderate long-term help:	24%
Provided temporary help:	0%
Ineffective:	12%
Made patient feel worse:	6%

The fitness boom has resulted in the creation of thousands of spas and health clubs. Chances are that you have at least one such facility (including the local YMCA) near your home, complete with an exercise expert who is willing and able to work with back sufferers.

Three key factors determined the relative success that survey participants had with physical fitness instructors.

(1) *Self-assessment.* If you have serious back problems, *say so.* Heroic attempts to join a class of superfit people who look like Jane Fonda and Richard Simmons got participants into trouble. You

need to assess the specialized training or the instructor who will be working with you.

(2) *Self-protection*. Ask questions; the degree of back-care expertise among physical fitness instructors varies widely. Also, if the instructor seems disinterested in your special circumstances, move on. The risks are too great. Find someone who takes the time to learn about your back and then proposes a sensible progression of exercises. Participants called this kind of individualized program the best insurance they could buy.

(3) *Self-indulgence*. If going to a health club is fun and relaxing in general, and you feel as if you're "getting away from it all," you'll benefit more than you would by doing the same exercises at home.

The "Y's Way to a Healthy Back" at YMCA's appears to be an excellent program, rated well by the ten survey participants who went through it. But, again, remember the collective wisdom of all survey participants: only you can judge how fast and far you can go with exercise. If you have to compete with someone, compete with yourself. Do not push to keep up with other members of an exercise class.

DANCE INSTRUCTOR

- For people who occasionally have minor aches and pains, but nothing more serious, dance can be a pleasurable form of exercise therapy.

Number of dance instructors in this survey:	10
Provided dramatic long-term help:	50%
Provided moderate long-term help:	40%
Provided temporary help:	0%
Ineffective:	0%
Made patient feel worse:	10%

Dance movements are too strenuous and advanced for most people with back problems. However, if you're up to it, dance instructors (teachers of modern dance and ballet) know how to transform your body from so-so to excellent condition and do wonders for your back in the process.

The nine out of ten survey participants who found success by following the advice of a dance instructor had the following in common:

(1) They went for instruction after a painful episode had ended, *not* in the throes of back pain.

(2) They enjoyed the idea of learning to dance and of practicing at least three times a week.

(3) After a month's time, they experienced substantial improvement in their posture, abdominal strength, and overall flexibility, along with a substantial reduction of back pain.

OTHER NONMEDICAL-DOCTOR PRACTITIONERS

Survey figures on other non-physician practitioners are not statistically significant, but participants' comments are revealing.

NURSE

• All nine survey participants treated by nurses were helped substantially.

"I got more advice from my orthopedist's nurse, while putting on my hat and coat after an appointment, than I did from the orthopedist himself," reported a young mother. The nurse gave her helpful tips about how to cope with her infant and her back at the same time. For example, the nurse asked the patient how she lifted the baby and how she positioned herself while bathing the baby—then suggested ways to perform these procedures without back strain.

Many a doctor's nurse has long experience with people who suffer from back pain. The nurse *may* have some answers for you, or at least the time and inclination to talk.

If you work for a large corporation with a physical fitness program or a competent medical department, you may be fortunate enough to find a nurse specifically trained in practical aspects of back care. Of the nine survey participants who sought help from nurses, five saw corporate nurses and wound up with a comprehensive—and successful—rehabilitation program.

KINESIOLOGIST

- With their special training in muscles and movement, these specialists can alleviate many kinds of back pain.

The eight kinesiologists seen in this survey were chiropractors who had received an additional degree in kinesiology—the study of the mechanics and anatomy of movement. They were able to help six of the eight participants, which is impressive considering that all of these patients were severely limited by low back pain, sciatica, or a ruptured disc.

Kinesiologists usually employ all the same techniques as chiropractors, including a gentle form of manipulation. But their expertise in the area of movement seems to give them a substantial added advantage.

Note: Chiropractors who advertise the *use* of kinesiology usually do not have a degree in kinesiology.

One disabled back sufferer, a health educator, was in severe pain during the five years that she saw chiropractors, orthopedists, neurosurgeons, and physical therapists. After a few months of treatment by a kinesiologist, she made a complete recovery. "Applied kinesiology—heat, massage, acupressure, gentle adjustments, and stretching exercises—finally helped me," she said.

Although it may not be possible to find a listing of kinesiologists in the telephone directory, residents of the USA, Canada, Australasia, the United Kingdom, and some European countries can learn the name of one practising in their area by contacting the International College of Applied Kinesiology which is based in the United States. Those in North America should telephone (913) 384–5336. On the same number you can obtain details of offices in other countries around the world. In the United Kingdom, the local office telephone number is (01835) 823645. More details can be obtained from the ICAK's extensive website, www.icak.com.

ROLFER

- This holistic therapist uses fingertips, knuckles, elbows, and philosophy, but offers no lasting relief to the average back sufferer.

Rolfing is to Swedish massage what a hurricane is to a calm summer breeze. You *know* your body is being worked on. There is pain as fingertips, knuckles, and elbows dig into you. This raises two questions: Why the pain? Is the treatment worth it?

The pain comes from having to probe deeply into your muscles to free them of tightness, adhesions, and malfunction, Rolfing patients say. In theory, this makes sense, because if the muscles that support your spine are not working properly, you could have back pain. In practice, however, only one of the eight survey participants who tried Rolfing got long-term results, and four got nothing positive at all. The technique, also called Structural Integration, was developed in 1940 by Ida P. Rolf. Since Rolfing is defined by its proponents as "an approach to the personality through the components of the physical body," it is also considered a form of psychotherapy.

ALEXANDER INSTRUCTOR

- If you feel that bad posture is causing your back pain, Alexander instruction has minor value.

You have backache because you are misusing your body—standing and moving incorrectly, according to the theory of the Alexander technique. And this misuse can be brought about by physical or emotional factors, both of which can be treated by Alexander instructors. Five out of six survey participants who tried it—all of whom had chronic but not disabling low back pain—were helped slightly in the long run. The technique is named for Australian-born Frederick Matthias Alexander, a nineteenth-century actor who created it in ten years of exhaustive self-exploration. Doctors' advice could not keep Alexander from losing his voice on the stage, so he worked at correcting his total musculoskeletal technique until he cured himself.

PSYCHOTHERAPIST

- More *have* back problems than *solve* back problems.

More than 300 participants in this survey felt that stress played a role in increasing their back pain. Yet only six of these back sufferers went to a psychologist or psychiatrist for help. Of the six, four felt that their backs were slightly improved in the long run by "talk therapy." Many more psychotherapists (fourteen) were involved in the survey as participants than were cited as practitioners (six). Still, if you feel that your emotional problems are causing back pain, talking to a psychotherapist about these problems might help.

FELDENKRAIS THERAPIST

- Only one of five participants was helped in the long run.

Considered by some to be a psychotherapist and by others to be a kind of posture, movement, and awareness instructor, the Feldenkrais therapist did not provide back sufferers in the survey with substantive help. One, a renowned foreign correspondent and author, was personally instructed by Moishe Feldenkrais, the founder of this therapy, without nearly the success she later obtained from back exercises prescribed by a young orthopedist just starting his practice.

PODIATRIST

- "Instant cures" for back pain caused by short-leg syndrome.

Make sure that the length of your legs is measured during any examination for back pain. A difference of one-half inch is considered significant, although some survey participants and their podiatrists felt that even one-sixteenth of an inch was significant. In these cases, a simple heel lift can work miracles. So can an orthotic, which is a prescribed insert for your shoe. Podiatrists also relieved participants' back pain by advising them about proper shoe height and support.

NATUROPATH

- Three out of four participants got long-run help for minor but chronic low back pain.

Numerous drug-free means of treatment are used by naturopaths to treat back problems and most other disorders and diseases. Techniques include manipulation, diathermy, massage, diet, stress-reduction techniques, and exercise. If there is a naturopath near you who comes recommended by another back sufferer, you might get some long-run support and relief.

Indeed, about a half century ago, you might very well have taken your back pain to a naturopath. Naturopaths were more popular then for their drugless "whatever it takes that won't harm you" approach to chronic medical problems. Today, however, in spite of the swing back to natural means of healing, the number of naturopaths is held in check by legal restrictions on their diagnosing and treating disease.

TAI CHI INSTRUCTOR

- All three Tai Chi devotees in this survey felt that Tai Chi helped their backs and overall state of well-being.

Tai Chi is a blending of martial arts and dance that can help increase your strength and flexibility *if* your ability to move is not overly restricted by pain at the outset. The instruction covers an intriguing way to progress from so-so to excellent shape. "Tai Chi movement, in addition to regular back exercise, is essential," commented a rehabilitation counselor who improved with this combination regimen.

BIOFEEDBACK INSTRUCTOR

- There is no indication that the flood of publicity heralds a breakthrough for most back sufferers.

It is almost impossible to distinguish the well-trained instructor from the imposter. Overall, biofeedback instructors help occasionally—more through personal interaction than by the technology they apply. The technology usually consists of an electrical device that resembles a stereo tuner and connects to some part of your body via wires and electrodes. These monitor one or more vital signs, from heart rate to skin temperature, and the machine gives out a visual or auditory signal as the reading changes. The instructor can theoretically help you learn how to control yourself on many "involuntary" levels, such as increasing the flow of blood to an injured body part.

Virtually anyone with a machine or gadget can claim to be a biofeedback instructor. So . . . *caveat emptor.* Judging by the overall reactions from survey participants, it would seem that practitioners who don't use biofeedback, but who are receptive, compassionate listeners, will assist you as much with stress-related back pain as will the average biofeedback instructor.

Part Three

Back Treatments

"All treatments [for back pain] are controversial, and the reason is an almost complete lack of controlled clinical trials. Treatments have been based on the bias of the particular physician."

—Murray Goldstein, DO,
  Director, National Institute of
  Neurological and
  Communicative Disorders and
  Stroke

"Even after the trouble is diagnosed, the patient is confronted with a baffling choice of therapies."

—Time magazine cover story,
  July 14, 1980,
  "That Aching Back"

"I can't get the same answer twice about what I should and shouldn't do to help myself."

—A survey participant

Chapter 5

The Most Widely Used Treatments for Back Pain

Although you've no doubt heard of every treatment in this chapter, you probably *don't* have enough information to decide whether any one of them will help or hurt you.

Take manipulation, for example. Is it the quackery some doctors claim, the cure-all some chiropractors proclaim, or something in between? Just what *is* its value?

How about heat? Should you use it? If so, when and for how long? Is wet heat really better than the old-fashioned heating pad? And what about electronic means of delivering heat—diathermy and ultrasound?

Do drugs alleviate back pain? Analgesics are routinely prescribed for severe back pain, but do they work? How about anti-inflammatory drugs and muscle relaxants? Is Valium® a good muscle relaxant? How does aspirin compare to its prescription counterparts?

Can traction harm you? Are back supports worth trying? What can massage do for you? Are "off-the-rack" back exercises the answer for most back sufferers?

Here, at last, are answers to these and other questions.

Note: Treatments in this chapter are arranged according to their frequency of mention in the survey, beginning with the most popular ones.

The order does *not* reflect relative effectiveness of the treatments for helping
back sufferers.

DRUGS

- There is no indication that prescription analgesics (pain
  pills) work for the average back sufferer.

- Prescription anti-inflammatory pills have less value than
  placebos. And one out of nine patients suffers adverse effects.

- Aspirin turns out to be the *only* effective anti-inflammatory
  agent, causing only a fraction of the side effects of prescription drugs.

- Muscle-relaxant pills and Valium® have minor value for a
  minority of back sufferers. But they also make one patient in
  every ten feel worse.

	Analgesics	Muscle Relaxant	Prescription Anti-Inflammatory	Tranquilizer	Aspirin
Number of treatments:	138	95	70	25	32
Provided dramatic long-term help:	0%	0%	0%	0%	0%
Provided moderate long-term help:	0%	0%	2%	0%	0%
Provided temporary relief:	30%	36%	24%	36%	78%
Ineffective:	61%	55%	60%	44%	19%
Made patient feel worse:	9%	9%	14%	20%	3%

Pills are the most popular form of treatment for back pain. Yet, according
to survey participants, no prescription drug is significantly more useful than
a placebo. (A placebo is a pill or treatment with no active ingredients or

known medical value, but that nevertheless helps about one-third of patients who receive it.) And, of course, the harmful effects of prescription drugs far outweigh those of placebos.

This doesn't mean that you should refuse to follow a doctor's advice about taking medication for back pain. It is to say, however, that the survey results have shown the odds are poor that pills will help you, especially if you have non-arthritic, muscular aches and pain. And the level of relief, if any, is likely to be minor and temporary. Moreover, it means that you should question those drugs that failed and even harmed some survey participants.

Data about side effects may also give you pause, since the chances are one in ten that you will experience an adverse reaction to a drug prescribed for back pain. Most side effects reported were of the "unpleasant but temporary" variety, although some survey participants suffered serious damage to internal organs. We don't know how many survey participants would have refused to take drugs had they been informed beforehand about side effects. But we do know, according to a survey released in 1983 by the National Council on Patient Information and Education, that nearly three-quarters of all patients are *not* told about the possibility of drug side effects. Furthermore, the same study revealed, only 2 to 4 percent of all patients question their doctors about prescribed medications.

Following is an account of which drugs made survey participants feel worse—and why:

Analgesics—*nausea and other gastrointestinal disturbances, impairment of mental clarity.* Different combinations of acetaminophen with codeine, and aspirin with codeine, were prescribed most frequently. For most survey participants, there were no significant differences between prescription and over-the-counter drugs in reducing pain. And the majority of survey participants who took pain pills considered them ineffective. Highly potent painkillers are available and are necessary in some instances, but back sufferers raised two warning flags about them: (1) be aware of the possible side effects of what has been prescribed for you; and (2) remember that a pill powerful enough to mute pain will also deprive you of helpful warning signals. In other words, if you take a strong analgesic, you should greatly reduce your physical activities and movements.

Muscle-Relaxant Pills—*dizziness and light-headedness, drowsiness, impairment of mental clarity*. Robaxin® and Parafon Forte®* were the brand names mentioned most frequently, but the majority of survey participants could not remember the name of the muscle relaxant prescribed for them.

Prescription Anti-Inflammatory Agents—*gastrointestinal disorders, including aggravation of ulcers and gastritis, as well as a few cases of rectal bleeding*. Motrin®, Indocin®, and Naprosyn®* were the pills taken most. Although we could not determine which brand names or generic classes carried the greatest benefit or did the most harm, our correspondence and conversations with back sufferers convince us that most people should shun *all* anti-inflammatory pills except aspirin. For the most part, only those whose back problems are caused by arthritis can hope to gain anything by taking these drugs.

Aspirin—*gastrointestinal disturbances*. The number of survey participants who took aspirin is certainly higher than our reported figure. Many participants didn't include aspirin in their list of drugs simply because aspirin is used so commonly and is often not considered a "real" drug. In fact, most participants who mentioned aspirin said it had been recommended by a doctor. But the vast majority of medical authorities agree that aspirin is a powerful drug, and that regular, long-term use requires the approval and supervision of a qualified practitioner.

Valium®—*drowsiness, light-headedness, impaired mental clarity*. When Valium® is prescribed for back sufferers, it is usually meant to act as a muscle relaxant with stress-reducing qualities. It is thought to act on the part of the brain thought to influence emotional stability. Individuals who take Valium® during the day should not be surprised if they cannot function as usual. Few doctors told them that it can be dangerous to drive while using Valium®.

There is a growing consensus among medical professionals, and among informed consumers, that drugs are being overprescribed for ailments such as back pain. For years, patients who went to a doctor wanted to come away with something concrete—and that something was a prescription. But this

---

*We don't have enough survey data to know whether any particular brand name is better or worse than any other in its drug family.

attitude seems to be changing. A survey conducted by researchers associated with Johns Hopkins Hospital found that "patients who did not receive prescriptions reported more satisfaction with their visits to physicians than patients who did receive prescriptions. Patients may not be as prescription-oriented as many physicians believe."

MANIPULATION

- Reduces pain temporarily in a majority of treatments but is *not by itself* a long-run solution.

- Best for low back pain and neck pain.

- Beware of practitioners using manipulation to treat acute pain caused by a herniated disc.

Number of treatments:	333
Provided dramatic long-term help:	5%
Provided moderate long-term help:	7%
Provided temporary help:	44%
Ineffective:	34%
Made patient feel worse:	10%

Manipulation, used alone as a means of relieving back pain, is not what it's cracked up to be. When it relieves pain it does so temporarily—from a few hours to a few days. Manipulation used as one element in a well-rounded program of total back care, however, helped about 25 percent of people in this survey to function normally over the long run—with only minimal back pain and without the need for regular treatments.

The two kinds of medical specialists who make the greatest use of manipulation are chiropractors and osteopaths. But other specialists, including small groups of physical therapists and "Manipulating Orthopedists," also manipulate the spine as part of their recovery programs for back sufferers.

Although manipulation is a discipline that requires extensive training, it is also, like so many other medical procedures, an art form. Perhaps this explains why the average chiropractic patient in the survey went to at least two chiropractors or osteopaths before finding a manipulator who got results.

Nevertheless, participants' experiences show how to cut down on the amount of running around it takes to find a practitioner skilled in manipulation. The best and surest way is to get a recommendation from another back sufferer.

An alternate approach is to arrange an appointment for consultation purposes, rather than for treatment. This allows you to gauge the practitioner's receptiveness to spending time learning about you and your problem, as opposed to getting you on the table posthaste. You'll also get a chance to ask the practitioner about his philosophy of manipulation. The gentler forms produced the most satisfactory results for survey participants. One specific technique mentioned frequently and favorably was "directional non-force manipulation," but try not to get caught up in the manipulation name game.

There are dozens of names used for manipulation techniques. Some are technical and others imply merchandising ploys. The differences separating one from another are usually indiscernible to lay people (and to some manipulators, for that matter). Promise-laden brochures proclaiming the unique healing powers of this or that form of manipulation are fairly common. In short, ignore claims that border on the miraculous, be skeptical of supposedly documented success rates of 90 percent or higher, and look for a professional who is interested in you and in an overall program of back care.

BACK EXERCISES

- For the vast majority of back sufferers, appropriate exercises are essential to lessening or ending back pain.

- People with debilitating back pain have far more success with individually prescribed exercise programs than with exercise routines in self-help books and articles or in health club classes.

- See the low back exercise program in Chapter 10.

- See Chapters 11–14 for advice about exercises for ruptured disc, arthritis, neck pain, scoliosis, sciatica, and spondylolisthesis.

Number of survey participants who exercised regularly:	278*
Got dramatic long-term help:	45%
Got moderate long-term help:	32%
Got temporary help:	10%
Saw no effect:	7%
Felt worse:	6%

Much has been written about the preventive and rehabilitative aspects of exercise for back sufferers. In fact, over the last two decades, more than a thousand books and magazines have featured an X-minutes-a-day exercise program, each one ballyhooed as *the* plan for you.

Since most people with activity-limiting back pain do back exercises on a regular basis—*and still have limitations*—it is obvious that the whole story about back exercise hasn't been told. So let's try to sort out the misconceptions from the facts by examining some commonly held but erroneous beliefs about exercise and back pain.

If you are athletic and fit you won't have back pain. False. The physical fitness boom that took hold in this country ten years ago, galvanizing some 55 million Americans into regular fitness activities, has not banished back problems by any means. There are no statistics to show that the back pain epidemic has diminished or even slowed in its rate of growth.

Lost playing time because of back pain among professionals is rampant in every sport, so much so that the daily sports pages often sound as though they were filed from a back clinic. Here are just a few of the athletes whose back problems were mentioned in the media during the summer of 1983:

- One of America's greatest heroes, Joe DiMaggio, didn't play in a Yankees' Old-Timers game. Why? Although Jolting Joe was fit at age 68, back trouble had been a factor in keeping him out of Old-Timers games since 1975.

*These statistics are limited to traditional forms of back exercise prescribed by practitioners ranging from orthopedists to chiropractors to physical fitness instructors. Excluded are less traditional forms of exercise, such as yoga, which are covered in the next two chapters.

- Yankee pitchers Ron Guidry, Rudy May, and Matt Keough missed games because of back pain.

- Milwaukee Brewers All-Star shortstop Robin Yount was out of action with back pain.

- After three ruptured discs, the American League rookie of the year in 1980, Joe Charboneau, was reported playing semi-pro ball.

- Tracy Austin, the world's third-ranked women's tennis player, couldn't compete in the U.S. Open because of back pain.

- Star goalie John Davidson announced his retirement because of injuries to his knees and back.

- Former heavyweight champion Mike Weaver canceled a fight because of an injury to his lower back.

- Future Hall-of-Famer Steve Carlton departed early from a National League playoff game because of back spasms. He is considered one of the best-conditioned athletes in professional sports.

- And the list of other athletes who have had back pain goes on too long, including pro football Hall-of-Fame coach Chuck Noll, New York Jets punter Pat Leahy, tennis star Hana Mandlikova, and baseball greats Pete Rose and Reggie Jackson.

Incapacitating back pain among weekend athletes is also common-place. According to the Health Insurance Association, an estimated 20 million sports injuries, including back injuries, occur each year. And according to our survey participants, tennis, squash, and racquetball—with their sudden lunges, starts, and stops—seem to be especially risky for back sufferers.

Any reputable book, magazine article, or printed sheet handed to you by a doctor can teach you the back exercises you need. This is only half true. Roughly half the people who get advice this way are not helped much by it—and about 10 percent are injured by it. If you have ordinary low back pain that is more annoying than incapacitating, and if you are in relatively good shape, chances are that a conservative plan calling for slow increments may help you a great deal. But if you have activity-limiting episodes of back pain, or chronically disabling back pain, you probably need an exercise plan prescribed specifically for you, lest you risk serious injury, or minimally, fail to make progress.

Practitioners are interested in giving you an exercise program; the problem is that people are too lazy to do what they are told. This is mostly false. Only 13 percent of physicians and 26 percent of other practitioners seen by survey participants recommended an exercise program. Most practitioners have no training at all in the science of back exercise. According to a study reported in the *Journal of Medical Education* in 1975, "very little time—an average of about four hours, usually in conjunction with a medical physiology course— was spent studying the effects of exercise." And according to Dr. Arthur Michelle, professor and chairman of the Department of Orthopedic Surgery at the New York Medical College and author of *You Don't Have to Ache,* doctors spend only one percent of study time learning about muscles, but then find that the vast majority of their patients have pain relating to the musculoskeletal system.

Fully 61 percent of participants in this survey exercised regularly, from four to seven days a week, with the vast majority exercising daily. And many of these people exercised after simply being handed a sheet of exercises or told to get a certain exercise book.

Fifteen percent of participants were told to exercise . . . did so at first . . . but stopped after they felt improved. "I should exercise, but I'm lazy about it," they told us.

Of the remaining 24 percent, 13 percent were totally unaware of the therapeutic value of exercise; 5 percent were told *not* to exercise; and 6 percent stopped exercising after finding that the activity made them feel worse.

As for specific exercise advice, survey participants' experiences show that two "non-back" exercises do help just about everyone with back pain— walking and swimming. Even the twenty-six back sufferers who couldn't lead normal lives because of back pain *all* improved in the long run by following their practitioners' advice to walk or swim regularly. At least a half hour of brisk walking every other day is recommended, or building up to fifteen minutes of non-stop swimming three times a week.

Personally tailored exercise advice is most likely forthcoming, participants say, from one of the following exercise experts:

(1) Physiatrist (medical doctor specializing in physical medicine and rehabilitation)

(2) Physical therapist (practitioner trained in natural means of rehabilitation, who usually requires a doctor's authorization to treat you)

(3) Sports medicine specialist (medical doctor trained to prevent and repair sports injuries, including back problems)

(4) Kinesiologist (expert in the principles and mechanics of movement)

(5) Yoga teacher*

(6) Physical fitness instructor*

HEAT

- Wet heat is slightly more effective than dry heat.

- Electronic means of dispersing heat into muscle— diathermy and ultrasound—require professional supervision *and are less effective* than simple home remedies.

- Don't apply heat to a severe and acute spasm without professional advice. The heat can cause the spasm to "lock."

	Wet Heat	Ultra-sound	Dry Heat	Diathermy
Number of treatments:	118	71	51	30
Provided dramatic long-term help:	1%	0%	0%	0%
Provided moderate long-term help:	0%	2%	0%	0%

*Not all yoga teachers and physical fitness instructors have the experience or the desire to work with back problems. On the other hand, some physical fitness instructors have advanced degrees in exercise physiology or kinesiology, and may be especially qualified to prescribe exercise.

Provided temporary help:	71%	35%	67%	43%
Ineffective:	25%	62%	32%	57%
Made patient feel worse:	3%	1%	1%	0%

"Get out the heating pad."

"Soak in a hot tub."

These two pieces of advice for back sufferers turn out to be as wise as they are commonplace. Both of these heat treatments are simple, effective, and cheap.

Apply a hot, wet towel or soak in the tub. You'll give the same relief to your tired, overworked back as you would if you invested money in hot packs or whirlpools.

A heating pad is also a worthwhile investment, according to survey participants. And although there is a trend among practitioners of all kinds in recommending wet heat over dry (heating pad), our data show only a slight difference in effectiveness.

You might expect that since heat applied to the surface of your skin provides relief, deeply penetrating heat would help even more. And it would seem that the use of expensive machines and a trip to a practitioner's office would further magnify your relief, whether by "power of suggestion" or technological healing magic.

But this is not the case. As you can see from the figures above, the results of using electronic heat conveyors are unimpressive when compared with home remedies. The sophisticated techniques are ultrasound (sound waves that cause cell molecules to vibrate and produce heat) and diathermy (short waves of heat that penetrate and warm deep tissue). Participants who suffered from sciatica and osteoarthritis derived the greatest benefit from ultrasound (a temporary relief rate of 50%), but the average back sufferer will likely discover that home remedies surpass both ultrasound and diathermy, are less time-consuming, and are far less expensive.*

*A 1970 issue of *Physical Therapy* reported that over 90 percent of patients with osteoarthritis showed improvement when lower-than-usual frequencies of ultrasound were used. However, there is no indication from our survey results that ultrasound offers that degree of help to back sufferers, whether or not they have arthritis.

MASSAGE

- Shiatsu, or acupressure massage, is the most successful, drug-free treatment available for temporarily relieving low back and neck pain.

- Swedish massage is soothing and relaxing, if not healing and pain-relieving.

- If you have severe low back pain, here's how to position yourself for maximum comfort and safety during a massage.

	Swedish	Shiatsu
Number of treatments:	95	29
Provided dramatic long-term help:	2%	3%
Provided moderate long-term help:	3%	7%
Provided temporary help:	61%	69%
Ineffective:	31%	14%
Made patient feel worse:	3%	7%

With its low level of long-run success, Shiatsu wouldn't normally get much acclaim in a report of this kind. But its value has to be taken seriously for three reasons.

First, its "temporary help" rate of 69 percent is surpassed only by aspirin and wet heat for short-term relief.

Second, wet heat was usually the *first* step taken by back sufferers to alleviate pain. Shiatsu, on the other hand, was usually the treatment of last resort for survey participants with the most intractable problems. And it typically got results where heat did not.

Third, the temporary help provided by Shiatsu usually lasted long enough for participants to get involved in long-run rehabilitation programs.

A close relative of acupuncture, Shiatsu is applied along meridians, or pathways through which energy is said to course through the body. Like acupuncture, it can create a dramatic cessation of pain for weeks or months at a time, allowing the back sufferer to make considerable progress.

Shiatsu may feel a little like "bad medicine that must be good for you." The pressure of the massage, usually exerted with the ball of the thumb, sometimes elicits a few ouches and grimaces from back sufferers with tight muscles. This minor pain hardly ever persists after the treatment, but excessive pressure on the lower back can be injurious and did cause an increase in pain for two of the twenty-nine survey participants.

Swedish massage, by comparison, with its mostly smooth-gliding movements, is virtually pain- and risk-free. The one exception—which applies *only* to severely disabled back sufferers—is that lying on your stomach for up to one hour, even with a small pillow tucked under you, can aggravate lumbar pain. Shiatsu also carries this element of risk. But the risk can be minimized or avoided as follows:

(1) When you're on your back, put a folded towel or small pillow under your neck and head, and one or two pillows under your knees.

(2) If you think you can lie on your stomach without aggravating your problem, tuck a pillow under your abdomen. If the pillow is thin, and you feel a pull on your lower back, fold the pillow in two. In any event, make sure the pillow is under your abdomen and not under your chest.

(3) If you feel uncomfortable lying on your stomach, try lying in an oblique position: lie on your side, tuck a folded pillow against your abdomen, and lean into it. Keep leaning toward the stomach-down position as far as you can without turning onto your stomach. Experiment with different positions for your legs, making sure that you keep at least one of them bent.

Note: Many massage therapists, and virtually all chiropractors, feel they cannot work on you unless you lie on your stomach. So check before you go.

As with every other aspect of back care, remember to believe in *your* judgment about yourself.

TRACTION

- *Danger:* Back traction makes more people feel worse than any other widely used form of back treatment. Its use warrants a second opinion.

- Cervical (neck) traction is only slightly less hazardous.

Number of traction procedures:	78
Provided dramatic long-term help:	1%
Provided moderate long-term help:	2%
Provided temporary help:	22%
Ineffective:	52%
Made patient feel worse:	23%

"Traction was pointless and painful physically and mentally," commented a coal miner with a ruptured disc who spent four weeks in traction at a hospital. "I have dead tingly nerves where my legs meet my hips from the traction belt. Traction weakened and stiffened my back."

A respiratory therapist also had harsh words for traction: "The treatment which left me with excruciating pain was suggested by an MD and consisted of neck and back traction with weights."

Even brief forms of traction can be injurious, as in this typist's experience: "At the start of ten minutes of traction at a chiropractor's office, I felt a sharp pain in my lower back and this pain continued to bother me for almost two months. I didn't even know I was getting traction until I yelled for help and asked what was happening."

Granted, patients who have traction prescribed for them are often in excruciating pain, where instant miracles could hardly be expected. Granted, too, that some participants' perception that they felt worse because of traction may be wrong. Perhaps they were confused by the contrast between moderate relief during traction and the return of their "old pain" immediately afterward.

But no matter how we try to give this procedure the benefit of the doubt, we have to conclude that the use of traction for back and leg pain should probably be avoided. "Why not just bed rest?" and "What are the risks of becoming worse?" are two specific questions you should ask any practitioner who advocates traction.

Why is traction used fairly often? According to survey participants, back practitioners offered three major reasons:

(1) Traction can keep antsy patients in bed and assure complete bed rest.

(2) Light weights can help tilt the pelvis slightly upward, thus flattening the curve in the lower back and relieving pain.

(3) Heavy weights and special traction equipment can pull apart vertebrae enough to ease pressure on a nerve, thus relieving pain.

Assuring complete rest is the most often cited reason for prescribing back traction. It implies that a certain number of adult back patients won't follow orders just to rest. We suggest, based on what survey participants have told us, that you forgo weights and substitute willpower if complete bed rest is what you need.

Neck traction, on the other hand, substantially helped three of nine survey participants who tried it.

A housekeeper who suffered a whiplash injury found that using light-weight traction three times a day solved her problem where all else had failed. Even so, she said, "I was scared to death of using a pulley with weights attached to my neck."

Neck traction also harms people, though, with two or more survey participants reporting injuries from it. See Chapter 12 for details.

One do-it-yourself form of traction that has mushroomed in popularity among back sufferers is *inversion traction*—also known as "anti-gravity," "hanging," or "gravity inversion." See Chapter 7 for details.

BRACES AND SUPPORTS

- These usually provide some relief during acute episodes of back pain.

- Back supports may be good preventive measures during physically demanding or emotionally stressful times.

- Overuse is self-defeating and risky, weakening the muscles needed to support the spine.

Number in the survey:	70
Provided dramatic long-term help:	0%
Provided moderate long-term help:	6%
Provided temporary help:	50%
Ineffective:	32%
Made patient feel worse:	12%

Picture a foolproof way to keep your posture perfect—tummy not protruding, rump tucked in, body relaxed and properly aligned. This foolproof technique ultimately comes from the proper conditioning of your abdominal, back, and buttock muscles—not from a back support.

But if your muscles temporarily cannot do this job, then a back support can help in the short run. Supports for your back are really supports for your abdominal muscles. If these muscles aren't strong enough to keep your tummy "in," your spine will not be adequately supported and all kinds of back problems can ensue.

"A simple rubberized brace with Velcro® fasteners provided instant relief for the first few weeks I was out of bed," commented a chemical engineer who was recovering from a bout of severe low back spasms.

"I wear a girdle when I know I'm in for a taxing day," said a waitress.

Rigidly constructed back braces, fit to your exact proportions, perform the same abdominal-holding function and more—keeping you aligned in a manner that a practitioner feels is right for you.

Many different kinds of back supports are available, including some that you can purchase at a surgical supply store without a prescription. Most survey participants who were helped by these aids, though, used back supports that had been prescribed for them.

The risks of supporting yourself artificially are clear.

"After wearing a brace for two months, and not exercising, my muscles were so weak that my back pain worsened greatly after the brace was removed," commented a professional athlete who had been through disc surgery.

In summary, if your muscles are strong enough to provide you with a built-in back support, you will only weaken this natural mechanism by using an aid. But if you're not in shape, a support can help you until you feel well enough to strengthen your muscles through exercise.

Chapter 6

Less Common (and More Controversial) Treatments for Back Pain

Only in the field of back care, where the variety of treatments is as extensive as it is bewildering, could yoga, surgery, and acupuncture attract about equal numbers of individuals desperate for relief. And only in the field of back care, where documentation about treatment effectiveness is generally unavailable, could there be so many people promising to banish pain in so many different ways—injecting it (triggerpoint, cortisone, and muscle-relaxant injections), numbing it (cryotherapy), unknotting it with electrical currents (electric muscle stimulation), and healing it with spiritual power (meditation).

The extent to which there is back-fitness value behind all this controversy is explored in this chapter.

Note: Treatments in this chapter are arranged according to their frequency of mention in the survey, beginning with the most popular ones. The order does *not* reflect relative effectiveness of the treatments for helping back sufferers.

SURGERY

- Even if a doctor tells you that you have a ruptured or degenerated disc, there is a 75 percent chance that you will *not* need surgery.

- One-quarter of surgical procedures provide dramatic long-run help.

- One out of seven patients winds up significantly worse in the long run.

- The absence of skilled physical therapy is one major reason for a poor outcome from surgery; scarring is another reason.

- Survey participants who didn't fare well after surgery tended to be abandoned—in spirit if not in fact—by doctors.

Number of treatments:	65
Provided dramatic long-term help:	25%
Provided moderate long-term help:	25%
Provided temporary help:	28%
Ineffective:	8%
Made patient feel worse:	14%

Perhaps the most important fact to know about disc surgery is that you probably don't need it. For every survey participant who had disc surgery, three others were told they probably had disc problems requiring surgery but found successful alternatives.

This widespread use of ruptured disc as a diagnosis isn't surprising for two reasons.

First, participants with severe, chronic back pain were typically referred by a GP to an orthopedist or a neurosurgeon, either of whom was more likely than any other practitioner to suspect a ruptured disc or suggest surgery.

Second, most survey participants who were told they needed surgery were misinformed. They received a tentative diagnosis that proved incorrect or was never borne out by diagnostic procedures.

There is a growing consensus among medical authorities that many of the approximately 200,000 disc operations performed annually are unnecessary. Currently, the rule of thumb is that no more than 5 percent of back sufferers require surgery. But Dr. Norman Shealy, president of the American Holistic Medical Association, is even more optimistic. He believes that fewer than one percent of back sufferers have disc problems requiring surgery.

If surgery has been advised for you, survey participants' experience can help you choose a surgeon and avoid postoperative complications. You may also be interested to read about helpful alternatives to surgery that some of them tried.

Choosing a surgeon

For most people, disc surgery *is* elective surgery, even though severe pain may make them feel as though they have no choice. And that means you can probably choose your own doctor.

But how? You're hardly up for arranging consultation appointments and asking surgeons about their accreditation or the quality of their training. In fact, if you're really caught up in pain, you may go along with the electrical engineer who said, "I didn't care at a certain point whether a monkey with a Boy Scout knife operated on me. I just couldn't take it anymore." In that case, try to have someone close to you—someone whose judgment you trust—do the investigating.

Begin by asking friends, relatives, and acquaintances whether they know of anyone who has had disc surgery. If you find an individual who is pleased with a particular surgeon—and the outcome of the surgery—your search may be over.

If you don't find a helpful recommendation, call the chief orthopedist at three hospitals near you. Take a positive attitude. Try to phrase the inquiry something like this: "A relative of mine was told he needs disc surgery. I've heard wonderful things about your orthopedics department. Could you possibly recommend a surgeon for us to consult with? And could you give us some idea of your success with disc cases?"

If the orthopedics department is in a teaching hospital, ask if the surgery would be performed by the orthopedist in charge of your case or by a resident. Residents have to practice on someone, but not necessarily on you.

It is extremely important to learn about the rehabilitation process. Again, try to be positive and specific with your questions. Ask about the range of time usually needed for partial and complete recovery, and what kind of physical therapy is offered. Remember that a good physical therapy program is crucial; it can make a competent surgeon seem like a genius.

Two disabling postoperative problems . . . and how to avoid them

Of the thirty-three survey participants who failed to improve in the long run, or who became worse after disc surgery, only six felt they knew the reason for their problems. CAT scans revealed that these six individuals had formed scar tissue from the surgery, and this tissue was apparently generating pain by pressing on nerve roots. In some cases, nerve root pressure causes worse pain than a ruptured disc.

It seems that no one who has a disc removed surgically can avoid the formation of scar tissue. But why scar tissue is a problem for some people and not for others remains a mystery.

Most survey participants who recovered fully from disc surgery shared two key elements in their rehabilitation process: (1) ice massages during the first weeks after surgery; and (2) a supervised, daily physical therapy and exercise program that included an emphasis on building abdominal strength. See Chapters 10 and 11 for tips on how to do appropriate exercises.

Two survey participants who fared poorly with surgery later were told that they had arachnoiditis—scarring of the spinal column apparently caused in these cases by an allergic reaction to Pantopaque®, the oil-based solution once used routinely in myelograms. Not one of the forty-three survey participants who had myelograms was warned of this possible side effect, which is both painful and seemingly irreversible.

Caution: A myelogram is a test that attempts to determine the precise location of the ruptured disc. It is a required procedure at most hospitals, but it can be performed with safer, water-based solutions. If you must undergo myelography, find out which kind of solution will be used. Oil-based solutions are seldom used anymore. But don't assume anything. *Ask*. And see Chapter 8 for further details about myelography.

How to avoid surgery for a ruptured or degenerated disc

Talking about how to avoid surgery may seem out of place in a section *about* surgery, but most people considering surgery are secretly or openly wondering whether they can avoid it. Approximately half of sixty-five survey participants with positive myelography or CAT scan results did just that. After hearing they had a ruptured disc, they opted against surgery. Most were functioning well an average of five years after the initial diagnosis. And they attributed their success in avoiding surgery to one of the following approaches or procedures, listed according to their frequency of use. (You'll find a thorough look at how best to recover from a ruptured disc, and achieve fitness, in Chapter 11.)

- Everyone who avoided surgery started his or her recovery with *bed rest,* for an average of one to eight weeks.

- *Strong pain medication* (Percodan®, for example) was another important factor. Prescription pain pills don't work well for most back conditions (see Chapter 5 for details). But in the case of debilitating, acute sciatica caused by a ruptured disc, potent pain medication is essential. Milder analgesics usually don't help sciatica. The result is that some patients are unnecessarily driven to surgery by intolerable pain before bed rest has had a chance to work.

- Having a *supportive practitioner* who wants to avoid surgery as much as you do is extremely helpful. Otherwise, you will have to deal with the physical pain *and* the pressure to "get back on your feet quickly." Doctors of physical medicine are rated best by survey participants on this score.

- Survey participants also stress the need for carefully planned and supervised *physical therapy,* covering everything from the length of time you should walk each day to the therapeutic use of ice and graduated exercise. Professional help during this stage of your recovery is almost essential. The right help for a few weeks can enable you to take charge of your recovery more effectively.

- *Chymopapain injections* may be tried if you are in too much pain to tolerate bed rest, or if the ruptured disc is causing troublesome nerve impairment such as loss of bladder control.

- *Inversion traction,* or hanging upside down, in one of the many harness-type devices now available may be attempted—

but *only* with medical supervision when you're in acute pain. Note that regular traction is a poor bet.

YOGA

• An extraordinarily high percentage of survey participants who practice yoga get good results in the long run.

• Individualized, modified yoga instruction is the key to success since many *regular* yoga positions are the route to serious injury.

• Modified yoga therapy helped back sufferers with osteoarthritis, neck pain, and scoliosis. (See Chapters 12–14.)

Number of participants:	45
Provided dramatic long-term help:	51%
Provided moderate long-term help:	42%
Provided temporary help:	3%
Ineffective:	0%
Made patient feel worse:	4%

Many disciplines other than yoga integrate help for the spine, the mind, and the spirit. But none comes close to matching the widespread appeal and positive results of yoga.

If you haven't tried yoga because it seems mystical or somehow peculiar to you—an activity associated with ex-flower children or Indian fakirs—consider these comments:

A union carpenter was surprised and delighted to find that yoga suited him. "Yoga has helped my back more than anything," he said. "I stumbled on it by accident as a back pain remedy. I was curious and took a class."

"Yoga is a wonderful way to keep your back limber and your whole body in good shape," commented a house cleaner. "It is such a wonderful experience—my spine and muscles feel so much improved and my head feels clearer. It is the best thing to do for your back as well as your spirit."

A manual laborer said, "Yoga seems to have strengthened my back. It certainly brings a lot of temporary relief from tension. But if not practiced regularly and carefully, I believe it is possible to harm the spine with 'overenthusiastic' yoga."

How to get the most benefit from yoga

A few survey participants learned yoga entirely on their own. But those who were helped the most got started with professional and personalized instruction.

If there is a yoga institute near you, it is best to drop by and discuss your needs with an instructor. Participants report that telephone inquiries seldom reveal whether the staff members have the expertise to provide individualized therapy.

The yoga instructor's willingness to *modify the therapy* cannot be emphasized enough. At least two generally accepted forms of yoga therapy for back sufferers could actually cause further injury if you try them while you are in pain or before you have the necessary flexibility. One is the Cobra, in which you lie on your stomach and arch your back by raising your head and chest. The other is the Plough, where you lie on your back and raise your straightened legs up and over your body and head, until your toes touch down behind your head.

However, if you are able to do regular back exercises, and seem to have progressed as far as you can with them, yoga is an excellent and proven-effective way to further both your physical and emotional well-being.

If professional yoga instruction is not available to you, here are exercises you can try on your own:

(1) *Relaxation position.* This deceptively simple procedure tells you as much about the meditative yoga philosophy as does any yoga exercise. Lie on your back with a pillow under your knees. Keep your arms at your sides and your legs slightly apart. Let your body go limp, with neck, arms, and legs allowed to shift naturally into the most comfortable position possible. Now *think* about muscle relaxation. Start with your feet, ankles, and legs. Concentrate on making the individual muscles and joints relax. Work your way up your body to your neck and head. Take a few minutes to do this. When you are finished, your concentration and energy will be directed toward the exercises to come.

(2) *Stretching your spine from a sitting position.* Sit on the floor with your legs fully extended and your ankles touching each other. Raise your arms in front of you. Now slowly lower your upper body as far as you can while also lowering your hands to your knees. When you feel resistance, hold this position for a count of ten. Start with three repetitions and increase by one repetition every other day until you reach ten.

(3) *Flexibility twist.* Stand with your feet close together. Raise your arms to shoulder level and touch your hands together. Slowly turn your upper body to the left. When you meet resistance, hold for ten seconds. Return to the starting position. Drop your arms and relax for a few seconds. Perform the same movement to your right. Start with three repetitions and increase by one repetition every other day until you reach ten.

(4) *Modified Locust.* Lie face down with a pillow tucked under your abdomen. Keeping your knees locked, raise one leg about a foot off the floor. Hold for a count of six, then lower the leg slowly to the floor. Do the same procedure with the other leg. Start with three repetitions and increase by one repetition every other day until you reach ten.

Note: None of the above exercises, except the relaxation position, should be done by anyone whose activities or motions are greatly restricted by pain.

ELECTRICAL STIMULATION THERAPY

- Provides minor, short-lived relief about half the time for spasm-induced low back pain.

- Has no noxious side effects.

Number of treatments:	45
Provided dramatic long-term help:	0%
Provided moderate long-term help:	0%
Provided temporary help:	47%
Ineffective:	51%
Made patient feel worse:	2%

Electrical stimulation therapy is most often used by physical therapists and chiropractors. It is almost never offered as a sole means of treatment, but usually as a supplement to massage, manipulation, or triggerpoint injections.

Electrical stimulation equipment comes in all sizes and shapes—from small units that a physical therapist can bring to your home to hefty space-age-looking devices. All of them work by sending an electrical current into contracted muscle areas, causing the muscles to contract and relax. The current is applied for ten to fifteen minutes. One theory is that the current drives the muscles to contract themselves into a state of exhaustion, thereby ending the original contraction or spasm.

Electrical stimulation therapy works modestly well about half the time. But the relief isn't dramatic enough to elicit cheers from survey participants, except for one occupational therapist who reported complete relief from painful muscle spasm after one treatment of massage and electrical stimulation therapy.

If electrical stimulation therapy is offered as one element in a comprehensive back-care program that appeals to you, rest assured that there's no harm in trying it. It might speed up the healing process.

ACUPUNCTURE

- Fifty-four percent of survey participants who tried acupuncture treatments were helped by them.

- Acupuncture works for most kinds of back ailments. At least five to ten treatments may be needed to determine effectiveness in individual cases.

Number of treatments:	35
Provided dramatic long-term help:	6%
Provided moderate long-term help:	17%
Provided temporary help:	31%
Ineffective:	43%
Made patient feel worse:	3%

No one knows why acupuncture works. Traditional Chinese medical texts claim acupuncture corrects energy imbalances. According to some researchers, it releases endorphins—your nervous system's own painkillers. But some doctors maintain that the effect from acupuncture is purely psychological—you think it will work, so it does.

Also, no one knows who will benefit from acupuncture. One patient with sciatica will get relief; another patient with a comparable problem won't. The same holds true for other kinds of back pain.

What is clear from the survey is that acupuncture *does* work in some cases. It provides relief slightly over half the time. Occasionally, it eliminates pain for a patient's lifetime.

In most acupuncture treatments, thin needles are inserted into points along meridian lines designated by ancient practitioners as channels of energy. There were no complaints about pain from the insertion of the needles, which is most often described as a pinprick sensation that lasts an instant. During the treatment, patients say, a barely perceptible current or flow of pressure from one insertion point to another can be felt, but no pain is associated with this, either. Some practitioners twirl the needles; others attach electrodes to drive currents through the energy channels.

If you are leery of needles used for injections, rest assured that there is no comparison. Acupuncture needles are as thin as fine wires. They produce no bruising or bleeding. You are likely to feel comfortable, even relaxed and drowsy, during treatments, which can last anywhere from fifteen to forty-five minutes.

If you are not improved after five to ten sessions, you can assume that acupuncture—or at least the particular kind of treatment you are receiving—will not help you.

INJECTIONS

- Cortisone injections are occasionally useful, even curative, for inflammation and pain from arthritis, sciatica, and muscle strain, but side effects can be unpleasant and dangerous.

- Triggerpoint injections are a hit-or-hurt treatment. They can work miracles, but they usually make you feel worse before you feel better.

- Muscle-relaxant injections offer temporary relief only—from a few hours to a day.

- See Chapter 7 for details on chymopapain injections and nerve block injections.

	Cortisone	Triggerpoint	Muscle Relaxant
Number of treatments:	15	10	6
Provided dramatic long-term help:	7%	10%	0%
Provided moderate long-term help:	7%	0%	0%
Provided temporary help:	40%	40%	66%
Ineffective:	33%	20%	16.5%
Made patient feel worse:	13%	30%	16.5%

The three treatments grouped here are the most frequently used injection procedures, although they are *not* always similar in technique, objective, or effectiveness.

Cortisone injections—According to most survey participants who received cortisone injections, the procedure is a last-resort attempt to deal with painful inflammation. Positive long-run results from cortisone injections are the exception, and there were only two in this survey. A telephone repairman with severe hip pain from osteoarthritis received three injections, found immediate relief, and was still pain-free three years later. A homemaker with sciatica, who had seen everyone and tried everything to relieve the pain, said she was cured by a single cortisone injection.

Another survey participant, a retired engineer, reported great success with cortisone injections *after* disc surgery. Every year or so, when pain flared up in the area where his disc had been removed, a cortisone "lumbar puncture" saved him.

In most instances, though, relief from cortisone is fleeting—a few hours or days at most. Also, the hazards of cortisone and other steroids, especially when taken over time, are worse than most drugs prescribed for back pain. For example, a professor who received an injection every week for a month was hospitalized with extreme mental confusion attributed to cortisone.

And a housewife who received cortisone injections retained so much fluid that she gained over sixty pounds and developed kidney problems.

Triggerpoint injections—"When one small area of muscle near where my buttock joins my hip was touched by the doctor, it hurt like hell and pain radiated from that spot down my leg to my knee." This statement from a computer programmer probably defines a "triggerpoint" as well as or better than most technical explanations. Indeed, there is little agreement among doctors about what a triggerpoint is, or even whether such a thing exists.

Survey participants who had triggerpoint injections, though, all said they could feel small areas of soft tissue that seemed to be knotted, were extremely painful to the touch, and radiated pain to other areas of the back, buttocks, or legs. These points were injected with a solution of painkiller, often xylocaine or procaine, mixed with saline or cortisone. Participants warn that the insertion of the needle hurts about twice as much as an ordinary injection—uncomfortable but not unbearable. And for the first day or two after an injection, you can expect to feel worse before you feel better, with the triggerpoint area bruised and swollen. But when there is relief a few days after the injection, it usually represents a major step toward recovery.

Triggerpoint injections require considerable expertise on the part of the practitioner, although any medical doctor or osteopath can give them. And although triggerpoint injections have been used for decades to alleviate back pain, their effectiveness is still controversial and relatively few practitioners believe in them.

Muscle-relaxant injections—If specific muscles in your back are contracting or in spasm, some doctors may suggest injecting an anesthetic into the affected area. They believe this injection makes more sense than the "shotgun" approach of prescribed muscle-relaxant pills. There is usually temporary relief from a numbing agent such as novocaine, xylocaine, or procaine. And there is the added hope that during the several hours you're not in pain, the pain-spasm-pain cycle will be interrupted and possibly broken.

Survey participants stress the importance of avoiding normal activity while part of your back is numb. Until full sensation returns, you should do very little but lie in bed and rest.

FOOT ORTHOTICS

(Also called shoe inserts, lifts, and arch supports)

- These prescribed forms for shoes can correct imbalances and immediately reduce or end years of back pain.

- Find out whether you have short-leg syndrome. It sometimes causes severe back pain but is easily correctable.

Number of survey participants:	17
Provided dramatic long-term help:	18%
Provided moderate long-term help:	64%
Provided temporary help:	6%
Ineffective:	12%
Made patient feel worse:	0%

"None of the doctors to whom I brought my back problem ever measured my legs, with the exception of the meds at the National Institutes of Health in Bethesda, Maryland," reported a film editor. "The correction made [by varying the height of one shoe] was the only thing that really eased my pain. My orthopedist told me that many people go through life not knowing that one of their legs is shorter than the other. Even a slight difference can cause exhaustion and back pain."

"The most help I've received came from a half-inch lift in my right shoe," said a mechanic who had back pain for twenty years before he was virtually cured by this simple device costing less than a dollar.

"After enough doctors tell you that the problem is in your head," a clothing salesperson explained, "you start to believe it. Well, their thinking was upside down. Orthotics corrected my weak and painful arches. This let me walk normally. My back pain vanished and I haven't had any major problems for ten years."

An orthotic is a prescribed shoe insert. But for our purposes, let's define it as any corrective shoe form that can help your feet and your back, whether it's a commercially available heel lift or arch support, or a prescribed insert that runs the length of your shoe.

Clearly, anything that affects the way you stand or walk can affect your back. According to a recent study at Iowa State University, 90 percent of low back sufferers were free of pain one year after using the kind of arch supports you can find in any drugstore. Although we find this statistic overoptimistic, our findings support it in principle.

Can a shoe insert relieve your back pain? If you have low back pain, it's definitely worth trying to solve the problem from your feet up. Your best bet is to see either a sports podiatrist (a foot specialist with training in sports medicine) or an orthopedist who specializes in foot and ankle problems. One can be found in the yellow pages under "podiatrist," the other by consulting your county medical association.

It is important to note that orthotics do have an element of risk. Two survey participants were made worse—with markedly increased pain—because of inappropriately prescribed forms. Furthermore, any significant change needs to be made gradually, particularly if you have a lot of back pain at the time. Abruptly changing the way you walk can aggravate a back problem. With this in mind, and based on what survey participants told us, we suggest that you wear new inserts only thirty minutes the first day and thirty minutes more each day thereafter.

SELF-HELP STRESS REDUCTION

- *Any* technique that provides a break from stressful activities can help your back.

- "Visualization" was the most popular self-help, stress-reduction technique used by survey participants.

- Try the self-help technique described in this section.

- See Chapter 7 for details on biofeedback.

Number of survey participants:	17*
Provided dramatic long-term help:	18%
Provided moderate long-term help:	64%
Provided temporary help:	6%

*Limited to self-taught, stress-reduction techniques used in part to relieve back pain. Other disciplines that reduce stress and back pain, such as yoga, biofeedback, and psychotherapy, are tallied separately.

| Ineffective: | 12% |
| Made patient feel worse: | 0% |

Survey participants reported there is no single best way to reduce stress. But according to merchants of books, tapes, and gadgets advocating a particular stress-reduction technique, *theirs* is the best way.

It really doesn't matter which stress-reduction technique you use. Survey participants cited here practiced meditation, visualization, or prayer, and *each* of these approaches worked to some extent. Moreover, there is virtually no risk of stress-reduction therapy making you feel worse, unless, of course, you substitute it for needed professional help.

Technique is not the key: belief is. If you believe that a method of stress reduction will help you to relax—and control back pain—it probably will. It isn't a question of tricking yourself. It is, at the very least, a respite from the daily grind—a way to treat yourself well every day and interrupt the activities that allow stress to build up to unmanageable levels.

Several survey participants had success with this visualization/imagery technique:

Find a time each day when you will not be interrupted. That is easier said than done, but everything hinges on your having solitude. Even a few minutes is valuable, but half an hour is ideal.

Clear your mind of the day's activities and problems. Lie down in any position that feels comfortable. Take a few deep breaths. As you exhale, imagine that you're in a relaxing environment—perhaps on a beach or near a lake. See yourself there. Allow the image to become real to you.

Now, picture a soft breeze warming your body, one part at a time, relaxing you. Save your aching back for last. Then concentrate on making every inch of your back become more and more relaxed.

Imagine your back feeling well. Imagine it *being* well and pain-free.

COLD THERAPY

(Cryotherapy)

- Using ice (rather than heat) for the first twenty-four to forty-eight hours after an injury is widely accepted and successful.

- Ice also relieves certain kinds of chronic back pain. Here is a guide that cuts through conflicting opinions about when and how to use cold therapy.

• Combining heat and ice works well for some back sufferers.

Number of survey participants:	14
Provided dramatic long-term help:	0%
Provided moderate long-term help:	0%
Provided temporary help:	64%
Ineffective:	36%
Made patient feel worse:	0%

Almost everyone who has back pain can warm up to the idea of soothing sore, aching muscles with heat. But who ever heard of curling up in bed with a shockingly cold ice pack?

But if ice sounds bad, or temporarily feels bad, remember that it can do wonders for your back pain. Survey participants who used ice advise that you apply it immediately after you have strained a muscle in your back. Don't stop after the first twenty-four to forty-eight hours, *but use it on a regular basis as long as there are muscle spasms causing pain.*

Why use ice?

Integrating the opinions of survey participants, sports medicine specialists, physical therapists, and chiropractors, we come up with these reasons:

(1) Cold, like heat, is a counter-irritant, so you tend to feel the cold, not the pain. Moreover, when applied long enough, cold numbs all sensation.

(2) Cold reduces swelling, bruising, and the formation of scar tissue caused by the tearing of muscle fibers (muscle strain).

(3) Cold "shocks" a muscle spasm into relaxing.

(4) Cold lessens inflammation from muscle strain, which eases pain and can end the pain-spasm cycle.

How to use ice

The only real disagreement among survey participants about using ice revolves around *how* to use it.

Typically, participants under a chiropractor's care used a five-minutes-on, five-minutes-off, five-minutes-on technique. This total of ten minutes' application was then repeated every two hours.

Patients under the care of a medical doctor or physical therapist usually applied ice for ten to twenty minutes at a time, two or three times a day.

What should *you* do?

These rules of thumb evolved from our talks with survey participants:

If you're using ice to reduce the swelling and inflammation of a *newly incurred strain,* apply ice cubes in a plastic bag for up to ten to fifteen minutes at a time, every two hours, for the first thirty-six hours.

If you're using ice to treat chronic muscle spasm, apply an ice bag for ten to fifteen minutes, two or three times a day.

Try substituting an ice massage for an ice pack. To do this, you need a paper cup and a friend. Fill the paper cup with water and freeze it. Then tear off the top inch of the cup and have someone massage the affected area, in circular motions, for about fifteen minutes, always moving toward the heart.

Note of caution: Even though no survey participants who used ice were injured in the process, there is a risk of frostbite. Therefore, never apply ice directly on your skin, unless someone is continuously moving the ice from one area to another.

If you're using ice cubes, put them in an ice bag or plastic bag and place a thin towel (a dish towel or a diaper works well) between the bag and your skin. If your skin turns red, that's a warning. If it becomes white or numb, discontinue use.

If you have arthritis or another medical condition, don't use ice unless it is recommended by a specialist.

Combining cold and heat

In the preceding chapter, we talked about the widespread use of heat in combating back pain and relieving tired, aching, and sore muscles. Several back sufferers have successfully combined heat with ice to relieve severe and chronic low back pain, including both spasming and soreness. They first take a warm bath, or use a heating pad, to relax and relieve soreness and pain. Then they use cold treatments on the areas that continue to spasm and hurt. The result? Much more pain relief than when just heat or cold therapy was used. Also, survey participants who combined heat and cold found this form of therapy particularly relaxing.

Chapter 7

New, Unusual, and Seldom-Used Treatments for Back Pain

Many of the most widely debated and unorthodox ways to control back pain are explored in this chapter. You'll find last-resort ways to combat chronic pain, from transcutaneous electric nerve stimulation to nerve block injections. You'll learn about techniques that are new to most back sufferers, including chymopapain injections for ruptured discs and gravity-inversion traction for many different kinds of back pain. You'll hear what back sufferers are saying about the results of their illegal experimentation with substances such as marijuana and DMSO to treat back pain.

Indeed, sooner or later, if your back pain persists, one or more of the treatments or substances described in this chapter will be recommended to you by a practitioner or a friend. And you'll be able to make a more rational decision after reading the information that follows.

Note: Treatments in this chapter are arranged according to their frequency of mention in the survey, beginning with the most popular ones. The order does *not* reflect relative effectiveness of the treatments for helping back sufferers.

TRANSCUTANEOUS
ELECTRIC NERVE STIMULATION (TENS)

- Survey participants found less relief than has been reported in most other studies.

- TENS helped some post-surgery patients cut down on prescription painkillers.

Number of survey participants:	14
Provided dramatic long-term help:	7%
Provided moderate long-term help:	0%
Provided temporary relief:	29%
Ineffective:	57%
Made patient feel worse:	7%

The device is about the size of a TV remote control unit. You can hook it over your belt or conceal it under loose clothing. It runs on batteries, costs a couple of hundred dollars, and sends electric impulses to nerves through electrodes affixed to your skin.

The sensation you feel is not the least bit painful. "Buzzing" or "tingling" are the descriptions used most often by survey participants.

First made available to consumers over a decade ago, transcutaneous electric nerve stimulation was heralded as a miraculous, drug-free painkiller. Although the statistical information in this survey about TENS is limited, there is no indication that the treatment has value for most back sufferers—whether they have acute or chronic pain.

"It seems like many people are divided on the effectiveness of transcutaneous electric nerve stimulation," reported an artist who tried it because the formation of scar tissue after surgery was causing her severe pain. "Many feel it is all psychological," she continued. "But I was in pain for five months taking pills like one eats potato chips and I could get no relief whatsoever. With TENS, I was able to handle the pain and finally get rid of most medications."

An executive with low back pain had the opposite experience. His discomfort increased: "It felt like a vibrator on the place where it hurt."

(Note: TENS devices hardly ever cause pain; placing the electrodes differently might have prevented the problem in this case.)

Overall, most participants agreed with the electrical engineer who declared that "TENS is a waste of somebody's money. It did little more than distract me, rather than block pain."

"To me it was no more than wearing a toy buzzer," a copywriter said. "I don't think it's any more than a counter-irritant."

All TENS users in this survey worked with a medical doctor or a physical therapist who supervised the electrode placement for them. And still the TENS unit provided little benefit, if any. So the notion that TENS works *if* the electrodes are expertly placed doesn't wash. There is also a belief among TENS advocates that if one brand name fails to get results, another might work wonders. But survey participants who tried different brands didn't find this to be true.

In any case, if you plan to try transcutaneous electric nerve stimulation, we strongly advise against buying a device—unless you've already used one satisfactorily under the supervision of an experienced practitioner. At the very least, rent before you buy.

GRAVITY INVERSION

(Also called hanging or anti-gravity)

- Based on an ancient healing technique, inversion devices seem to have value for many kinds of acute and chronic back pain.

- Survey participants sustained no ill effects themselves, but a few reported injuries to other back sufferers they knew.

Number in the survey:	11
Provided dramatic long-term help:	0%
Provided moderate long-term help:	45%
Provided temporary relief:	55%
Ineffective:	0%
Made patient feel worse:	0%

"Anti-gravity" is a misnomer. So is "hanging." But never mind that. The procedures called anti-gravity and hanging do work.

A better term might be "reverse-gravity" or "inversion therapy." Your body is inverted during treatment, so that the ever-present pull of the earth's gravity tugs at all your tissues and vertebrae from the opposite direction, often with therapeutic effects. Whether you're hanging upside down or tilted just enough so that your head is lower than your feet, the inverted position can allow gravity to decompress your vertebrae and stretch your muscles.

Naturally, anything that promises new help to back sufferers is mired in the usual profusion of confusion, claims, and competing products and techniques.

Comprehensively tested and researched, the daddy of the many posture-inversion systems is the Gravity Guiding System®. Now widely imitated, it was developed by an orthopedist, Dr. Robert M. Martin, who, in his youth, was a skilled acrobat and expert at handstands. Under proper supervision, the most disabled back sufferers — even an individual in the throes of ruptured disc pain—can attempt to be treated with Dr. Martin's technique. In part, the procedure is similar to the vertical traction used in many hospitals, with one obvious exception. Instead of being tilted toward a standing position, you are tilted toward a standing-on-your-head position in an effort to create more space between vertebrae and to diminish nerve root pressure.

"The Gravity Guiding System® is more than just a safe way to hang upside down," an attorney who used it told us. "It has added a helpful new dimension to my daily exercise program and has turned a chronically bothersome back into one that is virtually pain-free."

A film editor raved about the system: "It helped me to stretch myself out every day when I got home from work. It's not only great for your back, but for your head, too." (According to yoga philosophy and to research done recently at the University of Chicago, the rush of blood to the head from inversion is invigorating and perhaps therapeutic.)

Another survey participant, a jeweler, also liked the Gravity Guiding System®. "The boots help a great deal. I recommend them along with massage, proper nutrition, attention to posture, and exercises that are not too strenuous."

Many mail order and medical supply companies now sell posture-inversion systems based on Dr Martin's idea. Some can be found on the Internet. But if you have substantial back pain, or if your health is impaired, do not use this or any other reverse-gravity device or procedure without a go-ahead from a medical practitioner. Research on reverse-gravity at the Chicago College of Osteopathic Medicine reveals that *any* inversion procedure may especially pose risks for people with high blood pressure or glaucoma.

More comments about inversion

Many participants improvised well, attempting reverse-gravity via jungle gym bars, chinning bars, back swings, and miscellaneous contraptions, including one devised by a mechanical engineer who says he hung from his ice skates on a suspended wire. Mail order and medical supply companies also offer various devices, some advertised on the Internet.

The enthusiasm for inversion seems almost boundless. Said a dog trainer, "My chiropractor told me about hanging by my feet. At first I thought he was nuts. But I must say that it really works. It seems to decompress the spine. If it is hard at first, hang from the backs of your knees."

The least amount of enthusiasm came from a teacher who makes regular use of gravity inversion. According to her, "Inversion is of some help but yoga is best."

In addition, two survey participants talked about injuries to acquaintances who did inversion exercises. Said one of these survey participants, "A friend of mine went from bed rest to a half-hour workout on an anti-gravity machine and the exercises were much more than she could tolerate. You need to be gradual about it. But once you can do some regular back exercises, then you're ready for anti-gravity."

NUTRITION AND VITAMINS

- Most survey participants were uncertain about the extent to which nutrition and vitamins helped prevent or relieve back trouble.

- The most popular suggestions: take calcium and vitamin C supplements, particularly after an injury or surgery . . .

avoid processed foods, sugar, alcohol, and chemical additives . . . eat more complex carbohydrates, less protein, and fat.

Number of survey participants:	11*
Got dramatic long-term help:	0%
Got moderate long-term help:	27%
Got temporary relief:	9%
Ineffective:	64%
Felt worse:	0%

Here are specific recommendations from survey participants about the role of nutrition and vitamins in alleviating back pain.

For osteoarthritis

"Take large daily doses of vitamin E, vitamin C, vitamin B_6, dolomite, and calcium."

"Bonemeal, alfalfa tablets, and kelp reduce pain from spinal arthritis."

"Alfalfa tablets and vitamin B seem to help me more than anything else."

"Vitamins B_6 and C are essential for speeding recovery from back pain."

"Every day, take 500 mg of magnesium, 90 mg potassium, 1 gram vitamin C, and vitamin B complex."

"Magnesium oxide, pantothenic acid, and vitamin C are good for osteoarthritis sufferers."

"Avoid nightshade plants like potatoes, tomatoes, and peppers. If you're allergic to them, eliminating them from your diet will help pain."

There is no proof that any foods or vitamins can prevent, relieve, or cause osteoarthritis. It is true, though, that taking vitamins A, B, C, and E and calcium does make some osteoarthritis sufferers feel better.

Five participants in this survey found that adding calcium to their diet "cured" osteoarthritis-like symptoms. Possibly, what seemed like arthritis to these individuals was really a calcium deficiency, which is fairly common in older people. Still, if you have osteoarthritis, it might make sense to try a multivitamin and calcium supplement. Beware of taking megadoses, though.

*Dozens of survey participants experimented with nutrition and vitamins. The individuals represented here made a concentrated, long-term effort to relieve back pain by changing their nutritional habits.

It is known that megadoses of many vitamins and minerals can have serious toxic effects.

Also, in rare instances, nightshade plants like tomatoes, potatoes, and peppers can cause an allergic reaction that makes `muscles feel sore and inflamed. Again, consult an allergist or a practitioner trained in nutrition if you think this possibility is worth exploring.

For low back pain

"Diet is important. Avoid sugar, coffee, and too much alcohol."

"Constipation makes my back hurt more. Plenty of fiber and liquids solve the constipation and improve the way my back feels."

"I feel that calcium tablets helped me more than any other treatment."

"Take vitamin E when your back bothers you."

"Two grams of vitamin C every day are helpful for the pain of spondylolisthesis."

"Take bad back tea—a mixture of valerian and any other herbs."

"Massive amounts [prescribed by a chiropractor] of certain vitamins and minerals—such as magnesium orotate, zypan, and drenotrophin—have worked well from time to time."

There is no such thing as an "Eat Your Way to a Better Back" diet. But there are consistent indications that a bad diet can make back pain worse:

(1) Eating poorly—consuming a lot of sugar and junk foods and not receiving proper nutrition—can make you feel tired and out of sorts. And this can only make your back and the rest of you feel worse.

(2) Not drinking enough liquids and not eating enough fiber can constipate you. Constipation was mentioned by a dozen survey participants as a condition that aggravated or caused back pain.

(3) Being overweight can be tough on your back, especially if you wind up with a protruding gut. A lean body hardly precludes back pain, but a few overweight back sufferers did feel better after shedding surplus pounds.

(4) Alcohol and caffeine can lead to and aggravate ulcers, gastritis, colitis, and other gastrointestinal problems—all of which can

cause back pain. Medical treatment for these problems helped five survey participants to eliminate back pain.

Chiropractors offer the most advice about nutrition, according to survey participants, and it is not uncommon for them to "prescribe" vitamins and minerals. Most medical doctors, on the other hand, lack extensive training in nutrition.

Only one survey participant saw a nutritionist, and a famous one at that: Carlton Fredericks. A changed diet prescribed by Fredericks helped this back sufferer enormously.

BIOFEEDBACK

- Eight out of ten survey participants benefited somewhat from biofeedback when it was part of a total back-care program.

- Biofeedback works best for low back and neck pain.

- Technology and gadgetry are less important than the skill and concern of the therapist.

Number of patients treated:	10
Provided dramatic long-term help:	0%
Provided moderate long-term help:	50%
Provided temporary help:	10%
Ineffective:	40%
Made patient feel worse:	0%

Does anything give you conscious control over the physical factors that cause back pain? Is it possible to will a muscle to stop spasming? Can your mind prevent muscles from contracting, eradicate the sensation of pain, or keep stress from hurting your back?

The answer in many cases is yes, through biofeedback. This does not mean that biofeedback *alone* will cure back pain, but it can aid your overall recovery.

Just as you can be taught to raise the temperature of your fingers or toes with the help of a biofeedback device, so can you be taught to ease or prevent the tension that aggravates back pain.

But why not just use stress-reducing approaches like meditation or visualization? Why is a device needed to help you relax?

The value of the device, whether it is a 99-cent thermometer or a $20,000 electronic unit, is to measure specific information about your body—heart rate, for example, alpha brain waves, muscle tension, galvanic skin response, or the volume of blood in your veins—and then give you auditory or visual cues as the measures change. This feedback enables you to test new ways of "thinking relaxed" until the biofeedback gadgetry you're using tells you that you *are* relaxed.

The value of biofeedback in reducing back pain has not been scientifically documented. But survey participants were definitely able to articulate its benefits in an overall program of back care.

"Biofeedback offered me ways of calming myself with resultant reduced muscle tension and less pain," said a metallurgist who simultaneously used acupuncture and exercise. "Overall, though," he added, "acupuncture and an exercise program did the most for me to curb low back pain."

A social worker with low back pain also found biofeedback to be a useful part of her recovery program. "Biofeedback was effective because it dealt with the true cause of my problem—tension. It showed me how to deal with tension properly. Overall, though, yoga was the greatest help because I've learned to see that mind and body need to be in harmony."

And a professor who functions despite chronically painful spondylolisthesis reported, "Anxiety and tension do affect my back and I have worked with a psychologist using biofeedback techniques to control and relieve tension in my back. This has helped. But I think depression is a big problem, too, as well as anxiety and frustration."

Biofeedback was especially useful for survey participants with low back or neck pain caused in part by emotional stress. But this doesn't mean that any of the doodads you see advertised are worth owning.

For one thing, all biofeedback treatments covered in this section were professionally supervised—and participants felt that the quality of the biofeedback instructors meant much more than the sophistication of the biofeedback equipment. Moreover, according to research supported by the National Institute of Mental Health, "Biofeedback devices purchased and operated by consumers have not proven themselves to be valid means of treatment."

The recommendation of a health practitioner or friend is the best way to find competent biofeedback instruction—and to avoid the many shoddy clinics and unqualified instructors claiming expertise in this discipline.

MODERN DANCE

- Modern dance offers an invigorating form of help for back problems. But it is very definitely not for anyone still recovering from back pain.

- Look for an instructor who shows some understanding of back problems.

Number of survey participants:	10
Provided dramatic long-term help:	40%
Provided moderate long-term help:	50%
Provided temporary help:	0%
Ineffective:	0%
Made patient feel worse:	10%

Survey participants who enjoyed and benefited from modern dance generally agreed about these three things:

(1) If modern dance is to your liking, it is a wonderful way to fine-tune your body and protect it against recurrences of back pain.

(2) Modern dance is a buoying experience. It lifts your spirits and provides a healthy outlet for stress.

(3) It is dangerous for anyone in pain, or even anyone who can't already do a wide range of back exercises, to try modern dance.

"The warm-up exercises in modern dance are precisely those recommended by chiropractors I've seen," said an administrative assistant to a publisher. "Dance is a great form of relief with just the right combination of freedom and structure needed for a healthy body and mind. I recommend it strongly as a creative way to deal with back pain."

MARIJUANA

- Participants who used marijuana for back pain relief did not use it regularly for recreational purposes.

- No one had a middle-of-the-road opinion about marijuana. It either helped where prescribed drugs didn't, or it made the individual feel worse.

Number of survey participants:	8
Provided dramatic long-term help:	0%
Provided moderate long-term help:	0%
Provided temporary help:	65%
Ineffective:	0%
Made patient feel worse:	35%

All of the survey participants who turned to marijuana for pain relief treated it as a prescription drug. They approached it cautiously and used it for specific effects.

"Illegal though it may be," said a bookkeeper with sciatica, "marijuana helped relax me, especially during periods of extreme pain."

A paraplegic with chronic, severe pain throughout her back found marijuana an invaluable sleep aid on occasion: "When the pain is unbearable and I can't sleep, one marijuana cigarette makes comfort and relaxation quite easy."

An artist who underwent disc surgery and then suffered from scar tissue impinging on his nerves said, "When I'm in pain, nothing helps except smoking a little dope. Sometimes it's the only thing that helps me stand the pain."

"Instead of taking a strong prescription drug, smoke a small amount of marijuana or make a tea out of it," advised a salesperson with a ruptured disc.

"If the pain is bad, marijuana works the same as muscle relaxants without the side effects," noted a market researcher with severe low back pain.

An office manager with low back pain disagreed with all of this advice: "I experienced mild discomfort when I smoked marijuana. It seemed to make me more sensitive to pain."

A computer programmer also felt that marijuana could increase back pain: "I suggest that people with back trouble stay away from marijuana. It makes you feel the pain more."

A waitress with low back pain found marijuana harmful: "I suspect that the effectiveness of marijuana as a drug used for tension can create negative effects. I hold an opinion that marijuana has damaging effects to the spine. That is my idea from experience."

It would seem logical for the federal government to sponsor studies about the use of marijuana as a muscle relaxant/analgesic for chronic back pain. But this would have little meaning for back sufferers in the near future, for any research involving the use of controlled substances is hampered by their limited availability and the restrictions placed on the experimental conditions.

KINESIOLOGY

- Applied kinesiology integrates the advantages of manipulation and individualized exercise with knowledge about how to put your muscles in good working order.

- Here are specifics on how to find one of the relatively few kinesiologists who treat back sufferers.

Number of survey participants:	8
Provided dramatic long-term help:	50%
Provided moderate long-term help:	25%
Provided temporary help:	12.5%
Ineffective:	12.5%
Made patient feel worse:	0%

Few medical disciplines are as potentially useful to back sufferers as kinesiology—the study of the principles and mechanics of movement. Applied kinesiology involves the use of a wide range of non-drug, nonsurgical procedures, ranging from manipulation to massage to exercise. But what stands out most in the minds of survey participants who had kinesiology treatments was the kinesiologist's interest in and knowledge about muscles. For example, five out of six participants reported that muscles in their backs, hips, or legs were measured and tested for strength and flexibility; and that specific, corrective movements and exercises were prescribed after evaluation.

You can get the name of a practictioner in your area by calling the International College of Applied Kinesiology—(913) 384-5336 in the United States or (01835) 823645 in Great Britain. The US number can also provide details of local offices in Canada, Australasia, and some European countries. Alternatively, check the ICAK's website, www.icak.com.

ROLFING

- This is a painful but sometimes effective way to temporarily relieve minor or moderate—but not disabling—low back pain.

- Compared with other kinds of treatments, however, the results from Rolfing may not justify the discomfort.

Number of survey participants:	8
Provided dramatic long-term help:	0%
Provided moderate long-term help:	12.5%
Provided temporary help:	62.5%
Ineffective:	12.5%
Made patient feel worse:	12.5%

If you're not ready for the equivalent of an energetic workout, you are not a candidate for Rolfing—a deep tissue massage described by one pleased survey participant as, "Like someone was trying to reshape my muscles."

Push hard enough on tense muscles and you will feel pain. Offer resistance to a force being applied to your body and you will ultimately feel tired, even exhausted. Combine both these sensations and you have some idea of what Rolfing feels like.

Rolfing does get results, though. The most impressive pain relief from Rolfing was reported by a massage therapist with bad low back pain. Her comment about the treatment: "Rolfing helped quite a bit. But, after a few years, the pain returned."

Because of the degree of pressure exerted, one participant with sciatica reported an increase in pain lasting several days. And even some patients who were helped by Rolfing did not complete the full series of treatments. (Usually ten sessions are prescribed.) They stopped because they felt the discomfort from the procedure had become greater than the relief.

DMSO

- It is illegal to use DMSO for musculoskeletal injuries or arthritis pain.

- DMSO did help most survey participants who tried it, but there are risks and side effects.

Number of survey participants:	8
Provided dramatic long-term help:	12.5%
Provided moderate long-term help:	25%
Provided temporary help:	25%
Ineffective:	25%
Made patient feel worse:	12.5%

For more than two decades, astonishing tales have circulated about low back sufferers who thumbed their noses at the law and received miraculous cures by applying an industrial solvent called DMSO (dimethyl sulfoxide) to their skin. And for more than two decades, the country's medical authorities have pointed out that there is no proof that DMSO works, only proof that it can be hazardous.

Itchy, blotchy, and red skin as well as nausea are the most common problems among DMSO enthusiasts. Irreversible damage to the eyes of lab animals was reportedly found in early tests. And the long-run effects of using an industrial solvent on human beings are unknown. (All but one DMSO user in this survey bought the widely available industrial solvent, instead of the purer kind manufactured "For Veterinary Use Only"—a 90 percent solution or gel used to reduce swelling in injuries to animals.)

After decades of claims and counterclaims, DMSO remains controversial.

Meanwhile, survey participation have these opinions to offer:

"I have used DMSO for the past six months," reported a telephone salesperson with sciatica. "It takes several weeks of daily applications. But there is a decided increase in flexibility and lessening of pain."

Said a computer scientist with severe muscle spasms in his back, "I applied DMSO full strength (99 percent industrial solvent solution), left it on the spasming muscle group for twenty-five minutes, then wiped off the excess. It noticeably helped reduce the spasming. Let me add that I've been cautioned by friends to avoid putting anything on my skin that could be soaked in with the DMSO. So I wash the area first, then wear a clean, white cotton T-shirt afterward."

A disabled accident victim with low back pain claims that DMSO has been a blessing unmatched by prescription drugs. "DMSO works remarkably well," she says. "Apply a thin coat of it as often as necessary. Some may think it has a peculiar odor (like garlicky oysters or worse), so adding clove powder to the solution takes care of that problem."

A musician with low back pain also praises DMSO. "Twice-a-day applications of DMSO got miraculous results."

No user suffered anything worse than a bad itch. But it *was* a bad itch. Said a direct marketing consultant, "My skin itched so badly that I thought I was going to jump out of it. Even when I cut the DMSO to a 50 percent solution with distilled water, I couldn't tolerate putting it on my back."

A miracle painkiller? Many people think so, but there are dissenters. A housewife recovering from several operations on ruptured discs said, "DMSO did not help my pain nearly as much as Ben-Gay."

Survey figures on the following treatments are not statistically significant, but participants' insights and comments are revealing.

SCLEROTHERAPY

- This high-risk injection procedure is designed to cause the formation of scar tissue.
- Used mostly by osteopaths, sclerotherapy should be consid-

ered only as a final resort and a dangerous route out of
incapacitation.

Sclerotherapy involves injecting a chemical irritant and local anesthetic
into ligaments, usually around a joint thought to be unstable. Your body
reacts to this irritant by forming scar tissue, which is supposed to help stabilize
your back. The procedure was used fairly commonly several decades ago by
medical doctors to repair hernias (scar tissue covered the tear) and to
eradicate varicose veins.

A farmer who risked losing his business because of back pain, and who had
done virtually everything under the sun to keep working after disc surgery,
praised sclerotherapy. "The injection to build up scar tissue around the area of
pain helped the most. It relieved the pain, and I was able to work, drive a
tractor, trucks, and machinery."

A housewife who got the same level of long-term help remarked, "The
injections were somewhat painful, probably made worse because I was
terrified of them. But afterward, it was the first time in five years that I
could do a normal amount of housework."

On the other hand, two low back patients felt that sclerotherapy
treatments injured them permanently. "After the injections I couldn't
bend as well or perform my daily routines without greater pain," a nurse
reported. "Three years later, I'm still worse off for having had those idiotic
treatments." And a homesteader commented: "After a series of sclerotherapy injections, a CAT scan showed that the treatment caused a lot
of scar tissue to form in my lumbar area. This is why I have more severe
pain."

The reported long-term damage to two survey participants should give
readers pause about sclerotherapy. If the scar tissue that results presses on a
nerve root, you're in trouble. Moreover, although scar tissue resembles the
fibrous tissue in muscles, it lacks the "stretchability" of muscle and can
impede normal movement.

ALEXANDER THERAPY

- If you have a posture problem, Alexander therapy might be
  worth looking into.

- "Helped just a bit" reflects the reaction of most survey participants who tried this treatment.

Bad posture can cause back pain. And to the extent that it affects *your* back problem, postural therapy may help.

No strong opinions, pro or con, were expressed by the half-dozen participants in the survey who tried Alexander therapy. All were chronic back sufferers in search of help for a long-standing problem. None found substantial relief in Alexander therapy.

"Alexander therapy helped me to hold myself correctly and that helped some," a reading teacher commented. "But, in retrospect, I probably would have done as well if I had tried to change my lazy posture habits myself."

FELDENKRAIS THERAPY

- In theory, you'll learn to move in a way that will help your back and improve your self-esteem. In practice, your back pain is not likely to be helped by Feldenkrais therapy.

Like yoga, Rolfing, Tai Chi, and other disciplines, Feldenkrais therapy attempts to integrate physical, mental, and spiritual approaches to well-being.

An educator with chronic low back pain felt that "Feldenkrais therapy was very helpful. It unlocked tight muscles and tissues." However, none of the other four survey participants who underwent Feldenkrais therapy found it useful or even relevant to helping resolve chronic back ailments.

FOOT REFLEXOLOGY
(Also called Zone Therapy)

- Foot reflexology offers some relief for low back pain.

- Try the self-treatment described here to see if the procedure might work for you.

Zone therapy holds that every part of your body, including your back, is linked to a point in your feet. Massage that point and the related area of your body will feel better.

The idea does seem to have some validity. Two survey participants with low back pain reported moderate long-term relief through foot reflexology. Three others with low back pain got temporary relief. And none of the five suffered any discomfort from foot reflexology.

The duration of temporary relief from foot reflexology compares favorably to Shiatsu—ranging from a few days to several months—providing pain-free time to work on long-term corrective measures.

Try this foot reflexology technique for back pain:

Purportedly, the arches of the feet, including the sides of the arches, are linked to the back. So give the entire arch a good workout. Rub in circular motions and knead your arches to loosen them up. Then press with the ball of your thumb. If some spots are tender or painful to the touch, give them extra attention, gently though. Too much pressure can trigger pain.

CHYMOPAPAIN

- Injecting this papaya extract to remedy ruptured disc pain is less traumatic, invasive, and costly than surgery.

- Chymopapain seems as effective, but not more effective, than surgery. A summary of research findings follows.

- As with surgery, it is important to remember that chymopapain is just one step in the recovery process. It is not by itself a cure.

When we spoke to New York Ranger goalie John Davidson in 1982, after his ruptured disc had been treated in Canada with chymopapain, he was ecstatic. "I wish that everyone with a ruptured disc could have access to this treatment," he said. "It worked extremely well for me."

Months later, following years of controversy and squabbling, chymopapain did become available in the United States, thereby eliminating the need to travel to Canada for treatment while in agonizing pain. The Food and Drug Administration—after round two of research contradicted the supposedly poor results of round one—finally gave its approval.

Davidson eventually needed surgery to remove two discs. But if your line of work is less demanding than crouching over to stop speeding pucks, chymopapain offers you a good chance to get back on your feet.

How it works

Chymopapain injections sound almost too good to be true. "One injection completely cured me without the need for surgery," said a real estate broker in the survey.

A chymopapain injection is administered under local or general anesthesia by a neurosurgeon, orthopedist, or anesthesiologist. You lie on your side on an X-ray table. Depending on whether you are awake or asleep, different techniques are used to pinpoint the exact area where the gel portion of your disc has broken through its casing and is putting pressure on a nerve root. The injection itself takes about five minutes. The entire procedure, from entering to leaving the treatment room, takes about half an hour.

If the injection is successful, the chymopapain—a papaya extract something like the substance used in meat tenderizer—dissolves the gel from the ruptured disc. This in turn relieves the pain in your legs almost immediately.

Some patients who get chymopapain injections leave the same day they are treated, but most are hospitalized one to four nights for observation or for treatment of back pain caused by the procedure itself. Disc surgery patients, on the other hand, are hospitalized for an average of eight days.

And chymopapain patients have another advantage over disc surgery patients. They are usually back in full swing in six weeks, while surgery patients may need three to six months to resume the activities they pursued before the ruptured disc episode.

Highlights of some research findings

At the University of Wisconsin's Division of Neurological Surgery, 124 patients were treated with chymopapain and the results reported in the *Journal of the American Medical Association (JAMA)*. Fully 72.6 percent of patients experienced marked improvement, 16.9 percent had slight improvement, and 10.5 percent had no improvement.

Twelve hundred patients with ruptured discs were treated with chymopapain at Long Beach Memorial Hospital Medical Center and at the College of Medicine, University of California. On long-term follow-up, chymopapain appeared to be as effective as laminectomy (one form of disc surgery). Here, too, about 75 percent of the patients improved.

A widely quoted statistic on this treatment—"75 percent effective where bed rest and traction failed"—reflects the tests concluded in 1982 that won approval for chymopapain from the Food and Drug Administration.

Some negatives about chymopapain

Allergic reactions. In the clinical trials that led to approval of chymopapain, two out of 1,400 patients died because of allergic reactions to the enzyme. Such fatalities might possibly be avoided by proper testing to identify allergic patients and by administering preventive medication to them. About one percent of patients who have chymopapain injections have an allergic reaction, although most are not fatal. Overall, injuries and deaths from chymopapain are *not* substantially lower than from disc surgery.

Severe back pain. About one-third of chymopapain patients develop excruciating back pain from the injection. The pain lasts up to forty-eight hours and occasionally longer. Muscle relaxants and locally injected anesthetics used to relieve this pain don't provide much relief.

Inaccessibility to injection. Even when a myelogram or CAT scan can locate a ruptured disc, a syringe cannot always reach the offending gel.

Relatively poor success rate with surgery patients. If you've already had disc surgery and then another disc ruptures, the chances of success with chymopapain are probably less than 50 percent.

Not an all-purpose substitute for back surgery. Numerous back ailments such as degenerative disc, spinal tumors, spinal stenosis (a narrowing of the spinal column), and spondylolisthesis cannot be treated with chymopapain.

Read the fine print about "success rates." The most widely quoted effectiveness rate for chymopapain, 75 percent, does not exceed the comparable rate in this report for disc surgery. More to the point, this widely publicized rate does *not* mean, for example, that 75 percent of patients receiving chymopapain are in great shape three years after the injection. It simply means that, three years after chymopapain injections, 75 percent of patients were significantly better than they were when incapacitated with ruptured disc pain.

As with any pain-relieving treatment, chymopapain isn't a cure. It doesn't change the conditions that brought on the problem initially. But it does offer you a less invasive and debilitating alternative to disc surgery and an opportunity to rehabilitate your back and avoid future problems.

Success rates vary from hospital to hospital. More to the point, they vary from doctor to doctor. *And it is extremely important to find one of the relatively few doctors who has had a lot of successful experience using chymopapain therapy.* This doesn't mean that you have to find a Canadian doctor, but don't assume that any competent surgeon or anesthesiologist has adequate training in chymopapain therapy.

NERVE BLOCK

- This injection procedure has considerable potential for relief—but also for harm.

- Consider it only as a last-resort treatment.

Three participants in this survey had nerve blocks, which are injections, often consisting of alcohol or a steroid designed to numb the nerve center that is generating the pain. In addition, several survey participants talked to us about the effect of nerve block treatments on back sufferers they knew. What emerges from these discussions, and from available research, is a last-ditch effort to control pain—a best guess at precisely what to inject, and where, to help the patient.

Since there is so little known about what causes pain, and about what can stop it, nerve block injections involve artistry as well as science. The skill of the practitioner can make all the difference in the world. "The treatment of the most lasting benefit was the nerve block provided by the neurosurgeon," said a social worker in the survey. "I had three injections next to the spine. I can't say it cured me, but it helped tremendously."

Nerve block injections are usually given by neurosurgeons or anesthesiologists who work at this specialty regularly. Other medical doctors can administer nerve blocks, but since experience is critical to success, you really need to ask a doctor about his track record with this procedure.

TAI CHI

- For the overstressed, fairly able-bodied back sufferer, Tai Chi is a fascinating way to enhance and complement your back exercise program.

This intricate and disciplined form of exercise originated centuries ago in China. Tai Chi exercises are more reflective than vigorous. They will barely raise your pulse rate, according to cardiologists who have prescribed Tai Chi for their patients. Yet, after a workout, you feel as if you have reaped the rewards of vigorous exercise. Overall, the effect is one of relaxation and pleasure, a good bet for back sufferers who need a therapeutic routine to follow and who believe that stress is a major factor in their back pain.

According to a carpenter who suffered chronic, but not incapacitating, low back pain, "Tai Chi is the total solution to my back pain. It is a relatively painless treatment that has been the most thorough way for me to take control of my discomfort and has eliminated pain altogether for long periods of time."

Two other participants were equally enthusiastic about this graceful discipline that exercises virtually every part of your body—even your eyes.

Part Four

Categories of Back Pain

"Over 80 percent of low back pain is due to muscle deficiency."

> —Hans Kraus, MD,
> from *Backache, Stress
> and Tension*

"In most cases, a backache is just a tension headache that has slipped down the back."

> —John V. Basmajian, MD,
> Director Chedoke-McMaster
> Rehabilitation Centre
> Ontario, Canada

"You probably have one of the three most common types of back problems: A worn facet joint, Type One backache; a protruding disc, Type Two; or a pinched nerve, Type Three. And since Type Three accounts for only one case of common backache out of every ten, there is a ninety-percent chance that you have Type One or Type Two."

> —Hamilton Hall, MD,
> from *The Back Doctor*

"I've been to eight different practitioners and have gotten eight different diagnoses. It's difficult to know what you have and why you have it."

> —A survey participant

Chapter 8

Diagnosing Your Diagnosis

There is one thing about treating back pain that all practitioners, from neurosurgeons to faith healers, agree on. Simply, you can't treat someone without knowing what's wrong. You first need to diagnose the problem. But that's where the unanimity ends and the chaos begins.

Two hundred sixty-nine participants in this survey—*more than half the respondents*—received two or more *different* diagnoses from two or more practitioners. Most of the discrepancies represented vast differences of opinion, not just variations in terminology.

Of the remaining 223 participants, 32 (7 percent) had no diagnosis, 40 participants (8 percent) got a diagnosis from the one practitioner they saw, and only 51 participants (10 percent) received the same diagnosis from two or more practitioners.

No other major area of medical diagnosis has a comparably poor track record. In psychiatry, a field infamous for conflicting diagnoses, any two psychiatrists will agree on specific cases 43 percent of the time. But even when back diagnoses come from the same medical specialty, only 29 percent of patients receive the same diagnosis from two or more practitioners.

More to the point, you do not have to get mired in this confusion. And you *won't*, once you understand what commonly used diagnostic terms mean, how a practitioner's specialty can bias his diagnosis, what things go wrong in various diagnostic procedures, and other revelations from survey participants.

A specific diagnosis is usually not essential to successful treatment.

The maxim that you can't treat a patient without first knowing exactly what's wrong with him or her doesn't hold up in the field of back care. Most people never find out exactly what's wrong with their backs, and they get well nevertheless.

For example, a 60-year-old construction worker who saw a noted orthopedic surgeon received a diagnosis of severe osteoarthritis of the lumbar spine—good specificity. But after a few weeks of bed rest and exercise therapy, there was no improvement. A lesser-known orthopedic surgeon then diagnosed the problem as a general weakness of the lower back—not terrific specificity. But the result of his approach to treatment *was* successful.

What you need most is a diagnosis that rules out serious medical conditions.

When you're dealing with persistent back pain, it is essential to evaluate underlying medical causes of this pain. Chances are 95 in 100 that nothing of great consequence will be discovered. But if you have severe or chronic back pain, don't take chances. Any disease or disorder, literally from your head to your toes, can cause back pain. And some two dozen participants in the survey, about 5 percent of the total, needlessly suffered back pain for years because no practitioner made a thorough effort to identify the tangible—and treatable—cause. One was a writer whose neck pain caused him great anguish for five years. In all that time, no doctor tried systematically to rule out a tangible cause of his pain. The practitioners he saw talked continually about stress as a major causal factor, until the writer himself wondered whether the pain was "all in the head," or at least mostly caused by stress. Finally, common enough diagnostic measures revealed a large but nonmalignant tumor. When the tumor was removed, the pain eventually went with it.

A businessman who owned his own company spent years seeing virtually every famous back specialist in the country. As in the writer's case, he was repeatedly told that the problem wasn't physical but that he needed psychological help. Crippled with pain, depressed, and obsessed with thoughts about suicide, the patient tried one last specialist. A treatable neuromuscular disorder was discovered. In six months a prescribed drug brought him a 90 percent recovery. In a year the patient was fully recovered.

Colitis, an inflammation of the colon, turned out to be the cause of back pain for a secretary. She went to a general practitioner for a complete medical examination after years of chiropractic care failed to control her chronic back pain. Appropriate medication quickly solved her problem.

Perhaps the most frustrating story of this kind comes from a publishing executive who was warned by an osteopath that he would have to live in a wheelchair for the rest of his life. A "crooked spine," the osteopath said, "was combining with spondylolisthesis [see Chapter 14] to produce incapacitating and irreversible leg pain and numbness." But after ten years of agony, the last two of them disabling, the executive saw a chiropractor who diagnosed the problem as short-leg syndrome. The real culprit, again, was the lack of a thorough examination. The chiropractor prescribed a built-up shoe, and the patient fully recovered in two months.

So be *thoroughly* evaluated *once.* Then ignore diagnostic jargon and focus on getting well.

Some survey participants, *after receiving appropriate diagnostic tests* (discussed below) and after being bombarded with vague diagnoses that basically said, "You have pain, but nothing is seriously wrong," continued making the rounds of practitioners in search of the "right" diagnosis—one that sounded specific, tangible, and curable. Looking back, almost all of them found this to be a tremendous waste of time and money.

You should know that survey participants who received no diagnosis did just as well in the long run as patients who received one or more diagnoses. This is because a fancy diagnosis for low back pain usually does *not* have specific treatment implications. For example, an author with low back pain accumulated the following labels: low back syndrome, idiopathic lumbar-sacral radiculopathy, low back derangement, lumbar strain, myositis, and myoligamentous lumbar-sacral strain. All of these mean essentially the same thing: low back pain. Moreover, the patient got the best results from the practitioner who called the problem "low back syndrome." And the doctor didn't even mention this diagnosis until recovery was well under way and a health-insurance form forced him to give the problem an official name.

How to know your probable diagnosis before you are examined

As predictably as hairdressers focus on split ends and cobblers look for run-down heels, certain kinds of back practitioners tend to diagnose with tunnel vision. Survey results demonstrate graphically that the name of your problem may depend on the name of your practitioner's specialty, as follows:

Chiropractic diagnosis. The chances are nine out of ten you'll be told your spine is misaligned. "Misalignment" is the specific term chiropractors use most often to describe back pain. "Subluxation" is another, more impressive way of saying misalignment, but it means the same thing: two adjoining vertebrae are dislocated relative to one another. "Twisted pelvis" is another common way for chiropractors to describe a specific area of an improperly aligned spine. So is "spinal curvature," indicating either a slight scoliosis (lateral curvature) or lordosis (an overly pronounced inward curve in the lower back). Chiropractors also talk in terms of "pinched nerves" and congenital bone defects such as "malformed hips."

There is nothing inappropriate about these diagnoses. To the contrary, it reassures many back sufferers to know that the chiropractor feels something is wrong. Given a choice between having a "bad back" or a "subluxation of L4, L5" with a "twisted pelvis" to boot, many people prefer the latter diagnosis. After all, they *are* in pain, and they want to know why.

Surgeons. The two most common diagnoses from orthopedists and neurosurgeons are "low back syndrome" and "there is nothing really wrong." The latter diagnosis touches a raw nerve among back sufferers. "Why would I be wasting my time seeing a doctor if there wasn't anything wrong?" demanded a cashier who got this diagnosis. "It's patronizing. It puts you off. Why can't doctors say, 'There obviously is *something* wrong with you. I don't know quite what it is. But let's see what we can do about it'? When I pushed my doctor months later for a more specific diagnosis, he said, 'Don't worry about it. For insurance purposes I'll write idiopathic lumbar-sacral radiculopathy.' When I asked him what that meant, he replied, 'It means I don't know why you have low back pain.' " (Note: Idiopathic means cause unknown.)

Most back sufferers who get a "nothing really wrong" diagnosis are frustrated by it. But if you know beforehand that this diagnosis from surgeons is commonplace and that most surgeons are interested only in treating people surgically, you might be relieved instead of frustrated. Look at it positively. You now have ruled out certain known conditions and can either treat yourself or get some initial help from a practitioner who is interested in back problems that don't require surgery. And the vast majority of back problems *don't* require surgery.

General practitioners. This survey found that most general practitioners and internists tend to come up with a catchall diagnosis—low back pain or muscle spasms—with implications for treatment by prescription drugs. Low back pain, for example, is customarily treated with painkillers by GP's; muscle spasms are treated with muscle-relaxant pills.

Physiatrists, sports medicine specialists, physical therapists, and kinesiologists. These practitioners' diagnoses usually focus on the muscular status of different parts of the body, e.g., weak abdominal muscles, tight hamstrings, weak lower back muscles. And these diagnoses have specific implications for individualized exercise therapy.

Acupuncturists and Shiatsu therapists. These two specialists tend to offer no diagnosis at all. One would think this would frustrate patients, but it doesn't because the practitioners seem so willing to try to help. And their positive attitude gives patients the feeling that they have some diagnosis—and a corresponding course of treatment—in mind.

Holistic, alternative practitioners. For convenience, we use this phrase to describe practitioners such as holistic massage therapists, naturopaths, and Rolfers, and we find that unconventional diagnoses are the norm for this group. For example, a holistic massage therapist may attribute chronic low back pain to an excess of urea in the blood and a lack of ying energy. A naturopath may claim that low back pain is due to lethargy caused by a poorly functioning liver and a lack of zinc and magnesium.

And the offbeat diagnostic beat goes on. Posture therapists will point to posture deficiencies. Feldenkrais therapists will find fault with your awareness of how you move. Rolfers will declare that your state of mind and muscles are not in the best shape. Biofeedback therapists will tell you that your life is too stressful, and so on.

The point here is to demonstrate how certain practitioners follow predictable patterns in assessing your condition and framing a diagnosis. Of course, predictability does not make a diagnosis inappropriate or appropriate. Mostly, it means that you can easily wind up with more diagnoses than you would care to count, and that in most cases you need not be concerned about what your problem is called. Instead, you should focus on learning (in the upcoming chapters) what treatments are most likely to help you overcome different types of back pain.

Tentative diagnoses: take them with a grain of salt.

Some diagnoses are best guesses. They are subject to further diagnostic procedures, or they will be proven or disproven by the passage of time.

Take the case of a journalist who gritted her teeth through many years of back pain until the problem finally decked her. On the basis of X rays and a clinical examination, an orthopedist told her she had a ruptured disc requiring surgery.*

"The diagnosis terrified me," she recalled. "In retrospect, I feel that it amounted to a misdiagnosis, since I got well without surgery."

Whether the diagnosis was incorrect will never be known. What is known, though, is that it was a *tentative* diagnosis. The pain in the journalist's legs could have been caused by a hyperextended vertebra, a narrowing of the spinal canal, or numerous other conditions.

Another participant in this survey, a business owner, had the wits scared out of him by five diagnoses, none of which was based on concrete evidence: ruptured disc, spinal tumor, compressed nerve in low back, deteriorated disc, and Wilson's Disease (a serious and rare neurological disorder).

There is nothing intrinsically wrong with tentative diagnoses. They can simply indicate that your first visit, which usually consists of history-taking, direct examination, and X rays, signals the need for further diagnostic procedures.

So don't panic needlessly about think-aloud diagnoses. They tend to be less accurate than weather forecasts. They can also give you a headache that will make your back pain seem mild in comparison. And they turn diagnosis into a multiple-choice format—"It could be a disc, a facet joint, some arthritis, or a pinched nerve"—often without regard for the patient's feelings.

---

*X rays are ineffective in diagnosing a ruptured disc because the discs themselves cannot be seen on conventional X rays.

In fact, the way you are told about a tentative diagnosis can be frightening, even debilitating. It is one thing to say, "You may have a ruptured disc, Ms. Jones." But it is quite another matter to say, as a handful of doctors in this survey did before solid evidence was in hand, "Have an operation now or you'll be pleading for help in a few years."

Many practitioners don't bother telling patients whether diagnoses are tentative or documented. As a result, the patient may leave the office badly shaken, rather than informed, with a firsthand and unwelcome opportunity to learn about the role of stress in back pain.

What they see may not be what you've got.

Dr. Willibald Nagler, renowned physiatrist-in-chief at the New York Hospital–Cornell Medical Center, treated one of the authors of this book. After examining Art thoroughly, he asked whether his back had been x-rayed recently. It hadn't. Dr. Nagler thought for a few seconds and, reasonably certain that the problem was muscular in nature, said, "Let's skip the X rays. Even if we find a slight abnormality, we still won't know if it is the cause of your back pain."

Dr. Nagler's decision turned out to be sound. And his thinking makes an important point about diagnosis—namely, *what your practitioner sees may have nothing to do with your problem.*

Take the case of the fast-food franchise manager who had low back pain for the first time at age 45. An X ray showed that two of his lumbar vertebrae were fused and apparently had been so since birth. The practitioner attributed the pain to this congenital fusion. But the vertebrae had been fused for forty-five years without causing back pain. Furthermore, the patient's pain vanished in a few weeks while the fused vertebrae, of course, did not. So there's no way to know whether the malformation had anything to do with the episodes of back pain.

There are probably millions of people with visible conditions—mild scoliosis, lordosis, some osteoarthritis, and congenital malformations—who don't have back pain. There are also millions of people with these problems who do have back pain. And millions of people suffer terribly despite the absence of any obvious abnormality on which to blame the pain. So remember that your spinal curve or malformed vertebra may have nothing to with any given bout of back pain.

Here are some more illustrations:

A bookkeeper with low back pain saw three specialists, two of whom attributed the pain to a curvature in her upper back (scoliosis). The third practitioner agreed that there was a curvature but commented, "It is ludicrous to think that this mild a curvature could be the major cause of your problem." The patient's treatment and recovery had nothing to do with trying to correct, counter, or even consider her spinal curvature.

A farmer was told by one back specialist that his sciatica had been caused by a congenital hip malformation. Another specialist noted the malformation but didn't think it was congenital or worth talking about. The farmer recovered by devising his own treatment plan.

A 73-year-old retired hospital administrator was told that an extra lumbar vertebra was causing an unstable back with resultant low back pain. The patient asked her doctor why a structural oddity should suddenly be giving her trouble. There was no answer. There is no answer.

The moral: once you have a diagnosis that rules out *serious* structural abnormalities, you can probably afford to ignore the little curves and various whatchamacallits that practitioners like to point to as maybe, could-be, might-well-be reasons for back pain.

DIAGNOSTIC PROCEDURES

The first step: describing your pain

The overwhelming majority of survey participants felt that the quality of their dialogue with practitioners was more important in diagnosing a problem than any clinical or technical procedure. Why? Pain can't be seen, and its intensity cannot be measured. It has to be described, and you're the only one who can do it.

With this point in mind, here are suggestions from participants for making your examination more productive:

- If you've already seen several practitioners, or if your problem has lasted a long time, mention this in advance to the practitioner's receptionist, and request an appointment time that is either longer than usual or held during non-rush hours.

- Write a short chronology of your condition. This one-page report—at the most—isn't meant to take the place of your verbal explanation, but it will help you organize your thinking. And good practitioners appreciate a concisely written history.

- If a written report seems presumptuous to you, or if it's just not your style, consider making some notes for your own use.

- When you're in pain and in need of help, it's difficult to feel that you should examine the practitioner as carefully as you hope he will examine you, but try. The success or failure of treatment often hinges on your rapport with the practitioner. Trust your instincts. If you don't have a good feeling about the practitioner, no matter how esteemed his reputation, don't proceed with treatment or even with an examination. (Naturally, if you're in acute pain, you will want to get whatever immediate relief you can.)

In *Oh, My Aching Back*, the best-seller by Dr. Leon Root, the author states: "The inability of most patients to clearly explain what bothers them is a long-standing source of grievance to modern doctors."

Ironically, participants in this report had just the opposite complaint. In effect, "Modern doctors don't listen well, don't believe that you can contribute anything intelligent, and seem put off if you can."

The diagnostic examination

Observation is the first part of examination. That is, the competent practitioner will look at your posture, gait, and other movements from the moment you walk into view, as well as while taking your history and examining you. Then you will probably be asked to walk a bit, bend over gently from the waist, and bend to each side. Pain and lack of mobility, if any, will be noted. So will an absence of fluidity—tremors, lurching, or inability to perform normal movements.

While you're lying face down on the examination table, the practitioner will perform a hands-on examination. He will palpate (lightly tap) your back to determine the extent of spasming. He will probe your back, hips, and buttocks to check for tightness, "knotted" muscles, triggerpoints (small, extremely sensitive areas that are painful to the touch), and areas of referred pain. If lying on your stomach causes you pain, ask if you can lie on your side, or tuck a small pillow under your abdomen.

While you're on your back, the practitioner will raise each of your legs. Sharp pain felt during this procedure, as opposed to the slight pulling sensation of a tight hamstring, may indicate a ruptured disc. You will also be asked to bring both knees toward your chest simultaneously. If you have a plain old backache, you'll feel pulling and tightness in your lower back. If you have a ruptured disc, you may find this to be a relatively pain-free position. Your reflexes and neurological reactions will be checked with a small rubber hammer. Lack of appropriate knee-jerk response may indicate a neurological disorder. The same holds true if you show an abnormal reflex when tested in your Achilles tendon area.

Chances are about nine out of ten that the findings in your examination will be negative. From your viewpoint, however, the medical word "negative" means "positive"—no serious disease, neurological impairment, or structural abnormality.

X rays: their value and shortcomings

If you see an orthopedist or chiropractor, you'll probably be advised to have one or more pictures taken of your back. Actually, "advised" isn't the right word. "Told" is more accurate. You usually don't have a choice unless you forgo the examination altogether or see a back doctor who uses X rays sparingly—a physiatrist, for example—or see a practitioner who isn't allowed to take X rays, such as a Shiatsu therapist or a non-MD acupuncturist.

X rays usually don't reveal much about back pain. What can you expect X rays to tell you about your back pain? Chances are . . . nothing at all. But some important conditions can be seen this way. Osteoarthritis, for example, shows up on X rays. X rays are also crucial for checking out possible fractures.

Then there are the congenital "spondy" conditions, as confusing as they are hard to pronounce. Spondylolysis involves incompletely formed vertebrae. If you have spondylolysis, it can evolve into spondylolisthesis, where one vertebra comes into direct contact with an adjoining vertebra.

Spina bifida, an opening in the spine that can be serious enough at birth to cause paralysis below the lesion, is fairly common in a very mild form that seldom accounts for back pain. X rays will show that a portion of the spinal column failed to develop—a condition called spina bifida occulta—in perhaps 20 percent of the population. But it is just an X-ray finding, and no one knows how this painless anomaly is related to the full-blown spina bifida, if at all.

The risks versus the benefits of X rays. Keep these points in mind when deciding whether to have your back x-rayed:

- Less than 5 percent of survey participants who were x-rayed by medical doctors learned the cause of their back pain from these X rays.

- X rays neither spot nor rule out many serious conditions. For example, ruptured discs and spinal tumors are all but undetectable on X rays.

- A safe level of radiation has been established—*only to change time and time again as new evidence reveals new dangers*. For example, when X rays were first used, it was commonplace to treat a strep throat with them. Years later, the treatment was found to have caused cancer. It was also standard procedure to use X rays for the detection of breast cancer. Today, neither the National Cancer Institute nor the American Cancer Society recommends mammographs (X rays of the breasts) as annual procedures for most women. Even the routine chest X ray is under fire. The American College of Radiology recently condemned "automatic" chest X rays for any individual unless symptoms suggest X-ray examination. And a study by the Food and Drug Administration's Bureau of Radiological Health estimates that one-third of all X rays are unjustified, posing unnecessary risk from radiation.

- Two of the most common causes of back pain—muscle strain and disc problems—are *not* visible on X rays. A third cause of back pain—worn facet joints (the small joints that enable your movable vertebrae to function)—seldom show up clearly enough on conventional X rays to determine the extent of wear.

In conclusion, unless a practitioner is looking for a specific abnormality or disease—as opposed to taking an X ray "just as a precaution" or "just to have a look"—you probably won't gain anything in the process.

Don't get caught up in the doctor/chiropractor debate about X rays. If you see a medical doctor and then go to a chiropractor, the chiropractor will reject the doctor's X rays and insist on taking his own. The reverse is also true. Get X rays from a chiropractor, take them (if you dare) to an orthopedist, and "I'd like to take some X rays" is what you're likely to hear. To put it mildly, doctors and chiropractors disagree about how to take X rays and how to interpret them.

According to survey participants, most chiropractors take X rays while you're standing up; they feel it's pointless to "shoot" you when you're lying down, since most people don't feel pain when they're reclining. Doctors, on the other hand, complain that chiropractors take single pictures of small areas of the spine—too small to provide needed information.

In reading X rays, a doctor will tell you there is no structural malformation, while a chiropractor will see malformation in misaligned vertebrae. Neither believes the other's judgment nor accepts the other's interpretation.

If most doctors and chiropractors agree about anything, it's that X rays are valuable tools for diagnosing back problems and that radiation poses little danger. Many back sufferers don't agree with either conclusion. Minimally, if you have X rays taken, insist that a lead shield be placed over your reproductive organs. This should be done routinely, but it isn't.

CAT scanner: more "all-seeing"

The CAT scanner has been widely hailed as a landmark technological breakthrough in diagnosis. The latest model, when used for back diagnosis, can detect just about everything a practitioner might be looking for—ruptured disc, degenerative bone diseases, tumors, narrowing of the spine, and a host of other problems.

CAT stands for computerized axial tomography or computer assisted tomography. It is vastly more sophisticated and all-seeing than X-ray technology. The patient lies inside the CAT scanner, and radiation is beamed from several directions at once to produce a composite image. The computer part of the equipment analyzes the numerous views, combining them into a series of highly detailed pictures. Unlike X-ray images, a CAT scan shows soft tissue as well as bone. But like standard X-ray procedures, CAT scans involve appreciable levels of radiation exposure.

But not even a CAT scanner can show every possible view of the back, thereby leaving an opening for oversight and misdiagnosis. And even in cases where a CAT scanner helps diagnose a ruptured disc, patients about to enter surgery must undergo further test procedures—usually a myelogram (see below)—to pinpoint the location of the protruding gel.

Because a CAT scanner is costly to own and maintain, the machines tend to be clustered at major medical centers, and appointment time is limited. Survey participants reported waiting up to eight weeks for a CAT scan. They also said that unless their problem was deemed "serious" enough, their request to have a CAT scan was turned down.

Survey participants also suggested that doctors may give "phony" reasons to justify using a myelogram instead of a CAT scan. Indeed, it appears that the CAT scan is superior to the myelogram for most diagnostic purposes, and safer. So the only doctors who cling to myelography are those untrained in CAT scan interpretation or without access to a scanner.

Myelography:
what doctors don't tell you

The word "myelogram" sends chills up and down the spines of many back sufferers whose doctors recommend the procedure. A myelogram involves placing the patient on a tilting table and injecting a solution opaque to X rays into the spinal column. Tilting the table disperses the injected dye throughout the spinal column. X rays are then taken. The dye enables abnormal shapes—such as a ruptured disc or a narrowing of the spine—to show up.

About fifty participants in this survey had one or more myelograms. Highlights of their experiences follow.

Two survey participants reported permanent harm caused by a severe inflammation of the spinal cord from an allergic reaction to the oil-based myelography solution, Pantopaque®. This chronic condition, called arachnoiditis, results when drops of Pantopaque® remain in the spine. Arachnoiditis is often more disabling than whatever was causing pain in the first place.

Pantopaque® has long been banned in Sweden and other countries. More recently, it has been replaced in most American hospitals by water-based solutions. A water-based myelography solution can be put into the spine with a smaller needle, so there's less discomfort at the outset. It does not cause chronic inflammation, and it does not have to be removed after use. But remember, any procedure that entails inserting or withdrawing fluid from the spine can bring on severe headaches.

Ten survey participants got violent headaches after myelograms. Some back doctors mentioned the possibility of myelography-caused headaches to patients, but the duration and intensity of the pain often was glossed over. Three participants in this survey reported post-myelography headaches lasting from three to six *months*. About 20 percent of patients receiving myelograms got severe headaches lasting from twenty-four to forty-eight hours.

Doctors seldom mention the possibility of injury or increased back pain from myelography. If it is mentioned, the implication is that patients who claim they were hurt by myelography are hypochondriacs or malingerers. But survey participants believe that the risks are very real, and numerous articles in medical journals seem to substantiate their claims.

"I ended up extending my hospital stay for five days due to a spinal leak from the myelogram," said a nurse who had previously seen the same problem occur with her own patients.

"On one of three myelograms," recalled a housing administrator, "the nerves to my left leg were touched—oh boy! There was pain for months."

Said a service station owner, "The myelogram was pure hell at the time and for months afterward."

An editor remarked, "They would have to catch me for another myelogram. I suffered years of pain and discomfort from it."

You will seldom read about the extent to which myelography fails to pinpoint ruptured discs and other malformations. The percentage of diagnoses that myelograms miss is anyone's guess. According to one survey participant, a tree surgeon, "The medical people said I had all the symptoms of a ruptured disc, but a myelogram couldn't prove it. I was told that myelograms are 80 to 85 percent effective and that I had fallen into the 15 to 20 percent crack." And according to the *Manual of Acute Orthopedic Therapeutics,* interpreting myelograms is "fraught with the possibility of technical errors."

Although CAT scanning has not replaced myelography as a tool for evaluating disc problems, there is little question that it should. Myelography must still be used immediately before surgery, at least until a less invasive procedure comes along. But for initially evaluating the need for surgery, there is little or no call for a myelogram. It is doctor convenience, as well as the lack of available technology, that puts unnecessary pressure on patients to undergo diagnostic myelography.

A good deal of research underscores this point. In a study done at the Cologne University Clinic of Orthopaedics, from May 1980 to April 1982, a CAT scanner was found to be more accurate than myelography in pinpointing disc problems. "It seems possible that non-invasive computed tomography will eventually replace invasive myelography as a routine examination method," the study concluded.

A 1982 report in the *Journal of Computer Assisted Tomography* said that computerized tomography and myelography are both satisfactory methods of diagnosis, but that the non-invasive CAT scanner gives direct anatomical information and is more accurate at the area of the spine known as L5-S1 (the lumbar-sacral junction—the most common place for a ruptured disc to occur). The article noted that if the physical examination correlates with the CAT scan, myelography may be bypassed.

And a comparison of computerized tomography and myelography that appeared in the *American Journal of Neurology* in 1982 found that computerized tomography showed many lesions not discovered by myelography. The study suggests that computerized tomography "should be given serious consideration as the primary definitive radiographic examination of suspected lumbar disc disease."

Electromyography (EMG): painful and only moderately useful

Before the invention of the CAT scanner, some doctors thought that electromyography, the testing of muscle activity, would become the most accurate and least painful way to test for ruptured discs. This prediction hasn't come true, but electromyography remains a widely used neurological test. During electromyographic studies involving back pain, a fine needle is inserted into different muscle groups to test them both at rest and while contracted. The electrical activity of the muscles is then recorded as graphic waves and compared to normal patterns. Certain abnormal patterns can suggest anything from muscle disease to impairment of nerves supplying the muscles being tested.

The procedure has some value. For example, if doctors suspect that you have a ruptured disc, an abnormal EMG reading can increase the certainty of their diagnosis. However, according to participants in this report, doctors and technicians often differ in their interpretations of electromyography readings.

The comfort of this one- to two-hour procedure is also arguable. Doctors typically describe it as "annoying or slightly uncomfortable but not painful." Patients range in their reactions from "uncomfortable" to "very painful" to "excruciating"—agreeing with doctors about the thinness of the needles but not the degree of pain they cause when inserted into muscles.

Nuclear magnetic resonance (NMR)

No one in this survey was examined by nuclear magnetic resonance (NMR), which is currently available in only a handful of hospitals. But the *possibility* of diagnosing back problems with NMR—getting precise pictures of spinal tumors, discs, and muscle tears *without any radiation at all*—represents an extraordinary breakthrough.

With a combination of magnetic force and radio signals, NMR "sees" soft tissues—discs, muscles, and ligaments—better than any existing technology. A computer collects and interprets radio signals from the body, displaying on its screen a composite image of structure and function in the examined part.

Nuclear magnetic resonance has nothing to do with nuclear energy. "Nuclear" refers to the use of your body's own atomic nuclei as the basis for getting pictures. There is no pain associated with the procedure.

It is estimated that there will be about 150 NMR units in use by 1985. And it seems to us that back sufferers would benefit if NMR, as well as innovative ultrasound tools, were used for diagnosing back conditions.

Now *you* be the diagnostician. Then let's move on to getting rid of your pain.

At this point we hope you are clearer about the whole confusing saga of diagnosing back problems. But even if you're just clearly confused, don't worry. Pain may be invisible. But *you* know where *you* hurt.

Even if you don't have a concrete diagnosis . . . even if you don't believe the one that you have . . . even if you don't know which of several diagnoses is the "right" one . . . *you do know your own symptoms and, therefore, you can "categorize" your own pain,* as long as serious medical conditions have been ruled out as the cause of this pain.

The sole aim of the rest of this book, then, is to guide you to what other back sufferers know works for specific categories of back pain. These categories—low back, ruptured and degenerative disc, sciatica, osteoarthritis, neck, scoliosis, spondylolisthesis—cover the kinds of back problems that were mentioned most frequently by survey participants. Four categories—ruptured disc, osteoarthritis, scoliosis, and spondylolisthesis—were chosen for their obvious specificity. The remaining three categories—low back, neck, and sciatica—reflect how back sufferers themselves describe pain when back practitioners cannot agree on its cause.

If your back pain falls into more than one category, you'll find more than one chapter of value. If you suffer from low back pain *and* sciatica, for example, both those chapters will help you.

This much is certain. Whether you need professional help right now as part of your long-run, self-care program—or whether you need immediately applicable self-treatment techniques—you will have the benefit of other back sufferers' experience in eliminating or easing virtually every kind of back pain.

Chapter 9

How to Be Your Own Low Back Doctor for Acute, Severe Pain

Low back pain is not considered a disease. It is called by dozens of names, from old-fashioned lumbago to the fashionable facet joint syndrome, from misalignment to lumbar-sacral radiculopathy, from muscle strain to just plain low back pain.

No one knows for sure why people suffer from low back pain. Only colds and sore throats top it as reasons for seeking medical attention. It is the leading cause of disability in American adults under age 45. Yet there is no national research foundation worrying or wondering about it. It is, in short, America's biggest and most baffling pain. *And it can be controlled, reduced, or done away with altogether.*

You've no doubt heard that promise before. And you probably wouldn't be reading this book if the promise of this or that "X Minutes A Day Surefire Formula for Eliminating Back Pain Forever" program had come true. But the advice offered here is of a different sort, based on the experience of 272 survey participants with low back pain. They know all too well that no pill or potion, movement or motion is usually the *single* key to ending your troubles; that some little-known, self-help healing approaches work wonders; that an array of widely publicized treatments are ineffective and dangerous; that you can't necessarily end your back pain by yourself overnight. Many of you *will* make remarkable strides in just days or weeks, but not *everyone* can. If you are a chronic back sufferer, it may take months to recover, *but it can be done*. Some of you may also need professional treatment and advice at first. And knowing when and how to get professional help is an essential but often overlooked aspect of self-care.

This chapter will teach you how to become your own low back doctor. About 80 percent of participants in this report with low back pain either have eliminated pain completely or have reduced it enough so that it no longer seriously limits their lives. And we believe that what they know can help even the most disabled low back sufferers. Certainly, they can help you discover what steps you should take *right now* to keep your own back in good shape for years to come.

Nine myths about low back pain

So much misinformation plagues people with low back pain that we feel we must begin this chapter with facts, all based on our survey results, that dispel some well-established but unfounded myths.

Myth: You must know exactly what is wrong with your lower back in order to have a good chance of resolving the problem.

Fact: If you're in generally good health, an exact diagnosis is usually as meaningless as it is difficult to attain. What is meaningful is the nature of the treatment, not the terminology of the diagnosis.

Myth: Back specialists agree about what causes low back pain.

Fact: There is little agreement. People with bad posture, weak abdominal muscles, and unmanageable stress get low back pain. But so do people with correct posture, strong abdominal muscles, and well-handled stress. All that's known is some treatments and approaches work extremely well, while others are grossly overrated.

Myth: Back practitioners agree that for most people exercise is the long-run answer to low back pain.

Fact: The vast majority of practitioners who treat low back sufferers neither prescribe nor mention exercise to low back patients.

Myth: Most practitioners would prescribe exercises, but patients are too lazy to do them.

Fact: Nearly three-quarters of low back sufferers in this survey do back exercises regularly (at least four times a week), and most of these individuals exercise daily, even though their practitioners did not prescribe a regimen.

Myth: Any quality book, article, or instruction sheet from a doctor can teach you what you need to know about exercise therapy.

Fact: People with chronic, activity-limiting back pain recover more fully after receiving instructions and individualized attention from exercise experts. (The best of these experts are mentioned in this chapter and fully described in Chapters 3 and 4.)

Myth: If you need professional care, choose either an orthopedist or a chiropractor.

Fact: Neither orthopedists nor chiropractors were rated tops for low back pain by the back sufferers in this report.

Myth: Most people solve their low back problems with the help of medical doctors.

Fact: Most people start their treatment with medical doctors but *complete* it with a non-physician practitioner—many of whom have more training than doctors in musculoskeletal disorders and exercise therapy.

Myth: The most widely used treatments for low back pain are the most effective treatments.

Fact: Some extremely popular treatments, including prescription drugs and traction, have *no* value for the vast majority of back sufferers—and carry a greater-than-usual potential for harm.

Myth: Eighty percent of back sufferers recover within two months without any treatment.

Fact: This figure—an obligatory statistic in virtually every book and article on back pain—is misleading. The key is the word "recover." The truth is that 80 percent of back sufferers do get back on their feet within a matter of weeks. But the *quality* of their recovery is too often *incomplete* and *temporary*. Most of them continue to have episodes of recurrent back pain in the months and years that follow. What's more, "within two months" is a long time if *you* are the one who has to endure those weeks or months of pain, or if you lose your job during this time. And what about the 20 percent (no one knows *how* many) who do *not* recover from low back pain within two months?

HOW TO RELIEVE ACUTE, SEVERE LOW BACK PAIN

Important: The remainder of this chapter is devoted to those of you who *recently* have been incapacitated with low back pain.

However, it is also valuable if your activities have been *severely limited for a long time.*

If your pain is *chronic, but you can function in most ways,* you may want to skip to the next chapter.

Sometimes it happens out of the blue:

"While shaving one day, I bent over the sink and experienced a stabbing pain between my hips," said an attorney. "It took me ten minutes to get from the bathroom to the bedroom, which was only about twenty feet away."

A plant nursery worker had a similar tale: "I was lifting a small plant. My back wasn't properly lined up, as I was bending over at the hips. I suffered a muscle strain so severe that I could not sit or stand and had to actually crawl into the doctor's office."

Sometimes it happens after days or weeks of warning signs:

"I had been packing and lifting cartons for two weeks in preparation for moving," a pizza parlor owner reported. "My back felt like hell, but then it had always been a bother. I was a little worried about it, but I figured, 'I can stand the pain. It's just the price you have to pay.' Besides, I was doing my back exercises. Then one morning I woke up and couldn't believe the pain. There was no way I could move. I could barely breathe, the pain was so intense. It took me almost an hour to get out of bed."

"Back pain was nothing new to me," a sales representative said, "but if you had told me I could have been out of work for six weeks with it, and not even have something like a ruptured disc, I would have laughed. After putting in a lot of overtime, though, and gritting my teeth about the pain all that time, I got up from my chair, reached for my attaché case to leave for home, and wound up being taken to the hospital in an ambulance."

How to get rid of the pain

If you're literally knocked to the floor with severe muscle spasm and "locking" muscles, you have no alternative but to rest in bed. After a few days, however, if you're like most back sufferers, you will get "itchy"—bored, restless, discouraged, and depressed—and your mind will be filled with questions.

Here are some of the most frequently asked ones, followed by answers from back sufferers who recovered quickly and learned how to prevent relapses of low back pain.

Q. Should I seek professional help?

A. When you're really hurting so badly that you can't move, it's almost inevitable to want to ask your doctor or a back specialist for help. But most survey participants who sought professional help immediately after the onset of low back pain regretted getting out of bed. When your muscles go into spasm and contract to a point that you can barely move, the effort required to go to a practitioner's office usually offsets the value of any treatment. The ride, the wait to see the doctor, the need to stand or sit for a long time—all can make matters worse. In short, your severely contracted muscles are telling you to stay put.

If you are in more pain than you can stand, or if there is any chance that you have a serious medical condition, then you need professional help. But you should try to have your practitioner make a house call.

This is easier said than done, but according to survey participants, one out of four GP's will come to your home if he has treated you before. And some cities and towns have a house-call service, listed in the telephone directory, specifically designed for people in your situation.

If you want to increase the odds of a bedside visit, survey participants suggest that you *don't* say, "I'm in too much pain to move," even though that may be the case. Drastic descriptions may land you in a hospital emergency room, which is a disastrous place for any back sufferer to be. Instead, say something like, "I seem to have just a bad case of muscle strain. But when I try to get up the pain gets worse."

Q. What kind of mattress is best?

A. Most survey participants use a firm mattress with a half-inch plywood bed board between it and the box spring. But many of those who expressed the most enthusiasm about their sleeping arrangements suggest omitting the box spring and putting an extra-firm mattress on a platform bed.

If you have the option, don't use a brand-name mattress. Instead, have a foam-rubber company make you a six-inch-thick, extra-firm mattress. It's less expensive than purportedly corrective mattresses and at least as firm and comfortable.

Futon mattresses on platforms are the next choice of survey participants. But if your hips, buttocks, or thighs are painful, you will probably find the futon too thin and hard, and the cause of unwelcome pressure.

Of the fifteen survey participants who turned hopefully to water beds, eight switched back to firm mattresses and bed boards, complaining that the bed couldn't be made hard enough to suit them. They also said that the water produced a "rolling action" that made it difficult for them to control their movements and positions. The other seven were happy with their water beds so long as the mattresses were kept "filled to the top" and "firm." They said the water enabled the spine to align more comfortably, and that the floating sensation eased the pressure on the spine and muscles.

Some back sufferers give up mattresses altogether and take to the floor when their back pain flares up. But lying on the floor is not recommended for incapacitating pain and muscle spasm, primarily because getting up from and down to the floor may add to your pain. Also, if your low back pain is accompanied by pain and spasming in the hips and upper legs, even a carpeted floor can put too much pressure on inflamed and sensitive areas, causing more pain and spasm. Finally, if you need at least a week of bed rest, you may feel better psychologically if you can look people in the eye instead of the foot.

If, however, you find yourself stuck between a hard floor and a sagging mattress, take the floor until you can make other arrangements.

Q. What is the best way to get in and out of bed?

A. The stoop-and-roll technique works best, even when you can barely move:

Stand with your back to your bed, close enough so that the backs of your legs touch it. Look straight ahead, pull in your abdominal muscles, keep your back straight, and sit. (*Don't* twist around to see where you will land.) Then, in one easy, fluid motion, using your arms and hands to help support and guide you, roll onto your side and swing both legs onto the bed.

Never flop backward onto the mattress from a sitting position. Also, never leave your legs dangling off the bed, as that position is guaranteed to make your back arch painfully.

To get up, reverse the process: ease your way over to the edge of the bed, remaining on your side with your knees bent. If you're lying on your right side, place your left palm on the mattress next to your right shoulder. Then, in one easy motion, push down on your left palm, swing yourself into an upright position, bring your legs off the bed, and put your feet flat on the floor. Now keep your back straight and stand up, pushing off with your hands if that makes it easier for you.

One way to help yourself getting in and out of bed is to cut the distance you have to stoop or rise by raising your mattress to a height of thirty inches from the usual twenty-four. An admittedly expensive way to do this is to buy an old-fashioned poster bed, as most are six to ten inches higher than modern beds. Other ways to give yourself a lift: replace the detachable legs of a low, modern bed with taller legs, or have a taller platform bed designed for you. Then, when you feel well enough to do household chores again, the extra height will facilitate making the bed each day and changing linens.

Q. Is complete bed rest necessary?

A. It often is. Complete bed rest—which at home means not leaving bed except to use the toilet—was far and away the most successful approach among survey participants for helping them *start* to recover from newly incurred and severely restricting lower back pain.

Listen to what your body is telling you. If it says rest, then rest. That can be the only way to ensure that *this* episode of pain is your *last* one. Remember that in most cases of acute, severe pain, the quickest way back on your feet is to get off your feet and give your body a chance to repair itself.

"If it kills you to move, don't move," advises a roofing contractor who participated in the survey. "If you're worried about your job, your kids, or whatever, don't worry. Stay in bed, else you *really* won't be able to move and you'll *really* have something to worry about."

"My wife told me to stay in bed," he recalled. "My doctor told me to not even bother coming to his office—just stay in bed. But staying in bed made me feel like an idiot. Everyone I know has some back pain. My friends have problems with their backs and they still put in a full day's work. Anyway, I struggled out of bed the morning after my back went out, went to work, climbed a ladder to finish a job, and wham! My assistant had to call our volunteer ambulance corps to get me down from the roof and back into bed."

Q. How long should I stay in bed?

A. Sometimes a day is enough. Three to five days of complete bed rest is the average for low back sufferers who recover successfully. Here is the rule of thumb for you to follow: just as soon as you can move around in bed without severe pain, former back sufferers suggest, try walking for a few minutes. You'll feel achy, but if there's no substantial increase in pain, you're on your way.

In any event, now go back to bed. If you were able to walk, set up a gradually stepped-up activity schedule for yourself. Gradual increments are the key. The next time you're up, don't walk until you drop. If you do too much right away, you risk a serious setback.

Here are three brief case histories showing how back sufferers dealt with the difficult question "How long should I stay in bed?"

Case 1: A writer spent one day in bed, went back to work on the second day, spent all that day sitting at a meeting, and then spent the next six weeks in bed.

Case 2: A piano tuner awoke one morning barely able to move. The episode was like many he had experienced in the past. It took him fifteen minutes to get out of bed. A hot shower loosened up his back enough to keep him going. From experience, he knew that lying in bed, or remaining motionless for long, would just make him worse. And he was right. He made it through the day and his pain was gone in a week. (Caution: This gritting-your-teeth approach works for only about 5 percent of people with acute, disabling low back pain.)

Case 3: A boutique shop owner spent two weeks in bed. During the third week, she progressed from ten minutes an hour to thirty minutes an hour of walking or standing. During week four, she was out of bed almost all the time and sitting fifteen minutes an hour. In week five, she was well into an exercise program and back to work. Five years later, she was still free of back pain.

Q. Is there a "right" position to assume during bed rest?

A. Yes, because you can take the strain off your back by lying correctly. Lie on your side and keep your knees bent. Put a small pillow under your head. The pillow should be just plump enough to keep your head and neck level with the rest of your spine. Put another firm pillow between your legs so that it holds apart your knees and your feet.

You need not—in fact, should not—lie absolutely still. When your muscles are contracted and spasming, even a little movement can help you maintain some flexibility. For example, you can slowly and gently straighten out your legs and return them to a flexed position. Move your arms and torso a bit. Shrug your shoulders. Virtually any kind of shifting around, no matter how slight, can make you feel a little better.

It's also a good idea to change positions as you need to. The most basic way to change positions—and ease tightness and pressure—is to shift from one side to the other. To do this, keep your knees bent, roll slowly onto your back, and then roll onto your other side. Also, try lying on your back with a small pillow under your neck (but not under your shoulders) and two or three big pillows under your knees. The majority of acutely incapacitated low back sufferers are more comfortable in the side position. But if you can lie on your back for even a few minutes, the change will alleviate boredom and get you moving a bit more.

Don't try to sit up in bed to read or prop yourself up on an elbow to eat or drink. It feels awkward, but it really is possible to ingest and digest in a prone position. You can drink anything—even hot coffee—through a plastic straw with a flexible neck. And don't lie on your stomach. If you must do so for an examination, tuck a folded pillow under your abdomen.

Q. During bed rest, what can I do to speed up my progress?

A. *Use ice.* You can reduce the severity of muscle spasms by repeatedly icing the affected areas during the first forty-eight hours. Your best bet is to fill a plastic freezer bag with ice cubes and apply it to your lower back for ten to fifteen minutes every two to four hours. If your hips, buttocks, and upper legs hurt, use ice on these areas, too. If it's awkward to hold the ice bag in place, affix it with masking or surgical tape. (See pages 88–91 for more details about cold therapy.)

Try acupressure. You can reduce spasming by giving yourself Shiatsu (acupressure) treatments. You can also combine Shiatsu with ice, as follows:

Apply cold anywhere that hurts, from your lower back to your knees, for five minutes. Next, apply pressure to these same places with the ball of your thumb, using small circular motions for about ten seconds on each spot. Then reapply ice for five minutes more.

Apply heat. About forty-eight hours after the onset of pain, try using heat to relax your muscles and facilitate healing through increased blood flow. If you have spasming after heat treatments, apply ice to the painful spots. (Some people find that ice continues to soothe them more effectively than heat long after pain begins. If your body responds better to cold than to heat, stick with the ice pack.)

Wet heat is a drop better than a conventional heating pad, according to survey participants. Hot towels, hot packs, hot water bottles, and electric hydrocollators are all easy to use and effective. The hydrocollator, considered to be a good investment by many participants, allows you to have moist heat whenever you like without trekking to the sink. Hydrocollators are obtainable from most well-stocked medical shops and supply companies.

Heating lamps of various kinds are not recommended by survey participants. They're difficult to use when you're in bed, and their effectiveness is questionable.

A good massage is another drug-free muscle relaxant that will help your muscles unwind. A professional massage is best. But even a partner with no experience can improve your spirits and possibly rub away some tightness. Have your partner use a light oil and a fairly light touch. Too much pressure on your lower back can make matters worse at this point. Your partner should concentrate on three areas—your legs, back, and neck—massaging toward the heart, using either a long, continuous gliding motion with the palms or a circular motion with the fingertips and palms.

Q. How can I minimize the stress of lying in bed in pain?

A. There is no question that incapacitating back pain causes stress. And this stress, in turn, can magnify your pain. To minimize and control the stress-pain cycle effects, try some of the following stress-reduction approaches suggested by survey participants:

Do deep breathing exercises a few minutes each hour. Inhale through your nose for six seconds; hold your breath for one second; exhale through your mouth for seven seconds. Keep your eyes closed, and expect to feel more relaxed each time you exhale.

Visualize a state of relaxation and well-being. Once or twice a day, when you know you're not going to be interrupted (many survey participants suggest that you unplug your phone or take it off the hook), try to give yourself a vacation from pain. Concentrate on the thought that the pain is diminishing and leaving your body. Start with your forehead and facial muscles. Tighten them. Then let them relax completely. Using this same procedure, work your way down, relaxing your neck, shoulders, arms, chest, abdomen, pelvic area, legs, and feet. Now work on your back. Picture it relaxing, starting from the shoulder blades and working down. As an aid, some survey participants visualize a ray of sunlight touching each area that they want to relax. Others imagine a silky fabric or soft breeze helping each area to unwind and become pain-free.

Meditate, letting your mind go blank until you're unaware of pain or any thought or feeling.

Laugh. Find something to make you laugh or smile. Read a humor book, watch a comedy on TV, rent a videocassette or two from a home delivery company, and watch films that take your mind off your troubles and put you in an upbeat mood.

Listen to music that relaxes you.

Pray. Believe that your pain is easing and that you are on the road to recovery.

Q. Must I adjust my diet while I'm recuperating?

A. According to survey participants, the biggest risk you face from poor eating habits while inactive is constipation. Just being less active can, and often does, cause constipation, which in turn makes some people's back pain considerably worse.

To help avoid constipation, you need to drink a minimum of eight 8-ounce glasses of non-alcoholic liquid daily. And make sure you get plenty of fiber and roughage by eating a variety of whole-grain foods, raw fruit, and raw vegetables.

Some survey participants felt that supplementing their diets with vitamin C and calcium facilitated recovery from muscle strain. This isn't a widely accepted or well-documented theory, but there's probably no harm, and there just might be some good, in taking moderate amounts of these supplements every day—1,000 or 2,000 mg of vitamin C and 750 mg of calcium.

Of course, what you eat and how much you eat affect your weight, and back specialists are unanimous in their belief that excess weight can cause back pain. According to survey participants, however, weight is often not a *critical* factor in back pain. Of the eighteen people in the survey who dieted as part of their total program of back care, none felt that weight loss was nearly as important in reducing back pain as other factors mentioned in this chapter. Obviously, to be grossly overweight is to beg for a variety of medical problems. But weight loss alone is probably not a major factor in alleviating back pain.

Q. When can I start to exercise and what exercises should I do?

A. As soon as your contracted muscles have eased enough for you to move around in bed and be up and about for even a few minutes, you can try some of the pre-exercise "positions" that survey participants found especially useful. They are conservative but meaningful steps you can take even before your pain has lessened enough to allow you to exercise. In a week or two, when you have mastered these positions, you will be ready to attempt the exercises in the next chapter.

Position 1: Basic Exercise Position. From the fetal position, with both knees bent, simply roll onto your back. Position your feet flat on the mattress, with your heels about six inches to a foot and a half from your rump.

If you have been in severe pain, and the muscles and ligaments in your lower back have contracted, holding this position for a few minutes will set the stage for correcting the exaggerated "S" curve in your lower back, called swayback or lordosis, that contributes to back pain.

Keep your arms at your sides when you're in this position. But, for just a moment, to appreciate your ultimate goal, slip one hand, palm down, between the small of your back and your mattress. Then do it again after you've been in this position for a few minutes. The curve in your lower back should now be a trifle flatter just from the pull of gravity.

If you can lie in this position comfortably for five minutes, try Position 2 later in the day or the next morning.

Position 2: Basic Position with Pelvic Lift. Assume Position 1, but this time use a towel to raise your pelvis slightly, thereby flattening your lumbar curve a bit more.

Fold a bath towel once and slide an inch of the folded towel under the edge of your buttocks, at the point where they join your thighs. Do this for two minutes, once in the morning and once in the evening. If the position doesn't cause you discomfort, add one minute more each time, until you reach ten minutes in the morning and ten minutes at night.

At this point you can drop Position 1. You may discover, though, that even after you are recovered and exercising regularly, Position 2 will still be useful, helping to relax your back when it's tired.

Position 3: Basic Position with Knees Clasped. When you can maintain Position 2 for ten minutes twice a day, you might find, as many survey participants did, that it is useful to increase the amount of stretching you get from this position.

Immediately after completing Position 2, keeping the towel under you, bring one knee up toward your chest and hold it in place with your hand. Now bring the other knee up. Clasp your hands just below both kneecaps. Gently, *very gently,* pull your knees toward your chest *just a few inches.* Hold for a count of six. Return to the Basic Position. Repeat these steps six times. The slight amount of stretching involved here might be considered "exercising," but the real point is simply to relax in a comfortably flexed position, not to try to draw your knees toward your chest as much as you can.

Position 4: Basic Position with Legs Supported. This position is a slightly more difficult alternative to both Positions 2 and 3, primarily because you have to get up from and down to the floor. But because your legs will be supported, you might find it more relaxing and pain-reducing. If so, substitute it for Positions 2 and 3, and do it twice every day—more often if it makes you feel better.

Begin by lying in the Basic Position on a carpeted floor (or on a gym mat or two folded blankets) with your feet in front of a sofa or a chair. Support your neck with a folded towel, or support your head and neck with a small pillow. Put both legs, one at a time, on the chair seat or sofa. Your feet and calves—but not your thighs—should rest on the elevated surface. If you're using a chair with a hard seat, you will feel more comfortable with a towel or blanket on the seat.

Q. How do I make the transition from bed rest to being up and about a little bit?

A. *Walk your way out of pain.* As you recuperate, don't switch your environment from a bed to a chair. Walk as much as you can. Sitting puts much more strain on your back than standing. It slows rather than hastens your recovery.

Walk on level ground. When you venture outside for the first few times, avoid steep grades and uneven terrain. Walking up *or* down hills causes a noticeably greater strain on low back muscles. And uneven ground—like rocky or gravelly areas or beaches—tends to jar your back and make it difficult to relax and stride comfortably.

Stand with your weight unevenly *distributed.* Forget what you were taught as a child or in the armed forces. Most people with low back pain are much more comfortable if they shift their weight from one foot to the other when they have to stand for any length of time, for good reason: when you shift most of your weight to one leg, and bend that leg slightly at the knee, you lessen your lumbar curve. But don't favor one leg for more than a few minutes at a time. Shift back and forth as your comfort level dictates.

If possible, use a footstool, a book, your child's stuffed animal, or anything else that's lying around to prop up your foot. This further reduces your lumbar curve. Again, don't favor one leg; switch back and forth.

Also, wear a pair of well-made shoes. Don't pad around in old slippers, clogs, or run-down sneakers. Your footwear should have at least a one-inch heel and contain a cushioned heel and arch support. (Virtually all good shoes have these features; running shoes are also acceptable.)

Q. Once I'm out of bed and on the road to recovery, how can I maintain good posture?

A. Keep three things tucked in—your abdomen, rear, and chin—and the rest of your body will tend to line up properly.

If your abdominal muscles aren't strong enough to prevent a bulging belly, wear a back support until you can exercise and strengthen these muscles. If you can't keep your rear tucked in a bit (the more it juts out, the greater your lumbar curve and back pain), wear a back support that comes down low enough to position you properly. Tucking in your chin is important, because it helps you to maintain a proper cervical (neck) curve. Position your chin too high, or let it droop too low, and you'll add to the strain on your neck and the rest of your spine.

The importance of good posture cannot be emphasized enough. Survey participants mentioned it more than any other factor as a way to speed up recovery from acute episodes of low back pain. It gets instant results, costs nothing to learn, and will do more for you than most professional treatments.

Face what you want to see. While lying, standing, or sitting, turn your entire body, not just your head, toward anyone or anything you're looking at. Otherwise, the top part of your spine (your neck) will be going one way, the bottom part another way, which may increase spasming.

Q. How can I avoid reinjuring my back?

A. *Adapt easy-on-the-back dressing habits.* Low back sufferers reinjure their backs more from reaching the wrong way to put their shoes on than from lifting heavy objects. With this in mind, survey participants recovering from acute, severe low back pain recommended the following:

- Keep your next day's clothing—including your shoes—within reach of your bed. This way, you can start your day with relaxation and pre-exercise positions, not a hunt for what to wear. You can also give your back a break when you get dressed—as the next paragraph explains.

- If you are still very tight and prone to spasming, put on waist-to-feet clothing—underwear, socks, skirts, pants—while lying on your back in bed. Even put your shoes on this way, using an old towel to keep your sheets clean.

- If you feel comfortable enough to sit while putting on your socks and shoes, bring your feet to you, while keeping your back as straight as possible. Minimize bending from the waist to put on footwear. If need be, support the weight of your legs by propping your feet on a chair.

Keep your hands close to yourself. Don't reach out to pick up objects or perform an activity, no matter how light the object or easy the activity. For example, don't extend your arm fully to pick up a child's toy, water a plant, or answer the phone. Sidle right up to objects; the closer your arms are to your sides, and not to what you're reaching for, the better for your back. If you can't avoid reaching—to turn on a faucet, for example—turn to one side. It's easier to bend sideways than forward.

Also, until you're recovered, don't reach above your head for objects. If no one can help you, use a stepladder. Reaching for high objects arches your back—and that causes trouble.

SUMMARY OF TREATMENTS AND PRACTITIONERS FOR ACUTE, SEVERE LOW BACK PAIN

Best self-help therapies for acute low back pain

(1) Bed rest

(2) Cold therapy

(3) Acupressure

(4) Posture realignment

(5) Stress reduction

(6) Helpful habits and activities

Best professional treatments for acute low back pain

(1) Shiatsu therapy

(2) Chiropractic manipulation

Professional treatments worth trying
for acute low back pain

(1) Triggerpoint injection

(2) Muscle-relaxant injection

(3) Acupuncture

Widely used treatments best avoided during
episodes of acute low back pain

(1) Exercise

(2) Traction

(3) Anti-inflammatory pills

(4) Prescription pain pills (except in instances of extreme pain)

Best practitioners for acute low back pain
(See Chapters 3 and 4 for details)

(1) Physiatrist—Medical doctor who specializes in physical and rehabilitative medicine

(2) Physical therapist—Non-physician who specializes in reconditioning and rehabilitation

(3) Shiatsu therapist—Massage therapist who practices acupressure

(4) Chiropractor—Health-care practitioner who emphasizes spinal manipulation as a means of healing

Practitioners worth a try for
acute low back pain

(1) Sports medicine doctor—Medical doctor with special training in sports medicine

(2) Kinesiologist—Expert in the principles and mechanics of muscular movement

(3) Acupuncturist—MD or non-MD who is licensed to practice acupuncture

**Widely seen practitioners who sometimes make
acute low back sufferers feel worse**

(1) Neurosurgeons*

(2) Neurologists*

(3) Yoga instructors**

(4) Physical fitness instructors**

*Except possibly for diagnostic purposes.
**Outstanding for *chronic* low back pain but not for acute conditions.

Chapter 10

How to Be Your Own Low Back Doctor for Chronic Pain

Important: This chapter is specially designed to help you get rid of chronic low back pain—the discomfort and limitations that have bothered you for months or years.

If your low back pain is caused by a ruptured disc (Chapter 11), osteoarthritis (Chapter 13), spondylolisthesis (Chapter 14), or scoliosis (Chapter 14), we suggest that you read one of these chapters *first*, then follow the guidelines in this chapter.

If you are currently incapacitated with acute back pain, see Chapter 9 first.

If you have chronic low back pain—and most participants in this survey did—chances are that you . . .

- suffer some degree of discomfort every day;
- don't know what to do or where to turn to improve *substantially* your condition;

• find that certain days and weeks are more painful than others—or even incapacitating—and not always for obvious reasons;

• exercise on a regular basis (or at least know that you should) but aren't sure that the exercises you do are helping your back as much as possible;

• hardly expect a cure to drop into your lap, but are weary of getting simplistic and uninformed responses to your questions.

TWO PATHS THROUGH PAIN

Two cases offer some valuable insights.

Case 1: Kevin, a 34-year-old, long-distance independent trucker, had devoted his career and his life's savings to running his own business. But now it seemed that he might lose everything he had worked so hard for, because of a chronically and increasingly painful lower back.

Every year Kevin suffered two or three episodes of low back pain. Each episode either diminished his driving time or kept him off the road entirely. As the years passed, Kevin's pain grew worse. The muscle-relaxant pills prescribed by his family doctor made him more drowsy than comfortable. A back support that worked at first hardly helped at all now. Exercises that used to make him feel better caused severe spasming. And acupuncture wasn't making a dent in the problem.

Kevin asked his doctor to recommend a specialist. His GP, as could have been predicted, referred him to an orthopedic surgeon. The orthopedist examined Kevin thoroughly, found no "pathological anomalies," and told him that the only real answer was to get out of the trucking business.

Kevin went through the roof. "How would you feel if I told you that the only way to get rid of your back pain was to give up being an orthopedist?" he yelled.

The orthopedist was sympathetic but repeated his contention that sitting in a truck for long periods of time was extremely hard on Kevin's lower back. His recommendation stood.

Remarkably, by the time Kevin told us his story, his back had become pain-free.

"Did you change your job?" we asked.

"No, although I thought long and hard about it," he replied. "I was unbelievably depressed and frustrated at first. A couple of weeks passed and I was driving, with my lower and middle back taped up to hold out for the rest of the run, when a Peggy Lee song came on the air about 'Is that all there is?' That struck me. I couldn't believe that all modern medicine could offer was changing my job."

"How did you turn around a condition that had been deteriorating for eleven years?" we inquired.

"After the orthopedist," Kevin answered, "I went to a chiropractor. I tried manipulation and other treatments for six months. Each treatment made me feel better and I thought I was coming along. But then the amount of relief started lasting for just a couple of hours, rather than a few days or a week. I felt I wasn't really improving overall, and I was losing time and money by seeing the chiropractor three times a week, so I stopped."

"What did you do then?"

"Nothing. I mean, I didn't see anyone else. Who was I supposed to see? Instead, I talked to people with back problems and looked at some back books. By this time, my friends and relatives were clipping out and sending me any articles they saw about back problems. It took a long time to get better, but I got there. It was touch and go for two years, a lot of trying to figure out what I should and shouldn't do—everything from how I sat when I drove to doing back exercises that would help rather than just keep the status quo, to little things you can do for yourself without making yourself feel like an invalid or basket case.

"People should be realistic," he added. "Anything that causes you as much trouble as my back caused me, and for such a long period of time, is going to take a lot of changing. The question is what to change and how. And, for me, there was also the question of whether I would work it out first or drive my family and myself crazy in the process."

Case 2: Maggie, a 51-year-old management consultant, had been bothered by low back pain since she hurt herself leaning over a couch to force open a jammed window. That was twenty years ago.

At the time we talked to Maggie she rated herself 7 on a pain scale of 0 to 10—0 being pain-free and 10 being totally incapacitated. The long meetings and luncheons with clients required in her business were particularly hard to take. She had been doing back exercises every day for fifteen years—a smorgasbord learned from a variety of practitioners and books—and she felt these definitely helped to keep her pain from growing even worse.

Maggie had been examined or treated by eleven practitioners over twenty years. When she first experienced pain her family doctor had prescribed rest and medication. Soon afterward the parade started.

"After I saw my family doctor, I went to a neurologist, who prescribed more rest and more drugs. I took pain pills and muscle relaxants, the biggest change from these being that I couldn't think straight. The neurologist thought I might have a ruptured disc and sent me to a neurosurgeon. No luck there, so I decided to go it on my own. But after ten years of managing pretty well, including swimming every day at a health club and doing a lot of exercise, things started going downhill.

"I went the chiropractic route at this point and made some progress. Not enough though. A few years ago, my pain was consistently bad enough to affect my business. I couldn't make long plane trips and it was torture to sit through all-day meetings.

"A few months ago, I went to see a well-known back specialist. He sarcastically diagnosed my problem as 'treadmillitis'—running from doctor to doctor—handed me a sheet of exercises to do and told me to stick with him or any other competent doctor of my choice and get the problem resolved once and for all.

"I've also tried acupuncture, naturopathy, psychotherapy, and massage. I've had it. I don't know what to do now," Maggie concluded.

"Did the exercises from the latest doctor help?" we asked.

"I think they're actually making things worse," Maggie replied. "But I'm so frustrated I'm doing them anyway." Further conversation with Maggie revealed that she accepted everyone's judgment but her own about how to get well. She was always trying the "latest" exercise program. A water mattress suggested by a friend was bothering her back. She didn't take a back cushion to meetings or use a special carry-on seat for her frequent plane trips because such items embarrassed her, she said. Her footwear was appropriate for meetings but inappropriate for her back. Indeed, Maggie concluded that there were a dozen things she could do to help herself. And when we last spoke to her, she was doing those things and was in better shape than she could remember for ten years.

Note: The self-help techniques that low back sufferers found most useful are contained in this chapter as well as in Chapters 9, 15, and 16.

Kevin and Maggie are two of the 240 chronic low back sufferers in this survey. Their stories demonstrate patterns of success and failure, but *both* offer proven, concrete approaches that you can apply *right now* to cut short the recovery process and banish chronic low back pain from your life.

Since chronic low back pain is dramatically affected by what you do every day, we will begin with those daily activities, functions, and attitudes that have the most to do with back problems, listed according to their frequency of mention by survey participants.

Some of these points may seem mundane or even silly. But they play a crucial role in resolving low back pain. In fact, collectively, they may be more important than any other factor in determining whether your low back pain will continue, worsen, or improve. As you study these points, you might find it useful to check off the ones you particularly need to act on. Then, after completing this chapter, you might come back to the checked points and plan out corrective steps.

THE TWENTY-FOUR-HOUR-A-DAY BACK HELPER

When we reviewed the comments of survey participants who had found a way out of years or even decades of chronic low back pain, one thing above all stood out—their attitude.

It wasn't simply a belief they would get well, although that was important. It wasn't anything mystical. They simply had made up their minds to put themselves in charge of ending their back pain. They listened to the experts without awe and with the knowledge that they themselves ultimately knew more about their bodies than anyone else possibly could. Those who sought professional care did so for a limited time and acted as partners in the treatment, not as helpless victims looking to be cured. And all made the resolution of back pain a high priority in their lives.

These former back sufferers rejected as nonsense *any* claim of instant pain-banishing magic. They also rejected the idea that low back pain was common and inevitable. (Some noted that back pain is uncommon in many societies, including Japan and other Far Eastern countries.) They refused to believe that low back pain was the price they had to pay for walking upright, pointing out that walking upright a lot is a great way to *avoid* back pain.

They shunned the myth that low back pain is part of growing older. (The majority of back sufferers are under age 45.)

In essence, former back sufferers were determined to beat the rap. They took charge. They listened, learned, then decided for themselves what they needed to do to get well. They became their own low back doctors.

THE MOST POPULAR TIP
FOR PREVENTING LOW BACK PAIN

In the section of our survey that asked, "What are your most helpful tips for other back sufferers?" advice about lifting topped the list. The most often-stated advice was, in a phrase, to bend your knees and not your back. More emphatically, as one survey participant put it, "Never bend from the waist, not even to pick up a pin."

Some of the following advice about lifting is standard; you may have heard it before. Other suggestions are more unusual but equally useful. You will also receive advice about how to handle the three most common "back breaking" lifting activities mentioned in this survey—lifting a baby, lifting groceries, and lifting heavy objects around the house and yard.

How to pick up and carry miscellaneous objects

- Position your feet about shoulders' width apart with one foot a shoe length in front of the other. This position makes it easier to keep your back straight, to get up and down, and to maintain your balance.

- Keep whatever you're picking up close to your body. A ten-pound object extended just a few inches away from your body can strain your back.

- When lifting a heavy object, try to hold it *in back of you*, instead of in front of you or at your side. Lifting from the back may be impossible because of the size or shape of the object. But do it whenever you can; it will make a big difference.

If this "backward" position seems odd or illogical to you, perhaps the comments of one survey participant, a physical fitness instructor, will help explain its merit: "Remember the old strong man cliché—the bulging-muscles guy who picks up the front end of a car with his back turned to it? This same strong man would be reduced to picking up a truss or back support if he tried to lift the car when it was in front of him. Picking up an object behind you, or walking down the street lugging an object this way, may look funny. But better to look funny than feel bad."

Carrying groceries

It may be neat and efficient to have all your groceries packed into a single carton, but a loaded carton is a disaster for lifting and carrying. Instead, have your groceries packed into two bags of roughly equal weight, and use bags with handles. It is much easier to carry groceries with your arms at your sides than to clutch bags to your chest. Lifting your arms while holding heavy packages puts more strain on the back, participants say.

Driving to the supermarket would seemingly solve your grocery-carrying problem. However, taking a car on shopping outings actually causes back sufferers more problems. When you have to walk your groceries home, you tend not to take most of the store with you. Not so when you're driving. This leads us to one of the Top Ten Back Wreckers in our survey: getting groceries into and out of a car trunk. If the trunk of your car was at the level of your rear window, you wouldn't have a problem. Unhappily, though, no one has designed a car with the floor of the trunk at this height.

So, even if you're driving, avoid heavy cartons. Avoid bags that are weight lifters' specials or else, when removing objects from the trunk, you'll be bending perilously at the waist and leaning forward to grab the bottom of the bag or box. And that is trouble. Also, lift bags out of the trunk, one at a time, by the handles, or skip the trunk altogether if you can and put your groceries on the back or front seat close to the door.

If you are suffering an acute episode of back pain, have your groceries delivered. Don't worry about treating yourself with kid gloves. If it's strenuous exercise you want, work out on a Nautilus device under supervision at a health club. From what survey participants tell us, it seems safer to bench press a hundred pounds than to grunt and lift a twenty-pound grocery carton off the floor of your car trunk.

Lifting and carrying babies and children

To have them is to love them. And to love them is to want to pick them up, hold them over your head, and delight them by carrying them piggyback and giving them rides on your shoulders.

To not be able to do these kinds of things is the most heartbreaking situation a back sufferer can encounter. With this in mind, here is advice from survey participants about minimizing your back problems and maximizing your pleasure with your children.

- Avoid the bassinet. It is cute, charming, and possibly an even greater plague for back sufferers than car trunks. The bassinet is precisely the wrong height—too high to let you kneel on the floor and comfortably reach your baby, and too low for you to reach your baby without bending yourself out of shape.

  One solution is to use a big wicker laundry basket instead of a bassinet; line it with soft blankets and set it on the floor or at the level of a changing table—about midriff high. Fastening it securely to a platform or a sturdy, low table may do the trick. When the child is big enough for a crib, don't lean over the bars to lift the baby in or out. Instead, drop the collapsible side, get down on your knees, and go from there.

- Playpens are another macabre invention designed without parents' backs in mind. If you can't avoid playpens, at least get one with a side that folds down in seconds, allowing you to kneel, rather than lean over, to pick up your child.

- Changing tables take up space and aren't cheap, but most survey participants with children consider them essential. If you don't have one, you can kneel and change the baby on the floor or on a low bed.

- Sit in a rocking chair for feedings or to lull your baby to sleep. Rocking chairs were popular with back sufferers long before President Kennedy publicized their value for low back pain. The backs of these chairs are usually straight. The rocking movement, according to some back sufferers, may ease stiffness and discomfort for you while it helps calm the baby.

- The least stressful way to carry an infant a long distance is on your back in a carrier. It may seem impersonal not to wear the carrier in front where you can see your child, but babies don't seem to mind, and your back will thank you.

- Avoid the hip carry. A mother of twins in this survey routinely used to pick up and carry her 2-year-old twins, one on each hip, until a doctor who was a friend of the family pointed at her and exclaimed, "*That* is your back problem." The hip carry was used by many mothers and fathers in this survey. And most realized at some point that the technique was causing them pain.

- If your child and your back are acting up at the same time, and your child wants to be held, try to comfort him or her while you're kneeling or while both of you are lying down.

- Piggyback rides are easier on you if your child can climb up on a chair and then grab hold of you while you're standing.

- A top-of-your-shoulders ride isn't the worst thing for your back. It's lifting your child *onto* your shoulders that's the real problem. Again, have your child get on a chair and climb on your shoulders while you are kneeling with your back to the chair.

SITTING

"Take a seat and make yourself comfortable," the receptionist at one of the country's most prestigious rehabilitation clinics told the strong-backed husband of a low back sufferer. He did—in a plush, leather chair whose rounded back defied all attempts to get comfortable. An hour later, when the doctor was ready to see the patient—who because of her low back pain had chosen to stand rather than sit—the husband was sorry that he hadn't made an appointment for himself.

As every reader of this book already knows, sitting is hard on the back. Most low back sufferers would probably agree that the problem is not that we evolved into creatures who stood upright but that we decided to "take a load off our feet" and sit down on the job, in the car, and just about everywhere else.

A good chair gave some survey participants more help than a good back specialist.

Survey participants are almost unanimous about what constitutes a good chair:

Overall qualities. Look for a straight-backed chair with a back tall enough to support your lower *and* upper back, arms to support the weight of *your* arms, and a seat that is firm enough to keep you from sinking in, wide enough to shift around in, and deep enough to support your thighs almost to your knees.

The back of the chair. Most chairs that you find in homes, offices, and restaurants have as little backing as a bikini. Either there is enough room between the slats for a small child to crawl through or there is nothing but air at the point where the small of your back is yearning to make contact.

And as if all this weren't bad enough, most chair backs aren't straight, either. They are curved almost as much as the inside of a barrel, or they tilt back just enough so that you're neither reclining nor able to sit up straight.

Nevertheless, think straight and insist on adequate support when you shop for your own chair. Make sure the back of the chair extends down to, or almost to, the seat. Also see to it that the back of the chair is at least high enough to make contact with your shoulder blades, so that it can adequately support your upper back.

The seat. A chair seat should be firm enough for you to sit on without more than about a half-inch of give. For well-padded individuals, a hard seat without any cushioning is fine. The depth of the seat—measured from back to front—should be about eighteen to twenty-four inches, depending on your size. You want enough seat depth to support about three-quarters of your thighs. Less will create a pull on your lower back; more, extending to your knees or beyond, will also play havoc with your back.

When considering the depth of a chair, figure that you might be using a back support, which will take up some of this measurement. In fact, if the only problem with a chair is that it has too much depth, that's easy to solve. Add a firm pillow, a back support, or both.

Chair arms. Your chair should have them. Chair arms take the weight of your arms off your back. They're not critical, but they are a help. If you have to make do without them, rest your arms in your lap.

The back support. If there is a straight-backed chair that comes with a built-in adjustable back support, the authors aren't aware of it. Secretarial and executive desk chairs have lumbar-support contours, but even the best of them aren't as effective for most low back sufferers as the unadorned straight-backed chair with the back support of your choice—a rolled-up towel, cushion, pillow, or commercially available backrest. *Anything* that provides the hollow of your back with something to rest on tends to relieve (or prevent) nagging low back pain.

Chair foot support. If you are a fan of the *Tonight Show,* you've probably seen how Johnny Carson relieves the discomfort of diminutive, seated guests whose feet don't reach the floor. A push of the button and, poof, a footstool slides out from under the guest's chair. Survey participants who have low back pain also advise using a footstool. The point is not to help your feet reach the ground—although if you're short, a footstool is essential for that reason—but to raise your knees so that they are higher than your hips. Try it and you'll feel a noticeable and consistent increase in comfort. Of course, you don't have to invest in a footstool. A hefty book (about four to seven inches thick) will do just fine.

There is one difficulty with straight-backed chairs—namely, it isn't always possible to use them. For example, a straight-backed chair would be impractical to use at a desk, especially if you have to move back and forth between your desk and your typewriter or computer, turn to talk to people, or rummage through files.

For working at a desk, you might want a rolling office chair with a built-in lumbar support. Scores of different brands and models, ranging in price from modest to extremely expensive, are available at office furniture and department stores, and over the Internet.

How to choose a good desk chair

(1) *Never buy a desk chair sight unseen or seat untried.* Sit on it for thirty to forty-five minutes before buying it. One survey participant was reluctant to do this for fear of making a nuisance of himself. Another survey participant *was* mistaken for a salesperson sitting down on the job. But it's your back and your money. And an actual trial is the only way to make an intelligent selection.

(2) *Check the position of the lumbar support area.* This is the part that

bulges a bit toward you and *should* fit right into the small of your back. Lumbar supports tend to be positioned too low on most chairs, making contact with your sacrum (the protruding bony area of your spine directly below your lumbar curve) instead of with your lumbar curve. If the back support is adjustable up and down, that's a plus, but it's not a guarantee that the chair will feel right to you.

(3) *Try out the tilting action of the back of the chair.* Does it support your weight when you're sitting up straight? Or does it tilt back too easily under your weight and prevent you from sitting straight? You want to be able to vary your position from time to time by tilting back into a reclining position. But to reiterate, if the chair cannot support your weight and keep you at a ninety-degree angle, the undesired tilting will cause you back pain.

To maximize your comfort, whether or not you're a hotshot executive, put your feet up on your desk every so often. And think of other constructive ways to vary your position when you're sitting at a desk. For example, put your feet in an open bottom drawer, drape them across the wastebasket, or prop them up on the bottom of your typing table.

When you're not at your desk, and want to get away from a straight-backed chair, you might consider a reclining chair. They were popular among survey participants who wanted the comfort of an easy chair without its usual feet-down, sink-in-and-suffer quality. Reclining chairs are almost never as good as the best straight-backed chair, but they are usually better than other easy chairs for two reasons. They tend to have firm seats, and the reclining action puts your knees above your hips.

How to keep your car seat from driving you to a back doctor

An acquaintance of ours, a strapping, clean-living fellow in his thirties, recently threatened to put his moving business up for sale. If you do a lot of driving, you can probably guess what caused him to think about selling a successful enterprise. It wasn't the lifting, even though he routinely picked up thousands of pounds during the course of a day. It was sitting behind the wheel that did him in.

According to survey participants, car (and truck) seats are rivaled for back discomfort only by restaurant-booth seats, soft couches, and sofa beds.

What can you do about this? If you're wealthy, perhaps buying a Volvo or Mercedes will help. Survey participants mentioned the unusual comfort of these cars. But wealthy or not, there is a great deal you can do to improve your comfort in a car.

(1) *Buy or make your own car seat.* Probably the best way, and certainly the cheapest, is to buy two pieces of plywood from a lumberyard—one that is seat-sized, the other tall and wide enough to support your back. If you're handy, cover both pieces of wood with a half-inch of firm foam rubber and a cover, then connect the two pieces of wood with hinges. If you're not handy, simply place a chair back support or rolled-up towel between your back and the backrest board, and a seat cushion or a thrice-folded beach towel on the seat board.

(2) *Get as close to the wheel as you can without discomfort.* Never mind the image of the racing-car driver who holds the wheel at arms' length, or the feeling many of us have that the only people who sit close to the wheel are nervous wrecks who drive at 30 mph on expressways. The point is that sitting close to the wheel will elevate your knees and enable you to place your free foot flat on the floor.

(3) *Sit at a right angle.* Tilt the back of your seat so that it is nearly perpendicular (ninety degrees).

(4) *Use the armrest on the driver's side if you can.* You might also want to create an armrest to support your other elbow. Nothing fancy is needed—a towel-covered box, a couple of cushions or pillows—just about anything that comes up to armrest height will do.

(5) *If your back starts to feel tired, do something about it immediately.* Move around in your seat, readjust your back support, stretch, try reclining the back of your seat a bit—and take a break every hour. Just a few minutes of walking and shaking loose the kinks will help immensely.

EXERCISE

"I did my back exercises faithfully for ten years," reported a professor in this survey. "And they helped. A doctor gave them to me, and if I stopped doing them for a few days, my low back pain got noticeably worse. Still, over the course of the ten years, my overall condition slipped a bit. Working out with weights started to cause me pain. I could still do everything. But some days were bad and my back really hurt. I had to watch myself more, be more cautious about things like raking, shoveling, and sitting too long. The idea of having to be even a little less active bothered me, so I went to a back doctor with a big reputation. It seemed to me that he knew less than I did about backs and exercise. Finally I found a doctor who was an exercise expert and he individualized an exercise program that has made a tremendous difference."

Like this professor, many back sufferers in our survey relapsed but then made progress again after years of "doing the right exercises" failed to prevent deterioration. Obviously the exercises weren't right for *them*.

There were also many survey participants who recovered successfully from low back pain in large part by piecing together their own exercise programs. The comments of a draftsman typify this approach: "I've created my own back exercise program," he told us. "I learned a few exercises from a physical therapist and a couple from a chiropractor. But most exercises I picked up from doing a lot of reading and talking to other people with back problems."

Both these approaches to exercise therapy—learning on your own and receiving a professionally individualized program—are reflected in this section. Each exercise we present is accompanied by variations, to help you customize your own program. Collectively, these exercises have done the most good for the most survey participants. Equally important, they caused no known setbacks or injuries. These exercises aren't a cure-all—no exercise program is—but they *can* give you the strength and flexibility you need to function *much* more effectively.

To reiterate, these exercises, along with other suggestions described in this chapter, will *probably* provide you with all the help you need. *But we estimate that 25 to 50 percent of this book's readers will not achieve maximum gains without professionally prescribed, individualized exercise therapy.* (See pages

65–66 for the kinds of back-exercise experts who were rated best by survey participants.) If you do go the professional route, a single examination/consultation and a few demonstration sessions may be all that you'll need. This next point should be obvious, but it's worth stating anyway: you can be certain that seeking professional exercise therapy is decidedly *not* a case of your failing to take responsibility for your own problem. It is, instead, a proven way that some chronically limited individuals can, and should, help themselves. As Dr. Hans Kraus states in his landmark book *Backache, Stress and Tension*, an exercise program "is a craft, even an art." He adds, "An exercise prescription should be regarded as potent medicine, which it is if properly given."

We agree. And here, for the majority of low back sufferers, is the right medicine to promote optimum back fitness.

The most important back exercise is a mental one.

It has been said a hundred times by participants in this survey, and could be repeated a thousand times more, that your *approach* to back exercise—your attitude and preparation for exercise—is at least as important as the mechanical components of the exercise therapy itself.

Survey participants offer these ways of thinking about exercise:

- Exercise therapy, no matter how cautious it may seem to you, is almost always more beneficial than anything you can put into or onto your body.

- Try to ignore two mass-media concepts about exercise: (1) that it must be vigorous and competitive, and (2) that results have to be instantaneous. Back exercise runs counter to both these beliefs. As one survey participant put it, "Slower is better, gradual is faster, and vigorous is self-defeating." Properly done, back exercise will bring you small but noticeable improvement in a few weeks. And in three to six months, you can feel like a new person.

- It's okay to think that back exercises aren't exciting or that they are like bad-tasting medicine that is good for you. "I consider back exercise to be about as scintillating as going to the bathroom . . . but just as essential," said one low back sufferer. Of course, other survey participants disagree. They look forward to their fifteen to thirty minutes a day of exercise. For them it's quality time—time when they are alone, quiet, in touch with themselves, meditative, doing something good for themselves. The latter perspective certainly makes things easier. In any case, it is important that you exercise intelligently.

Here are some other suggestions to help you get the most out of your exercise program:

(1) *Try to perform back exercises daily.* About 70 percent of low back sufferers in this survey felt that they had to exercise every day either to achieve maximum fitness or because they felt, "If I don't make it a habit, I may not exercise at all."

(2) *Adjust the pace to your needs.* If you haven't been exercising regularly, or you're recovering from an acute episode of low back pain, you can speed up your progress with a twice-a-day exercise program—once in the morning and once in the evening. Not everyone can find the time to do this, but survey participants recommend it highly. Then, at the point you're exercising to *maintain* rather than reach a high level of fitness, cut your program to once a day.

(3) *Exercise when and where you like.* Pay no attention to what people say about the great importance of exercising at the same time every day, in the same room, and on the same surface. This kind of sameness is unnecessary and even counterproductive for many back sufferers, who believe it smacks of the same compulsive, driven behavior that aggravated their backs in the first place. What's more, a rigidly fixed routine can quickly become boring and stifling enough to be dropped. A beautician who exercises strictly as a preventive measure commented, "I do back exercises three days a week in a gym (once alone and twice as part of a group), two nights a week on my bed, and two nights a week on the living room carpet with my husband. According to what I've been told by back specialists, my routine, or lack of routine, is almost sinful. I say, nonsense."

(4) *Establish a logical exercise sequence.* Even though they may scoff at routinizing the time or place for exercise, most survey participants believe that an exercise regimen should always be done in the same *sequence.* A sense of logic and order—warm-ups, increasingly difficult stretching and strengthening, then cooling off—seems a necessary part of the therapy.

(5) *Create a good exercise environment.* Your exercise room should be warm and draft-free. If it isn't, turn up the heat or use a space heater about half an hour before exercising. Keep overhead lights off. Put the telephone out of reach and turn it off if possible. Tell the kids not to disturb you. (There's no harm in trying.) Try to free your mind from the problems of the day. Wait at least two hours after eating a heavy meal to exercise, an hour after a light meal or snack. It's not a good idea to watch TV while exercising. Aside from being distracting, watching TV while exercising can put a strain on your neck. Consider playing your favorite music instead.

(6) *Try warming up before doing back exercises.* Some survey participants felt that a warm bath or the use of a heating pad just before exercise enabled them to stretch more readily, get more from the therapy, and increase their rate of progress. Further, most survey participants agreed that starting their exercises immediately after awakening didn't give them enough chance to warm up. If you must exercise first thing in the morning, move around in bed, then walk for a few minutes before you begin.

(7) *Get the most out of your exercises safely.* Stretch to the point of resistance, then try to move just a fraction beyond it. But don't "go through" pain. Overstretching is worse than not exercising at all. It can cause great harm, including torn muscle fibers, spasming, and pain. Stay in touch with yourself and within yourself. Plan to expand slowly but continuously your limits of strength and flexibility. You *can* make tremendous progress this way.

EXERCISE 1
BREATH OF THE YOGI

For relaxation and abdominal toning

According to survey participants, this first exercise simultaneously relaxes and energizes your body, thus preparing you for the rest of the exercises to come. Lie in the Basic Position (on your back with your knees up, feet flat, arms at your side). Inhale through your nose. Allow the breath first to expand and fill your abdomen, then your chest. If you're not used to deep abdominal breathing, put a hand on your abdomen when you inhale; if your abdomen rises, you're breathing properly. Exhale through your mouth . . . slowly. Inhaling should take at least eight seconds, exhaling twelve seconds. When you exhale, let yourself go limp. Repeat three times.

EXERCISE 2
PELVIC TILT

To improve posture by reducing your lumbar curve and strengthening your abdominal and buttock muscles

Stay in the Basic Position. Slide one hand, palm down, between the surface you are lying on and the small of your back (lumbar curve). The space or hollow that you feel is what you're going to flatten away when you achieve the Pelvic Tilt. Then contract and pull in your abdominal muscles. This movement automatically tilts up your pelvis. (Don't try to raise your pelvis by pushing down with your legs.) If you're having trouble getting the feel of this exercise, pretend that you're trying to pull in your abdominal muscles so that they touch your spine. Relax.

Frequency: Week 1—three repetitions of three seconds each; by the end of Week 2, three repetitions of six seconds each; by the end of Week 3, six repetitions of six seconds each.

Advanced Version 1: Lying in the Basic Position, contract your abdominal muscles *and squeeze together your buttocks.* This buttock-clenching motion raises your pelvis and flattens your back. A handful of survey participants with unusually weak abdominal muscles found this variation easier to do than the basic Pelvic Tilt.

Comment: If human beings had perfectly straight spines, instead of an "S" shape, their movements would be severely limited. So the problem is not that you have a curve in your spine, but that your lumbar curve is probably exaggerated—a condition called lordosis, or swayback. At the other extreme, some people, including back sufferers who have been bedridden for years, may have an overly elongated (flattened) "S" curve. If you're one of these people, you won't be able to slide your hand between a firm mattress and the small of your back when you're in the Basic Position. And you will find that the Pelvic Tilt is either uncomfortable or pointless to do. For most low back sufferers, however, the Pelvic Tilt is an essential way to flex and strengthen the back.

Advanced Version 2: Stand a foot away from a wall and gently lean your back into it. Then try to flatten your lumbar curve by contracting your abdomen and buttocks. Some survey participants found this awkward or uncomfortable to do. Others raved about its value, not so much as an exercise but as a way to take the strain off their backs after they had been sitting for a long time. We suggest that you use this maneuver any time during the day that your back needs a brief respite.

EXERCISE 3
ONE KNEE TO CHEST

To stretch the lower back

Starting in the Basic Position, slowly bring one knee toward your chest as far as you can, without using your hands and without straining. Since you will be stretching slowly and fluidly, it will take you a few seconds to reach your limit. When you reach it, hold for one second. Then return your knee to—*and through*—the starting position, sliding your heel until your leg is fully extended and flat on the floor. Wobble the leg a few times, moving your ankle a bit to the left and right. (This "shaking loose" procedure helps keep you relaxed and flexible during the exercise.) Slide the leg back up to the starting position. Repeat this entire procedure with your other leg.

Frequency: Week 1—three repetitions of five seconds* each; by the end of

---

*From the time you start raising one knee toward your chest until the time you've stretched as far as you can comfortably, about five seconds will pass. But the specific number of seconds you need for the movement is not important; don't rush this exercise.

Week 2, six repetitions of five seconds each; by the end of Week 3, ten repetitions of five seconds each.

Comment: This is the most basic of low back stretching exercises. It seems simple, and it is. But don't underestimate its value. Most survey participants felt that if the knee-to-chest exercise were the *only* exercise they did, it would keep their backs in reasonable shape.

EXERCISE 4
KNEE SPREAD

To stretch hip, groin, and buttock muscles

Remaining in the Basic Position, and without exerting any effort, allow both knees to spread apart and lean downward toward the floor. The weight of your legs will spread apart your knees. When you feel resistance, hold for three seconds and return to the starting position.

Frequency: Week 1—three repetitions of three seconds each; by the end of Week 2, four repetitions of five seconds each; by the end of Week 3, six repetitions of five seconds each.

Comment: If you have tighter-than-average muscles, or if you're unusually tight now because of a recent episode of back pain, don't let your knees spread apart as far as they will go. Stop when you feel the slightest pulling sensation. Then stretch a little more each day until you achieve a wider but still comfortable position.

Many back books suggest a hip-stretching exercise that involves dropping *both* knees over to *one* side until they rest on the floor. This exercise will stretch your hips. But to the extent that it also twists your torso and arches your back, many survey participants feel it does not belong in a conservative back exercise program.

EXERCISE 5
KNEE TO SHOULDER

To stretch your hips, buttocks, and lower back

Lie on your side in the fetal position. Bend both legs at the knees slightly. Relax your arms, elbows bent, with your hands resting near your face. Slowly slide your top leg toward your shoulder. When you feel resistance, drop your knee on the floor, relax your leg completely for one second, then slide it back to the starting position. Do the number of repetitions suggested below. Then turn onto your other side and repeat the exercise.

Frequency: Week 1—three repetitions; by the end of Week 2, six repetitions; by the end of Week 3, ten repetitions.

Comment: Aside from the obvious stretching value of this exercise, it gets you off your back and prevents stiffness from exercising in one position for too long.

EXERCISE 6
MODIFIED BENT-KNEE SIT-UPS
To strengthen your abdominal muscles

Return to the Basic Position. Tuck in your chin and pull in your abdominal muscles while inhaling. As you start to exhale, simultaneously raise your head and reach your hands up toward your knees. You'll know you've raised your head far enough when you can see your navel. Hold this position for one second, then return to the Basic Position. Relax for a moment. Repeat.

Frequency: Week 1—three repetitions; by the end of Week 2, six repetitions; by the end of Week 3, ten repetitions.

Advanced Version 1: Instead of keeping your arms at your sides, and then extending them toward your knees as you raise your head, fold your arms across your abdomen. This increases the level of difficulty slightly. Also, with your arms in this position, you'll actually be able to feel your abdominal muscles contract and strengthen. We suggest you try this variation a month after being able to do the easier version.

Advanced Version 2: Clasp your hands behind your head. Raise both your head and shoulders until they are just slightly off the floor. Hold this position for three seconds rather than one second.

Comment: Every survey participant we talked to, and every back practitioner who treated these survey participants, agreed that strong abdominal muscles are essential for low back fitness. However, there is also widespread disagreement about what is required to make your abdomen strong enough to help hold your spine in place and allow you to maintain good posture. A slight majority of survey participants we interviewed believes that the modified half sit-up recommended here will provide you with the strength you need without causing you harm.

A handful of survey participants and back practitioners feels that deep breathing alone can sufficiently firm up your abdominal muscles. A slightly larger group believes that doing isometric contractions (pull in your abdominal muscles for a few seconds; then push out) will do the job. And about 25 percent of back sufferers and back specialists believe in more strenuous abdominal-building exercises, such as full bent-knee sit-ups, sit-ups on slant boards, and sit-ups done from an inverted position.

Note: Don't even attempt straight-leg sit-ups. They put excessive strain on your lower back and take away from your effort to strengthen your abdominal muscles.

By following our suggested plan, and exercising twice a day, you'll be doing twenty modified half sit-ups a day. At that point, if you're pain-free, you may choose to switch to regular bent-knee sit-ups, with your feet held down by a partner or hooked under a bureau or couch. However, based on the comments of survey participants, we don't recommend it for the average back sufferer. Modified half sit-ups will safely give you all the abdominal strength you need to perform a full range of daily activities, from extensive sitting to manual labor and athletics.

EXERCISE 7
SINGLE KNEE TO CHIN: EXTRA STRETCH
To stretch your lower back

This exercise is the same as Exercise 3—with one important difference: after you raise one knee toward your chest as far as you can, clasp your hands just below that knee and apply gradual upward pressure. By using your hands and arms this way, you'll find you can move your knee several inches more toward your chest and stretch your lower back more fully.

Frequency: Week 1—three repetitions of three seconds each; by the end of Week 2, six repetitions of six seconds each; by the end of Week 3, ten repetitions of six seconds each.

Advanced Version 1: Keep one leg fully extended and flat on the floor during the exercise. This enables you to stretch the lower part of your spine even more. However, it also increases the risk of injury to your lower back. So if you're in the process of rehabilitating your back, this variation is *not* recommended. But if you want to get from fit to fitter, add this version to your routine after a month of doing all the exercises in this chapter.

Advanced Version 2: As you bring your knee to your chest, simultaneously raise your head and try to touch your chin to that knee. This variation increases the amount of flexing you do. It also strengthens your abdominal muscles. The only major drawback, according to survey participants, is a psychological one. In all other exercises we've mentioned, there is no set "athletic goal," such as having to touch your chin to your knee. And the absence of this kind of goal is a plus, because it allows you to find and slowly expand *your* own limits. If you're in reasonably good shape, try the variation we just described, but don't get competitive and overstretch in an effort to "do it successfully." You have but one goal: *progress.* We suggest that you try adding this variation to your routine two months after being able to do all the exercises in this chapter.

Comment: If you watched a group of people do the exercises and variations described in this section, you would note tremendous differences in the degree to which people can stretch. Some people can touch their knees to their chests on the first try; some take six months to do it; others are never able to do it. It doesn't matter which group you fall into. Simply move to your point of resistance and try, gradually, to expand it.

EXERCISE 8
KNEE TO SHOULDER

(Repeat Exercise 5)

EXERCISE 9
BOTH KNEES TO CHEST

To stretch your lower back

Starting from the Basic Position, put your knees together, clasp your hands around them, and pull them toward your chest. If it's awkward to clasp your hands around your knees while you're lying in the Basic Position, raise your knees a few inches first and then clasp them. When you feel some resistance, pause. Then try to gently stretch your way past that level for six seconds. If you can't stretch any farther without pain, then just hold the position for six seconds.

Frequency: Week 1—three repetitions of six seconds each; by the end of

Week 2, six repetitions of six seconds each; by the end of Week 3, ten repetitions of six seconds each.

Advanced Version: Same as above except that you keep your knees shoulder-width apart rather than together and clasp a hand around each knee. With your knees apart during this exercise, you'll be able to stretch farther than you can when keeping them together. Based on the experience of survey participants, we recommend that you substitute this variation for the knees-together version after you can comfortably do all the exercises in this chapter.

Comment: If you've never done back exercises before, it may seem that bringing both knees to your chest does no more or less for you than the single-knee-to-chest exercise. Not so. When you actually perform these stretching exercises, you'll feel differences. And you'll discover that the differences will add new dimensions to your flexibility and suppleness.

EXERCISE 10
MODIFIED HALF SIT-UPS

(Repeat Exercise 6)

EXERCISE 11
HAMSTRING STRETCH

To stretch the backs of your thighs

If your hamstring muscles are tight, and they most likely are if you have low back pain, it is important to find a way to stretch them without straining your lower back in the process. That is why, although the following exercise is the safest way we know of to stretch your hamstring muscles, *we suggest that you NOT do this exercise until you have first done all the preceding exercises for one month.*

Start in the Basic Position. Raise one knee toward your chest. Fully extend and straighten your leg toward the ceiling at a forty-five-degree angle. Then, keeping your knee locked, try to move your leg up toward a ninety-degree angle.

Frequency: Week 1—three repetitions of three seconds each; by the end of Week 2, six repetitions of six seconds each; by the end of Week 3, ten repetitions of ten seconds each.

Comment: The safety feature here is *initially* to extend your leg at a forty-five-degree angle—*even though you can go higher*. At this angle there is virtually no risk of overstretching your hamstrings. And you must avoid the risk, because overstretching, or "popping," your hamstring muscle can set you back weeks or even months. Better to wait until your flexibility increases before attempting to extend your leg all the way up to a ninety-degree angle.

There are three other commonly used hamstring-stretching exercises, none of which is recommended by most survey participants. But we will briefly describe these variations, because you're likely to run into them and want to know why they might not be advisable.

(1) A straight-leg lift done from the Basic Position, locking your knee and raising your straightened leg from the floor toward ninety degrees

(2) Sitting in a chair, bending from the waist, and lowering your head toward your knees

(3) Sitting on the floor with your legs straight out in front of you and leaning forward

Survey participants felt strongly, however, that these movements, compared with the recommended exercise, placed unnecessary stress on the lower back and hips.

SUMMARY OF TREATMENTS AND PRACTITIONERS FOR CHRONIC LOW BACK PAIN

Note: Items in each category are listed in order of their effectiveness, based on survey data.

Best self-help therapies for chronic low back pain

(1) The right attitude about self-care and about being a partner in any professional treatment or guidance you may seek

(2) Mastering proper lifting, carrying, sitting, and driving habits

(3) Knowledge about what kind of back exercise routine you need

(4) Back exercise therapy

(5) Gravity inversion (if pain is not severe)

Best professional treatments for chronic low back pain

(1) Instruction about the impact of daily activities on back pain

(2) Individually prescribed back exercise therapy

(3) Individually prescribed yoga therapy

Professional treatments worth trying for chronic low back pain

(1) Shiatsu

(2) Acupuncture

Widely used treatments best avoided during episodes of chronic low back pain

(1) All prescription drugs, including painkillers, anti-inflammatories, and muscle relaxants

(2) Sclerotherapy

(3) Surgery

Best practitioners for chronic low back pain

(1) Physiatrist

(2) Physical fitness instructor

(3) Yoga instructor

(4) Physical therapist*

(5) Shiatsu therapist

Practitioners worth a try for chronic low back pain

(1) Sports medicine specialist

(2) Kinesiologist

(3) Chiropractor

Widely seen practitioners who sometimes make chronic low back sufferers feel worse

(1) Neurologist

(2) Neurosurgeon

(3) Orthopedist

(4) Osteopath

*Physical therapists rank second for helping low back sufferers with especially severe or disabling conditions.

Chapter 11

How to Recover from a Ruptured Disc

"The pain I felt during this time was something I hope not to experience again in my lifetime," said a restaurant owner of the first surge of severe pain from a ruptured disc. "There was virtually no position for comfort, and only the slightest relief from pain while lying on my back with my knees bent."

This description could just as easily have come from any of the other sixty-four survey participants who suffered a ruptured disc. Readers who are familiar with the agony of disc pain will certainly empathize.

The pain and incapacitation caused by a ruptured disc are well established. So is the frequency of the disorder: there are about 200,000 disc operations every year in the United States and perhaps three times that many people suffering acute or chronic pain from a ruptured disc who never undergo surgery. But concrete and accurate information about how to recover from a ruptured disc has *not* been available, obscured as it has been by a storm of conflicting opinions and data.

In particular, survey participants found themselves searching, often in desperation, for answers to the following crucial questions:

- How can I resume everyday activities as quickly, safely, and productively as possible?

- What are the alternatives to surgery?

- Is chymopapain as good as its favorable publicity indicates?

- To what extent can I treat myself?

- Which of the many different kinds of practitioners are best for ruptured disc sufferers?

- What steps can I take to prevent further injury?

Most survey participants were not able to get adequate answers to these or other more specific questions when they needed them. Usually they had to learn the hard way—from unhappy experiences, through trial and error.

Thanks, however, to what these individuals eventually learned—and shared with us—the information that follows can provide the clarity you need to take charge of, and resolve, your own case.

We have divided this chapter into two sections: acute and chronic pain from ruptured disc, each with its own summary.

ACUTE PAIN: HOW TO RELIEVE IT

Bed rest is still best . . . even with the availability of chymopapain.

In an age of genetic splicing, heart transplants, and myriad other medical wonders, it may seem absurd to you to be told that bed rest is still the best first step in trying to recuperate from a ruptured disc. In fact, if you're like survey participants who had ruptured discs in the past several years, you may be wondering, "Why should I lie in bed when I can get a chymopapain injection and be done with the problem? Isn't chymopapain supposed to be able to 'fix' a ruptured disc?"

The answer, however frustrating it may seem, is *no*. Bed rest is best because it works and because any alternative almost always involves more risk. For example, a chymopapain treatment is a less invasive and time-consuming procedure than surgery. But chymopapain can cause allergic reactions, injuries, heightened pain, and, in rare cases, death. So although the odds of being helped by chymopapain are in your favor, bed rest is usually your best bet at first.

Ironically, bed rest can also get you on your feet faster than any other treatment. After just a week to ten days of bed rest, you might have enough relief from pain to start a light recovery program. And, two weeks later, you might be well enough to perform most day-to-day activities.

After a chymopapain treatment, on the other hand, you would be unable to resume all regular activities for about six weeks.

See Chapter 7 for further details about the pros and cons of chymopapain treatments.

Home bed rest versus hospital bed rest

When considering how to recover as quickly as possible, another question that survey participants had was, "Should I stay at home or go to a hospital?" The question has nothing to do with how brave you are, or how stoic about pain you might be, because most pain medication can be administered just as easily at home as in the hospital. What matters, according to survey participants, is that the following conditions prevail:

- *You do not get up for any reason.* For bed rest to have the best chance of working, you really need to stay in bed. Actually, slightly more than half of survey participants with ruptured discs, whether they stayed home or in a hospital, got out of bed whenever they had to use the bathroom. But many of these people felt that getting up, at least during the first week, did them more harm than good. So, if you choose home over hospital, they advise you to get a practical nurse, or count on a spouse or friend with a lot of free time—as well as the willingness to empty bedpans, bathe you, and do all the tasks you would ordinarily do for yourself. You may find lying on your back with two or three pillows under your knees to be the least painful position.

- *You are able to reduce the pain as much as possible.* Most ruptured disc patients do get some relief from strong painkillers such as Percodan® or Demerol®. Medication of this potency is potentially addictive, but survey results indicate that the advantages far outweigh the risks. If you can take the medication orally, then you can use it by yourself at home. If intramuscular injections or intravenous drips are called for, however, your doctor will probably want you to go to a hospital. Remember, though, if good nursing service is available to you, *any* kind of pain medication can be administered at home. The most commonly prescribed analgesics—aspirin or acetaminophen with codeine—are hardly ever strong enough to counter acute, severe ruptured disc pain.

- *You have the best odds of avoiding surgery.* Some 55 percent of survey participants with acute ruptured disc pain had hospitalized bed rest; 45 percent had bed rest at home. Of the thirty-six people who went to a hospital, twenty-six (72 percent) eventually had their bed rest interrupted by surgery. Of the twenty-four individuals who stayed home, only six (25 percent) wound up in surgery. (Not everyone can avoid surgery. But later in this chapter, we will show that ruptured disc patients who forgo surgery do better in the long run than those who consent to operations.) Those individuals who chose hospitalization, or had it chosen for them, might have had more painful conditions than those individuals who remained at home. If so, comparing the incidence of surgery between the two groups would be unfair. But there is no question that the chances of your agreeing to surgery, instead of waiting it out, are greater in a hospital. As a statistician said, "By nighttime your tolerance for pain can be so low that you'll tell the next person you see to knock you out and operate. If that next person happens to be a doctor it's bye-bye baby. The next thing you know you'll be awakening from surgery. I would rather be home and complain to my wife."

- *You feel emotionally comfortable.* "I felt I would be a nuisance to my family and that my child would be constantly reminded of what bad shape her mommy was in if I stayed home. My doctor also felt I would get better care in the hospital and that it would be easier to carry out any necessary tests," stated an advertising account executive. A telephone company worker felt differently. "Hospitals are bad places for body and soul," he said. "They are depressing, routinized, and coldly inefficient. I know because I was there for two weeks. In retrospect, I know I would have done better at home. Tell other back sufferers that hospitals are *not* restful places to be. The one good night's sleep I almost got was interrupted by a nurse walking into my room. She came in to inquire whether I wanted a sleeping pill."

You have to gauge your own feelings, your family situation, and your past experience, if any, with hospitals to decide where you should get your bed rest.

Now that you understand the goal and requirements for total bed rest, you can make the most personally satisfying selection.

Remember that *you can take diagnostic tests as an outpatient.* " 'I suggest you go into the hospital because we need to run tests and it's easier to monitor your condition,' was the pitch my doctor used to convince me to go into the hospital," said a voice-over announcer who wished he had stayed home.

If you need tests and you're in too much pain to get to and from the hospital, you obviously have no choice about hospitalization. But if you can travel a bit—even if that means lying on the back seat of a car, for example, and requesting a stretcher bed once you reach the hospital—you may not have to be hospitalized.

Note: A few survey participants who took diagnostic tests as outpatients were put in wheelchairs when they mentioned how difficult it was for them to walk. *Don't allow this to happen to you.* Sitting in any chair, and especially a wheelchair, which has very poor back support, will almost inevitably make your pain worse. Again, ask for a stretcher bed. If you're told that one isn't available, suggest that you will have to lie on the floor. Not so miraculously, a stretcher bed *will* materialize.

If you are told, as many survey participants were, that you should be hospitalized in order to have bed rest *and* traction, then another question arises: do you need traction?

Traction: the most ineffective and risky of all common back treatments

Twenty-seven of the sixty-five people in our survey with diagnosed ruptured discs were put in traction. Of these, two reported enough relief from pain to aid their recovery; one reported relief from pain during traction but said the pain returned full force immediately after treatment; three felt that traction injured them; and twenty-one rated traction ineffective.

Considering that only 22 percent of survey participants with ruptured disc were helped by traction—and that 11 percent were injured—we strongly advise against this procedure as it is traditionally used in hospitals. Moreover, when we measure the effects of all traction treatments on survey participants, including those with low back pain and sciatica pain not caused by a ruptured disc, the results are even more forbidding: 23 percent of participants who had traction reported that it made them feel worse.

See Chapter 5 for additional information on traction.

Surgery: should you or shouldn't you?

Most back problems cannot be resolved by surgery. But if you're one of the estimated one million back sufferers every year who receives at least a tentative or best-guess diagnosis of a ruptured disc, you will need to consider the decision with as much background information as possible.

For starters, you should know that a diagnosis of a ruptured disc—based on a manual examination, with or without X rays—is *not* definitive. Among our survey participants, for example, ninety-eight received a preliminary diagnosis of a ruptured disc, but only sixty-five of these underwent either further tests to confirm the diagnosis or disc surgery, or both. The comments, statistics, and recommendations in this chapter are based on the experiences of these sixty-five individuals. Among them, thirty-three had surgery and thirty-two did not.

Those who decided against surgery had these outcomes after an average of six years:

—52 percent were virtually pain-free;

—27 percent were functional but limited in activities such as sitting, housework, yardwork, lifting, and athletics;

—21 percent were more disabled than functional.

Now look at the outcomes for the surgery cases that were evaluated an average of five years after hospitalization:

—33 percent were virtually pain-free;

—30 percent were functional but limited*;

—37 percent were more disabled than functional.

On a scale of 0 (pain-free) to 10 (disabled), survey participants who had surgery had an average pain rating of 5.0, five years after surgery. On the same scale, nonsurgery patients had a lower average pain rating of 3.9. Both groups had identical diagnoses based on comparable tests. And in both groups, acute pain required an average of four weeks' bed rest.

These statistics will help you make an informed decision about whether or not to have surgery to correct a ruptured disc. But statistics never tell the

---

*Included here are two participants who were operated on *twice* and two participants who underwent surgery *three* times. All four were better off for having had more than one operation, and three of the four felt that their initial surgery had been "botched." It is interesting to note that the usual statistics on success rates for multiple-surgery disc patients—not to mention surgeons' expectations for these patients—are extraordinarily discouraging.

whole story. Insights, attitudes, and feelings also have a lot to do with decision-making. That's why we think you'll be interested in the anecdotes that follow. They let you listen to others in your situation—to know how they felt while grappling with different options, and how they feel now in retrospect.

A small minority of ruptured disc patients view surgery as a cure.

Doctors themselves hardly ever refer to surgery as a cure. No matter how optimistic a surgeon might be, he knows he can't restore your back to its original condition. He also knows that surgery cannot create the kind of fitness you need to prevent further injury to your back. Yet, with some individuals, for reasons no one can pinpoint, surgery does seem to "cure" ruptured discs.

Take the case of an appliance store owner. She couldn't be more pleased with the results of her laminectomy—surgery that removes the gel portion of a disc as well as a small amount of bone that blocks access to this disc. Twenty years ago, as a young woman, she bent over one morning and collapsed to the floor in pain. The next day she was hospitalized. The following day she underwent surgery. Two months later she went back to her job. Now looking back at her pell-mell rush to the operating table, she says, "I don't know why people are afraid of back surgery. It literally cured me. I'm overweight, I don't exercise, and I haven't had a single ache or pain for twenty years."

Is this survey participant a rare exception? Most definitely, but she's not alone. From our survey data, we estimate that about one in twenty ruptured disc patients makes a complete and permanent recovery from surgery, even when he or she goes back to doing the very same things that caused problems in the first place.

An artist in our survey did almost as well as the appliance store owner. "A laminectomy caused *instant* relief," she told us. "I sit and paint all day, and I have had very little pain for the past five years. I was taught exercises but I don't do them."

Will lack of fitness catch up with this survey participant? Probably not. But keep this in mind: for every *one* individual who resumed full activity after surgery—*without* making any effort at rehabilitation—there are *nineteen* others who were much worse off because they didn't work hard to put their backs in good shape.

For most people, surgery is just one step toward recovery.

Here is a more typical experience. A self-employed businessman struggled through episodes of incapacitating pain from a ruptured disc for ten years before he had a laminectomy. "The blinding pain in my buttock and leg vanished almost immediately after surgery," he said. "My back hurt some, it was kind of sore all over, but I thought it was mostly from the surgical procedure itself."

What were the next several weeks like?

"When I got home ten days after surgery," he continued, "I felt pretty good. Then, about a month later, when my activity increased, I started to get muscle spasms. The pain was moderate, but it really frightened me. Oh, no, here we go again, I thought. My surgeon told me that some spasming after back surgery was normal and that I shouldn't try to do so much yet. When I went back for a two-month postoperative checkup, I asked about back exercises and was given a pamphlet containing some. The exercises didn't help. There was still some pain from spasming, and I lived in constant fear of reinjuring myself and not being able to make a living. I decided to join the YMCA and take their back exercise program. That worked for me and I've been pretty much unlimited in my activities ever since."

We had one more question for this survey participant: did he think, in retrospect, that a laminectomy had been his best bet?

"Yes," he answered, "although it's possible that if I had been able to tolerate bed rest longer than four days, the pain might have subsided. But I felt that surgery would correct the problem, once and for all, and I was right."

A produce manager also found himself in moderately good shape after a diskectomy—removal of the gel portion of a disc without cutting through bone. "I got 10 percent disability from insurance after the operation. But my back doesn't bother me now unless I overdo it or try to lift something heavy. I waited six months between the rupturing of the disc and the surgery, but bed rest didn't work for me. Every time I left bed to go back to work I got laid up again."

Some 30 percent of individuals can carry on—but with difficulty.

An unemployed amusement park worker, now age 25, had a disc operation nine years ago. She looks back at her surgery this way: "I have been able to work since then, but there is always pain. I was young when this surgery was done, and my parents and I felt overwhelmed by a group of orthopedists who said I was too far gone even for traction. Now, just a few months ago, a surgeon recommended that I have fusion.* I refused, probably not for logical reasons, but who knows? You see, nothing is ever really explained to you. You're just a patient, so what's the point of telling *you* anything?"

A public parks worker also keeps at his job in spite of chronic back pain since a laminectomy five years ago. "My pain continues to interfere with my job performance," he commented. "But I don't complain and I do work, even though I could be put on disability."

An electrician also reported that there is never an absence of pain after disc surgery. "All that my laminectomy did was get rid of the pain and tingling in my legs for a while. Other people I've talked to say the exact same thing. First the sciatica vanishes and you're really pleased. Then you realize that your back pain hasn't subsided at all. Then some leg pain comes back, and even when it's not there, the back pain is. I work because there's no alternative. It's unbelievable to me that nothing else can be done and that I'm stuck with being limited, having to lie down every day after I get home from work, for the rest of my life. Maybe other areas of medicine have become advanced, like heart operations and transplants, but not back medicine. I don't mean to trot out the cliché about 'If they can send a man to the moon, how come they can't fix your back?' But is an artificial disc really implausible?"

More than one-third of disc surgery patients have remained disabled.

"The surgery seemed to relieve pain and pressure for a few weeks," a housewife told us, "but it has left me mostly disabled. I wish that an exercise

*Fusion joins together spinal vertebrae with pieces of bone taken from another part of the body, often the pelvis.

program had been emphasized more." Five years after surgery, this woman is still struggling to be able to function even modestly as a mother and wife. Her experience typifies the disastrous long-run outcome of more than one-third of people in our survey who had surgery for a ruptured disc.

Another young housewife talked about the incapacitation she has lived with: "When you start thinking about back surgery, doctors don't tell you, but I know for a fact, that one operation can lead to the need for another. I have been unable to work six of the last twelve years. A partial diskectomy just relieved the pain for a couple of weeks. Then I had microsurgery, which was supposed to remove the rest of the disc material that hadn't been taken out during the first operation. The microsurgery didn't work. Then, a while later, an orthopedist removed two ruptured discs and fused my vertebrae. This last operation helped the most, but I continue to have back pain, sciatica, and muscle spasms."

"I have been mostly disabled for twenty-two years," the former owner of a successful construction company told us. "When I hear stories of people bouncing back after surgery, I can't help being bitter. I was operated on for a ruptured disc in 1960 after trying to avoid surgery for eight months. I had a laminectomy and it failed. There wasn't even a small amount of relief. At this point another group of surgeons told me I may have waited too long to have the surgery, and that the eight months of bed rest had made it possible for too much scar tissue to form. Now, how the hell was I supposed to know that! [Note: Eight to ten weeks of bed rest is the upper limit recommended by most survey participants with ruptured discs.] This new group tried cortisone shots at the site of the surgery. These shots helped me temporarily. I also saw a physiatrist. His exercises didn't relieve the pain, but they kept me mobile enough to hang on to my business. Swimming is good, too. Buying a firmer mattress and using a bed board, two things I was told about only a couple of years ago, helped even more than the exercises and the swimming. Now a surgeon tells me that three of my discs have flattened, causing the vertebrae to move closer together and push on nerves. He wants to cut away parts of the vertebrae to relieve the pressure, but admits there isn't a terrific chance of doing much for me because of the number of years I'd been in pain. I told him no thanks."

One-third of nonsurgery patients would have had surgery if they had followed their doctors' advice.

Eleven out of thirty-two survey participants decided against their doctors' recommendations of surgery. Here are a few of their stories.

"After three weeks of bed rest in a hospital, I was to have surgery the next morning," a bookkeeper told us. "That night, when the nurse took my temperature, I had a fever. It turned out that I had bronchitis and the next morning's operation had to be postponed. I was sent home to rest for three weeks, at which time I was supposed to return for the operation. Fortunately, during that time, the rest relieved the pressure and I could walk. I've been walking a lot since and have not needed any surgery."

A farmer with a ruptured disc had compelling reasons for not following his doctor's recommendation to have surgery. "I needed to plant my crops or risk losing everything. So I rested a bit and planted in spite of the pain. Then things improved, so I never did need surgery."

" 'You need surgery,' an orthopedist told me after giving me a diagnosis of ruptured disc," an executive reported. "I mentally wasn't ready to have my back opened up so I rested for two weeks and then gradually started to exercise. My pain has now dropped enough to let me function, though with limitations."

"You won't believe what an orthopedic surgeon told me twenty years ago," a commercial artist remarked. "The doctor said that it might take months, or even years, but that sooner or later I would crawl into his office on my hands and knees, begging to be operated on. I've had episodes of pain that keep me from working a few weeks every year. So, even now, more than twenty years later, I'm still not sure I made the right choice about not having surgery. But can you believe that doctor's incredible attitude?"

A few survey participants avoided surgery with their surgeons' encouragement.

A periodontist told us, "My neurosurgeon felt that surgery should not be done at all because pain persists in 80 percent of cases. I was happy to hear this. However, all he offered was a corset and Ascriptin®. Then I saw a physiatrist who referred me to a physical therapist and I am gradually improving without surgery."

"I was glad I found an orthopedist who believed that surgery was an absolutely last resort," said a writer who started to recover after three weeks of bed rest, Valium®, and pain medication. "He believed in movement and exercise, once I could leave bed, and this helped a lot, too."

A lecturer also appreciated his orthopedist's caution about surgery. "It took me almost a year to get back to 'normal.' Maybe surgery would have speeded up my recovery, but I doubt it. I attribute my progress to increasing daily activities and to working with a physical therapist on an exercise program."

Beware of chiropractic treatment for acute, ruptured disc pain.

No discussion of how to recover from the initial, incapacitating phase of ruptured disc pain would be complete without special mention of the role of chiropractic care. Half of our survey participants with ruptured discs sought help from chiropractors. Unfortunately, *the results from spinal manipulation for people in severe pain were too often injurious.* In addition, some conditions were misdiagnosed and opportunities for effective treatment were lost.

Keep in mind that the statistics below apply only to chiropractors who treated ruptured disc pain during the initial phase, when patients were partially or totally disabled with sciatica.

Number of patients:	24
Temporary relief:	5 (21%)
No relief:	12 (50%)
Injuries or significant increase in pain:	7 (29%)

Here are some of the stories behind these numbers.

A dentist told us, "The chiropractor made my problem worse. At the time I was treated by him, pain was severe in my lower back and right buttock. During the process of manipulation, the condition became worse, with sciatica pain radiating down my leg into my foot."

"I already had a diagnosis of a ruptured disc when I saw a chiropractor," a company owner reported. "Relatives and friends had convinced me that I should stay away from doctors and also not waste my time lying around in bed. I was limping badly with sciatica and could barely make it under my own power to the chiropractor's table. After my spine had been adjusted, the pain was worse to the extent that I had to be carried out. If I hadn't been overwhelmed by the pain, I think I would have tried to kill the guy."

A lawyer said, "I had a series of treatments from a chiropractor for my ruptured disc. The pain got progressively more severe during the treatments until I stopped them. It is aggravating, and it also seems unprofessional, that a ruptured disc is not seen as a ruptured disc by chiropractors, or at least not by my chiropractor. Misalignment was the diagnosis. I think if I had walked in without a head, I would have been told that the top of my spine was misaligned."

SUMMARY OF TREATMENTS AND PRACTITIONERS FOR ACUTE, SEVERE RUPTURED DISC PAIN

Note: Because of the intensity of pain during the initial, incapacitating stage of a ruptured disc, as well as the risks of neurological impairment, "self-treatment" is not advised. Bed rest is almost always indicated, however, and you need to be thoroughly informed and involved as a partner in your recovery.

Best professional treatments for acute, severe ruptured disc pain

(1) Strong prescription pain medication such as Percodan®

(2) Chymopapain*

(3) Surgery*

Widely used treatments best avoided during episodes of acute, severe ruptured disc pain

(1) Manipulation

(2) Traction

---

*Most survey participants felt that it was worth trying to wait out the intense pain from a ruptured disc, for as long as two months, before considering more invasive treatments such as chymopapain or surgery.

(3) Acupressure

(4) Anti-inflammatory and muscle-relaxant pills*

Best practitioners for
acute, severe ruptured disc pain

(1) Physiatrist

(2) Orthopedist

Practitioners worth a try
for acute, severe ruptured disc pain

Any nonsurgically oriented medical doctor or osteopath who has experience with disc problems and who has the skill and interest to supervise the rehabilitation process

Widely seen practitioners who sometimes make
acute, severe ruptured disc pain sufferers feel worse

(1) Chiropractors

(2) Osteopaths**

(3) Shiatsu therapists

COPING WITH CHRONIC DISC PAIN:
HOW TO MANAGE IT

Special exercises are called for.

The exercise needs of people who have ruptured discs—compared with people who have low back pain without disc pathology—are different. And in order to maximize your chances for a complete and lasting recovery, it is

---

*Their "temporary relief" rate fails significantly below the placebo effect, and they may cause adverse side effects.

**Osteopaths who *don't* use manipulation for ruptured disc—and who have an understanding of physical medicine—*can* be of help.

important that you know about the differences and act on them. Here are highlights of what we will discuss further in this chapter about exercise:

Back exercises are not always the answer, but some form of exercise is essential. Fewer ruptured disc patients than low back sufferers follow a regular exercise routine—51 percent compared with 72 percent. One key reason for this disparity is that 15 percent of ruptured disc patients injure themselves with exercise, while only 3 percent of low back sufferers are harmed by it. The point is not to avoid back exercises, but to know which exercises to do and when to do them.

Ruptured disc patients need more exercises aimed at building abdominal strength. Although both strengthening and stretching were important to survey participants recuperating from ruptured discs, most felt that strengthening their abdominal muscles took priority. Low back sufferers, on the other hand, put greater emphasis on stretching lower back muscles.

There are two 100-percent effective "non-back" exercises for chronic ruptured disc pain. Fully one-third of ruptured disc patients acclaimed swimming and walking as 100 percent effective for improving their condition in the long run. Only 5 percent of low back sufferers performed these exercises regularly.

Movement of some kind is absolutely essential.

Learning how to perform movements that enhance flexibility and strength as well as reduce stress—as soon as possible and as much as possible after acute pain ebbs—is critical to recovery and renewed fitness for practically everyone who has had a ruptured disc. Why *practically* everyone? No one knows. As we mentioned earlier, about one in twenty survey participants who had a ruptured disc, and who was in bad physical shape to start with, got well and stayed well for more than five years without doing anything about fitness. *But this is the exception that proves the rule. The odds are overwhelming that if you don't start a fitness program as soon as you're out of bed, you will remain considerably limited.*

How to avoid practitioner-caused injuries from back exercises

"My internist told me to do three exercises—sit-ups, single-leg raises, and double-leg raises," said an assistant TV producer. "This was after a diagnosis of ruptured disc and three weeks of bed rest. The doctor probably wouldn't have said anything about exercise. But friends had told me so much about the importance of exercise that I asked him to suggest a program. I did five repetitions of each exercise and the pain immediately afterward was great. These exercises set me back two weeks. A month later, I went to an orthopedist and he assigned me to a physical therapist who provided me with exercises that helped a great deal. They weren't difficult and I felt at first that was a bad thing. But I could do them and they helped. I still do them ten years later."

Specific exercise suggestions

Full bent-knee sit-ups are not recommended by most survey participants. And straight-leg sit-ups are taboo. See Chapter 10 for instructions on how to do the *modified* bent-knee sit-ups recommended by a majority of survey participants. (You may find that full bent-knee sit-ups are feasible for you after at least a month on the modified version.)

Single- and double-leg raises are *not* recommended by most survey participants with disc problems. In fact, judging from the comments we received, it seems safe to say that the excessive pressure exerted on discs by double-leg raises should be enough to have the exercise outlawed for these back sufferers.

The value of single-leg raises is more debatable. About one-third of survey participants who had surgery for ruptured discs felt that this exercise (described below) helped prevent excessive postoperative scarring and subsequent limitations. And these individuals had much better outcomes than their counterparts who underwent surgery but didn't do single-leg raises.

On the other hand, a majority of ruptured disc sufferers who did *not* have surgery considered single-leg raises potentially harmful. Our conclusion? We suggest that you do the more conservative hamstring stretch described in Chapter 10. If you have had disc surgery, we further suggest that you be willing to try single-leg raises *cautiously*—if they are prescribed by a competent exercise expert as part of your rehabilitation or maintenance program.

How to do a single-leg raise: Lie on your back. Keep one leg bent and extend your other leg flat on the floor. Lock the knee of your extended leg and raise the leg slowly until your foot is about two feet off the floor. If you stop the upward motion at this point, you will minimize the pressure on your discs. Holding your leg here—at about a thirty-degree angle—for three seconds is a good exercise for strengthening your hips. (By the end of the first week, build up to five repetitions with each leg. Then build up to ten repetitions by the end of the second week.)

If you continue raising your leg toward ninety degrees, you will be strengthening your hips *and* stretching your hamstring muscles. *This* is the exercise that was recommended, and done successfully after surgery, by one-third of the survey participants covered in this chapter.

Note: Not many back practitioners recommend stretching your hamstrings by bending over and touching your toes. But you may be told to do this by some specialists. You'll also find this exercise in a number of best-selling exercise books. Our advice: don't do it. It simply isn't worth the risk of injury. "I was in an exercise class touching the floor with the palms of my hands when I heard a 'pop,' " a business manager wrote. "I had ruptured my disc and could not straighten up. I wound up in bed. The *right* exercises are crucial."

Everyone can exercise his or her back . . . even without doing back exercises.

An insurance executive summed up the thinking of twenty-two of sixty-five ruptured disc patients in our survey: "I feel that walking and swimming are more constructive than regular back exercises. They are more relaxing and they keep me in top shape."

Many survey participants who do back exercises regularly concur. Said a chemist, "Back exercises help, but walking and swimming are even more essential to maintaining my mobility."

And survey participants who were in too much pain to do back exercises felt the same way. One retiree said, "The only exercises I can do without experiencing pain are walking and swimming. Back exercises aggravate my problem (pressure on a nerve from scar tissue). The only thing approaching a back exercise that works for me is lying on the floor with my lower legs draped on a couch. This procedure done a couple of times every day relaxes my back muscles and eases the pain."

Should every ruptured disc sufferer do back exercises?

Yes, in theory. No, in reality. A social worker told us, "After surgery I was given instructions on exercise and scheduled for a few more appointments for instruction after that. Then I was on my own, but I was never able to be free from strain when I exercised. Even though the exercises were taught to me, their risks, benefits, and alternatives were never explained. I was simply told that there should not be as much pain as there was."

A psychologist noted, "I find that back exercises increase my pain each time I have tried them over the past twenty-five years."

On the positive side, about 60 percent of survey participants with ruptured discs did back exercises regularly and successfully. The following comments illustrate their range of positive feelings.

An author: "I do my back exercises faithfully twice a day and believe that they help slowly and undramatically."

A college teacher: "Sit up! Sit up! Sit-ups help the most for recovery, although it took me a year after I started to exercise for my back to become reasonably normal. Most people don't realize how sophisticated the back structure is and that strengthening the abdominal muscles is essential." This professor noted that a year and a half after surgery, he could barely walk. No exercises had been recommended by the operating neurosurgeon. Exercises he learned from a physical therapist gradually brought him back to normal functioning.

A periodontist: "Daily calisthenics—progressively increasing the workout—is the best way to prevent a recurrence of ruptured disc pain. The most important thing is to strengthen the abdominal musculature so that it can help support the upper body. Also, do flexibility exercises to stretch large muscle groups such as the glutei [in the buttocks] and hamstrings. Sit-ups are best for abdominal muscles. Back sufferers only delude themselves if they remain ignorant of the value of exercise and if they do not become aware of what *they*—and not someone else—can do to relieve their problems." This survey participant learned the general principles of exercise, as well as specific exercise routines, from a physiatrist and physical therapist. He then went on to shape his own daily routine.

One final point about back exercises: even if you haven't been able to do them, there may still be hope.

If you have not been able to do back exercises because of chronic pain from a ruptured disc, don't quit yet. Several survey participants with ruptured discs, who were *initially* discouraged or negative about back exercise, eventually found it to be of great value. Some weren't aware of the potential benefits of exercise. Others were told never to exercise. Still others were given the wrong exercises, or were not taught how to exercise, or tried to exercise too soon after the onset of ruptured disc pain. Here are some of their comments:

A management consultant: "I can function as long as I am faithful *(absolutely)* to the exercises prescribed by my practitioner. I do them for about forty-five minutes each morning and evening."

A lawyer: "Go very slow at first and then build up the number of repetitions. I started off at the so-called recommended number of exercises and repetitions, and it cost me another week in bed."

A truck driver: "I recommend heat first, then exercises to strengthen abdominal muscles, which relieve pressure on the lower back."

And a pharmacist who had trouble exercising at first: "Exercise does not relieve pain, but I push the exercises somewhat in order to keep limber. I also don't do the exercises that everyone else does. My program is prescribed for me, and it works for me."

If you aren't doing back exercises, the program in Chapter 10 may put you on track. These movements are conservative, proven-effective, and easy to individualize. If, for any reason, you find the exercises hard to do, stop immediately. If this happens, or if you are not satisfied with your progress, or if you have been advised not to exercise, we urge you to consult one of the six best kinds of back exercise experts revealed by this survey: physiatrists, physical therapists, sports medicine specialists, kinesiologists, yoga teachers, or physical fitness instructors.

Other approaches to chronic disc pain

Two chronically disabled ruptured disc patients in our survey sought medically supervised gravity inversion, with fair to good results. (The treatment is described in Chapter 7.) It is admittedly difficult to find a medical doctor to oversee this approach to relieving back pain, because gravity inversion has not been widely accepted by the medical profession. Chiropractors and physical fitness instructors, however, are making increased use of the technique. You can also attempt to use gravity inversion on your own if you are relatively pain-free.

Spinal fusion, an extreme measure that permanently joins together spinal vertebrae and limits your movement, is a last-ditch measure that fails as often as it succeeds. However, we mention it because three survey participants found that this surgery restored them to the mainstream of life after all other appropriate measures, including excellent rehabilitation programs, had failed.

They report that getting opinions from at least two surgeons is essential, and they recommend an orthopedic surgeon rather than a neurosurgeon.

SUMMARY OF TREATMENTS AND PRACTITIONERS FOR CHRONIC RUPTURED DISC PAIN

Best self-help therapies
for chronic ruptured disc pain

(1) Swimming

(2) Walking

(3) Back exercises that emphasize abdominal strengthening as much as or more than stretching

(4) Gravity inversion

Best professional treatment
for chronic ruptured disc pain

Individualized back exercise therapy

Professional treatments worth trying
for chronic ruptured disc pain

(1) Gravity inversion

(2) Spinal fusion

Widely used treatments best avoided
for chronic ruptured disc pain

(1) Traction

(2) Painkillers, muscle-relaxant pills, and anti-inflammatory pills

(3) Cortisone injections*

(4) Nerve block injections*

---

*These techniques have resulted in a few successful outcomes, but the risks are extremely high. See Chapters 6 and 7 for details.

Best practitioners for
chronic ruptured disc pain

(1) Physiatrist

(2) Physical therapist

Practitioners worth a try for
chronic ruptured disc pain

(1) Physical fitness instructor

(2) Chiropractor*

(3) Kinesiologist

Widely seen practitioners who sometimes make
chronic ruptured disc pain sufferers feel worse

(1) Neurosurgeon**

(2) Neurologist**

*The chiropractor's poor record in dealing with *acute* pain from ruptured disc is discussed on pages 190–191. However, once you're out of bed and no longer suffering sciatica pain, chiropractic care can be useful.

**An excessive reliance on drugs, poor interpersonal skills, and disinterest in the rehabilitation process are the negatives most often mentioned by survey participants.

Chapter 12

How to Get Rid of a Pain in the Neck

"What we have here is low back pain that has traveled north," said a doctor to a warehouse foreman who couldn't move his neck without feeling severe pain.

"There may be some truth in what you say," replied the survey participant, who had never suffered low back pain. "But what should I do about it?"

"A good question," the doctor said, reaching for his prescription pad.

It is a good question. The answer, according to survey participants, has almost nothing to do with viewing neck pain as a bad back problem that just happened to land higher up on the spine.

There are similarities, of course, between neck pain and low back pain. But mostly there are differences—major differences in self-help therapies (including the kinds of exercises to do), in practitioner effectiveness, and in the success rates of a wide variety of treatments.

Who can be helped by the information in this chapter?

About half this survey's 492 participants had neck pain at one time or another: a stiff neck when they woke up, a painful neck after painting a ceiling, a "crook" in the neck after holding the telephone in an awkward position during a long conversation. If you are like these people, the first half of this chapter should prove helpful. The second half of the chapter is designed for—and based exclusively on the experiences of—*chronic neck pain sufferers*, people who have neck discomfort all the time, or who suffer activity-limiting episodes of neck pain.

One-third of the thirty-six chronic neck sufferers in this survey injured their necks in accidents. And they usually suffered years of pain before learning how to improve their conditions.

"My problems stem from a minor car accident at which time I was rear-ended while stationary in my vehicle," a human resources director told us. What happened to her reflects the experiences of many people with neck pain: "I felt fine at first, but the next morning I could barely move my neck." After trying manipulation, physical therapy, prescription drugs, and acupuncture—and after "a period of being totally immobile due to the most excruciating pain I have ever felt," this survey participant found the help she needed.

A construction worker's injury also typifies the traumatic origins of most neck pain. "I was hurt on a construction job and was in the hospital forty-one days," the worker wrote. "I saw many doctors. Most had different opinions of the extent of damage done to my back. All I know is that I have suffered severe pain."

Another one-third of survey participants attributed the onset of neck pain to emotional stress. For example, a television personality suffered neck pain while two members of her immediate family were gravely ill. A teacher linked her neck pain to working with highly disturbed and handicapped children. An executive experienced severe neck pain while going through a painful divorce.

The remaining survey participants in this chapter just "found" themselves with neck pain one day. Some had had the pain for years, but at a nuisance level. Others found that it seemingly struck full blown out of the blue.

"I woke one morning and, for no apparent reason, could not raise my head or move it from left to right," said a family therapist. Other participants who echoed her words endured pain for months or years before obtaining relief.

Don't let them play
diagnostic games with your neck.

It is essential for your peace of mind and your bank account to know that *you are not likely to get a highly specific diagnosis for neck pain.* In fact, nine out of ten times you will not get the same diagnosis from two different practitioners.

Fortunately, though, this lack of diagnostic specificity has little bearing on what you can do to improve your condition. Fortunately, too, there is widespread agreement among neck pain sufferers about which self-help and professional treatments can reduce neck pain.

All this having been said, it is still useful to know about the kinds of diagnoses you are likely to receive from various practitioners. At the very least, this knowledge can keep you off the treatment treadmill.

If you see a medical doctor for neck pain, you will probably be told you have cervical strain, muscle strain, cervical derangement, or a pinched nerve. If your pain started right after an accident, whiplash will probably be mentioned also. Just what in your neck is strained, deranged, pinched, or whiplashed? And to what extent? With implications for what treatment? It is a rare doctor who can answer these questions.

If you see a chiropractor for neck pain, your diagnosis will probably be misalignment, vertebrae displacement, or subluxation. To the uncommon extent that chiropractors agree with doctors, they both may attribute your pain to a pinched nerve. Congenital birth defects such as incompletely formed vertebrae are also popular diagnoses among chiropractors. And no matter what diagnosis you get from a chiropractor, it is likely to be "pointed out" to you on your X rays.

Of course, there are cases where the need for diagnostic specificity is critically important. This is especially true if you are the one in perhaps ten neck pain sufferers with a "treatment-specific" problem such as a ruptured cervical disc, fractured cervical vertebrae, infection, arthritis, or tumor. Of the thirty-six survey participants whose experiences are recounted in this chapter, one had a fractured cervical vertebra, two had ruptured cervical discs, and one had a benign tumor; the remaining survey participants had vague, general diagnoses.

HOW TO RELIEVE
ACUTE, SEVERE NECK PAIN
Avoid bed rest,
except when disabling accidents require it.

We said at the outset of this chapter that the means to successful recovery from neck pain are considerably different from those for low back pain. And the relative value of bed rest is just one indication of this.

Virtually all low back sufferers benefit to a degree from bed rest, but the only neck pain sufferers in this chapter who benefited from it were those involved in disabling accidents. These ranged from car and truck accidents to falling off trampolines and ladders. Most other neck pain sufferers reported that bed rest made them feel worse.

Here, for example, a chemist details his experience with neck pain and bed rest:

"I woke up one morning with an incredibly stiff neck. I had had this kind of pain before from time to time in the morning, although not as intensely, but it had always lessened once I started moving. My neck would bother me some that day and the next day, but that would be it. This time the pain was unbelievable. It took me fifteen minutes to reach out a few feet to the phone on the night table. When I reached my family doctor, he suggested that I rest in bed for two days and then come see him. It didn't work. The longer I lay in one position the stiffer my neck got, so that when I finally wanted to move even a bit, it was all but impossible. I was miserable but better off sitting and walking around. Not *much* better. But it beat lying there."

Sleep in a pain-preventing position.

The best sleep position is on your back, according to survey participants. The fetal position is next best. Lying on your stomach is the worst position, as it puts the most pressure on your neck. It also strains the rest of your spine.

Use the right pillow.

A relatively flat pillow is the first choice of survey participants who lie on their backs or sides. A plump pillow raises the head higher than the spine and tends to strain the neck.

Not using any pillow worked for a minority of survey participants who slept on their backs. You might try this for a few nights and see whether it works for you.

If you're accustomed to sleeping on your stomach, make an all-out effort to change this habit. If you cannot, at least avoid using a pillow. Elevating your head while lying on your stomach is bad for your entire spine.

Several orthopedically designed neck pillows are available. However, no survey participant felt that using a special pillow helped much to relieve pain or prevent further problems.

Any pillow you use should be positioned under your head and neck, *but not under your shoulders*. If the pillow is just under your head, your neck won't be supported. If the pillow is under your shoulders, neither your neck nor your head will be adequately supported.

Get a second opinion about neck traction, which hurts as many people as it helps.

Of the eleven neck pain sufferers in our survey who had traction, three received substantial help, three were set back due to injuries from traction, and five found that traction made no difference. "I asked my doctor about the advisability of using traction for my pinched nerve," said a jeweler who decided against the treatment. "He said that the relatively light weights used for neck traction weren't enough to decompress vertebrae and relieve nerve pressure, and that very heavy weights are risky to use."

"My neck has never been the same since it was in traction on and off for two weeks," reported a road maintenance worker. "I've been told that no permanent harm was done, but I can tell you that the pain afterward was greater."

Nevertheless, neck traction did provide enough relief to promote long-term recovery for three survey participants.

A geologist whose neck pain became unbearable at times learned from a physical therapist how to use a traction device at home. "Nothing but traction worked," he commented, "and I did neck exercises every day and also tried Shiatsu and yoga."

"Traction provided the most immediate results and relief from pain," said a teacher of the emotionally impaired, "although the relief didn't last that long."

And a land surveyor overcame months of "pinched nerve" pain by using traction at home for a week. "Traction was a godsend," he told us. "It enabled me to get back to work."

Should *you* consider neck traction? Yes, but with caution. First try the less risky healing approaches discussed in this chapter. Then raise questions of any practitioner who recommends traction. Remember that the use of traction is not a precise science; it is a sometimes necessary but close-to-last-resort way to try breaking out of a prolonged episode of neck pain. Finally, if you elect to try neck traction, and you feel it's hurting you, never accept a practitioner's word that the pain is "necessary" or "temporary" or "an inevitable part of freeing up tightened muscles." *You* will know whether the treatment is helping or hurting you.

Use ice rather than heat.

Ten survey participants used ice for neck pain and all of them reported good, if temporary, results. Six of these people turned to cold therapy after heat therapy failed to help them. Only ten of twenty neck sufferers who used heat found that it provided relief. Apparently, heat is less effective for neck pain than for back pain. And cold therapy should be tried by more neck sufferers.

For sure, unless your medical condition dictates otherwise, you should try cold treatments for the first forty-eight hours after the onset of neck strain. You can assume that ice will outperform heat for easing spasming and contracted muscles in your neck and shoulders. (See pages 88–91 and 142–143 for details on self-help cold therapy.)

After the first two days, experiment with both ice and heat. Wet heat is the best bet for neck pain—a shower, steam, hot towels, hot packs. Any of these will give better results than a conventional heating pad. (Also, there is no indication that deeper forms of heat, such as ultrasound and diathermy, are more effective than wet heat.)

Try self-massage for neck pain.

Nine neck pain sufferers in this survey had success with self-massage. There is no single magical technique to use. But there are proven-effective guidelines to follow:

(1) Lie in a fetal position with a small pillow under your head and neck and another pillow between your knees. This is a more relaxing position than standing, sitting, or lying on your back.

(2) Begin by lying on your left side, using your left hand to apply oil or lotion to the right side of your neck, the back of your neck, and your right shoulder.

(3) Start the massage directly below your right ear. Apply gentle to moderate pressure with your fingertips, making small circular motions as you work your way down to your shoulder.

(4) Go slowly. Relax.

(5) Repeat this procedure until you have done as much of your neck and shoulder as you can.

(6) Turn onto your right side and complete the massage with your right hand.

Avoid prescription analgesics.

Of the thirteen neck pain sufferers who took pain medication, nine took prescription painkillers and got no relief at all. Two adverse reactions were reported—dizziness and headaches—from prescription drugs.

There *are* painkillers strong enough to provide some relief for most kinds of severe pain, including debilitating neck pain. But the medications prescribed for survey participants with neck pain, including aspirin with codeine and acetaminophen with codeine, didn't work. To make matters worse, some survey participants tried to carry on all their regular activities while taking these prescription analgesics—and were disturbed to find their level of alertness slowed down by the medication. According to these survey participants, aspirin is the best painkiller to take if you want to function *and* get some pain relief.

Don't expect much help from muscle relaxants and anti-inflammatories.

Not one of the four survey participants who took prescription muscle relaxants for neck pain got relief. The same is true of the three neck pain sufferers who took prescription anti-inflammatory drugs. We don't have enough survey data to make recommendations about the effectiveness of these drugs for neck pain, but it seems unlikely that they will help.

Consider trying manipulation, the most common treatment for acute neck pain.

Manipulation works relatively well. Thirty chiropractors and five osteopaths mentioned in this survey used manipulation of the neck to help promote recovery from neck pain. Some 60 percent of these practitioners were able to offer real help. And about 25 percent of those survey participants who were helped reported that their problems were substantially improved for *years*, not just for days or weeks.

"I went to a chiropractor, and his manipulation treatments helped tremendously," said a rugby player who once had severe neck pain. "I still go every once in a while when I feel it's needed, and the result is that I feel great!"

A warehouse supervisor noted, "Manipulation helped my neck pain when it was so bad it was painful to breathe."

We don't have enough data to tell you whether chiropractors or osteopaths are the most successful in using manipulation, but the survey did reveal other important conclusions about neck manipulation:

- Manipulation alone is not a complete answer for a majority of patients. However, it is more effective for neck pain than for back pain, and it gives most neck sufferers enough relief to further their recovery.

- There is a considerable risk of injury or pain. About one in seven survey participants who had neck adjustments told us they had been "injured" or made to feel worse by these treatments. They complained of increased pain for a few days, although they reported no lasting damage. "I hate the feeling of my neck being 'cracked' and I thought it just made the pain worse," was a typical comment from these participants.

- About one-third of survey participants who were helped by neck manipulation reported temporary, minor aches from the treatment for twenty-four to forty-eight hours, followed by relief. "Sometimes a treatment hurts, maybe for a while, but by the next day I feel great," a broadcaster told us. And a manufacturer's sales representative also felt that some aches were a small price to pay for excellent results: "No treatments really injured me, although all chiropractic treatments left me stiff for a day or so."

- *Gentle* manipulation works best. Most survey participants who had neck manipulation felt strongly about this. In fact, the average survey participant who received neck manipulation went to two or more chiropractors before obtaining good results. The most effective of these chiropractors manipulated in a relatively gentle manner, usually *after* promoting relaxation with heat and massage. Word of mouth appears to be the only way to find this kind of practitioner.

"Gentle manipulation helps the most," concluded a caterer. "Anything else is too nerve-wracking. You can't call and ask, 'Are you gentle?' But I regret having seen chiropractors who used rougher techniques."

An importer who suffered terrible neck pain and headaches despite more than two years under orthopedists' care, found relief after treatment by chiropractors. "Look for a chiropractor who will take his time," he advised. "That is the key because it does take more time to adjust your neck in a nonstressful way."

Don't automatically rely on a cervical collar.

You've probably seen someone at one time or another wearing an awkward, bulky-looking collar around his or her neck. If you currently have acute and severe neck pain yourself, this recollection can immediately turn into a question, "Would a cervical collar help me?"

Probably not. Medical research offers no conclusive indication that the average neck pain sufferer would benefit from wearing a cervical collar. And of the five survey participants who wore collars for pinched-nerve neck pain, only one found it helpful.

If the point of wearing a collar is to keep you out of physically stressful positions—dropping your chin toward your chest when reading, for example—you would probably be better off learning to hold your neck properly without an aid. Eventually you will have to learn to do this on your own anyway.

If, on the other hand, there is a compelling medical reason for immobilizing your neck—the risk of permanent nerve damage, for example—then you will need to wear a cervical collar. After you remove it, however, you must still work to restore lost muscle strength and flexibility. The exercises in this chapter will help you achieve that goal.

WHAT YOU SHOULD KNOW ABOUT THE MOST WIDELY SEEN PRACTITIONERS FOR NECK PAIN

Chances are only one in ten that an orthopedist can help you . . . even temporarily.

The orthopedist's track record with neck pain sufferers is dismal. The fact is that twenty-six out of thirty-six survey participants covered in this chapter saw orthopedists for neck pain—and only three of these individuals (12 percent) got any help at all—either temporary or long-run. Of the remaining twenty-three cases, not one got any kind of positive or useful advice or treatments—not so much as an encouraging word.

"Orthopedists will say almost anything to get rid of a chronic neck sufferer," said a typist. "Their knowledge about muscle strain, necks, or chronic pain is close to nil, and, furthermore, they could care less."

An editor also found a lack of skill and constructive attitude: "The orthopedist was very offhand about my injury. He called it mild whiplash and said it would improve by itself within a few months. But it turned out that the pain was very intense for a year."

In case after case, orthopedists' negative attitudes toward chronic neck pain precluded any effort on their part to help, unless obvious pathology, malformation, or injury was present.

Said a management consultant, "The orthopedist acted as though I was there just for the insurance claim."

A musician wrote, "The orthopedists acted as if I were faking my pain. They said they saw nothing at all."

There are a few positive points to be made. Two survey participants with

ruptured cervical discs got excellent results from surgery performed by orthopedists. And one survey participant felt relieved of stress after an orthopedist
conducted a thorough examination that ruled out any serious medical
problem. However, there is no escaping the reality that in nine out of ten
instances orthopedists are not helpful for neck pain.

Holistic chiropractic care surpasses
medical care in restoring neck fitness.

The results of chiropractic care for low back pain weren't especially
impressive, falling far short of physical medicine and other disciplines for
relieving back pain. Too often, chiropractic care came up short for low back
sufferers because (1) improvement was short-lived; (2) patients were in
constant need of additional treatments—with no end in sight; and (3) the
vast majority of patients were not helped to reach what presumably was their
ultimate goal: *self-sufficiency*, or knowing how to take care of themselves in
the long run.

However, these factors do *not* apply to total chiropractic care (as opposed
to manipulation alone) for neck pain. Here, results are enduring more often
than not. Most patients completed their treatments in less than eight weeks.
And nearly half of all patients learned how to prevent pain from recurring.

On the negative side, the "made patient feel worse" rate of 13 percent
from chiropractic care is alarming but no greater than the comparable rate
for physical therapists. Moreover, a chiropractor who uses "gentle" manipulation, who avoids traction, and who emphasizes self-care education, is likely
to give you the help you need.

Massage therapists are remarkably effective
in providing substantive, temporary relief.

Seventeen of nineteen survey participants reported a 90 percent chance
of getting badly needed relief for neck pain from Swedish massage. Most
individuals who received Swedish massage for neck pain got one or two full
days of relief. This contrasts sharply with the effect of Swedish massage on
low back pain—where a lower percentage of people were helped and where
only a few hours' relief was the norm. And neck pain sufferers, who are dealt
additional pain all too often by a variety of practitioners, reported "no harm
done" even when the massage brought no relief.

Shiatsu, or acupressure massage, was tried by four survey participants with neck pain. And the results, though statistically insignificant, are promising. Three of the four got enough temporary relief to further their progress, and the other reported dramatic, long-term relief after five treatments.

The chief drawback of professional massage therapy is its cost.

Almost everyone with neck pain who tries massage benefits from it and wants more. But the relatively high cost of professional massage—and the likelihood of a surcharge of 50 percent or more for residential calls—prevents many people from getting even the occasional treatments they need. Compounding the problem, many health-insurance companies, including Blue Cross/Blue Shield, will rarely reimburse you for medical massage therapy, even if it is prescribed by a doctor. (You can, however, claim the cost of the therapy as a medical tax deduction.)

Self-massage for neck pain is one solution. In addition, survey participants strongly recommend that you do some comparison shopping among massage therapists. Prices vary widely. A higher price often means a more expensive environment rather than a higher-quality massage.

Here are additional suggestions from survey participants:

- Have a full body massage. A complete massage, with special attention to your neck, is more relaxing and beneficial than a neck massage alone.

- Find a massage therapist you like and respect. Then stay with that person for a series of massages. It takes time even for a skilled practitioner to know your body and your needs.

- Consider trying Shiatsu therapy. It is highly effective for relieving low back pain, and it seems promising for neck pain sufferers as well. One note of caution: reject any Shiatsu therapist who is applying too much pressure. Some discomfort from Shiatsu therapy is normal, but your judgment about pain tolerance is superior to any practitioner's.

A family doctor is seldom helpful for treatment or referral.

Unfortunately, you can't expect much help for neck pain from your family doctor. Treatment from GP's, consisting mostly of drugs or traction, was harmful to four of twelve neck sufferers in our survey. And no effective referrals were made.

SUMMARY OF TREATMENTS AND PRACTITIONERS FOR ACUTE NECK PAIN

Best self-help therapies for acute neck pain

(1) Cold therapy

(2) Self-massage

Best professional treatments for acute neck pain

(1) Holistic massage

(2) Manipulation preceded by heat and massage

Professional treatments worth trying for acute neck pain

(1) Shiatsu

(2) Kinesiology

Widely used treatments best avoided during episodes of acute neck pain

(1) Traction

(2) Cervical collar

(3) Anti-inflammatory drugs

(4) Muscle-relaxant drugs

Best practitioners for
acute neck pain

(1) Holistic massage therapists

(2) Chiropractors*

(3) Physical therapists

Practitioners worth a try for
acute neck pain

(1) Shiatsu therapists

(2) Kinesiologists

Widely seen practitioners who sometimes make
acute neck pain sufferers feel worse

(1) Orthopedists

(2) General practitioners

HOW TO BANISH CHRONIC NECK PAIN
You must integrate different therapies.

No matter where your back hurts, it takes more than one kind of therapy—making more than one change in your life—to free yourself of pain. This is especially true of neck pain, *where no single approach to healing provided long-run help for the majority of neck pain sufferers in this survey.*

Chronic neck pain sufferers who did away with disabling pain included at least two, and often all three, of the following changes in their lives:

(1) physical change—posture and exercise;

---

*Osteopaths may manipulate as well as chiropractors, but total chiropractic care for neck pain seems more effective than osteopathic care.

(2) emotional change—relaxation through exercise or stress-reduction techniques;

(3) attitudinal change—a different philosophy about everyday activities.

Survey participants reiterate that change in any *one* of these areas is
unlikely to control chronic neck pain—that the "single magic step" to relief
is more myth than reality. But positive steps in all three areas will give you
an excellent chance for a total recovery.

Reduce stress—a greater factor in neck pain than in any other kind of back pain.

"Does your back get worse when you are under stress?"

We asked this question of every survey participant. And 83 percent of
neck pain sufferers answered, "Yes."

Not only is this statistic a full one-third higher than the average for all
back sufferers, but neck pain sufferers were also more vocal about the pain-
causing role of stress and the consequent need to change their lives in order
to reduce stress and promote recovery.

A children's author told us, "All the physical therapy and neck and back
exercises and everything else you can think of did not get rid of my neck
pain, because it failed to touch the basis of the pain—stress. In spite of all my
good intentions, I sit over the typewriter, tense up, become absorbed in my
work, and by the time I realize it, my neck is in grim shape. What worked for
me—in addition to everything else I was doing—was taking breaks every
hour and jogging (which I love) in the middle of the day to prevent the
buildup of accumulated tension."

"What helped me the most was learning to relax," a clerk typist wrote.
"Other things helped—professional massage therapy, my own exercises, and
not sleeping on my stomach. But the biggest improvement came after I
found a way to leave my troubles behind by joining a health club. There, I
could really relax."

"The worst neck pain I ever experienced occurred when two members of
my immediate family were gravely ill and I was functioning under the
assumption that I did not need to slow down under stress," an assistant
professor commented. She added, "A psychotherapist explored the emo-

tional stress of these crises with me, and that helped. On the other hand, an orthopedic surgeon discouraged my thinking about psychosomatic factors. He seemed to want to convince me that a medical injury in childhood accounted for my problem."

This latter point—the inability or refusal of some doctors to talk about stress—fueled the anxiety felt by many neck pain sufferers. It also tended to delay their seeking ways to control stress. In answer to another survey question about stress, neck pain sufferers reported that only five of forty-six medical doctors "mentioned stress in a constructive way."

An office manager underscored this point when she reported, "I have seen many physicians. Their attitude is that I am a healthy-looking and athletic young woman, so I can't have back or neck problems. It is all in my head. I therefore suffer from 'neurosis.' (This word is mine; doctors dare not actually say neurotic. They just hint at it.)"

And an electrical engineer explained, "It isn't a question of wanting your hand held or having a daddy figure tell you that everything will be okay. It's a matter of respect for another person's pain. Anyone who can lift your spirits can also help you to mobilize your own resources against pain. But this seems to be too much to ask of a doctor. At least it was more than I got from the doctors I saw for chronic neck pain!"

Because of the high incidence of stress among neck pain sufferers, it is important to keep three points in mind:

First, if and when a medical doctor talks to you about stress, it is unlikely that what he says will be helpful or accurate.

Second, there is a small but significant chance that a serious medical condition is causing your neck pain and that this condition will be overlooked because your pain will be dismissed as stress-caused. So if you have doubts about *your* medical problem not having been taken seriously, dispel these doubts by getting a thorough checkup—more than a quick look and another X ray to add to the pile—including a CAT scan or whatever else is needed to provide an answer.

Third, you will need to take decisive steps to manage your stress.

A slight majority of neck pain sufferers were able to manage stress by themselves, simply by doing something pleasurable and athletic. They joined a health club. They walked, swam, or jogged. They took up Tai Chi or modern dance.

Other survey participants got short-term professional help. One learned visualization techniques from a mental health counselor. Another learned yoga from an instructor. Two survey participants underwent psychotherapy. Still another got instruction in meditation.

Since stress management is a burgeoning and chaotic industry these days, we think this final comment, from a horticulturist, provides some needed perspective: "Yes, I think that stress aggravates my neck pain. And, yes, I have learned to control it with a three-mile walk every day, come rain or shine. But I feel humble about this. I don't think that anyone, professional or otherwise, should get too preachy about stress. It is an area where there are more unknowns than knowns. The existence of stress is sometimes an excuse to treat back and neck sufferers poorly, or not treat them at all. On the other hand, the individual with an ulcer or heart condition caused by stress will be taken seriously because his problem is now a disease that can be seen and treated. My advice is to do something nice for yourself every day, some kind of exercise that will restore you, please you, and put you in control. In other words, don't let about a million stress experts out there drive you crazy."

Improve your neck posture—an effective but seldom used way to ease chronic pain.

With all the talk about the need for good posture to reduce back pain, correct alignment at the top of the spine got little attention from most survey participants. But take a moment now to consider your neck posture because those few survey participants who improved theirs, no matter how slightly, reaped great dividends in comfort.

"I looked in the mirror one day and realized I always cocked my head to one side, and that was the beginning of the end of twenty years of neck pain," an assembly line worker told us.

And a court stenographer found that the key to alleviating neck pain as well as low back pain was to follow a physical therapist's advice to "keep your chin in line with the rest of your body instead of jutting out in front."

Here are two specific suggestions from survey participants for facilitating good neck posture:

(1) *Maneuver your way into correct posture.* Try to make yourself an inch or so taller for an instant by stretching your neck and head skyward. Now relax and let your chin tuck in slightly, instead of

jutting or drooping. Doing this a few times during the day is a good way to position your neck correctly.

(2) *Use the ball-on-flagpole concept.* Another good way to check and correct your neck posture is to visualize a ball (your head) perched on top of a flagpole (your spine). Keeping this image in mind will help you to maintain good neck posture and avoid future episodes of neck pain.

Perform neck exercises—often overlooked but effective and helpful.

Only 35 percent of survey participants with neck pain did exercises to improve neck fitness. And only about half of neck pain sufferers were even aware that exercise could add strength and flexibility to their neck muscles.

But neck exercises offer proven help. Of the seventeen survey participants who did neck exercises, four (24 percent) had temporary relief, seven (41 percent) reported moderate long-term improvement, and three (18 percent) showed dramatic long-term improvement.

These results don't match the gains from doing exercises for low back pain, but they are impressive, nevertheless, since 59 percent of survey participants with neck pain who exercised *showed some long-term improvement.* When you consider that there was no difference in success between survey participants who learned neck exercises on their own and survey participants who got professional instruction, you may decide to include the easy-to-learn neck exercises explained on the next page in your daily routine.

Before you try them, however, keep the following general rules in mind: *Neck exercises are best combined with low back exercises.* Most survey participants with neck pain also had low back pain or occasional low back discomfort. And it helped them to combine neck exercises with back exercises in a regular routine. Later in this chapter, we will suggest how this can be done.

Neck exercises are as important for promoting relaxation as for building fitness. Most neck exercises are designed as much to relieve tension as they are to stretch and strengthen muscles. A few should be incorporated into your exercise routine, but the rest may be done as your stress or discomfort dictates—while at work, during a break, upon awakening, before bedtime—anytime.

Neck exercises can be learned in minutes. You may recall from the chapter on low back pain that survey participants with activity-limiting pain maximized their progress with the help of professional exercise instruction. This is usually *not* the case with neck pain sufferers. You can quickly learn most neck exercises on your own.

Try these neck and shoulder exercises along with the low back exercises in Chapter 10.

We feel that the best place in the low back routine to add the following neck exercises is right after Exercise 3 on pages 170–171. Or you can add them to any back exercise routine after doing a few warm-up stretches.

Prone shoulder stretch. Lie in the Basic Position (on your back, knees bent, feet flat on the floor, arms at your sides). Raise one arm and lower it to the floor behind your head, stretching but not straining to extend the arm fully. Relax for a second. Repeat this exercise with your other arm. Alternate arms and do five repetitions with each.

Prone shoulder shrug. While in the Basic Position, count slowly to five while shrugging your shoulders toward your ears. Lower your shoulders and relax for a second. Repeat five times.

Prone neck roll. Start from the Basic Position, but with your chin tucked in about an inch toward your chest. Turn your head toward one shoulder. When you feel resistance, hold there for three seconds. Return to the Basic Position and relax for a second, then turn your head toward the other shoulder. Do five repetitions.

Comment: The objective of these exercises is to relax you and keep your neck muscles stretched and flexible. A few survey participants asked us if they could do these exercises when they had *some* discomfort. We put the question to other survey participants, and they said yes. In fact, they tended to do these exercises more *when* they had discomfort. Keep in mind, of course, that no exercise should be done if it turns mild discomfort into pain.

You can do the following neck and shoulder exercises at work and on the go.

Note: All exercises in this section are done from a standing position unless otherwise noted.

Bobbing. Lower your chin toward your chest until there is resistance. Then "crane" your head and neck forward as far as you can without bending or moving your torso. Hold for three seconds. Relax. Do three repetitions.

Bending. Tilt your head toward one shoulder. After you feel resistance, pause for three seconds. Return to the straight-ahead position and relax. Now tilt your head toward your other shoulder. Continue to alternate and do five repetitions on each side.

Standing shoulder roll. The objective here is to move both your shoulders in a small circular motion at the same time. Simply shrug your shoulders up, roll them forward as if you were trying to make a circle, then return them to a normal position. Relax. Repeat three times. You can vary this exercise by shrugging and rolling one shoulder at a time, backward or forward.

Standing head roll. If you've ever watched a boxer loosen his neck muscles before a fight by making circular motions with his head, then you know how this exercise works. First move your head clockwise, down toward your chest, then back again. Now do this same movement counterclockwise. Three repetitions in each direction are suggested.

Range of motion movement. If you tend not to move around much on your job, and you feel your neck tightening up, here are four easy movements you can do while standing or sitting: turn your head as far as you can to the left, then as far as you can to the right. Lower your head toward your chest, then raise it until you are looking straight up.

Remember these do's and don't's that can benefit you every hour of every day.

Don't talk your way into neck pain. Survey participants with neck pain were unanimous in pointing out that the telephone is not "user friendly." To put this another way, if you bend someone's ear on the phone, you are likely to bend your own neck out of shape. Indeed, long telephone conversations gave more survey participants a pain in the neck than did any other daily activity.

What to do? Don't cradle the phone between your head and shoulder. This position puts tremendous and continuous strain on your neck muscles. If you must keep your hands free while you're talking on the telephone, get a speaker phone. A wide range of speaker phone equipment is available at telephone and electronic retail stores, and over the Internet.

(Cradle-shaped objects that attach to your phone make it slightly easier to hold the phone without using your hands, but they don't prevent neck pain.)

Finally, if you're talking for more than ten minutes, switch the telephone to your other ear. This may feel awkward at first, but will save your neck a lot of grief.

Do learn how to read without straining your neck. Reading is the next biggest source of trouble for neck pain sufferers. "I start off in a straight-backed chair at a desk. I hold the book on the desk. And I vow to keep my head straight, instead of bending my neck toward the book. Then, I become absorbed in the reading, and before I know it, the book is in my lap and my chin is almost in my lap, too." So said an executive search consultant who finds, as do many other survey participants, that exaggerating the downward tilt of the chin while reading causes and aggravates neck pain.

The best solution, of course, is to will yourself not to read or do paperwork with your chin on your chest. Another solution, if willpower alone won't suffice, is to buy a book holder from an office supply store and prop it on your desk.

"Getting nice and comfortable and reading in bed" is virtually impossible if you have neck pain. It is absolutely impossible if you have neck pain *and* low back pain. Avoid putting reading material on your abdomen and straining your neck downward to see it. Likewise, avoid holding reading material over your head while you're lying down; the strain on your shoulders will affect your neck and your back. (Reading while lying down and looking up can also cause eyestrain.)

Don't get your neck out of whack watching TV. Improper neck position while watching television is another common cause of neck strain. So sit in a good chair and keep your television at or near eye level. If you must watch TV in bed, the least stressful way is to lie on your side with a pillow under your neck. (A rule of thumb: if you would not be able to sleep comfortably in the position you're lying in to watch TV, you're lying in the wrong position.)

For sure, don't lie in bed or on a couch in a position that requires you to look down to watch TV. You shouldn't have to peer over your feet, or anything else, to see the screen.

Do relax your neck and shoulders while driving. Driving long distances, especially during bad weather or in heavy traffic, can cause a troublesome neck to flare up. Using a headrest can help. But it is even more helpful to take an adequate number of breaks—preferably every hour—and do some of the neck and shoulder exercises explained in the preceding section.

SUMMARY OF TREATMENTS AND PRACTITIONERS
FOR
CHRONIC NECK PAIN

Best self-help therapies
for chronic neck pain

(1) Stress-reduction

(2) Changing daily activities and habits

(3) Posture improvement

(4) Neck exercises

Best professional treatment
for chronic neck pain

Manipulation

Professional treatments worth trying
for chronic neck pain

(1) Shiatsu

(2) Holistic massage

Widely used treatments best avoided
during episodes of chronic neck pain

(1) Drugs: prescribed or over-the-counter

(2) Cervical collars (unless needed to prevent nerve damage)

Best practitioners for
chronic neck pain

(1) Chiropractors

(2) Holistic massage therapists

(3) Yoga instructors

(4) Physical fitness instructors with credentials in sports medicine

Practitioners worth a try
for chronic neck pain

(1) Physiatrists

(2) Kinesiologists

(3) Shiatsu therapists

(4) Acupuncturists

(5) Physical therapists

Widely seen practitioners who sometimes make
chronic neck pain sufferers feel worse

(1) Orthopedists

(2) General practitioners

Chapter 13

How to Relieve Osteoarthritis-Based Back Pain

In spite of the hundreds of millions of dollars devoted to arthritis research, osteoarthritis back sufferers still have more questions than answers. The most frequently and vehemently asked question concerns the seemingly wide gap between what the Arthritis Foundation preaches and what the medical profession practices.

An investment counselor in our survey described the situation this way: "The Arthritis Foundation is supposed to reflect the views of the medical profession. Certainly, it is more closely allied with physicians than with alternative practitioners. But, according to the Arthritis Foundation, arthritis should be taken seriously. And, according to three doctors I've seen, arthritis is 'inevitable,' 'the price you pay for getting older,' and 'wear and tear you can't do anything about except take drugs.' Is that taking the problem seriously?"

As we said, osteoarthritis back sufferers have a lot of questions. Do doctors take osteoarthritis of the spine seriously? Should you, as the Arthritis Foundation recommends, see a doctor? If so, what kind of doctor? And for what kind of help? This chapter provides answers, not from practitioners or from the Arthritis Foundation, but from other, clearer voices—osteoarthritis back sufferers themselves.

Please note: The information and tips in this chapter apply *only* to individuals with osteoarthritis, and *not* to those with any other forms, such as rheumatoid arthritis or ankylosing spondylitis.

Taken as a group, the forty-seven survey participants with osteoarthritis can answer your questions, bolster your spirits, and alert you to specific, practical techniques on shaking free of the pain and restrictions you encounter daily.

Here are a few of the questions they've answered:

(1) How effective are various nonmedical practitioners in helping osteoarthritis back sufferers? And how do they compare with medical specialists?

(2) Which of many treatments touted as curative actually help back sufferers with osteoarthritis? Which have no effect? Which make matters worse? And which are at least worth a try?

(3) What about diet and nutritional remedies? Do they have any value?

(4) To what extent can exercise affect the outcome of spinal arthritis cases?

(5) Should you ignore health-care professionals and treat yourself?

Do you have osteoarthritis back pain by any other name?

Osteoarthritis was the diagnostic term applied most commonly to survey participants who had a wear-and-tear disorder of the joints in their spines. But even medical doctors didn't use the same terminology to describe the same condition. Hence you may have osteoarthritis-based back pain if you were given any of the following diagnoses: degenerative arthritis . . . degenerative joint disease . . . degenerative disc disease . . . spondylitis (literally means inflammation of the spine, although some doctors use the term to describe a bacterial infection of the spine) . . . spondylosis (not to be confused with spondy*lolysis*, or defective vertebra) . . . degenerative hydrotrophic spondylitis . . . or bone spurs.

If you're thinking that this amounts to another confusing and unfunny back-pain name game, you're right. It's hardly funny and it is confusing, but don't let it throw you. Although you can't cure osteoarthritis, you can reduce or eliminate its symptoms and its physical limitations. Read on.

Professional versus self-care

According to the Arthritis Foundation, "It's best to consult a physician as soon as possible." Survey participants, even those who feel that their own self-care does them far more good than any professional treatments, also emphasize the need to form a partnership, even a temporary one, with a health-care practitioner.

But which one?

PROFESSIONAL CARE:
CAN A MEDICAL DOCTOR HELP YOU?

Most kinds of medical doctors *cannot* help you, survey participants avow. Only a few kinds of medical specialists can. Three out of four medical doctors seen by survey participants failed to provide them with any degree of long-run help. The major reason was ineffectual treatment consisting almost exclusively of drug therapy, which by itself did relatively little to curb osteoarthritis pain.

These doctors did not prescribe physical therapy. Most didn't so much as mention the need for movement, exercise, weight control, or corrective daily habits and activities. They presumably knew these factors were important—usually essential—to a successful outcome, but they chose to start and end their treatment with drugs.

It can be misleading, of course, to talk about medical doctors in general. So let's look at how well the most frequently seen doctors actually did, with an eye toward specific recommendations for you.

Medical doctors who work with
physical therapists: a winning formula

The odds of your controlling the symptoms of osteoarthritis, and living without limitations, increase dramatically if you see a medical doctor who either assumes the role of a physical therapist or refers you to a therapist. In fact, you have a 90 percent chance of getting long-run help from physical therapy under medical supervision.

Physical therapy, which uses natural means of healing to help you move more freely—and which depends a great deal on good rapport between practitioner and patient—was the key to success for the majority of spinal arthritis sufferers in this survey.

Physiatrist and rheumatologist: the two best medical doctors for osteoarthritis sufferers

The physiatrist, because of his expertise in physical medicine and rehabilitation, has a superb record in helping spinal arthritis sufferers. Eight osteoarthritis sufferers in our survey saw physiatrists, and all eight achieved moderate or dramatic long-term success.

The rheumatologist, with his specialty in arthritis and related diseases, can provide you with a complete recovery program, from a specific diagnosis (and a better explanation of that diagnosis than you would get from other medical doctors) to the information you need to be your own doctor as much as possible.

Of the eight survey participants with osteoarthritis who saw rheumatologists, five got moderate long-term help and one got temporary relief.

Orthopedists: better than GP's but not especially helpful

The orthopedist's record of success with osteoarthritis sufferers is better than his record with all other categories of back pain. Yet the chances are only about three in ten that you will receive long-term help from an orthopedist for spinal arthritis.

Of the fifty-nine orthopedists who treated osteoarthritis sufferers in this survey, thirteen (22 percent) helped bring about moderate long-term improvement and four (7 percent) helped patients achieve dramatic long-term improvement.

What do successful orthopedists know that the others don't? Probably nothing at all. The difference between effective and ineffective orthopedists in treating osteoarthritis usually depends on the individual doctor's *willingness* to apply his knowledge. Chronic back problems such as osteoarthritis take real effort on the part of both the patient and the practitioner. And the outcome of any case depends largely on what you come away with from the doctor's office, not what is "done" to you during your visit.

GP's, family doctors, and internists: inadequate skills and a lack of interest and knowledge

"Take two aspirins and call me" might not be bad initial advice from a general practitioner who tells you that you have osteoarthritis-based back pain. Aspirin and other anti-inflammatory drugs are, at best, merely a starting point for treating osteoarthritis. Yet a full 80 percent of doctors limited their treatment solely to drug therapy. Sometimes these doctors *mentioned* the need to lose weight, reduce stress, or increase exercise activities. However, no therapy other than drugs was specified.

Of the thirty-four GP's who treated osteoarthritis sufferers in this survey, five (15 percent) provided moderate long-term relief and two (6 percent) provided dramatic long-term relief. It would seem, then, that the Arthritis Foundation's slogan, "It's time to take arthritis seriously," applies more to most doctors than to arthritis sufferers themselves.

The failure of the general practitioner even to make an appropriate referral all but guarantees that some patients, out of sheer frustration, will eventually seek help from the "quacks" inveighed against so strongly by the Arthritis Foundation.

Osteopaths: better for osteoarthritis than for most other back ailments

If you are seeking *temporary* relief from acute osteoarthritis symptoms, an osteopath is a better bet to provide it than a GP, orthopedist, or chiropractor.

Of the thirteen osteopaths who treated survey participants with this problem, six (46 percent) provided temporary relief, usually through a combination of manipulation and medication. Osteopaths can prescribe any drug that medical doctors can, but they seem to prescribe medication more cautiously than other doctors, with fewer subsequent side effects.

Nevertheless, only one osteopath in our survey helped an osteoarthritis sufferer make lasting progress. The osteopath's poor record of long-term help applies to all back problems except sciatica.

Comments from osteoarthritis sufferers about medical doctors

All but two osteoarthritis sufferers in this survey were treated by medical doctors. On average, each of these survey participants saw more than three doctors. Unlike most low back sufferers, who wound up being treated by nonmedical practitioners, most spinal arthritis sufferers limited their care to physicians.

Osteoarthritis-based back sufferers also had the highest average pain rating—6 on a scale of 0 to 10—of any category of back pain in this survey, including ruptured disc and sciatica. So it is hardly surprising that most of these survey participants were antagonistic toward medical doctors. Nor is it surprising that the reasons for this antagonism go much deeper than their resentment about having a disorder that can't be cured.

An executive with spinal arthritis summed it up: "I have read extensively of the literature published by the Arthritis Foundation, and I am impressed by the soundness of their research and advice. I have also personally received excellent suggestions from my local Arthritis Foundation chapter. My source of anger is not that doctors can't perform miracles. It is that a chasm-like discrepancy exists between what the Arthritis Foundation espouses and what most individual medical doctors actually carry out in the way of treatment. In short, if you are a model patient in the eyes of the Arthritis Foundation—receptive to medical care and eager to learn how to help the doctor help you—you're still in for a rude awakening when a prescription and some banalities about taking it easy and learning to live with it are *all* that you are offered. I went to four doctors, all of whom have particularly good reputations, before I found one who was willing to really work with me. (Running through an alphabet of drugs is not working *with* me.) It's a damn shame. It makes a mockery of the information being directed at lay people with arthritis, telling them to see their doctor if they seem to have arthritic symptoms. The Arthritis Foundation's campaign would be more purposeful and productive if it tried to convince doctors to see their patients. I mean *really* see them."

This sentiment was echoed by a retiree: "The truth is that most doctors have no interest in treating you." By a housewife: "I would like to find an orthopedic doctor who is considerate and concerned." A child-care worker: "Doctors seem more interested in specific symptoms—not in the whole person. More interested in surgery and pills. More into 'you just have to live with it.' " And by an engineer: "My orthopedic surgeon was hostile at first and never prescribed physical therapy once I got out of the hospital."

Conclusions about medical doctors

- If your family doctor can't give you the help you need, and he probably can't, see a physiatrist. (If you need the name of one, consult your county medical association.) Or see a rheumatologist. (Your regional arthritis self-help group may be able to help you with a referral.) See Chapter 3 for further information about physiatrists and rheumatologists.

- Be skeptical about suggestions that pills and rest, or surgery, are the only answers. They seldom are. Minimally, get a second opinion from a physiatrist or rheumatolgist about the need for drugs or surgery. *No one should limit his or her recovery program to drugs or surgery alone.*

- Try not to let the gloom-and-doom attitude of some medical doctors ("I can only promise you a continuation of pain because there is no cure for osteoarthritis") sink you into despair. There are almost always ways to live a full life in spite of severe spinal osteoarthritis. The answer is appropriate information. And this information *is* available.

- You probably can enhance any doctor's course of treatment by looking over the self-help approaches presented later in this chapter. They represent the most popular suggestions made by osteoarthritis-based back sufferers who learned how to overcome disabling pain.

NONMEDICAL PRACTITIONERS

Chiropractors: even less effective than medical doctors

Chiropractic treatments for osteoarthritis-based back pain are usually a waste of time and money. Of the twenty-seven chiropractors who treated osteoarthritis back sufferers in this survey, only four (15 percent) provided moderate long-term relief and none provided dramatic long-term relief. The four chiropractors who helped did *not* rely exclusively on manipulation. They offered counsel about exercise and lifestyle, and this advice was the key to whatever success the patients achieved.

Eight of twenty-seven chiropractors (30 percent) provided survey participants with *temporary* relief through manipulation or, more commonly, through a combination of manipulation and other treatments such as massage, ultrasound, and electric stimulation. But the duration of this relief was brief—often just a matter of hours, and not enough to help survey participants make long-run gains.

A newspaper columnist expressed the feelings of many survey participants about chiropractic care for osteoarthritis: "The chiropractor seemed to help a bit, but I needed to learn to deal with the problem myself as my back would slip out after I left the office." And an artist cautioned that, "Arthritis can be worsened when manipulation strains joints because the manipulator doesn't know exactly where the pain is coming from and what his pressure is affecting."

Physical therapists: a superior record for helping osteoarthritis sufferers

Physical therapy for osteoarthritis-based back pain is given considerable emphasis in medical textbooks and in the literature of the Arthritis Foundation. The major stumbling block, as we have pointed out, is that most medical doctors neither prescribe physical therapy nor make appropriate referrals. Also, most other health-care professionals lack physical therapy skills.

Of the fifteen physical therapists who treated survey participants with osteoarthritis-based back pain, fourteen (93 percent) succeeded in improving the long-term quality of the patients' lives. Individualization was crucial, especially in areas of movement and exercise, as well as in teaching patients to make adjustments in the way they went about their everyday activities.

Who else can help?

Nine yoga instructors and physical fitness instructors treated osteoarthritis sufferers in this survey—and all nine helped these individuals to get better and stay better.

When you consider the high success rate of these yoga and physical fitness practitioners in helping low back sufferers—and their skill in teaching movements that foster fluidity and fitness—it becomes even more apparent that your opportunities for improvement are excellent.

Two participants found similar help from Tai Chi instruction.

PRESCRIBED AND RECOMMENDED TREATMENTS FOR OSTEOARTHRITIS-BASED BACK PAIN*
Anti-inflammatory drugs rarely work well.

Although "arthritis" means joint inflammation, most medical authorities agree that the typical osteoarthritis sufferer does *not* have inflammation. Nevertheless, doctors routinely prescribe anti-inflammatory drugs for osteoarthritis, as well as for other kinds of non-inflammation back conditions, including low back pain.

Half of the survey participants mentioned in this chapter took prescription anti-inflammatory drugs such as Motrin®, Indocin®, and Ascriptin®. Here is the outcome:

Number of osteoarthritis sufferers who took prescription anti-inflammatory drugs:	22
Temporary relief from pain:	7 (32%)
No relief from pain:	11 (50%)
Adverse side effects:	4 (18%)

These ratings are comparable to those in Chapter 5, for all participants in the survey who took prescription anti-inflammatory medication. So, for back pain in general, anti-inflammatory drugs seem to have no greater value than a placebo.

Aspirin, which has both anti-inflammatory and analgesic value, was taken by thirteen survey participants with osteoarthritis—and provided relief in ten cases (77 percent). This parallels the 78 percent relief rate reported by all survey participants who took aspirin for back pain.

*The following topics are arranged according to their frequency of mention in the survey.

Tips on how to take the only
known "miracle drug"

Aspirin is the only medication that relieved pain for a majority of participants in this survey. Its use is so widespread that Americans consume about 50 billion tablets of this "miracle drug" every year. Assuming that you may want to take aspirin on occasion, but find that it upsets your stomach, we are including tips from survey participants about ways to minimize discomfort from the drug:

- Take buffered aspirin.

- Take aspirin with baking soda. Dissolve two tablets with one-third teaspoon of baking soda in eight ounces of water.*

- Take aspirin with an over-the-counter antacid.

- Ask your health-care practitioner about enteric-coated aspirin. The coating lets the aspirin pass through your stomach and into your small intestine, where it dissolves and is absorbed into your bloodstream.

- Take aspirin while sitting or standing rather than lying down. Remain upright for about two minutes. An upright position speeds the tablet's trip through the esophagus, thereby preventing irritation of this organ.

Prescription analgesics get results
but have their drawbacks.

Prescription analgesics (painkillers) are more effective for osteoarthritis than for other kinds of back pain. Twenty-five survey participants in this chapter took prescription painkillers—including Darvon®, Darvocet®, Equagesic®, codeine, and Tylenol®-codeine combinations. Here are the results:

Number of spinal osteoarthritis sufferers taking
prescription analgesics: 25

---

*This is a medically approved procedure if you're not on a low-salt diet and you don't take aspirin every day. If you take aspirin regularly, baking soda is not recommended. Its salt content is too high. And its alkalines can accumulate and reduce the amount of aspirin in the blood, according to Dr. Kevin Ivey, professor of medicine at the University of California, Irvine.

Relief:	12 (48%)
No relief:	11 (44%)
Adverse side effects:	2 (8%)

Any drug with codeine in it is potentially addictive. So it is important to note that only three of twenty-five survey participants took analgesics for more than a month at a time. Nausea and constipation were the two noted side effects.

Muscle-relaxant pills do little.

Muscle relaxants don't seem to have value for osteoarthritis-based back pain—or for any other kind of common back ailment for that matter.

Twelve of this chapter's survey participants took prescription muscle-relaxant pills, including Robaxin® and Parafon Forte®. The results are comparable to those reported by all ninety-five survey participants who took this type of medication:

Number of spinal osteoarthritis sufferers taking muscle relaxants:	12
Relief:	4 (33%)
No relief:	8 (67%)
Adverse side effects:	0

Traction usually does more harm than good.

It is highly doubtful that traction has medical value for osteoarthritis sufferers. And there's no doubt at all that traction caused more harm than any other treatment mentioned by survey participants.

Of the fifteen osteoarthritis-based back sufferers who had traction, five (33 percent) got temporary relief, five (33 percent) were made to feel worse, and five (33 percent) felt no change in their conditions.

"Allowing me to just lie in bed and have a witch doctor apply essence of elephant toenails at least would not have made one of my hips go numb," commented an unemployed painter who regretted having had traction.

The most favorable comment about traction by an osteoarthritis sufferer came from a pet-obedience school owner: "Traction reduced my pain for a week, then I was right back where I started."

Massage gets few raves
from survey participants.

In every category of back pain we have covered thus far, Swedish massage was effective at least for its relaxation value. And Shiatsu therapy got outstanding ratings for short-term relief, with some promise of lasting results. However, there is no indication that any form of massage is worthwhile for helping spinal osteoarthritis pain.

Of the eight survey participants with this problem who tried Swedish massage, only two felt slight relief. And in no case was pain markedly eased.

None of the five who tried acupressure and other forms of massage such as polarity and connective tissue massage reported any gains whatsoever.

Ultrasound holds some promise.

Ultrasound, diathermy, electric stimulation, TENS, heat lamps—do any benefit the osteoarthritis sufferer? Do any provide the temporary relief promised or implied by medical doctors and nonmedical doctors alike?

Based on the limited data in this research, the answer would seem to be, no, these devices are not really worth the bother, with one exception—ultrasound.

Of the eleven spinal osteoarthritis sufferers who had ultrasound treatments, six got some relief. The level of relief wasn't great enough to warrant your making trips to a practitioner's office for ultrasound alone. But it does appear that ultrasound is more likely than not to have value for you as part of a comprehensive recovery program.

Surgery may not be worth the risks.

As anyone reading this chapter knows, osteoarthritis is hardly the "minor aches and pains" ailment some people believe it to be. Several survey participants with osteoarthritis had disc degeneration, bone spurs, and other arthritis-related problems that put pressure on nerve roots—resulting in pain, disability, and questions about surgery.

The pros and cons of having ruptured disc surgery are relatively clear-cut. (See Chapters 6 and 11.) But the advantages and drawbacks of surgery for nerve compression caused by degenerative discs and bone spurs are far less obvious.

Five osteoarthritis sufferers in our survey had surgery. There was one striking success which transformed a patient's life, one case where the patient became worse as a result of surgery, and three cases where the survey participants themselves weren't sure whether surgery had done them any good.

Let's look at the two extremes:

Case 1: Osteoarthritis of the spine had increasingly disabled a 39-year-old man who worked as a trucker and loader. Over a period of years, he had been treated by a general practitioner, a physical therapist, and a chiropractor. An orthopedist then pinpointed his problem as degenerative arthritis, with a bone spur and segments of broken disc causing excruciating sciatica pain. The orthopedist referred the patient to a neurosurgeon, who corrected the problem by surgically removing the bone spur and shattered disc.

"The neurosurgeon was my salvation," the trucker told us. "The operation provided me with the first relief from years of agonizing and sometimes paralyzing pain. I can only recommend seeing the appropriate specialists who can correct the problem, rather than waste time, money, and prolong the agony like I did."

Happily, judging from research published in medical journals, this success is not a rare, isolated instance. Numerous similar cases have been reported.

Case 2: A 58-year-old housewife had basically the same diagnosis as the trucker mentioned above—disc degeneration as well as bone spurs that were putting pressure on her sciatic nerve. After seeing orthopedists, a neurologist, a rheumatologist, and a chiropractor—and becoming increasingly incapacitated with pain—she agreed to have exploratory surgery to see if the nerve pressure could be relieved.

The surgery wasn't successful. There was no relief. In fact, the pain seemed worse after surgery. "I suffered terribly after surgery," this woman told us. "I have been on strong pain medication and a tranquilizer for the past five years. I have bought everything on the market trying to get rid of pain. I still suffer each day when I walk, sit, or stand."

What conclusions can we reach about the role of surgery in helping spinal osteoarthritis?

Nerve root pressure occasionally requires surgery. Crippling sciatica, caused by pressure from a bone spur, does not always respond to rest, medication, and physical therapy.

Rates of success are arguable. Differences in the kinds of surgery for osteoarthritis, and in the reported outcomes of these cases, make it impossible to give you a rule of thumb about the chances for a successful recovery.

If osteoarthritis is taken seriously at the outset, surgery can almost always be avoided. There is no question that osteoarthritis of the spine can cause severe impairment of normal functioning. But if the proven treatments and approaches discussed in this chapter are applied when symptoms first appear—and if activity and exercise are emphasized—there is almost never a need for surgery.

SELF-CARE

Exercise, though not a panacea, is essential.*

"I can't emphasize enough how important exercise is to anyone with osteoarthritis of the spine," an assistant museum curator told us.

A retired florist wrote: "Exercise does not make me feel better per se, but I believe that it prevents further deterioration and it also helps me to live as actively as possible."

"Exercise therapy recently reaggravated my problem and caused me a lot of discomfort," commented a real estate agent.

The facts: two out of three survey participants with osteoarthritis did back exercises regularly, and were helped by them. More important, four out of five survey participants with osteoarthritis did *some* form of exercise on a regular basis—with excellent results.

Unlike low back sufferers, osteoarthritis-based back sufferers who performed back exercises did *not* have a lower pain rating than those who shunned exercise. *Nevertheless, there is widespread agreement among spinal arthritis sufferers that back exercise helps them function better.*

For sure, you should do gentle stretching exercises. Survey participants found them essential for continued flexibility. And according to Dr. Lawrence E. Lamb, medical columnist, stretching exercises are important because many osteoarthritis deformities can be avoided by gently and regularly stretching each movable joint to its full range of motion.

The exercise routine outlined in Chapter 10 should suit your needs.

*Exercise is considered self-help therapy here, because only 20 percent of osteoarthritis-based back pain sufferers in our survey were *taught* what to do.

However, osteoarthritis sufferers we spoke to advise doing just *one* set of ten modified bent-knee sit-ups.

What other kinds of exercises should you do?

You should walk. Walking at least a mile a day helped eight out of eight survey participants make long-term progress.

You should swim. Five survey participants in this chapter swam at least fifteen minutes every other day. And all five were convinced that swimming, a nonweight-bearing exercise, was the ideal therapy for osteoarthritis sufferers.

Dr. James F. Fries, author of *Arthritis: A Comprehensive Guide*, points out that activities such as walking and swimming increase strength in the bones and ligaments around worn joints. Dr. Fries also believes that activity helps cartilage (which has no blood supply) to obtain the nourishment it needs to prevent deterioration.

Note: If you haven't had a thorough examination, the extent of your joint damage should be evaluated before you start any exercise program. And if your condition is severe, we strongly recommend trying to have an exercise program prescribed for you by a physiatrist or physical therapist.

Nutrition and vitamins: cures or quackery?

The Arthritis Foundation reports that for every dollar spent on research, $25 is spent on quackery—useless potions and devices that promise easy cures. Twelve survey participants with back pain from osteoarthritis were promised an end to their symptoms if they ingested—or stopped ingesting—certain foods, supplements, or vitamins.

All of these promised cures came from books, magazine articles, friends, or relatives. No practitioners were involved in "total cure" promises, although five chiropractors made dietary recommendations in their attempts to help osteoarthritis sufferers.

Only one survey participant with osteoarthritis-based back pain felt that a change in diet (taking a calcium supplement) had helped. Six participants were uncertain of the results, but reasoned that they were not doing themselves any harm. (See Chapter 7 for specifics.) An urban planner who took vitamin C said, "It's not just the old 'tiger's milk' crowd that believes in the curative powers of nutrition anymore. Remember that three winners of the Nobel Prize in medicine, including Linus Pauling, believe that megadoses of vitamins can be useful for many purposes. So maybe there is something to this, or maybe there will be someday."

Maybe, but there is no proof at present. And there is evidence from our survey that fad "arthritis diets" fraudulently raise hopes. Moreover, false promises about diets convinced a few survey participants that they no longer had to work at keeping fit or at controlling their symptoms.

TIPS FROM SURVEY PARTICIPANTS *

Know yourself well.

- Stay in touch with how you feel. Don't take your "mental temperature" all the time, and ignore minor aches and pains when you can. But slow down when you must.
- Find a middle ground between being Superman or Wonder Woman (doing everything yourself, no matter what the price) and being an invalid (letting every twinge stop you in your tracks).
- Keep a realistically positive attitude.
- Develop the capacity to distract yourself so that you can keep your mind off your pain until the pain really needs to be dealt with.
- Experiment with ways to better yourself mentally, spiritually, and physically to any degree possible . . . and try never to feel sorry for yourself.
- Work hard at making progress. And never give up!

Keep active.

- Warm up, start slowly, avoid sudden movements, and keep moving as much as possible throughout the day.
- Do daily back exercises that emphasize flexibility. (See Chapter 10.)
- Walk at least a mile every day, bicycle at least three miles every day, or swim a minimum of fifteen consecutive minutes three times a week.
- Keep active even while resting and relaxing by turning often to prevent stiffening.

---

*Listed according to frequency of mention. The most popular tips for all back sufferers are presented in Chapters 15 and 16.

Keep warm.

- Wear several layers of clothing during cold weather. Layers tend to keep you warmer, and you can always take off a layer or two if you're too warm.
- Use a space heater in the room where you spend most of your time. (To be on the safe side, and to conserve energy, turn off the heater when you leave the room and when you go to sleep.)
- Use an electric mattress cover. It keeps your body heated from underneath and can prevent morning stiffness.
- Use flannel sheets. They really do feel warmer than regular sheets.

Use heat therapeutically.

- Two warm baths a day—one in the morning to get started and one before bedtime to relax and loosen up—are of great value. Use warm rather than hot water, and soak for about twenty minutes. Long, hot soaks can tire, rather than relax, your muscles. (For tips on how to position yourself comfortably in the tub, see Chapter 15.)
- Use a heating pad. Some survey participants used heating pads for hours at a time, but most recommended no more than thirty minutes every two hours. If you are using a heating pad more than this, try reducing the amount of time. You may get more relief and have less fatigue.
- Don't spend a lot of money on heat-producing devices. None surpasses the tub or heating pad for effectiveness or affordability.

Get enough sleep and rest.

"My arthritis feels worse when I don't get enough sleep" and "Make sure you get enough rest" typify comments made by about half the survey participants covered in this chapter. In short, both exercise *and* rest are important. The resting position suggested the most is lying on a mat on the floor with a small pillow under your head and neck and two pillows under your knees. Sleeping positions are discussed in Chapter 9.

Keep your weight down.

Being overweight puts a strain on anyone's back. But spinal osteoarthritis sufferers mention the need to stay trim far more than any other group of back sufferers. Since the pain in your back is caused in large part by damage to weight-bearing joints, it makes sense that carrying less weight around could help your condition in the long run.

Look for ways to minimize stress.

Stress, according to survey participants, affects spinal osteoarthritis more than any other category of back pain except neck pain. Negative feelings about having a chronic disease associated with old age (although osteoarthritis is by no means limited to old age) are one factor. Having a disease for which there is no cure is another. "I concentrate on taking each day in a calmer way," commented a homemaker. "I try to get away now and then and ease up on worries and stress," said a shopkeeper. In general, most survey participants with osteoarthritis reduced stress simply by adding a few breaks to their daily routines. For tips on how to minimize stress, see "stress-reduction techniques" in the Index.

Ask questions about any medication prescribed for you.

"If an anti-inflammatory drug makes you feel worse, or has destructive long-term effects—and your doctor did not warn you about these possible effects—you are as much to blame as your doctor if you didn't ask questions or become informed on your own," observed an airline executive on the need to question any and all medications, be they prescription or over-the-counter.

According to our research, the odds are less than fifty-fifty that any drug except aspirin will help osteoarthritis pain. And there can be serious side effects from medication.

"After taking arthritis drugs for twenty-five years, I now have other critical medical problems, probably as a result of taking all these drugs," commented a practical nurse. She added, "I think it's high time that people stopped acting like children and started asking questions. I don't think that anyone should take any drug without first having information in writing about it and understanding what they need to know. Your doctor should provide this information. If you can't learn what you want from him, ask your druggist. If that fails, check one of the consumer guides on prescription drugs. If you still can't find out, don't take the drug."

Try using liniments.

Nine survey participants used liniments on their backs once or twice a day and got minor but welcome relief from pain.

There are no magic potions. All liniments produce a warm or glowing sensation that masks pain for a short time. Liniments also increase the flow of blood to the affected area and this seems to help. "Just the feeling of touch and warmth that you get from using a liniment makes you feel good," said an assistant chef. "Any other benefits are a bonus."

Ben-Gay® was the most popular liniment among survey participants. Mobisyl® was mentioned with great enthusiasm by three survey participants. Two others highly recommended Salon Pas®, a "wafer liniment" available in some health-food stores and Oriental food shops.

Wear a back support occasionally.

A corset, girdle, or specially fitted back brace was used by five of this chapter's survey participants. All found these devices helpful *if* used sparingly.

A babysitter's comment is typical: "If I know I'll have to be on my feet for more than a couple of hours being active with children, I wear a lumbar support. It reduces strain and has the added benefit of keeping the most painful part of my back warmer."

Try heel cushions.

Four survey participants with spinal osteoarthritis were helped by heel cushions. They used ready-made products available at drugstores—Dr. Scholl to name one. These people felt that heel cushions helped lessen walking's jarring effect on their spines.

Have an active sex life.

A drug company salesperson spoke for many spinal osteoarthritis sufferers about the benefits of regular sexual activity: "The 'old person' image associated with osteoarthritis is depressing enough. If this is accompanied by a reduction or absence of sexual activity, the negative psychological factors you suffer will probably literally make you feel like you're in more pain.

"Aches and pains, if they're not severe, shouldn't stop anyone from having sex," he continued. "You need it to feel whole, to have a better sense about yourself. Stay within your limitations, and the gentle rocking motions of sex will do wonders for your body and your mind."

TWO SPECIAL PLEAS FROM SURVEY PARTICIPANTS

If you need professional care, insist on being a partner in that care.

If you can talk to your health-care practitioner, and can feel like an equal in making choices about your case, you have the best possible chance of keeping osteoarthritis from limiting your activities.

"The role of interpersonal relationships between doctor and patient is more important than the medical society realizes," noted an editorial researcher. "The practice of medicine is impersonal, and that single factor has much to do with why people are not 'learning to live with arthritis.' "

Survey participants make it clear that if osteoarthritis were treatable primarily by medical means—drugs and surgery, for example—rapport between patient and doctor would be a nice fringe benefit, but one that patients could do without. This is not the case, however.

"We are people, not just cases," a farmer with spinal osteoarthritis said. "We need things that doctors often choose not to give: physical therapy, emotional therapy, and just the hope and optimism you feel when someone cares about you. On the other hand, maybe it would be more realistic to try to 'solve' this problem by changing our expectations of doctors. Let's just expect them to deal with technical matters and let's realize that most of us need other kinds of help, much of which we ourselves can provide."

Avoid the "I give up" syndrome.

Based on our survey data, we estimate that one out of five spinal osteoarthritis sufferers has, for the most part, given up. The reliance of these people on drugs that fail them—and their discouragement when so-called miracle remedies don't work—leaves them feeling defeated. Here are some conclusions:

A housewife: "I am 64 years old and can't expect any change."

A retired person: "Nothing can be done to help me, except maybe one thing. I have in my possession a diet which cures people of arthritis. Maybe some day I can afford to buy all the things in this diet. It's my only hope."

A night watchman: "There is no cure for arthritis at this time, so I suppose there's nothing I can do."

It is easy for well-wishers to say, "Don't quit." But it is a fact, documented in this chapter and in other research, that osteoarthritis sufferers can do much to combat this degenerative disorder.

SUMMARY OF TREATMENTS AND PRACTITIONERS FOR OSTEOARTHRITIS-BASED BACK PAIN

Best practitioners for osteoarthritis-based back pain

(1) Physiatrist

(2) Physical therapist

(3) Rheumatologist

Practitioners worth a try for osteoarthritis-based back pain

(1) Yoga instructor

(2) Physical fitness instructor

(3) Kinesiologist

Widely seen practitioners who sometimes make spinal osteoarthritis sufferers feel worse

General practitioners

Best professional treatments for osteoarthritis-based back pain

(1) Physical therapy, emphasizing proper movements and activities

(2) Individualized exercise instruction

Professional treatments worth trying for osteoarthritis-based back pain

(1) Yoga

(2) Tai Chi

Widely used treatments best avoided for osteoarthritis-based back pain

(1) Prescription anti-inflammatory drugs (unless there is concrete evidence of inflammation)

(2) Traction

(3) Muscle-relaxant drugs

Best self-help therapies for osteoarthritis-based back pain

(1) Walking

(2) Swimming

(3) Daily back exercises

(4) Stress reduction

(5) Heat therapy

(6) Adequate sleep and rest

(7) Weight reduction

(8) Heel cushions

Chapter 14

Advice from Survey Participants About Sciatica, Scoliosis, and Spondylolisthesis

The three categories of back pain covered in this chapter have little in common medically. What ties them together is the lack of reliable information about treatment—an even greater vacuum, judging from the comments of survey participants, than exists for other categories of back pain.

For example, sciatica is often caused by a structural anomaly, such as a ruptured or degenerated disc. However, *none* of the sciatica sufferers in this section was able to learn, with any degree of certainty, the cause of the pain.* All found the search for help slow and frustrating, waiting years to discover a pain-relieving approach.

Scoliosis sufferers have an equally difficult time finding information about how to relieve their pain, although they have little problem in getting a precise diagnosis. Why is there a lack of helpful advice? An auto mechanic in our survey spoke for many scoliosis sufferers when he said, "There is a great deal that can be done. But the attitude of many doctors seems to be

*Those survey participants with sciatica caused by a ruptured disc are included in Chapter 11. Those whose sciatica resulted from arthritis or degenerated discs are included in Chapter 13.

that nothing can be done unless you want to risk surgery. As for chiropractors, too many promise more than they can deliver."

Spondylolisthesis sufferers also encounter a lot of blank gazes and shrugs of the shoulders when seeking advice. "If you don't want surgery, then don't complain" was a comment heard by one survey participant.

The content in this chapter helps to fill the information gap about treating sciatica, scoliosis, and spondylolisthesis. In some instances, we do not have the statistically significant data needed to provide you with definite conclusions. However, even in these cases, you are likely to find value in the insights and suggestions of people with problems like yours.

SCIATICA

Sciatica is a knifelike pain running down your buttocks, down the back of your thigh, continuing into your calf, sometimes into your foot—and, at its worst, into every waking second of your day. It can be pain of a hellish quality—a bad toothache of your hind quarters and lower limbs. Caused by pressure on your sciatic nerve where it emerges from your spinal column, sciatica can also be crippling.

Ask the average doctor how to treat sciatica, and you will probably get a prescription drug and be told to rest. What you won't get, usually, is relief from your sciatica.

Turn to most books on back care, and you will learn that sciatica is typically caused by a ruptured disc. And if you don't have a ruptured disc? End of information.

Let's start by looking at five brief but representative cases of nonspecific sciatica, then proceed to suggestions, rules, and insights gleaned from these and other cases.

Case 1: Twenty-five years on the treatment treadmill without results

For twenty-five years, a 56-year-old wholesale jobber has struggled through painful and disabling episodes of sciatica—without ever finding a way to break this cycle. She has been treated by many practitioners, including an orthopedist (diagnosis: arthritis and calcification of the spine), a physical therapist (diagnosis: neuritis and sciatica), a chiropractor (diagnosis: pinched nerve and spinal curvature), and a GP (diagnosis: neurotic).

Cortisone made her feel depressed. Motrin®, a prescription anti-inflammatory drug, gave her gastrointestinal problems. Chiropractic manipulation was "helpful but short-term." This survey participant regularly practices yoga, which she taught herself from a book. No exercise program has ever been prescribed or recommended for her.

Conclusion: Although the self-taught yoga therapy helps a bit, no treatment has brought about substantial long-term gains.

Case 2: Individualized exercise therapy restores full activity.

A 61-year-old writer had chronic back pain for more than two decades. The pain was manageable, but then it became crippling when accompanied by "pins and needles and agonizing pain in my legs and sharp muscle spasms in my back." Feeling no better after treatments from two orthopedists and a neurosurgeon—all of whom felt that he needed surgery for degenerative discs—the patient sought help from a physiatrist. "He recommended a course of treatment which included electric muscle stimulation, a trigger-point injection, and an exercise program. The exercise program really did the trick. I suggest that most sciatica sufferers get into the hands of a good physiatrist and physical therapist. I believe I would still have a severe problem if it were not for the wonderful treatment I received."

Conclusion: "After eight years I have very little pain, often none at all. It is necessary to do *recommended exercises.*"

Case 3: Disabled by inappropriate exercises . . . then helped by the right ones

The orthopedist who first saw this 28-year-old artist told him his problem was "psychosomatic." A second orthopedist said there was "nothing to worry about." A third orthopedist told the patient he had a ruptured disc. "A prescription of 'back arches' (lying on my stomach and raising my chest and legs) from this orthopedist seemed to lead from mild lower back and leg sensations to such pain that I literally could not walk." Another orthopedist prescribed two and a half months of bed rest, which started to alleviate the pain. Then pelvic tilts, mild stretching exercises, and swimming brought about slow but major improvement.

Conclusion: "One must learn his own exercise needs and limitations and individualize a program accordingly. What aggravates my problem does not bother my friends who have comparable back pain. My pain often increases when I push exercise too far."

Case 4: The patient's own good judgment proves crucial.

Four orthopedists attributed this 35-year-old law student's sciatica to a "minor but inoperable disc protrusion in the lumbar region." Not one of the doctors, however, spelled out a comprehensive recovery program. The patient then went to a private sports rehabilitation clinic, where he was advised to take two aspirins a day. The aspirin was useless. However, the patient did eventually recover. He attributes his success to: (1) swimming three-quarters of a mile per week ("Swimming is the only safe form of exercise I can indulge in. When I miss more than two or three days, my back tightens up noticeably."); (2) a series of stretching exercises prescribed by a chiropractor; (3) a change of attitude ("In general I try to take things a little easier. I slow down or rest when I am fatigued, and spend more time standing or walking rather than sitting for long periods of time.").

Conclusion: Professional input helped some, but in the final analysis, the patient used his own judgment to shape an exercise program and a lifestyle that assured him long-term progress.

Case 5: Individualized rehabilitation comes to the rescue.

A 31-year-old restaurant worker with sciatica saw a group of doctors at a major medical college. A neurologist there diagnosed her problem as "perhaps disc" and an orthopedist called it "muscle sprain." Treatment consisted of "some pills—muscle relaxers." According to this survey participant: "The neurologist and the orthopedist sent me back and forth, suggesting the need for time, surgery, etc." The patient later saw a chiropractor, who reported "a misaligned vertebra putting pressure on a nerve root and disc." Massage, whirlpool, and electric muscle stimulation helped in the short run. An individualized exercise program, prescribed by the chiropractor, finally turned things around for this woman. Her severe pain is gone; she experiences only occasional discomfort.

Conclusion: Once pain subsides, a comprehensive and appropriate exercise program for each individual is the key to success.

Three important conclusions

(1) The dismissal by most doctors of sciatica as something caused by a ruptured disc—and treatable solely by rest or surgery—leaves sciatica sufferers in the lurch. If a disc problem *isn't* found, some doctors are quick to label the patient neurotic. The label seems unfair. Slightly more than one-third of all participants in this survey had some sciatica at some point. And the majority of these individuals did not have a confirmed diagnosis involving a disc problem. It would seem that doctors sometimes explain the unexplainable by blaming the patient.

(2) Exercise therapy—the right exercises at the right time—is crucial. The rate of injury from inappropriate exercises is higher for sciatica than for any other kind of back pain.

(3) The "pill-and-surgery" approach was unconstructive and frustrating for most survey participants with sciatica. Moreover, it caused people who were already in great pain to feel helpless and demoralized. But there are practitioners with a positive attitude about sciatica—and the skills to justify this attitude.

Who *can* help you?

The physiatrist is the only medical specialist we can recommend with confidence. Eight survey participants were treated by physiatrists, and all eight got long-term help. In contrast, only 20 percent of GP's, 20 percent of orthopedists, and 20 percent of neurosurgeons helped sciatica sufferers in the long run.

The cases we presented touched on the negatives of being treated for sciatica by most medical doctors. The following comment from a nurse offers a summary: "I don't know why I have sciatica. Spina bifida (a congenital defect of the spinal column), pinched nerve, muscle strain, and stress are but a few of the diagnoses I've received. What I haven't received is useful information. You see, doctors' egos can't take it when they don't know what is wrong. Therefore, in their minds, *you* are what is wrong. And, therefore, you are not worth treating, or else you're too much trouble to have to deal with. My advice for most sciatica sufferers: Stay away from most doctors."

In providing long-term help to six of eleven sciatica sufferers in our survey, the physical therapist stands out among nonmedical doctors. The Shiatsu therapist trained in exercise therapy may also be a good bet, promoting lasting recovery for three of six survey participants with sciatica.

To the modest extent that they are expert in the exercise rehabilitation process, chiropractors can help promote long-term results. Chiropractors helped thirteen out of forty-five (29 percent) of this survey's sciatica sufferers to improve substantially. In addition, twenty-one of forty-five sciatica sufferers got temporary relief through chiropractic care.

One final comment about chiropractic treatment for sciatica. In Chapter 11, we noted that manipulation for acute sciatica caused by a ruptured disc had an extremely high injury rate of 29 percent. But manipulation appears to be relatively safe and effective for sciatica that is *not* disc-related. The chiropractor's "made patient feel worse" rate for sciatica sufferers in this chapter is only 6.5 percent, compared with 7.5 percent for orthopedists.

The value—and risk—of exercise

Back exercises are essential. But you must proceed cautiously because injury from exercise is so common among sciatica sufferers.

It should encourage you to know that case after case of disabling sciatica improved when individualized exercise therapy was used as the major treatment after acute pain had eased. Virtually all these cases entailed guidance from an exercise expert, an individualized program, a conservative and progressive exercise sequence *that avoided single-leg raises (at least at first), double-leg raises, other straight-leg exercises, and full bent-knee sit-ups.*

Almost without exception, self-taught exercises are not as therapeutic as those worked out by you and an exercise expert. A physiatrist and physical therapist are your best bets. See page 66 for a list of other qualified exercise trainers.

A pianist who had sciatic nerve pain since age 15 made the point for professional exercise instruction: "I had tried back exercises on my own. They had worked, but not that well. The set of exercises I learned from a chiropractor are much more extensive and effective. The right exercises are the only sure way to help sciatica, except for ways to reduce stress. The chiropractor also urged me to ease up on jogging and to swim more."

A drummer agreed: "Nothing really worked except the back exercises prescribed by a physical therapist."

Exercises you see in the mass media are *not* for sciatica sufferers. "I do the exercises I see on TV," said a housewife, "but they make me worse. Some mornings I can hardly lift my legs." A survey participant on social security added, "I try to pick out exercises from magazine articles. But I keep being reinjured and it seems that nothing can help me."

Survey participants we spoke to agreed that the exercises outlined in Chapter 10 make up the kind of safe-not-sorry exercise program that can help a sciatica sufferer make meaningful progress in a few months' time.

Also, as noted in the case histories earlier in this chapter, swimming and walking are both highly recommended.

Other treatment approaches

- *Prescription drugs* taken by survey participants with sciatica failed to exceed the placebo level. Mild prescription analgesics, muscle relaxants, and anti-inflammatories don't usually help sciatica. Moreover, four of eight sciatica sufferers who took tranquilizers to lower the stress from their incapacitation reported adverse effects—the tranquilizers made them sleepy or distraught.

  We recommend one of two extremes: take aspirin for mild or moderate pain . . . or try to get a prescription for a strong analgesic to dull severe pain.
- *Heat* is usually soothing for sciatica. But for some people, heat makes an inflamed nerve *more* painful. Of seventeen sciatica sufferers in our survey, eleven benefited from heat and two reported that it made them feel worse.
- *Traction* carries considerable risk. Of the twelve sciatica sufferers who had traction, four felt worse. Of the remaining eight, four reported no change and four got temporary but not lasting relief.
- *Ice* eased pain for eight of ten sciatica sufferers. Three of these eight individuals used cold successfully, *after* heat applications, on small areas that remained painful after heat treatments.
- *Ultrasound*, which seemingly has no value for low back pain, brought temporary relief to four of eight sciatica sufferers.
- *Acupuncture* helped two of four sciatica sufferers. In one case cited earlier, ten treatments resolved more than two decades of intense pain.
- *Gravity inversion exercise* helped the three sciatica sufferers who tried it. See Chapter 7 for details, including a warning about unsupervised treatment for any painful back ailment.

• DMSO helped all three sciatica sufferers who used it. See Chapter 7 for further information.

SUMMARY OF TREATMENTS AND PRACTITIONERS FOR SCIATICA

Best self-help therapies for sciatica

(1) Swimming

(2) Walking

(3) Ice

(4) Heat

(5) Gravity inversion

Best professional treatments for sciatica

(1) Individualized back exercise therapy

(2) Shiatsu therapy

Professional treatments worth trying for sciatica

(1) Manipulation

(2) Gravity inversion

(3) Swedish massage

(4) Ultrasound

(5) Electric muscle-stimulation

Widely used treatments best avoided
for sciatica

(1) Prescription analgesics (except very strong ones in cases of severe pain), anti-inflammatories, muscle relaxants, tranquilizers

(2) Traction

Best practitioners for
sciatica

(1) Physiatrist

(2) Physical therapist

Practitioners worth trying for
sciatica

(1) Shiatsu therapist

(2) Chiropractor

(3) Acupuncturist

Widely seen practitioners who sometimes make
sciatica sufferers feel worse*

(1) Orthopedist

(2) GP

(3) Neurosurgeon

SCOLIOSIS

The information in this section focuses on practical approaches and therapies you can use to minimize or do away with back pain caused by scoli-

---

*The "feel worse" factor here stems from the practitioner's disinterest in seemingly intractable pain of unknown cause. Stated or implied accusations of neurosis, malingering, or hypochondria occur in about one out of three cases of chronic sciatica.

osis, a lateral (sideways) curvature of the spine that usually becomes apparent during pre-adolescence or adolescence. Our emphasis is on self-care. We do not have enough data from our research to pursue topics such as diagnostic testing, surgical implants and the desirability of surgery, corrective braces, or electric stimulation. Only two of the thirty-one survey participants in this section had surgery and only four used braces.

Scoliosis sufferers covered in this section had moderate to severe curvatures that were diagnosed by more than one practitioner as the cause of their back pain. Participants with minor scoliosis, which seemed not to be the cause of back pain, are not included here.

The question asked us most frequently by survey participants with scoliosis was, "Do you know what kind of practitioner can help?" (The most specific version of this question was, "Do chiropractors help?") We will begin by discussing the relative efficacy of widely seen practitioners, then explore professional treatments and self-help therapies.

Do chiropractors relieve scoliosis pain?

Please note that we are *not* addressing the question about whether chiropractors can *correct* scoliosis. *They cannot*, although some chiropractors promised to cure or correct scoliosis in a few survey participants.

The facts are clear.

Chiropractors treating scoliosis patients

Total:	31
Provided temporary relief:	9 (29%)
Provided moderate long-term improvement:	5 (16%)
Provided dramatic long-term improvement:	3 (10%)
Ineffective:	11 (35%)
Made patient feel worse:	3 (10%)

Chiropractors do provide some measure of relief 55 percent of the time, but the relief is mostly short-lived. Chiropractic manipulation, used alone, helped thirteen of twenty-seven patients in the short run. What helped in the long run was exercise therapy.

"My chiropractor says that manipulation will prevent scoliosis from worsening in the long run," said a tennis instructor. "But I have not found chiropractic manipulation to help."

"Chiropractic manipulation did nothing over the long run," said a student.

A fast-food restaurant employee concluded: "Manipulation gave very little help in the long run. Besides, the chiropractor proposed a long-range manipulation treatment at high cost, so I did not continue."

What level of temporary relief does chiropractic manipulation provide?

"A competent chiropractor can always get my back properly adjusted," said a microfilm technician. "Generally, one treatment a month is sufficient, although I have had periods where I needed an adjustment every day or so."

"The spinal adjustments helped a lot at first, but it seemed that I became dependent on the chiropractor," said a steel industry worker. "I got immediate relief but always began hurting again in a few days. Then it seemed that I hurt all the time anyway."

Added a gymnastics teacher: "The pain came back again in three hours." A warehouse worker: "Manipulation helped only temporarily, perhaps a day or two." And a retired painter: "Manipulation eliminates pain for days, but the pain always comes back."

Do orthopedists help?

Hardly ever—with the adult, nonsurgical cases covered in our data. They are much less effective than chiropractors. And the exercises they prescribed caused setbacks in three cases.

Orthopedists treating scoliosis patients

Total:	23
Provided temporary relief:	2 (9%)
Provided moderate long-term improvement:	1 (4%)
Provided dramatic long-term improvement:	2 (9%)
Ineffective:	15 (65%)
Made patient feel worse:	3 (13%)*

*These people were injured by prescribed back exercises.

Is *any* practitioner worth seeing?

Yes.

After unproductive years of seeing "mainstream" practitioners, twenty-two of thirty-one scoliosis sufferers in this section got long-term relief by receiving treatments from an alternative practitioner.

Practitioner	Number of scoliosis patients treated	Percentage who achieved long-term improvement
Yoga instructor	8	100
Physical therapist	7	57
Dance teacher	3	100
Tai Chi instructor	2	100
Naturopath	2	100

All these practitioners taught scoliosis sufferers gradual and graceful movements. And all kept morale high through heartening interpersonal skills.

Back exercises and scoliosis

Traditional back exercises seem to pose a greater than usual risk of injury to individuals with scoliosis. Of the twenty-two scoliosis sufferers who did back exercises regularly, six (27 percent) were injured by these exercises.

"The back exercises taught to me by an orthopedist were difficult for me to keep up," said a photographer. "They have caused recurrences of injury."

An editor who learned exercises from a popular back book commented, "I am still unsure about the advisability of back exercise. I don't know if stretching helps or hurts, although the books say that flexibility is important, and that is probably true. But stretching seems to be hard to do gently and correctly (for me anyway). I tend to overdo and my body reacts with a sore back."

A housewife expressed a more positive, more popular attitude about back exercises: "Back exercises are valuable, but they don't seem to work as well for me as for people I know who have 'regular' low back pain. And they don't provide the advantages of other forms of exercise—swimming, yoga, or Tai Chi."

In contrast with other kinds of back sufferers, survey participants with scoliosis had better luck exercising *without* professional input. These individuals also avoided all exercises that caused them discomfort—no matter how conservative and "universally safe" the exercises were reputed to be. Finally, most scoliosis sufferers who were successful with back exercises did *other* forms of exercise as well, such as swimming or bicycling.

Since back exercises help twice as many scoliosis sufferers (50 percent) as they injure, should *you* try them? We're going to hedge by saying that if yoga appeals to you, practice yoga instead. Otherwise, try the exercises in Chapter 10. But discontinue any and all of these exercises if you feel even the slightest bit worse.

Yoga: perhaps every scoliosis sufferer should try it.

Eight scoliosis sufferers practiced yoga regularly, and all eight found it helpful—more helpful than traditional back exercises.

"Yoga has done wonders for my back and well-being," a ceramic artist told us. "I used to be in pain almost constantly and now it is rare that my back hurts—just when I am overtired."

"The joy of discovering yoga is indescribable," a teacher commented. "I have been to dozens of doctors, all the top specialists, and then some. Now even the doctors in my family are believers."

These eight individuals got personal instruction from a professional. See Chapter 4 for information on how to select a yoga instructor.

Other helpful exercises

There is every indication that scoliosis sufferers who give their bodies a constructive workout every day have the least pain and lead the fullest lives. Swimming was as effective as yoga for eight survey participants. Walking and bicycling each helped five scoliosis sufferers. Dance helped three. Tai Chi and jogging each helped two. And, remarkably, *all* these activities, including yoga, helped every scoliosis sufferer in this survey—without exception. Moreover, scoliosis sufferers who had the most dramatic recoveries from severe and chronic pain participated regularly *in at least two activities*, such as yoga *and* swimming.

Tips from survey participants

Note: The order below reflects the frequency with which topics were mentioned.

(1) "Give your body a good physical workout every day. Be an athlete. There is no better answer for scoliosis pain."

(2) "Rest when the pain gets bad, because this will actually allow you more total active time than if you keep going until you drop."

(3) "Wet heat of any kind—bath, shower massage, whirlpool, Jacuzzi, hydrocollator—usually gives temporary relief."

(4) "Avoid favoring one side by shifting your weight from one leg to the other when you're standing still, by not overemphasizing one-sided sports like golf and by using light weights to help balance muscles."

(5) "Even when your back hurts, and all you want to do is sit in the most comfortable chair you have, sit for only twenty minutes to a half hour and then move around for ten minutes."

(6) "Don't listen to predictions from doctors about whether you'll have trouble delivering babies."

(7) "Don't agree to surgery just because you're told how much worse you'll be in ten years. No one but God knows that. And it isn't that you *have* to become worse."

SUMMARY OF TREATMENTS AND PRACTITIONERS FOR SCOLIOSIS

Best self-help therapies for scoliosis pain

(1) Yoga*

(2) Swimming

(3) Walking

(4) Bicycling

(5) Individualized back exercise instruction

---

*Professional yoga instruction is recommended, but most scoliosis sufferers in our survey believe that self-taught yoga is better than no yoga at all.

Best professional treatment
for scoliosis pain

Yoga instruction

Professional treatments worth trying
for scoliosis pain

(1) Dance

(2) Tai Chi

(3) Individualized back exercise instruction*

Widely used treatments best avoided
for scoliosis pain

No significant data

Best practitioner for
scoliosis pain

Yoga instructor

Practitioners worth a try for
scoliosis pain

(1) Dance instructor

(2) Tai Chi instructor

(3) Physical therapist

(4) Chiropractor

Widely seen practitioners who sometimes make
scoliosis sufferers feel worse

No significant data. It should be noted, though, that orthopedists are of almost no value to adult scoliosis sufferers who are not candidates for corrective braces or surgery. On the other hand, research elsewhere suggests that

---

*Caution: One in two survey participants with scoliosis was helped in the long run by traditional back exercises—but one in four was injured.

youngsters with signs of developing scoliosis should be treated by an orthopedist.

SPONDYLOLISTHESIS

The popular phrase "slipped disc" to the contrary, discs cannot slip. But vertebrae can. Hence the term "spondylolisthesis," derived from the Greek words for vertebra and slip. A vertebra, usually the lowest lumbar vertebra (L5), slips down to the uppermost position of the sacrum, pulling the upper spine downward in the process. Minimally, this slippage exerts great strain on your back muscles. It can also cause nerve compression and sciatica.

Spondylolisthesis is easier to diagnose than to pronounce, as it is one of the relatively few back ailments that can be spotted on conventional X rays. It is difficult to treat, however, since the slippage of the spine plays havoc with the back muscles.

Still, there are more successes than failures—albeit very hard-earned successes—among the ten survey participants with spondylolisthesis. These ten cases obviously cannot support definite conclusions, but the comments and suggestions have significant value. As one spondylolisthesis sufferer put it, "I don't know of anyone with a problem like mine. I wish I did, so I at least could compare notes. I'm sure people with spondylolisthesis could learn a lot from each other."

To enable you to hear from other spondylolisthesis sufferers, we will highlight each case, then provide a summary of findings.

Case 1

Age at diagnosis: 21

Current age: 51

Occupation: Lawyer

Practitioners: Chiropractor, orthopedist, physical therapist

Treatments: Manipulation, physical therapy emphasizing exercise training, back brace, shoe lift to correct pelvic tilt, bed board, changed daily habits—including proper lifting and sleeping in the fetal position

Treatment results: "Manipulation helped very little; shoe lift helped considerably; exercise program—prescribed by orthopedist and taught by physical therapist—helped dramatically."

Helpful hints: "Sleep on side in fetal position on a firm mattress and bed board. Bend your knees when you sneeze. Crouch, don't bend, to pick up objects from the floor. Lift carefully with your legs and arms, not your back. Reduce weight of objects lifted or weight carried if possible. Exercise to strengthen abdomen. Lose weight."

Emotional factors: "I'm a relaxed person. However, any substantial tension, rare as that is with me, seems to focus on my weak spot, i.e., lower back."

Outcome: "Ninety-five-percent cured ten years ago . . . no problem since except occasional low back twinge."

Case 2

Age at diagnosis: 24

Current age: 26

Occupation: Retail store employee

Practitioners: Three orthopedists, two neurosurgeons, two GP's, one chiropractor

Treatments: Exercise therapy, traction, ultrasound, massage, manipulation, muscle-relaxant drugs

Treatment results: "Manipulation worsened my condition. Traction helped temporarily, as did ultrasound and massage. The muscle relaxants helped, but side effects were bad so I quit taking them. Exercise, learned mostly from my own research, helped greatly."

Comment: "All doctors except a GP and a neurosurgeon treated me coldly."

Helpful hints: "Exercise is a must—walking, swimming, and back exercises in particular. Also, two to three grams of vitamin C daily help me."

Emotional factors: "Stress is a factor. In this area, though, for the most part, doctors did more harm to me than good."

Outcome: Functional, with pain mostly under control.

Case 3

Age at diagnosis: 55

Current age: 58

Occupation: Homemaker

Practitioners: Orthopedist, physical therapist, acupuncturist

Treatments: Traction for six weeks, physical therapy including exercise instruction, TENS used for two months, back support worn for two months, acupuncture

Treatment results: "The bed rest and traction helped me as far as standing straight. But after all the therapy, bed rest, and traction, I still was not able to sit. The acupuncturist, after the first treatment, helped me. I had to go only about ten times. Exercise, a combination of back exercise and yoga, is also useful."

Comment: "For years I did not listen to my body. I tried ignoring certain signs. When on my feet for a prolonged time or doing heavy work, there was burning in the thighs and pain in the calves. I now know one thing if nothing else—I listen to my body and back off and rest when it starts to act up."

Helpful hints: "Listen to your body."

Emotional factors: None.

Outcome: Fully functional with some pain.

Case 4

Age at diagnosis: 21

Current age: 26

Occupation: Electric utility manager

Practitioners: Chiropractor, orthopedist

Treatments: Prescription drugs, exercise, back brace, diathermy, electric muscle stimulation

Treatment results: "Chiropractic treatments felt okay for a while but really didn't do much. The orthopedist, through the use of a back brace and exercise instruction, really helped."

Comment: "The orthopedist was correct in his diagnosis and treatment. The chiropractor didn't know what he was talking about." (Author's note: The chiropractor's diagnosis was lateral curvature of back.)

Helpful hints: "Keep good posture and maintain your center of gravity when lifting objects."

Emotional factors: "My back sometimes gets worse when I am under stress. Stress was not mentioned to me in a constructive way by either practitioner."

Outcome: Active and relatively pain-free.

Case 5

Age at diagnosis: 21

Current age: 61

Occupation: Not stated

Practitioners: Four orthopedists, neurosurgeon, physical therapist

Treatments: Physical therapy including exercise training, prescription drugs including Indocin®, and Clinoril®, surgical procedures including spinal fusions and a "stepladder" inserted in the spine, ultrasound, TENS

Treatment results: "Three spinal fusions did not work. The fourth one—involving the insertion of a 'stepladder'—worked very well. None of the treatments injured me. I could not tolerate Indocin® or Clinoril®. The TENS unit works well for me."

Helpful hints: TENS therapy

Emotional factors: "Stress affects my back."

Outcome: Somewhat incapacitated with persistent pain.

Case 6

Age at diagnosis: 10

Current age: 55

Occupation: Unable to work; disabled from spondylolisthesis

Practitioners: GP, chiropractor, osteopath, orthopedist, gynecologist

Treatments: Anti-inflammatory drugs, physical therapy, exercise (walking), heat, electric muscle stimulation, massage

Treatment results: "What helps me the most is the heat and massage and electric stimulation from the chiropractor. I have been seeing him for eight years. The prescription drugs were not effective."

Comment: "The chiropractor has helped me very much. When I first went to him I couldn't hold my head up. Now I can turn it from side to side, and the chiropractor is keeping me walking. He calls it maintaining me."

Helpful hints: "Keep moving."

Emotional factors: "I was told that I was a mental case and that there was nothing wrong with me. One thing that was wrong was a large tumor that had to be removed."

Outcome: Poor. The patient is disabled.

Case 7

Age at diagnosis: 22

Current age: 28

Occupation: Student

Practitioners: Orthopedist, physical therapist, chiropractor, Alexander instructor, Feldenkrais instructor, Rolfer

Treatments: Manipulation, Alexander technique instruction, Feldenkrais instruction, Rolfing, physical therapy

Treatment results: "Alexander technique helped the most. Physical therapy made no difference. Rolfing hurt me and set back my gains (in terms of pain) months from what I had achieved from the Alexander work. Needless to say, I discontinued Rolfing after two treatments."

Comment: "The Alexander instructor was the only one who looked at my body as a whole. He was also the only one who gave me the responsibility of working things out myself with the proper input."

Helpful hints: "Making love loosens up the hips. Try to do things an easier way, rather than straining your back when it is not necessary to."

Emotional factors: "My back pain is worse when I'm under stress."

Outcome: Functions well with a minimum of pain.

Case 8

Age at diagnosis: 24

Current age: 28

Occupation: Not stated

Practitioners: Five GP's, chiropractor

Treatments: Ice, heat, exercise, drugs—Valium®, Darvocet®, Equagesic®, Soma®

Treatment results: "The exercises and muscle relaxants were most effective. None of the other treatments mattered."

Comment: "I went to four doctors complaining of back pain before one took me seriously. By that time, I was almost crawling. The doctor X-rayed my back, gave me exercises to do, and explained that the problem is progressive and that exercise minimizes or stops the progression. About six months later I went to a chiropractor who would not accept the X rays taken by the doctor (pecuniary reasons I suspect). I didn't continue with the chiropractor."

Outcome: Fully active with some chronic pain.

Case 9

Age at diagnosis: 26

Current age: 33

Occupation: Sales representative

Practitioners: GP, chiropractor, yoga instructor

Treatments: Traction, manipulation, ultrasound, prescription muscle relaxants, yoga

Treatment results: "Yoga worked best—it is tremendously effective and, in my opinion, more effective than regular back exercises. The muscle relaxants were useless. I received just the tiniest amount of assistance from the chiropractor and stopped seeing him after six visits."

Comment: "In the long run, it is imperative that you see somebody who actually knows more than you do about exercise and rehabilitation. In my case I saw a yoga instructor who understood back problems. It should be obvious to all back sufferers that the average doctor, and chiropractor for that matter, knows less about exercise than the average well-informed back sufferer."

Helpful hints: "A cautious, progressive, and complete exercise program."

Emotional factors: None.

Outcome: A complete success with minor lower back ache when tired.

Case 10

Age at diagnosis: 38

Current age: 44

Occupation: Professor

Practitioners: Chiropractor, massage therapist, physical therapist, GP, psychologist

Treatments: Chiropractic manipulation, massage, electric muscle stimulation, moist heat, ultrasound, back brace ("Warm and Form" belt), muscle relaxants, anti-depressants, biofeedback

Treatment results: "Different treatments helped at different times. At first, bed rest, aspirin, moist heat, and muscle relaxants (Parafon Forte®) worked. Later, intense massage helped, although after a while it began to feel too intense and was stopped. Chiropractic did no harm but seemed not very effective. Physical therapy has been the best bet, particularly the combination of ultrasound for getting heat in deep to affected muscles, a 'Warm and Form' back brace to help stabilize the L5/S1 vertebral joint, and a regular routine of gentle exercises (e.g., knee to chest and pelvic tilt ˛while lying flat on the floor). I have been wearing the back brace now for almost two years with good results, keeping it on when I am at work and any time when I sit for extended periods (meals, driving, movies, etc.).

"The effectiveness of drugs has been mixed, and I think my GP was too ready to prescribe new and powerful drugs. Some that he has prescribed have very unpleasant effects. Ironically, it was for a newly discovered side effect that he prescribed an anti-depressant, because it has been found that this drug also helps irritated nerves and nerve roots. This is true, but the drug's main effect was to make me very dopey. Parafon Forte® seemed effective but not to a very noticeable degree. The trouble with a relaxant is that it does not relax just your back but everything else, too. I think such medications are desirable right after an injury or reinjury when you don't mind being knocked out. Otherwise, my experience is that it is best to trust your own resources for relaxing and avoiding stress."

Comment: "Understanding friends and family are an immense help. My experience is often one of isolation in my contacts with the medical profession, the result of the widespread attitude that medicine means treating an illness rather than a person. To counter this, I believe that back sufferers could help one another a lot by sharing their experience. I know I would like very much to talk with people who have had, or still have, conditions like mine. If enough people join together in this kind of sharing, I think the benefits would be immense for everyone."

Helpful hints: "Everybody's lower back problem is different. But I think every back sufferer has to face up to some hard facts: (1) No matter what the problem is, it requires continuous care, not just when it hurts. (2) It means change, sometimes drastic, in one's self-image—I went through a period of intense mourning for myself and my body. (3) And it means struggle—not in the ordinary sense that more work, more activity and effort will overcome the problem, but just the opposite: a struggle to combat and reverse macho, workaholic, self-driven ideas about what one can and must do, ideas that probably were important causes of the back problem in the first place. High on the list of such inappropriate ideas I would put the assumption that one can just go to the hospital for a quick fix and then go back to a life of business as usual."

Emotional factors: "Stress plays a role in my back pain."

Outcome: Functional with considerable pain and effort.

Summary of findings

As we mentioned earlier, our data for spondylolisthesis are not statistically significant. However, tentative conclusions about practitioner and treatment effectiveness—based on the ten cases above—are of value.

Widely seen practitioners: Orthopedists were seen the most frequently, and their effectiveness in promoting long-run progress was good—better, in fact, than their record in helping any other kind of back pain except spinal osteo-arthritis. Judging from the comments of spondylolisthesis sufferers, the reason for this seems to be that spondylolisthesis (like osteoarthritis) can be seen on X rays, hence is taken more seriously by orthopedists.

Chiropractors weren't of much help. And only two of ten diagnosed the problem correctly.

GP's were of little help, relying mostly on prescription drugs that seldom helped and sometimes had adverse effects.

Physical therapists had the most success in helping spondylolisthesis sufferers. The best results of all were obtained when a physical therapist worked with an exercise-oriented orthopedist.

Widely used treatments: Manipulation was of virtually no value. Drugs of all kinds were of little use, although muscle-relaxant drugs used during bed rest helped to some extent.

Individualized exercise training was crucial to recovery. Only one survey participant with spondylolisthesis was able to recover without making back exercise part of his life.

Back supports were helpful to all five participants who used them.

Deep forms of massage—other than Swedish and Shiatsu—were injurious and probably should be avoided.

Traction helped two incapacitated patients to get back on their feet.

Part Five
Self-Healing

"We feel it is the consumers' responsibility to inform themselves about their own care."

—Patricia Phelan, Director,
Planetree Health Resource Center

"Ultimately, nobody can do as much for your back condition as you can do for it."

—A survey participant

Chapter 15

The Twenty-Five Most Often-Mentioned, Proven-Effective Ways to Free Yourself of Back Pain

Our questionnaire asked survey participants, "Do you have any 'helpful hints' or home remedies for other back sufferers?"

Almost everyone had something to say. Comments ranged from the important but commonplace—advice about lifting, posture, sitting, and exercise—to the unusual but important—have your leg length measured to see if a shoe insert is needed—to the frustrated—"Everyone gives advice, but it's impossible to know which to follow"—to the desperate—"No, I have no advice, but I pray that you have some for me."

We do have advice—the twenty-five most popular and proven suggestions from the 492 participants in our survey. And to our satisfaction, almost everyone agreed about the points that we cover in this chapter.

This near-unanimity is important, as it does *not* exist among back practitioners. Even if you have seen some of these tips covered in self-help books, you may have had trouble judging their significance—figuring out how much emphasis you should give them, or how you should think about them. The advice in this chapter is different. It combines the mechanics of back care—correct posture when you stand or sit, for example—with the perspective you need to make each tip work for you.

1. The most frequently mentioned helpful hint involves an intangible: attitude.

Your attitude about your body is the basis for improvement. A college professor summred up the feelings of hundreds of survey participants about the importance of attitude when he said, "In order to get rid of back pain, you have to be willing to learn and unlearn. You need to be receptive to looking at new ways to do things that have become ingrained over your entire lifetime. This is as much a matter of attitude as of mechanics, because attitude determines whether or not you will learn and apply what you need to know to reduce or eliminate back pain.

"You can have the best exercise instruction in the world," the professor added. "But only you can ultimately decide whether to exercise, and how much, and at what pace—and whether certain exercises just aren't right for you. You can buy yourself the best chair ever made for back sufferers, and then sit in it for three hours at a time, even though you know that taking a break every half hour is the only way to keep your back pain-free. You can consult gurus galore about stress and then blow it all simply by not being in touch with yourself, by not even being aware that you are under stress."

The point is well made. You have to know yourself. You have to be sensitive to your condition. Then, and only then, can you learn to beat back pain. This isn't to say that self-awareness can cure you, but if you're not aware of how you feel, then you can't make decisions about what you must do to maintain back fitness.

2. When lifting, bend at the knees, not at the waist.

Survey participants were adamant about lifting properly. They talked more about this activity than about exercise, posture, or any other physical aspect of promoting back fitness. Here are pointers for lifting all sorts of objects:

- Bend at the knees to pick up anything, whether it's as light as a tissue or as heavy as a baby or a potted plant.

- If it's difficult for you to squat, or to get back up, place a chair or stepladder near you and lean one hand on it for support. Keep your back straight when doing this.

- Use a mechanical "grabber" to retrieve light objects—anything from a pen to a magazine to a small book—from the floor or high shelves. (The Reach It—now called the E-Z Reach—available through the mail from Colonial Garden Kitchens, is recommended by survey participants, as it is less expensive than many other grabber devices, lightweight, and durable.)

- Keep the object you're lifting as close to your body as possible.

- When lifting a heavy object, if possible, turn your back to it and extend your arms behind you.

- Instead of lifting and carrying something heavy, see whether you can slide it to its destination. If so, turn your back to the object and pull it as you would a wheelbarrow. Don't push it with your foot or leg. And don't pull it toward you while facing it.

- Ask yourself whether the object to be lifted really has to be lifted by you. If there is doubt, ask for help.

See pages 157–160 for additional information about lifting.

3. Change your sleeping arrangements to suit your back.

As the saying goes, you spend a third of your life in bed. So it isn't surprising that your sleeping arrangements can have a great impact on your back.

Keep in mind the following recommendations from a majority of survey participants:

Even if your mattress is firm, use a bed board. The best kind comes from a lumberyard and is cut from ¾-inch plywood.

Sleeping in a bed away from home is particularly troublesome. To prevent problems when you travel, carry along a portable bed board. Some furniture stores sell them, or consult a specialist medical or back shop. Internet sites such as www.backsaver.com are also worth checking.

Some survey participants travel with their regular bed boards loaded on top of their cars. Others reserve rooms at hotels or motels where bed boards are supplied on request. If all else fails, and you feel you're in for a bad night, slide the mattress off the bed—or ask a bellhop to do it for you– and sleep on the floor.

No matter how much support your bed gives you, though, you have to position yourself to take advantage of this support. About three-quarters of survey participants do this by sleeping on their sides. The remainder sleep on their backs with pillows under their knees.

See Chapter 9 for additional information on mattresses and how to get in and out of bed without aggravating your back.

4. Learn how to sit . . . and how much to sit.

The best sitting apparatus ever invented is a combination of a place to rest yourself and the knowledge and awareness you carry around with you. Even though you have the finest chair available, all is for naught if you don't get up and stretch instead of trying to sit through an aching back. All is for naught if you don't get up and get that footstool from across the room, sit up straight, and avoid crossing your legs. The potential for harm from bad sitting habits is tremendous.

Always sit on a firm seat. Too soft and your back will feel the strain. Too hard, like uncovered wood or metal, and you can literally get a pain in the rear.

If your chair seat is too soft, a piece of plywood covered with foam will firm it up. Or you can buy a seat cushion to keep you from sinking into soft chairs or sofas. They are obtainable from specialist medical and back shops or Internet sites.

Use a back support. Office chairs are usually the only ones that come with built-in lumbar supports. If you use an office chair, make sure its support fits your back, for unless the back of the chair is adjustable, the lumbar support is likely to be too low for you. Also, make sure that the back of the chair does not tilt *until* and *unless* you want it to.

With most other chairs, you need to supply your own back support. Following are some of the products that meet this need. Several different manufacturers now make back support aids, so shop around for the product that matches your needs and pocketbook.

- Lumbar cushions were mentioned by the largest number of survey participants. These moulded cushions are designed to fit the contours of your lumbar spine. They are usually lightweight, comfortable, have removable and/or washable covers, and can easily be taken to luncheons, meetings and shows. Various makes and models are available from medical and back shops and from Internet sites.
- "Collapsible" cushions are available in a variety of shapes and sizes, if a cushion is needed that will fit into an attaché case or overstuffed suitcase. The better sort inflate with a detachable hand bulb rather than by mouth.
- If a chair has the kind of back that your back dreads—curved or without much to hold you up—then one of the many adjustable back supports may work where other cushions don't. These are designed to act as a substitute for the kind of chair back you need. Depending on the make and model, they may come with attachment straps, attachable cushions for the small of the back and shoulder area, and a choice of washable fabrics. They are usually lightweight and can be obtained from medical and back shops and Internet sites.

See Chapter 10 for additional information about sitting.

5. Correct posture, including "slouching," can ease back pain.

If you have chronic low back pain, a slight change in the way you stand can help ease this pain. For example, a jutting rear emphasizes the "S" curve in your lower back. So keep your rear tucked in a bit. Practicing Exercise 2 (Pelvic Tilt) in Chapter 10 will make it easier for you to maintain this "tucked-in" alignment.

More good advice: Tuck in your chin, tighten your abdominal muscles, and keep your knees unlocked—bent just a trifle.

Finally, don't believe the myth that good posture means that your weight must be evenly distributed on both legs. Believing this can cause you great discomfort when you're standing in one place for a long time. Shift your weight from one foot to the other every few minutes. Some experts consider this to be "slouching," hence bad for you. But since your "S" curve is less exaggerated when you stand this way, you will probably feel better.

See Chapter 9 for additional information about posture.

6. Turn your tub into a
pain-relieving hydrotherapy center.

Being in a bathtub is painful for some people. If your muscles are contracted, you might find it difficult to sit up and bathe or to lean back on the hard surface and relax. Moreover, just lying in a tub can put pressure on tight muscles or inflamed nerves. But there usually are ways around all these problems.

About half of the participants in this survey got backache relief from taking baths. Their suggestions should help you find more enjoyment in the tub:

- Warm water is better than hot. Hot water *is* more effective as a counter-irritant—you feel the heat and not the pain—but too much heat can tire your muscles to a point that spasming starts up or increases. Also, lying in a hot tub for a long time is risky if you have high blood pressure or medical conditions that are affected adversely by excessive heat.

- A twenty-minute bath is ideal, say most survey participants. Longer than this is potentially more harmful than beneficial.

- Using an extra-thick bath mat and filling the tub as high as possible will minimize pressure on inflamed muscles and nerves.

- Instead of reclining with your legs fully extended, lean your back against one end of the tub, raise your knees, and keep your feet flat.

- Tuck a folded hand towel between the small of your back and the end of the tub. Just this much support can greatly increase your comfort.

- To avoid stiffness from being in one position too long, prop your feet on the sides or edges of the tub from time to time.

- A small, inflatable bath pillow that attaches to the tub with suction cups will allow you to lean back more comfortably and avoid straining your neck and upper back. Medical and back shops and mail-order suppliers sell them.

- A body-length inflatable cushion that attaches with suction cups is a good bet if you can't tolerate pressure on your hips, buttocks, or back.

7. Apply moist heat while in bed.

It's not always convenient or desirable to get into a tub to soothe your aching muscles with moist heat. So here are alternatives:

- Apply a hot, wet towel to your back. One way is to soak a towel in the hottest water you can tolerate, wring it out, and apply it to your back. The effect is likely to feel wonderful but short-lived—only about three minutes—and become annoyingly cold shortly thereafter. A slightly longer-lasting technique is to boil water, dip all but the ends of a towel in it, wring the steaming towel by twisting the ends, wrap it in a dry towel, and apply. You might get five minutes of therapeutic heat this way, *but exercise caution.* The wet towel, even though it is wrapped in another towel, may be scalding hot at first and could irritate or even burn your skin.

- Use a manual heat hydrocollator. The special gel in this device retains therapeutic heat longer than a towel—about fifteen to twenty-five minutes. Also, the hydrocollator won't drip, and it costs less and feels moister than electric moist heat hydrocollators. The only drawback is that you have to get out of bed to heat the manual hydrocollator in hot water.

- Try an electric moist heat hydrocollator. These emit a constant amount of moist heat and come wrapped in a special covering that absorbs moisture from the air. The better sort have a hand-held pressure switch or automatic cut-out, which is a good safety feature because if you fall asleep the unit will turn itself off. A pad of approximately 13-by-13 inches will cover your lumbar area. One of approximately 13-by-26 inches is large enough to cover your upper and lower back. One make is the Thermaphore®, available on the Internet from www.painreliever.com and also by mail order. Their website has the details.

See additional information about heat therapy in Chapter 5.

8. Use cold therapy to reduce muscle spasm.

The value of cold therapy for many back sufferers, contrary to common wisdom, is not limited to the first twenty-four to forty-eight hours after injury. In fact, cold therapy remained more effective than heat therapy over long periods of time for survey participants with neck pain, sciatica, and severe muscle spasms.

- Large freezer bags filled with ice were the top choice among survey participants who used cold therapy. Zip-lock bags all but assure that icy water won't leak out. Rather than empty the bag after your treatment, try laying it flat in the freezer for reuse. (The rubber-screw-top ice bags available at drugstores have limited value, primarily because they are usually not large enough to cover the entire affected area.)

- Instant cold packs are especially useful when you don't have quick access to a freezer—on car rides or camping trips, for example. These gel packs turn cold in seconds when you squeeze and shake them. One popular brand is Jack Frost cold packs, available at some drug stores, camping stores and supermarkets. Other, equally effective brands are available in both North America and overseas.

- Cold hydrocollators may be the best bet of all if you want to apply ice to a large area—your lower and middle back for example. A brand name that comes well recommended is Hydrocollator® ColPac®, available at surgical supply stores in both North America and many other countries, and on the Internet. The oversize version, 21-by-11 inches, suits most back sufferers. There are smaller sizes, too, including one that wraps around your neck. Further information can be obtained from the Chattanooga Group, Inc. (1–800–592–7329; international calls, 1–423–870–7200; website with product and distribution details, www.chattanoogagroup.com).

See additional information about cold therapy in Chapter 6.

9. Use self-massage to ease pain and promote relaxation.

Rubbing away pain on a daily basis with self-massage is a popular and proven remedy among survey participants. Various self-massage techniques, as well as techniques that require a partner's help, are discussed fully in Chapters 4 and 9. The two most effective involve: (1) applying acupressure with the ball of the thumb to areas of pain caused by muscle spasm; and (2) ice massage, using either a paper cup filled with ice or a "friction mitten" available at surgical supply stores.

In addition, fifteen survey participants got instant pain relief by using the Ma Roller, a wooden body roller specially designed to apply acupressure to the long muscles on either side of the spine.

Body rollers of different kinds are available at most health-food stores. They are well worth trying, with this one note of caution: if you are in the recovery stage, do not place a roller under your middle or lower back. The pressure from it, and the degree to which it arches your spine, might be more than you can tolerate.

See additional information about massage in Chapter 5.

10. Exercise regularly.

Survey participants all advocate regular exercise. Chapter 10 sets out a complete low back exercise program—including how to think about exercise, how to warm up, what exercises to do, what exercises to avoid, how to know when you need professional help, and where to find this help. In Chapters 11 through 14, you'll find specific advice about exercise for pain caused by ruptured disc, neck ailments, osteoarthritis, spondylolisthesis, sciatica, and scoliosis.

11. Give yourself a break.

"Two 10-minute back breaks each day are the difference for me between progress and deterioration," said a church choir conductor. And a majority of survey participants agree that giving your back a few respites every day is the best way to lower the stress that heightens back pain.

The most popular and helpful way to take a back break is to lie on the floor with your calves and feet propped on a chair or sofa. The effect is even better when you combine this strain-easing position with deep breathing.

See the Index for additional information about stress reduction.

12. Walk at least two miles a day.

Walking was helpful in the long run for 98 percent of survey participants who made it a regular part of their routine. The activity not only added strength and flexibility to their backs but improved their muscle tone overall. Equally important, walking at least thirty minutes a day, four times a week, greatly reduced stress for these people.

Standing or walking a lot on your job "doesn't count," according to survey participants. What does count is brisk, mind-clearing, arm-swinging, uninterrupted walking.

13. Carry common objects comfortably.

Those things you hold near to you every day as you go through your activities at work or home could be contributing to back discomfort. A few precautions here can make a noticeable difference.

- Lighten shoulder bags and pocketbooks. Ten women and two men in our survey got relief from back pain when they cut down their everyday load. They switched to lighter-weight pocketbooks or shoulder bags, carried fewer objects, and shifted the pocketbook or shoulder bag from side to side to avoid muscle imbalance. Using a backpack instead of a pocketbook or shoulder bag may make you look less elegant, but backpacks are the most comfortable way for some people to carry weighty necessities.

- Watch where you put your wallet. Sitting on a bulky wallet all day can literally cause or aggravate sciatica pain. The solution is not, as some survey participants quipped, to give everything in your wallet to a back specialist. Instead, keep your wallet someplace else—in your jacket pocket, side pocket, or a shoulder bag.

- Divide up groceries. Carry your groceries in two shopping bags with handles and distribute their weight evenly. Don't clasp shopping bags to your chest or walk with them balanced on your hips. Avoid cartons. And, in general, keep the tonnage to a minimum. "Buying everything you need for the week doesn't mean that you have to carry that week in one trip," said a housewife. "No medals are given out for wounded backs incurred while carrying an extra case of dog food," she added.

- Get yourself a wheeled shopping cart for bringing home the groceries.

- Put your laundry on wheels, too. You can buy a laundry cart at hardware and department stores, or you can put your laundry bag in a shopping cart.

14. Avoid surgery.

Proportionately more disc operations are performed in the United States than anywhere else in the world. Moreover, most studies about the incidence of back surgery conclude that too much of it is done.

Certainly, many participants in our survey believe that back surgery is often recommended without good reason. Of every four participants who were advised to have disc surgery, only one elected to have it. See Chapter 11 for steps you can take to avoid surgery.

15. Learn more about drugs before taking them.

Aspirin is more than twice as effective as prescription anti-inflammatory drugs for back pain. Most prescription pain pills fall below the placebo level. All of these drugs have risks and side effects that your doctor may not explain to you.

These are highlights of some of our survey's general findings about drugs. For details—and for specific information about the efficacy of different medications for different kinds of back pain—see the entries under "Drugs" in the Index.

16. Treat your feet well and your back may be the better for it.

More than a dozen survey participants reported major relief from back pain when they switched from relatively high-heeled shoes (clogs, boots, or women's high-heeled pumps) to shoes with heels only about ½ inch higher than the soles.

Another ten survey participants were helped by heel lifts, heel cushions, arch supports, and prescribed shoe inserts (orthotics).

A wide range of custom shoe insoles are available, made from highly shock-absorbant materials such as Sorbothane. These lessen the impact on your spine of walking or running. Ask at drugstores, specialist sports and supply shops, or check the Internet.

gradually. Start out with a half hour the first day and use your new footwear a half hour more each succeeding day.

17. Join a health club.

"It's not that I can exercise any better at the club, at least in terms of doing back exercises," said an attorney. "But the camaraderie, the whirlpool, and the change of environment are good for me. I'm as stress-free as I can be after a workout at the club, and the same is not true after a workout at home."

Almost 12 percent of participants in this survey joined health clubs. Most initially doubted they could find the time for this activity, but they viewed the time spent working out as essential to their physical and emotional well-being.

18. Enjoy the healthiest exercise ever invented.

"If someone announced the invention of an activity that was non-weight-bearing, had great aerobic value, and stretched and strengthened virtually every muscle in your body, everyone would want to join in and it would make jogging seem like a medical disaster by comparison," said the owner of an excavating company who eliminated his back pain by adding swimming to his back exercise routine.

There was not a single naysayer about swimming in our survey. There were, however, these cautionary notes: avoid the breaststroke and butterfly unless your back pain is unquestionably a thing of the past. (Even then, you might have difficulty with these strokes.) Also, avoid the overhand crawl until you're pain-free. Then work at it gradually. The sidestroke is easiest on your back; the backstroke is next best if you keep your arms close to your sides and use a short fluttering stroke.

19. Participate in a mind-body activity.

Some 10 percent of survey participants had a remarkable degree of success with yoga, and, to a slightly lesser extent, with modern dance and Tai Chi.

These three very different activities have one thing in common: they help the whole person. They increase back fitness while they bolster spirits and reduce stress.

Although some survey participants taught themselves yoga, modern dance, or Tai Chi, professional instruction invariably made the experience more beneficial.

20. Eat properly.

Dietary habits that were viewed just a few years ago as the offbeat fetishes of health-food fanatics are now increasingly accepted by back sufferers, the general public, and even the medical establishment: go light on junk foods and processed foods. Eat more fruits, vegetables, and whole grains. Cut down on animal fats. Reduce your intake of caffeine, sugar, and alcohol. Substitute poultry and fish for beef.

What does this advice about nutrition have to do with your back? No one knows for sure. But, as a computer industry worker said, "Eating properly makes you feel better about yourself and that just might help your back."

It certainly can't hurt.

21. Lose weight.

"I think losing weight helped me some," said a railroad employee who shed twenty-five pounds in an effort to curb back pain. "But," she added, "losing weight seemingly should have done more than it did. I keep thinking of all the thin people with back pain, and all the fat people whose backs never bother them, and I wonder if losing weight matters."

Carrying less weight around can't hurt your back. And according to survey participants, it is likely to help a bit.

Be careful though. The *process* of losing weight can hurt your back. Three survey participants who were overweight, and who tried to lose weight, were injured while doing exercises from trendy diet and fitness books. These exercises are not meant to be rehabilitative, and their adverse effects actually discouraged some back sufferers from learning more appropriate exercise routines.

22. Wear a back support . . . on occasion.

Back supports should *not* be used by most back sufferers. But back supports benefited survey participants who:

(1) had not yet recovered from an episode of back pain; or

(2) had not yet strengthened their abdominal muscles enough to perform certain activities.

Back supports are not sold at most drugstores, and many surgical supply stores won't sell them unless you have a prescription. You may well be able to find a nonprescription support but *caveat emptor*: medical practitioners do not recommend them.

23. Try reverse-gravity relaxing and exercising.

Advertisements for back-care products sometimes exaggerate reality by multiples. But, according to survey participants, reverse-gravity equipment is even better for your back than it claims to be. Exercising or just relaxing while hanging upside down or tilted toward the inverted position may ease pain appreciably.

Proprietary inversion devices can be expensive and take up a lot of room. Even a compact unit may need four square feet or more of floor space. Those who have neither the money nor the room for a full-up system may be interested in a doorway chinning bar and inversion boots combo. The EZ-UP Inversion Rack and a choice of inversion boots can be browsed and ordered online from websites such as www.bodytrends.com or www.gravityplus.com. Alternatively, ask at a medical or back shop; there are plenty of other brands available.

See additional information and cautions about gravity inversion in Chapter 7.

24. Hanging from a chinning bar can increase your mobility and flexibility.

A few osteoarthritis back sufferers and low back sufferers found that a minute or two of hanging—gripping a chinning bar and suspending themselves with their feet off the ground—reduced low back pain.

Non-inverted hanging has the potential to stretch out and relax the muscles and ligaments that support your spine. If you want to try it, follow these tips from back sufferers:

• Make certain that the bar is secure. If the frame of your doorway is not in the best shape, don't even try to install a chinning bar there.

• Position the bar so that you can just reach it on your tiptoes.

Lower than this and you'll have to tuck your knees under you, a more awkward way to hold yourself up.

- Start by hanging for only ten to twenty seconds. Even if you feel terrific, go slowly. Increase your hanging time by ten seconds a day until you can hang for one to two minutes, twice a day.

- If you feel more than a little achy eighteen to twenty-four hours after hanging, figure that the routine isn't for you and isn't worth trying again even when your aches have gone away.

25. Try these miscellaneous tips mentioned by three or more survey participants.

- If you have a very tight lower back, do slow, gentle shoulder shrugs and knee-to-chest stretches while reclining in a warm tub. (A body-length inflatable cushion makes it easier to do these warm-ups.) Then do your regular back exercise routine immediately after the bath.

- *Before* attempting unusually strenuous activity (anything from tennis to snow shoveling) take two aspirins. The anti-inflammatory and analgesic properties of this drug may subdue aches before they can start up.

- At a time when you're feeling fit and optimistic about your back, make a tape of all the things you should think and do daily to keep your back in good shape. Then play the tape on days when you need positive feedback and reinforcement.

- Be a smart dresser. Wear an extra layer of clothing that you can take off if you're too warm. Bring along a jacket, sweater, or warm-up suit to put on after athletic activities. Getting chilled may never give you a cold, but it can play havoc with muscle spasms.

- Avoid constipation by drinking enough water and including enough bulk and fiber in your diet.

- Use a liniment to temporarily take your mind off aches and pains.

- Meditate. Even if you don't learn meditation from a professional, you will find it relaxing to take time every day to free your mind of all thoughts and concerns.

- If you don't own a firm mattress, a bed board, a straight-backed chair, a back cushion, and a footrest, you should invest in these items. If your doctor prescribes them, the cost may be tax-deductible.

Chapter 16

Helping Your Back: Tips for Performing Twenty-Five Common Activities

If you lived in Sweden and had a chronic back problem, a physical therapist might spend an entire day and evening with you just to observe how your activities affect your back. Wherever you went, whatever you did, the therapist would be there. Then he or she would compile detailed recommendations about what you should and shouldn't do to help your back around the clock.

In America, backs tend to be observed by X rays rather than eyes. Back sufferers usually have to compress their medical histories into a few minutes of hurried conversation. Back practitioners rarely if ever get to see their back patients in action—sleeping, walking, working at the office, watching TV, eating, making the bed, driving, playing tennis, gardening, and picking up the baby. As a result, the real culprits behind back problems are seldom seen, discussed, pinpointed, or—most important—eliminated.

What should you do? Become your own back doctor. How? By making use of the most potent diagnostic skill of all: *direct observation*. Watch yourself from morning till night. Track yourself from room to room, place to place, activity to activity. That's what this chapter helps you to do. While reading it, you may want to write some notes about specific changes you can make to help yourself.

Of course, there is no quiz at the end of this chapter. But do try to think of the material as a test of how serious you are about self-care, about taking responsibility for yourself to the greatest possible extent, about changing your life to reflect the proven principles of good back care recommended by survey participants and discussed throughout this book.

More than 95 percent of participants in our survey who got dramatically better—and who no longer have back pain—literally had to change their lives to achieve this new level of back fitness.

The following suggestions and guidelines are based on advice from about a hundred survey participants. We have tried to organize the tips by the places in and around your house where you may need specific information. We begin in the bedroom with positions for sex, because survey participants mentioned these more than any other topic covered in this chapter.

All the back-care products recommended below are described fully in the Appendix, along with information for ordering them by mail.

THE BEDROOM

Note: For tips about sleeping positions, watching TV in bed, and maneuvering your way into and out of bed, see Chapters 9 and 12.

1. Making love

"To the extent that the body is not flexible, the mind has to be," commented a commercial artist who couldn't work for six months because of a ruptured disc. "You can almost always find a way to have sex if your attitude about it is flexible and if you realize that your mind is the key to sexual pleasure. Some sex of any kind is better than deprivation, which can cause depression and bring about a heightened sense of pain."

Most back books make much ado about the physical aspects of sex, including how a wide variety of intercourse positions can restore your sex life. Here are the three positions for intercourse recommended most by survey participants:

Face to face

Lying on your side with your knees bent, facing your partner, is the least risky sexual intercourse position for a back sufferer. Since the position is also a natural one for nonsexual intimacy, it avoids the need, as one survey participant put it, "to make a big deal about rearranging yourself in order to have sex."

Front to back

Lying front to back, nestled like spoons, with the man behind the woman, is another safe position for sexual intercourse. Many couples feel that this position also facilitates penetration.

Modified missionary

If you are comfortable lying on your back with your knees elevated—and if your partner is strong enough to keep most of his or her weight off you—then this is also a safe position for sexual intercourse.

If the woman is the back sufferer, she assumes the bottom position, and places a small pillow under her head and neck and two plump pillows under her knees. Her partner lies on top *if he can support most of his own weight.* The easiest way for the man to do this is to get into what looks like a push-up position, with his hands placed on either side of the woman's shoulders.

If the man is the back sufferer, he lies on his back and his partner lowers herself on him in a seated position, with her knees and legs bearing most of her weight. If the woman cannot bear most of the weight herself, this position should be avoided.

Although these sexual intercourse positions topped the list of suggestions by survey participants who had an active sex life despite back pain, many survey participants declined to recommend specific positions. They felt it best to talk in terms of what you should *not* do and leave the rest up to individual preferences and limitations. "As long as I don't arch my back excessively during sex, I'm fine," said an accountant. "I would only suggest that back sufferers do whatever they feel like doing, and know they can do, at any given time."

A marine biologist said, "The fear of injury during sex had a disastrous effect on my sex life for years. The solution is not to read a manual about sex, or try to hide from it, but to talk about it openly with your partner. And once you've discussed what you can't do, talk a lot about all the wonderful pleasures you *can* have. Then stop talking and start doing."

"Keep in mind that intercourse is not the only option," noted a physics teacher. "Masturbation, whether alone or mutual, is a healthy option. So is oral sex, which can be done comfortably in the fetal position."

And a federal employee concluded, "The rocking motion of gentle sex is the best therapy ever invented for a back sufferer's body and mind."

2. Making the bed

Bend your knees instead of bending at the waist to reach the bed. Get into a kneeling position and stay there as you make your way around the bed. Work slowly and keep repositioning yourself to avoid overstretching your back.

Unless your bed rolls effortlessly, it's best to keep it freestanding, away from the walls. Otherwise you'll be forced either to reach too far in smoothing sheets and blankets, or to move the whole bed each time you want to straighten it.

Don't make the bed at all if you're in severe pain. And don't bother turning over your mattress every few months unless you have someone there to help you.

3. Staying warm in bed

Survey participants with muscle spasms or osteoarthritis-based back pain are quick to feel the painful effects of a chilly night. Appropriate sleepwear, blankets, and room temperature are usually enough to avoid problems. But if you can't get comfortable, back-care products are available that may generate more warmth under and around your body, such as mattress pads, both electric and nonelectric.

4. Getting enough rest

Nearly all back sufferers report increased back pain when they get less sleep than usual. On days when you don't get enough rest, you can protect your back simply by easing up on strenuous activities that tend to cause you problems. Also, survey participants note a tendency to "slump" into poor posture when tired, and need to watch extra carefully how they stand and sit.

5. Reading at bedtime

Reading in bed is one pastime most survey participants have had to learn to live without. If you like to read just before going to sleep, they advise, get a good chair for your bedroom. It is all but impossible to read in bed without hurting your back. And if you need a little extra push to make this change, remember that most sleep experts blame reading or working in bed as a major cause of insomnia.

6. Organizing your bedroom closet

If you're recovering from a bad back, have someone help you rearrange your closet so that you can reach the things you need without effort. For example, instead of keeping your shoes on the closet floor, put them in a shoebag on the door.

If it is a strain to reach for objects on a high shelf, move them to a more accessible spot or leave a small footstool in or near your closet.

It may be worth purchasing a "gripper" device such as an E-Z Reach. This can extend your arm's reach by over two feet. It will help you retrieve objects from the floor or high shelves without the need to arch your back, bend, or stoop.

THE BATHROOM

Note: See Chapter 15 for suggestions on how to turn your bathtub into a therapy center for relieving back pain.

7. Using the toilet

Toilet seats are rather devilish devices for back sufferers. They are awkward to get down to, unsupportive to sit on, and difficult to get up from. But just as there are easier ways to get into bed, so there are ways to take the strain off a painful back when using the toilet.

For example, until you are free of disabling pain, rails on both sides of the toilet can be helpful. They are safe and simple to install, and are reasonably inexpensive.

Another way to ease the pain of getting on and off the toilet is to raise the seat itself, and there are at least two ways to get around the discomfort of not having your back supported on the toilet. One is to wear a lumbar support belt whenever you use the toilet. Another option is to wedge a lumbar cushion between your back and the back of the toilet.

8. Bathing

When you're recovering from a back injury, getting into and out of the tub can also be a problem. Bathtub safety rails are available and are not too difficult to fit.

9. Cleaning the bathroom

To avoid back strain when you clean the tub or toilet, kneel rather than bend over. Instead of stretching across the tub with a sponge, use a scrubber with a long handle.

THE KITCHEN

10. Washing the dishes

Leaning over the sink to do the dishes is difficult for most people and especially so for back sufferers. And dishwashers don't completely solve the problem. However, here are some helpful suggestions:

- Turn your body to one side before you stretch to reach the faucets. It's easier to lean sideways.

- Belly up to the sink counter. Standing even a few inches away from the sink can vastly increase the amount of back pain you feel. (A plastic apron will keep you drier and more comfortable than distance from the sink.)

- Lift whatever you're washing out of the sink and hold it close to your body as you clean it. (A mat on the floor will keep the linoleum dry.)

- Shift your weight from one foot to the other every few minutes.

- Support one foot on a footstool.

- Soak whatever pots and pans may take long to clean—and go back to them later.

- The minute your back feels tired, switch to a less stressful chore, or simply take a break.

11. Sitting at the table

If you are uncomfortable sitting at the table, especially during long meals, follow suvey participants' advice about straight-backed chairs, back cushions, and footrests. See pages 160–164 and 274–275.

12. Washing the floor

Use a sponge mop that can be wrung dry with a gadget high up on the handle. These are available in most supermarkets and hardware stores.

Think about your posture as you work. Keep your abdominal muscles tightened and your spine leaning forward only slightly. You may find you can stand straighter if you hold the mop with one hand instead of two.

13. Sweeping

The real stickler here is collecting what you have swept while remaining upright. You can do this with a long-handled dustpan.

14. Reaching food on high shelves

Standing on your tiptoes and reaching as far as you can to get boxes and jars down from shelves can aggravate pain in your back. One solution is to use a footstool. Human nature being what it is, this tends to work only if you keep the footstool right where you work—and keep plants and other decorative objects off it.

Another solution, especially if you're too uncomfortable to climb steps, is a "gripper" device such as the E-Z Reach, mentioned earlier in this chapter.

THE LIVING ROOM

15. Sitting

If you have lovely-looking but unbearably soft chairs and couches in your living room, try concealing a ¾-inch piece of plywood under their cushions to provide more support. Even then you should still keep a good straight-backed chair—or at least a firm reclining chair for yourself—in the living room.

If you don't usually sit in the living room—and you don't have a good sitting arrangement for yourself there—make one up *before* company comes.

A printer explained why: "My wife and I like our living room to look nice, and frankly, a straight-backed chair doesn't fit into our decor. Of course, my back is more important than appearances. But I have found that if I don't get a chair, back support, and footstool set up before company comes over, I'm not likely to do it at all. This may sound silly, but it embarrasses me to bring in 'special provisions' for my back. It means having to talk about my back, and few subjects are as boring to me and to my company. However, if one of the wooden kitchen chairs is already in place in the living room, with a nice footstool as well as the plain black lumbar cushion that I have, then I'll sit the way I should and not have any problem the next day.

"To help my back and my wife," the printer continued, "I'm the one who asks people if they want more of anything. This is an unobtrusive way for me to take a break from sitting. People who don't know me that well may think I'm a good host or a liberated husband. But the point is that I've been a good host for ten years and I haven't had a backache after a party for ten years. I would like to address a final comment to your male readers. I don't lift the groceries out of the car. My wife does. If that sounds bad, so be it. The truth is that some men would rather wind up in traction than harm their macho image."

16. Vacuuming

Enough vacuuming will give almost anyone a backache. And judging from comments of survey participants, it is clear that the people who suffer the most back pain from vacuuming are those who are compulsive about this chore. If this description fits you, try to change your *attitude* about routine chores by following these suggestions from survey participants:

- Don't vacuum when you're in pain. "Resist, relax, take a bath— stop being so compulsive," said one housewife.

- Invest in a vacuum cleaner that you can push with minimal exertion and bending. Work with one hand at a time, if you can. You'll feel better with one hand at your side.

- Don't vacuum more than fifteen minutes at a stretch. And stop sooner than that if your back feels fatigued.

17. Dusting and window washing

The strain of dusting or cleaning high places can often be reduced simply by using a longer cleaning tool, especially one that combines a duster/ squeegee on the head. Long-reach window washers are also available.

18. Moving furniture

When you want to redecorate your living room, or any other room for that matter, don't try to push furniture around. Buy a small dolly mover and wheel it to and fro.

19. Painting

There's no easy answer to the many problems your back can encounter while painting, but here are some helpful suggestions from survey participants:

- Stand as close as possible to what you're painting. Your posture will be better and your arms will remain relatively close to your body.

- When you're painting walls, position yourself so that your arms are at a level between your chest and waist.

- Use whatever apparatus will get the job done fast—brush, roller, or paint gun. Rollers are usually best. Brushes can take too long, and paint guns are too heavy to hold for any appreciable time.

- Know your limits. The rest of the wall does *not* have to be completed immediately if finishing it will finish you.

- Hire someone to do the ceilings. If you can't, find a friend with a strong back. That failing, look down every few minutes, take a one-minute break every five minutes, take a ten-minute break every half hour, and do the standing neck and upper-shoulder exercises described in Chapter 12.

OUTDOORS

20. Raking leaves and

21. Shoveling snow

According to our best estimates from survey data, these two seasonal activities cause several million people a year to seek professional treatment for their backs. The strain of raking and snow shoveling comes from excessive forward leaning and arm extension. In this awkward and unsupported position, your back is extremely vulnerable.

One obvious but usually impractical solution is to avoid these tasks altogether, either by neglecting them or hiring someone else to do them. You could also invest in blowers, tractors, and other expensive outdoor equipment.

However, there are rakes and shovels with a gooseneck bend design that allows you to stand up straighter and shift some of the lifting *oomph* from your back to your arms.

For either raking or shoveling, you'll be warmer and more comfortable if you dress in layers. You can always remove outer clothing to avoid getting overheated. Several survey participants recommended wearing a long undershirt made of a "wick-through" fabric that keeps moisture away from the skin and thus helps prevent chills and spasms. Cotton may feel best next to your skin when dry, but it loses most of its insulating properties—not to mention its nice feel—when it gets wet.

When you shovel, remember to:

- bend your legs and not your back;
- keep the shovel as close to your body as possible;
- keep the size of each load modest.

For raking:

- keep your knees unlocked (slightly bent);
- position one foot in front of the other;
- avoid excessive leaning;
- kneel or squat—don't stoop—whether you're lifting one leaf or one million.

When you rake leaves into piles, never attempt to move an entire pile with your rake. Use a long-handled scoop or "claws" to pick up leaves, grass cuttings, pine needles, and garbage spills.

To carry bags of leaves, take two small bags of equal weight at a time, leaving your arms at your sides. Holding a large bag out in front of you can readily harm your back.

If you have to carry the leaves of autumn any distance, a cart built for this purpose will save you wear and tear.

22. Splitting and carrying firewood

Chopping wood is a wonderful activity that can benefit many back sufferers. "It's a great outlet for stress," said a bank manager, "and far better than jogging to let out aggression."

"Chopping wood is great for getting the kinks out and maintaining muscle tone," said a chemical factory worker. "You're outside and doing something vigorous and constructive."

But there's a darker side to the story for back sufferers, because for every survey participant who extolled chopping wood, another reported an injury from it.

Here are some suggestions to help you enjoy yourself safely:

- Find an ax with a weight you can mange. A heavier ax may save you swings, but your back will feel better wielding a lighter weight through more swings of the ax.

- Keep your knees bent and your feet shoulder width apart.

- Avoid swinging exclusively from one side; a muscular imbalance may result that could cause or aggravate back pain.

- Stop when you're tired.

23. Picking up and hauling debris

Don't try dragging garbage or other items around youself. Invest in a "wheelie-bin" or a cart.

24. Gardening

"If there's a gardener someplace out there who has never clutched his sacroiliac after being in a stooped position too long, let him come forward now," a watercolor artist commented about the relationship between gardening and back pain.

"There are two givens about gardening," a retiree and avid gardener told us. "Physically, it isn't good for your back. Spiritually, it is good for your back."

And a paper products manufacturer observed, "Only one thing motivates me to do my daily back exercises . . . and that's to keep in good enough condition to continue doing more gardening . . . which in turn continues to threaten my back with mayhem."

Clearly, gardening is a thoroughly enjoyable activity for many. Equally clearly, it caused survey participants more back pain than any other popular pastime, including jogging and team sports.

What can be done? Quite a lot.

According to most survey participants, the paper products manufacturer quoted above had the best suggestion: *exercise your back to keep it in shape for gardening*. Do not follow in the footsteps of one survey participant who, speaking from his bed while recuperating from a bad episode of low back pain, said: "Gardening is all the exercise my back needs. I may have overdone it again, but in any event, my back is always too tired after gardening to do back exercises." (See Chapter 10 for a complete back exercise program.)

Think of gardening activities as a way to strengthen your arms and legs—not your back. In other words, use your legs and arms to lift, carry, pull, dig, and scrape—and try to give your back a free ride. Kneel and squat. Don't scoop or slouch. Don't garden with your back.

Face the fact that gardening is physically stressful—and be realistic about what you can accomplish. As we mentioned above, it is theoretically possible to work in the garden without bending at the waist or working your back into a state of protest. But that's like saying you could garden without getting your hands dirty. You could—but no one does. An airline stewardess found this way out of the dilemma: "If you like gardening as much as I do, you're going to ache the next day. I try to tell myself that my back will be okay if I treat it only half as well as I treat my plants. This basically means trying to keep my back straight. I do this by thinking about posture, as well as by using tools with long handles and keeping them close to my body. As a last resort, if my back really hurts and there is more weeding to be done, I plant myself in the garden—on my side—and get the weeds up that way. I look funny. I might even smell funny. But I'm back gardening the next day."

Use the right tools. Long-handled "claws", mentioned in the preceding section, are useful for more than picking up leaves. They also help you pick up weeds, stones, and other objects that shouldn't be in your garden. Invest in other long-handled tools to keep you upright while you cultivate, weed, and aerate your garden. One such is the E-Z Reach Pruning Stick. This, or a similar tool from a different manufacturer, comes with a long, telescopic handle.

Finally, the right equipment for watering your garden can help keep back problems at bay. Many devices for this purpose are available at garden centers and hardware stores—including lightweight hoses on retractable reels, inexpensive connectors for hard-to-reach outside spigots, and elaborately timed sprinkler systems.

25. Sitting at outdoor events

Many survey participants suffered more back trouble from observing sporting events than from participating in them. For example, parents who sat in school bleachers to watch the kids play ball had a tough time on these "backless" back breakers. Beach lovers found it more uncomfortable to read at the beach than to take a long swim. And back sufferers at picnics found it more difficult to sit unsupported than to make a long hike to the picnic grounds.

There is an obvious solution: bring along your own sitting arrangements. But most survey participants were too embarrassed to do this. Even back sufferers who were willing to bring a good folding chair to the beach wouldn't bring the same chair to a picnic or to an athletic field with bleacher seats.

But since the essence of sitting comfortably at outdoor activities is to care more about being good to your back than about what others think, prove it by bringing along whatever it takes to make yourself comfortable. This might be a favorite folding chair or an exercise or insulation mat.

Appendix: Update of Treatments and Diagnostic Procedures

Chapter 4

The relative success of chiropractors and medical doctors

In the most comprehensive and scientific study to date of relative outcomes and costs for treating low back pain, patients rated chiropractors more helpful than primary care physicians. This rating was given in spite of the higher cost and typically longer duration of chiropractic care.

New England Journal of Medicine, 1995, 333: 913–17

Chapter 6

Comparative results of surgery and conservative treatments for herniated discs

Long-term results of surgery are only slightly better than non-surgical treatments. What accounts for successful surgical outcomes for lumbar discectomy? According to this source, it's *not* the skill of the surgeon, the reputation of the medical center or the innovative qualities of the surgical microscope. "The outcome depends more on patient selection than on surgical technique." In short, you've got to have the right kind of herniated disc and psychological make-up.

Spine, 1996, 21: 45S–56S

Microsurgery v. standard laminectomy discectomy

The outcomes of these two widely accepted kinds of surgery are about the same. However, the patient who undergoes microsurgery is usually better off because there are fewer postoperative problems, an earlier discharge from the hospital and a quicker return to work.

Drawbacks to microsurgery include: A limited field of view and "work area" for the surgeon, thus the potential to miss some problems or fail to remove all disc fragments and pathologies. On the plus side, microdiscectomy has improved recently through the use of better surgical microscopes and lighting.

An, Howard S., MD. *Principles and Techniques of Spine Surgery*, Williams & Wilkins, 1998, chapter 37

Chapter 7

Chymopapain

Chymopapain is still with us, still controversial after all these years, still a godsend to some and a bust for others.

The jury is out, deadlocked and bickering. Worse, medical researchers consistently come up with strikingly different outcomes from using chymopapain to ease ruptured disc pressure on nerve roots.

Consumers hardly know what to think. Ten back patients were surveyed on the Internet by the authors of this book in December 1998. Of those 10 patients, four said, in effect, to run for your life; four reported considerable discomfort for

30–45 days (post-injection spasms are common), then relief for one to three years. Two weren't sure what they thought.

For certain, indications for using chymopapain are limited. These limitations include large herniations, disc fragments and bony encroachment or calcification of the disc fragment. "Thus it would seem to the skeptic that the procedure is best indicated for small disc protrusions that often respond to conservative treatments."

> An, Howard S., MD. *Principles and Techniques of Spine Surgery*,
> Williams & Wilkins, 1998, chapter 20

Chymopapain can cause serious complications. It is not yet recommended for areas other than the lumbar spine. It should not be used when the bulging disc gel has broken away from the disc.

> *Drug Information for the Health Care Professional (USPDI)*,
> United States Pharmacopeial, 1998, vol. 1

Of course, good results also are part of the chymopapain story. "Long-term results show that improvement after chemonucleolysis (injection with chymopapain) is maintained, whereas the outcome after laminectomy is reported to deteriorate with time."

> *Spine*, May 1996, 12(9): 1102–5

Chymopapain became unfashionable in the United States in the 1980s because of shock reactions and other difficulties. However, improved techniques have reduced the risk of complications and "chemonucleolysis remains a minimally invasive therapeutic modality with extensive worldwide use but variable acceptance in this country."

> An, Howard S., MD. *Principles and Techniques of Spine Surgery*,
> Williams & Wilkins, 1998, chapter 36

Intrathecal pumps

A small pump is surgically placed under the skin of the abdomen. This enables medication to be delivered around the spinal cord. Because the medication goes directly to the site where pain signals travel, the procedure can significantly control pain with lower doses of medication.

> Medtronic Web Site, December 1998

In a study conducted by the Department of Anesthesiology, Sahlgrenska University Hospital, Goteborg University, Gothemburg, Sweden, approximately 95 per cent of patients obtained 60–100 per cent pain relief from intrathecal pumps. Average sleep increased from four to seven hours. Medication consumption was reduced by half.

PubMed Medline, December 1998

Laser energy for treating herniated discs

Laser-assisted back surgery—using a pulsed beam of light to "vaporize" disc gel and diminish disc pressure on nerve roots—requires only simple local anaesthesia. Patients can go home one or two hours after completion of the procedure.

Because laser treatment can bring about major reduction in pressure on spinal discs, it might be especially useful for treating pain from herniated discs in weight-lifters and others who exercise strenuously. One technique for doing this, devised by Dr. Harcharan Singh Ranu and his colleagues at Columbia University College of Physicians and Surgeons, in New York City, is called "laserectomy percutaneous decompression." The laser beams are used to reduce the size of the bulging tissue that is putting pressure on a spinal nerve.

Studies show a 65 per cent reduction of pressure and some degree of pain relief in 80 per cent of the patients tested.

The entire procedure takes less than 45 minutes. Patients are discharged the same day and able to resume normal activity after four days.

Journal of the American Medical Association (JAMA), June 10, 1998,
"Oh My Aching Back"

A more extensive report on 333 patients undergoing laser discectomy showed a "good or fair response," but significantly less effective, than open laminectomy procedures. The amount of disc removed by the laser method is "quite modest," according to this report, but it can diminish disc pressure by more than 50 per cent. The risks to patients of laser discectomy are relatively low. There is some discomfort after the procedure and "there is anecdotal evidence of two cases of bowel perforation."

Menezes, Arnold H., MD & Sonntag, Volker K. H., MD.
Principles of Spinal Surgery, McGraw Hill Text, 1998, vol. 1

Myeloscope

In spite of advanced imaging technology, not all spinal disorders can be diagnosed without direct visualization of the area. The myeloscope, based on recent advances in fiber optics, provides detailed information about the subarachnoid space. It also can reveal changing conditions that cannot be identified during open surgery.

An, Howard S., MD. *Principles and Techniques of Spine Surgery*,
Williams & Wilkins, 1998, chapter 5

Percutaneous discectomy

By using arthroscopic techniques, surgeons are able to operate on herniated discs in a relatively less invasive way. However, this method, sometimes called endoscopic discectomy, has not been as successful as open-surgery procedures and is still considered experimental. "The future may bring improved techniques, with arthroscopic visualization minimizing risk and improving the root decompression. At present, however, the open techniques prevail."

An, Howard S., MD. *Principles and Techniques of Spine Surgery*,
Williams & Wilkins, 1998, chapter 20

Spinal cord stimulation (SCS)

There is still considerable dispute about the effectiveness of spinal cord stimulation. In a study conducted by the Department of Neurological Surgery, University of Pittsburgh, 22 out of the 24 patients enjoyed reduced pain and continued to use the stimulator.

"We conclude that rigid selection protocol can maximize the proportion of patients with intractable pain who are successfully treated with SCS. Strict neurosurgical technique eliminates infection risk. Hardware selection minimizes incidence of malfunction."

Neurological Research, July 1998

Chapter 8

Computerized motion diagnostic imaging (CMDI)

This new test, not yet widely accepted, looks at how well your body functions while in motion. Light reflectors are attached to the different parts of your body causing you difficulty. You are then videotaped "while walking, sitting and bending." The video signals are computered and your movements are studied in detail.

Cole, Andrew J., MD & Herring, Stanley A.
The Low Back Pain Handbook, Hanley & Berfus, 1997

Computed tomography (CT)

With CT, cross-section images are created at different levels of the spine. The outcome is the most effective noninvasive modality for evaluating abnormalities of the spine. CT is especially useful for differentiating between hard discs and herniated discs. However, when dyes are used to increase the contrast of different images, a small percentage of patients suffer allergic reactions and scarring.

An, Howard S., MD. *Principles and Techniques of Spine Surgery*,
Williams & Wilkins, 1998, chapter 5

MRI—the new standard for diagnosing soft-tissue disorders.

Called Nuclear Magnetic Resonance (NMR) in the first edition of this book, Magnetic Resonant Imaging (MRI) has become the imaging test of choice for its remarkable ability to see and "read" soft tissue such as nerves, muscles and herniated discs.

For the claustrophobic, MRI "open" systems are available, although the clarity of imaging detail is relatively low.

MRI may have even greater value when it is used with patients positioned in more "dynamic" (movement-oriented) ways—sitting and extended, for example.
Spine, February 1996

Myelogram

This invasive procedure highlights nerve roots clearly. However, since the MRI also outlines nerve roots impressively, the need for a myelogram must be clearly demonstrated to patients before they risk headaches, nerve pain and allergic reactions.

Standard X rays for low back pain

In early 1997, the Agency for Health Care Policy and Research (AHCPR) published guidelines for dealing with low-back pain patients. They recommended increased use of lumbar radiographs (X rays of the lumbar spine) to search for fractures, tumors or infections.

However, it turns out that the ability of X rays to predict spinal damage or back pain is far too low to justify extensive use of low-back X rays.

Journal of the American Medical Association (JAMA), June 11, 1997

Somatosensory evoked potentials (SSEP)

This diagnostic procedure, which uses electrodes and gentle electric stimuli, is becoming more popular for preoperative clinical assessment of myelopathy, and can precisely pinpoint an overt myelopathy. It also is used for the continuing monitoring of neurological function.

Electrodes are placed on the scalp and on different parts of the body. Normal and abnormal responses are measured in the brain. These responses gauge the health of sensory impulses coursing through the body.

An, Howard S., MD. *Principles and Techniques of Spine Surgery*, Williams & Wilkins, 1998, chapter 2

SSEP is used basically because no other electrodiagnostic studies effectively detect damage involving sensory nerve fibers. There are problems, though: SSEP readings vary widely in normal subjects and are difficult to record, or absent, in up to 40 per cent of normal patients

Cole, Andrew J., MD & Herring, Stanley A.
The Low Back Pain Handbook, Hanley & Belfus, 1997

Thermograph (TMG)

This diagnostic procedure helps to distinguish a peripheral nerve injury from a nerve root injury. It is not used often for low-back pain sufferers.

Chapter 9

Bed rest v. daily activity as pain allows

A study reported in the February 9, 1995 *New England Journal of Medicine* reveals that bed rest should not be prescribed for patients who are well enough to get to a health center for treatment.

In a controlled trial, doctors randomly assigned patients to either bed rest, back exercises or the continuation of ordinary activities as pain tolerated. The patients who rested in bed took longest to recover.

Starting an exercise regimen for individuals still in considerable acute pain didn't bring about good results.

Authors' note: Prescribing back exercises for acute low-back pain sufferers seems unwise. What's more, poor results are likely to discourage these people (who need exercise) from starting a routine after their acute pain subsides— when exercise could be of considerable help.

Chapter 14

Pros and cons of spinal fusion for spondylolisthesis sufferers

The majority of people with spondylolisthesis can be treated without surgery. Spinal fusion should be considered "only after failure of a trial of nonoperative treatment lasting more than 12 months." Fusion has a low rate of success when used to treat back pain seemingly caused by multilevel disc degeneration.

Journal of the American Academy of Orthopaedic Surgeons,
May/June 1995

Index

Backache

WHAT EXERCISES *REALLY* WORK

CONTENTS

PART
ONE

The Magic Bullet

> *There is indeed a "magic bullet" that can effectively cure back pain. It is called exercise, and it works.*

A NOTE FOR THE UK EDITION

Throughout the book, some terms common to the US rather than the UK are used. Your physical therapist means your physiotherapist, and orthopedist is an orthopaedic surgeon, for example. The term physiatrist does not have an exact equivalent in the UK, the closest probably being a physician who specializes in rehabilitation. In addition, the symbol # is sometimes used to indicate 'number'. There are also references to private health care costs which do not apply to the UK in the same way.

Many of the exercises in this book involve getting on to the floor. To help you get down to this position, we advise you to: drop down on to your hands and knees; then roll on to one side by first lowering your bottom, then your shoulders, to the floor. You can then roll on to your back. Keep your knees bent all the time. To get back up, bend your knees and roll on to one side. Push up on to your bottom, and swing round on to your hands and knees, from where you can now stand up.

At the end of the book you will find some useful contacts for those with back pain in the UK, as well as a short Recommended Reading list.

CHAPTER 1

Exercise by Prescription

Are you in bed? Right this moment, are you suffering spasms of incapacitating back pain? Wondering how long you'll have to lie there this time? Worrying about when you can get back to work?

We hope not. But if you are, or if the memory of such an incident is still all too fresh in your mind, we believe this book can give you the help you need to end your episodes of back pain once and for all.

Indeed, the long-awaited, highly touted cure for back pain—the treatment that could relieve the agonies of an estimated 80 to 90 percent of the American public and save the country between $16 billion and $50 billion annually in medical expenses and lost work time, according to figures from the American Academy of Orthopædic Surgeons—has actually been discovered. It is called *exercise*. And it works.

Unfortunately, few people really understand the enormous benefits to be gained from exercise, and even fewer people with back pain, therefore, are willing to invest any time or effort in an exercise program specifically aimed at controlling their painful symptoms. Most of the 80 million people who suffer from periodic bouts of back pain continue to think that there must be a more scientific or perhaps even a surgical solution to their woes. They cannot accept the fact that exercise is simply the best, most potent medicine available to treat a back problem.

We consider this lack of knowledge about exercise a national tragedy. The fact is, as little as ten minutes of exercise a day for two weeks will bring about a striking degree of improvement for most people.

When we undertook our landmark study of back pain, we interviewed individuals from all fifty states who had tried literally everything to lead a full life despite a bad back. Our research exploded many popular misconceptions about back care. We showed, for example, that neither orthopedists nor chiropractors usually made the best back doctors, and that the most widely used treatments for back pain were either ineffective or downright dangerous. We also discovered that the right exercises, performed the right way, were the *only* key to a pain-free back.

Our recommendations, published in our book *Backache Relief*, reflected the positive experiences of many survey participants who enjoyed dramatic, long-term relief from back pain, without suffering repeat collapses. What accounted for these individuals' successful outcomes? In a word, *exercise*. The secret to remaining pain-free, they told us, lay in learning —and sticking to—a well-designed exercise program.

The book in your hands outlines just such a safe, sane

exercise program. It gives clear, simple instructions and step-by-step drawings to help you learn the exercise routines with ease. It will also help you devise your own individually tailored exercise program to accomplish any or all of the following goals:

- Prevent back problems from plaguing you in the future
- Treat a disabling episode of acute pain
- Achieve lasting relief from chronic backache
- Make lifestyle changes that can put an end to back pain

Our advice and suggestions about exercise are based not only on our own survey research, but also on our continuing review of recent hospital studies investigating the value of exercise for back pain. Numerous studies, completed since the publication of *Backache Relief*, add further proof that exercise can succeed in helping to alleviate back problems—even after other treatments have failed. Medical researchers all over the world now state confidently that a combination of aerobic, stretching, strengthening, and endurance exercises can bring about genuine improvement for most painful back conditions. Instead of dismissing back pain as "the price we pay for walking upright," specialists are at last coming to see back pain as the consequence of *not walking upright enough*—of spending too much time sitting at the desk, in front of the television, or behind the wheel.

For example, a recent study conducted at the University of Copenhagen, divided 105 patients with chronic low-back pain into three groups. One group underwent three months of intensive exercise training, which entailed thirty workout sessions. The second group attended just as many sessions in the gym, but were asked to perform only a fraction of the activity. The third group had the most sedentary time of all, performing some mild exercise at their sessions, but spending more time receiving heat treatments and massage.

As the doctors reported in 1991 in the journal *Pain*, the subjects in the active-exercise group who continued in training at least once a week over the follow-up year were in the best shape, with less pain and greater mobility than they had at the study's outset. The positive result held as true for women as for men, regardless of age. The researchers also noted that the patient's preexisting conditions had little bearing on their improvement. Indeed, even some veterans of chronic back syndromes got better as a result of the increased activity.

The program we offer in this book is neither rigorous nor difficult. Some of the exercises may seem no more strenuous to you than an everyday activity such as getting out of bed or shopping for your groceries. Yet the simple act of stretching your legs and strengthening your abdominal muscles will have profound effects on the way you look and feel. A small amount of effort will pay off in a noticeable improvement in well-being.

More validation for exercise emerged from a study at Sweden's Sahlgren Hospital. The participants there included 103 industrial workers who had been out of work for eight weeks because of low-back pain. The doctors instructed half of this group in gentle, individually tailored exercises and safety tips for avoiding injury. Not surprisingly, this half wound up going back to work sooner, feeling better. Over the ensuing year, those who exercised and "watched their backs" lost fewer work days than others who did not learn such precautions, according to the researchers' 1992 report in the journal *Physical Therapy*.

In the United States, where back pain accounts for 40 to 50 percent of all lost work days, and as many as one-third of all workers' compensation payments, employees in all sorts of industrial and office settings could be helped by performing exercises at home and learning the back-kindest ways to go about their jobs. You will find tips of this sort in chapters 14, 15, and 16.

When medical studies compare exercise to no exercise, few researchers are surprised to find that the exercise effort paid off in terms of pain relief. Other studies we reviewed went even further in establishing the importance of exercise—by comparing exercise to other widely used treatments for back pain. For example, Dr. Richard A. Deyo of the University of Washington School of Medicine and School of Public Health has tested exercise against transcutaneous electrical nerve stimulation, called TENS. In treatment, the TENS device, about the size of a television remote control, is hooked up to the patient's back via wires and electrodes that gently and steadily jolt the areas of muscle spasm. The electric current is said to confer relaxation and relief. Our own investigation of TENS had convinced us that the units worked —at most—50 percent of the time.

For his research project, Dr. Deyo gave each of his subjects either a real TENS device or a sham TENS unit that gave no jolt but looked like a working machine. Since he never told patients of the differences, each expected some help to come from the little machine. At the same time, Dr. Deyo also put several of the participants on a program of stretching exercise to be performed in addition to the TENS treatments. After one month, the subjects who had exercised were better off than those who hadn't, regardless of whether they had the real or false TENS units. Only the exercise proved valuable. But the subjects didn't seem to understand the connection. Despite the improvement, most of them had quit exercising by the time of the follow-up exam two months later—and their pain had returned.

To help you stick to your exercise program, we've come up with ways to work it into your daily routine, so that you won't look at exercise as just another impossible demand on your time. Chapter 5 gives the details of these strategies, and chapter 6 offers tips on sustaining your motivation to exercise through times when people or problems may tempt you to quit.

Another "treatment" long advocated as a way to beat a bad back is weight control. Doctors have suggested that dieting to lose five to ten pounds would reduce the strain on the back and therefore ward off future episodes of back pain. In our research, we determined that doctors who gave this advice were usually trying to pass the buck—to shift the blame to the patient instead of offering helpful exercise advice. Dr. Deyo later backed us up, when he used national survey data to show that only the very obese stand to gain back-pain relief from losing weight. The person who is just a few pounds above ideal weight is at no greater risk for back trouble than is a thin man or woman. And besides, exercise and increased activity tend to bring weight under reasonable control without the stress of dieting.

Dr. Deyo, who has probably conducted more research into back pain than any other American medical doctor, has also compared exercise to bed rest. He led a series of studies over the last ten years that have helped direct the tide of treatment away from prolonged bed rest and toward an active, healthful lifestyle. He wrote a widely acclaimed report published in 1986 in the *New England Journal of Medicine* that showed two days of bed rest to be sufficient in most cases of back pain. At that time, doctors were routinely recommending two *weeks* in bed for just about any back problem.

Prolonged bed rest for back pain is now recognized as the culprit in causing a host of other unwelcome problems, including bone loss, general weakness, and blood clots in the legs. The risks of prolonged bed rest make it too dangerous a treatment to consider lightly—unless it is attempted as an alternative to an even more dangerous procedure, such as surgery for a ruptured disk.

In other words, even if you are staying home because you have too much pain to go to work, and you cannot manage to sit in a chair, you will probably do better if you spend a good part of each day standing up and resting on your feet, as opposed to staying in bed. In chapter 6 we offer a few preliminary "exercise positions" for people who have been confined to bed by intractable pain, and who are just beginning to be able to exercise.

Further endorsement for exercise activity emerged recently from the so-called Quebec Task Force, a large consortium of researchers and back doctors who reviewed a worldwide collection of clinical reports. They concluded that only two things truly aid the person with common low-back pain: aerobic conditioning (exercise, that is) and education about the proper way to sit, stand, lift, and carry. You will find a guide to appropriate aerobic exercises in chapters 10 and 11, and tips on performing everyday activities, from working at a desk to holding a baby, in chapters 14, 15, and 16.

If you have consulted a doctor about your back pain, you may have received some exercise advice already. We hope so. If, however, your doctor has not mentioned the importance of exercise in alleviating back pain, we urge you to raise the subject yourself. Take this book along to show the doctor, and get his or her opinion of the safety of the program for your specific condition. We feel strongly that the exercises contained here are safe and will pass any practitioner's cautious inspection. We even include, in chapter 11, exercises particularly recommended for specific back-pain conditions, such as osteoarthritis-based back pain and scoliosis. Whatever condition your back is in, you can improve your condition with exercise. Even if you have not been able to exercise in the past, and feel limited by pain now, you can find suggestions in chapter 4 that will help you work a helpful amount of exercise into your life.

CHAPTER 2

Alternatives to Exercise

Exercise is almost invariably better for your back than anything else you can put onto or into your body. Compared with all other back-pain treatments, exercise makes the most sense because it is harmless, affordable, and effective.

The same cannot be said of painkillers and anti-inflammatory medications, for example, although these drugs are routinely prescribed for people with back pain. Indeed, drugs constitute the most widely used treatment for back pain. As we discovered in our Back Pain Survey and related research for our book, *Backache Relief*, they do practically no good at all, and their unpleasant side effects may cause considerable harm.

We have said that back pain afflicts an estimated 80 to 90 percent of the population at one time or another, and accounts for somewhere between $16 billion and $50 billion annually in medical expenses and lost work time. Many of the treatments that run up these high medical bills are the same ones we are calling ineffective and dangerous. Too many of them have come in and out of fashion like hemlines—proffered at the whim of the practitioners, with no basis in theories of back anatomy and dysfunction. Prolonged bed rest falls into this category. So does traction. So, too, do many varieties of injections and even surgical interventions.

If you are currently suffering from back pain, wondering what course of treatment to pursue or what kind of practitioner to consult, you no doubt have a lot of unanswered questions. Following are the questions we hear most often from people with back problems—along with the answers we've learned from our survey research and our reading of the medical literature.

How long should I rest in bed?
Unless you have a herniated disk, which may require you to stay in bed for a couple of weeks or more, two to four days is now considered ample time to rest a bad back. After that, try to get on your feet and walk around a bit. Sitting may be the last thing you feel like doing.

I want to see a doctor. Could my family doctor help me?
If your family doctor knows you and knows back pain, this may be all the help you'll ever need. If, however, your family doctor's answer to a back problem is to pull out a prescription pad—and this response is all too common among general practitioners—you will no doubt need to look elsewhere. (The pitfalls of prescription pills as a treatment for back pain are discussed in more detail later in this chapter.)

Your family doctor may decide to refer you to a specialist,

such as an orthopedist, a rheumatologist, or a neurosurgeon. Referrals make sense in medicine, so long as the family doctor is really trying to bring in an expert's opinion and assistance— and not merely dismissing you and your back pain by shipping you off to someone else.

General practitioners frequently refer their patients with back pain to an orthopedist, or orthopedic surgeon. Don't let the word *surgeon* scare you. Only about 1 to 3 percent of all cases of back pain can be treated surgically, so the odds of your needing an operation are slim. Instead, a well-informed orthopedist will try to diagnose your condition and prescribe the necessary exercises, or perhaps call in a physical therapist to work with you. An orthopedist who is less well informed— or less inclined to work with people outside the operating room—may say, "There's nothing really wrong with you." This throws the ball back in your court, so to speak, making you feel worse than ever. Now you not only hurt, but you've also been told that you hurt for no good reason. But don't lose hope if this happens to you! This is the time to work out a recovery plan, preferably with your family doctor's help, that involves a graduated program of stretching exercises plus walking.

Do I need X rays to discover what's wrong with my back?
Probably not. The very process of having an X ray may set you up for needless anxiety and disappointment—or worse. Since only a few back conditions show up on X rays, most X-ray findings are negative. In other words, they don't tell you any useful information.

About 80 percent of all cases of low-back pain can be traced to problems with the muscles, ligaments, or disks. And none of these soft tissues show up on an X-ray image. Only bones do.

In some cases, X rays reveal real conditions that may have nothing to do with the current source of pain. Suppose, for example, that you have mild scoliosis, which means that your spine is not perfectly straight. Somehow you have made it through life with no idea of this benign condition. Now that you find yourself in pain, however, some practitioner may be all too ready to blame your discomfort on the scoliosis. It is more likely that you have a muscle spasm or strain, unrelated to the X-ray finding.

Another common X-ray finding in practically anyone over the age of thirty-five is some degree of arthritis in the facet joints of the spine. The odds are still overwhelmingly in favor of your back pain being of a muscular origin—and having an exercise solution.

A real problem with X rays is that doctors who rely on them often conclude, from reading your X ray, that "there's nothing really wrong with you." But really, there *is* something wrong. *It's just that what's wrong with you doesn't show up on the X ray.*

What about chiropractors? Aren't they as good as—or better than—medical doctors for treating back pain?
Chiropractors fared slightly better, at least in the short run, than orthopedists in our Back Pain Survey, which compared and rated more than one hundred types of practitioners and treatments. They enjoyed their greatest success, among our participants, with acute cases of low-back and neck pain. They were less helpful to people who had severe chronic pain; in fact, they often proved counterproductive, as when they attempted to treat conditions such as herniated disk, sciatica, or severe arthritis pain. Likewise, they had little success in correcting scoliosis.

The hands-on manipulation for which chiropractors are famous worked best when it was done gently. Overall, chiropractic manipulation seemed less important, in terms of patient satisfaction, than these practitioners' holistic approach and willingness to listen. Chiropractors dispensed exercise advice as part of their treatments, which was all to the good, and sometimes they gave nutritional counsel as well as advice about lifestyle and the role of stress in aggravating back pain.

Chiropractors, like orthopedists, base their diagnoses on X rays, but, unlike orthopedists, they invariably see a specific cause of pain on an X ray. These causes are termed "subluxations" and "misalignments," often resulting in "pinched nerves," which the chiropractor aims to correct through manipulation of the spine.

The chiropractor's real secret of success, however, is a knowledge of exercise combined with the ability to build a good rapport with patients—and encourage them to exercise.

How can I find out exactly what's wrong with my back?
You may not be able to find out—ever. Our Back Pain Survey showed that practitioners made diagnoses based on their medical specialty and frame of reference. For example, neurologists and rehabilitation doctors frequently recommend an uncomfortable and expensive diagnostic procedure called EMG (electromyography) to check for nerve damage, while orthopedists and primary-care doctors, on the other hand, rarely go this route. This means that two doctors from different fields are more than likely to give you two different names for your condition, and two different explanations of what caused the problem. Or neither one will be able to pinpoint the cause of pain with any specificity.

Although some episodes of back pain can be tied to strains incurred during overexertion or in falls, at least as many bouts strike literally out of the blue. Even if you don't know exactly what laid you up, you can still get better with a brief period of rest followed by devotion to daily exercise.

Who are the back specialists who can help me the most?
The premier back doctor, according to the results of our survey, turned out to be a relatively little-known medical

specialist called a *physiatrist*, or doctor of physical medicine. These practitioners rarely prescribe drugs and do not perform surgery. They prefer instead to use individually prescribed exercise regimens and physical therapy—including ultrasound (heat) and massage—to treat back pain.

Shouldn't I get some kind of prescription medication?

Probably not. Our survey found no evidence that back sufferers gained any benefit from prescription analgesics (pain pills). Most of these drugs fail to relieve pain; those that do work may be so potent as to upset your stomach and cloud your thinking. If you are taking a drug powerful enough to mute pain, you won't have the warning signal of your pain to guide you, and so you must limit your physical activity in order to avoid further injury. And limiting your activity is ultimately bad for your back.

We found prescription anti-inflammatory drugs to have less value than sugar pills for most cases of back pain—but with far more side effects. Our participants complained of gastrointestinal upsets, including aggravation of ulcers and gastritis. It's not worth taking these drugs, especially when you consider that few back problems even entail inflammation in the first place.

Muscle relaxants, another favorite prescription item, offer some temporary relief to a minority of people with back pain, although these drugs cause potentially dangerous dizziness and drowsiness. Remember that muscles can also be relaxed with physical therapy, heat, massage, and gentle stretching.

Our survey participants found plain old, over-the-counter aspirin to be the most effective drug. And its price was the lowest of all these products.

If you have already received a prescription drug for your back pain, we urge you to discuss this point with your physician.

How do I know if I have a slipped disk? And what treatment will I receive if I do?

Many doctors diagnose a "slipped"—or, more correctly, a "herniated" or ruptured disk—by the degree and location of the patient's pain. This condition frequently causes numbness or tingling in the legs, all the way to the feet. The back, buttock, and leg pain may well be excruciating.

Although herniated disks do not show up on X rays, as explained above, they can be visualized with newer imaging procedures such as CT (computed tomography) scans and MRI (magnetic resonance imaging).

The disks, twenty-two in number, are sandwiched between the upper twenty-four vertebrae of the spinal column, where they cushion the bones and add mechanical strength to the spine. The structure of the disk itself—soft inside, firm outside—invites comparison to a jelly doughnut. An injury or deterioration can make the "jelly" bulge out into the spinal canal, where it may press on a nerve root, causing extreme pain and sometimes threatening paralysis.

A herniated disk is one of the few kinds of backaches that calls for more than two days' bed rest. A herniated disk often—but not always—warrants surgery. Because of the intense pain and the real risk of neurological impairment associated with herniated disk, you will need to seek a medical opinion. Remember, though, that many people have recovered by bed rest alone, or with the aid of strong pain medication. (This is one situation in which such drugs are clearly indicated.)

Since even herniated disks may right themselves, experienced physicians reserve surgery as a last resort, to be avoided until all other, safer approaches—including "tincture of time" in a six-week dose—have failed to deliver relief. Only about 5 to 10 percent of people with herniated disks actually require surgery, according to studies conducted at Harvard Medical School.

Advances in surgical technique have given rise to new, "scarless" disk procedures that can be performed on an outpatient basis, with tiny arthroscopic instruments and lasers. These operations promise fewer complications and faster recuperation at home than result from traditional disk surgery. But the new approaches don't yet match the success rates of the traditional operations. And instead of simply lessening the stress of surgery for those who need it, the seemingly benign procedures are more likely to be offered to people who don't really need surgery.

Manipulation, according to our survey results, is one treatment that can make the pain and disability of a herniated disk considerably worse. Traction is another.

Could my back pain be caused by some other health problem?
It could indeed, and that's why it makes sense to see a medical doctor for a thorough checkup when you have back pain. Conditions that can cause backache include arthritis, kidney disease, colitis, and certain forms of cancer.

I'm a bit overweight. Would dieting help my back pain?
It depends on how overweight you are. Many doctors say that losing five to ten pounds by dieting will reduce the strain on your back and help you avoid future episodes of back pain. But this comment seems to be another "blame the victim" strategy. Studies show that only the very obese stand to gain much pain relief from weight loss. And besides, exercise and increased activity tend to bring weight under reasonable control —*without* dieting.

How can exercise help my back pain?
Exercise stretches and strengthens the four sets of muscles that support the spine. Your abdominal muscles, for example, although they do not attach directly to the spine, are responsi-

ble for girdling your internal organs and contributing to good posture. The abdominals also assist the extensor muscles of the back, which flank the full length of the spine to maintain proper alignment of the vertebrae. Your hip and buttock muscles help support and govern the position of your back while you're sitting, standing, or walking.

Muscle pain typically arises from weakness, spasm or loss of elasticity due to age or inactivity. *All* of these conditions can be remedied through exercise.

A few people I know got over episodes of horrible back pain by trying nutty home remedies, and others got better without doing anything at all about it. So why should I bother exercising?

It's true that many—perhaps most—episodes of intractable back pain end of their own accord, regardless of the treatments applied. The on-again, off-again nature of some back problems, in fact, has given false endorsements to many dubious treatment modalities over the years, from corticosteroid injections to gravity inversion, from TENS to DMSO. Doctors and patients alike may attribute sudden improvement to the treatment of the hour.

Back pain can disappear, in time, with no treatment whatsoever. People who discover this fact for themselves may argue that exercise isn't worth the bother. But exercise can stave off *recurring* bouts of back pain, which tend to grow more debilitating with each successive onset. And back pain that goes away in response to exercise, studies show, tends to return when the exercise is stopped. In other words, your back will thank you for initiating and sticking to a safe exercise program.

CHAPTER 3

A Program for Permanent Improvement

By now you understand—intellectually, at any rate—the value of regular exercise in preventing and treating back pain. All that's left is to let us help you devise a personally tailored program that will fit into your life. Adopting the program is a commitment to performing a few stretching and strengthening exercises for ten to fifteen minutes a day—and engaging in aerobic activities for three to four hours a week. This is the biggest lifestyle change the program demands, but, as you'll see, the payoff is measured in an even bigger change in the quality of your life. If you've never exercised regularly before, get ready to feel great!

We urge you to ignore the popular image of exercise as

vigorous and competitive. For back sufferers, as one of our survey participants pointed out, "Slower is generally better, gradual is faster, and vigorous is self-defeating." We might well say, "Any pain, less gain."

All of the back exercises mentioned in this book were performed by the participants in our nationwide Back Pain Survey, who judged them safe and sound. We believe you'll agree. Not every participant performed every exercise, of course—nor should you expect to do so. From the full set, we will help you select those few that best suit your needs, depending on the location, type, severity, and duration of your back pain. Your exercise choices should match your level of fitness, comfort level, time schedule, and tastes. It must enhance your general health, too, so we urge you to check with your doctor about any special restrictions imposed by your personal medical history. Having a wide range of selections from which to choose will not only enable you to personalize your program, but also to change it from time to time—either to make your routine more challenging as you gain experience, or to introduce new exercises just for the sake of variety.

The stretching and strengthening exercises are all explained in detail in chapters 8, 9, and 12, complete with step-by-step instructions and line drawings. The aerobic exercise options are also discussed at length, in chapter 10, with specific suggestions for getting started. Our aim in this chapter is to explain the goals of the different types, and to show how they can work together to promote back fitness.

Your program will consist of three types of exercise:

1. *Aerobic activities,* such as walking and swimming, that increase your stamina and improve your cardiovascular fitness
2. *Stretching exercises,* typified by Knee Drops and Head Rolls, that keep your muscles limber and help prevent spasms

3. *Strengthening exercises*, including Push-offs and Bent-Knee Sit-ups, that firm up the muscles you need to maintain good posture and to carry out everyday activities without putting your back at risk.

Aerobic Exercise

You will spend most of your exercise time engaged in aerobic activities. In fact, aerobic exercise demands a certain minimum time period—at least twenty minutes per session, and preferably forty-five minutes to an hour, repeated three or four times a week. The sustained nature of the activity is what raises your heart rate and gets your blood pumping as you burn oxygen. These effects give aerobic exercise its other well-known name, *cardiovascular activity*. Indeed, the benefits of sustained activity for the heart and circulatory system have by now gained universal acceptance.

But for you, as a person with back trouble, aerobic exercise has another important value: Sustained aerobic activities nourish the disks of your spine by increasing the blood supply to these unique tissues. Much back pain emanates from the disks themselves, which contain abundant nerve endings. To treat your disks well, whether you are trying to protect them from deterioration or help them heal after injury, you do best to pursue aerobic exercise.

The strong relationship between cardiovascular exercise and the health of the spinal disks has implications for other lifestyle choices. You've probably heard at least a million times that smoking is bad for your heart and lungs. But the fact is, smoking damages the disks, too, through its effect on the blood circulation. Nicotine and other components of cigarette smoke compromise the microcirculation—the network of tiny blood vessels throughout the body that feed all the tissues, including the disks. Physicians' surveys have identified cigarette smoking as one of the major risk factors for back pain.

Among backache sufferers, smokers outnumber nonsmokers four to one. And in follow-up studies of people who have undergone operations for the repair of herniated disks, cigarette smokers prove five times more likely to have a poor outcome than postoperative patients who don't smoke.

Alcohol, like cigarette smoke, also constricts the blood vessels and can contribute to poor circulation around the disks. Moderate drinking in social situations probably contributes very little to disk degeneration, but alcohol abuse can aggravate back pain from this source.

You may feel immediate positive effects from aerobic exercise, in addition to backache relief. These could include increased energy during your waking hours, coupled with better sleep at night. You may find that you feel calmer during your aerobic activity period, and that you look forward to this time of day, at least in part, for the stress relief it brings. Over the long term, aerobic exercise will help you shed unwanted pounds, since such activity burns body fat and calories. Provided you don't simultaneously increase your food intake, aerobic exercise will gradually whittle away your excess weight.

Aerobic exercises tend to be everyone's favorites because they are intrinsically enjoyable, or can be made that way. Many of them can be done in the company of others, and therefore provide opportunities for pleasant social contacts. Walking wins our vote for the best aerobic exercise, since it is safe and effective and can be done virtually anytime, anywhere, indoors or out.

Stretching

Your muscles tend to tighten with disuse. If you lead a sedentary life, you can keep your muscles long and limber by intentionally stretching them with exercise. That primes them for action.

You probably already know too well what happens when you rely on overly tight muscles to help you make some sudden move: They fail you by going into spasm and slapping you with pain. Now they are in a state of painful contraction, and they may refuse to come out for a long time. The secret of successful treatment for spasm, just like the key to its prevention, lies in gentle stretching.

It's always a good idea to warm up before you stretch. Typical exercise programs for fit people often call for five minutes of jogging in place as a warm-up. But if jogging is too rough for you, or if you are starting out with very limited ability to move, you can warm up in any number of gentler ways. Some of our survey participants reported that they took a warm bath or used a heating pad just before exercise. This enabled them to stretch more readily, get more from the therapy, and increase their rate of progress. If you choose to exercise the very first thing in the morning, you may get an ample warm-up by moving around in bed and then walking for a few minutes before you begin.

When you stretch, try to concentrate on stretching to the point of resistance—and then moving just a fraction beyond it. But, we implore you, *don't push through pain.* Overstretching can be worse than not doing any exercise at all, since it can tear the muscle fibers or induce spasms and pain. Carefully executed back exercises can bring you noticeable improvement in just a few weeks. Please try to be patient. Remember that exercise therapy, no matter how cautious it may seem to you, is almost always better than anything you can put into or onto your body.

Although aerobic exercise can be limited to three or four days a week, stretching does the most for you when you do it every day. This is not just a physiological reality, but a mental one as well; by stretching every day, you make stretching a habit, and you are more likely to stick with it. In chapter 7 we'll discuss other strategies that can help you sustain your motivation to exercise.

You may choose to perform all your stretches at once, in a single session, or break up your exercise into two periods, one in the morning and the other at night. The twice-a-day approach works especially well for people who are recovering from an acute episode of back pain, because it helps them make speedier progress. Those who have already attained back fitness, however, and are exercising to maintain the good feeling, can do equally well with a once-a-day regimen.

Each exercise session needs to have its own internal order. After your warm-ups, we suggest you begin with the easiest, gentlest movements, and progress through the more difficult stretching and strengthening exercises. Then cool down by walking at a leisurely pace for about five minutes.

You will notice that many of the stretching and strengthening exercises call for you to make forward-bending movements with your spine, as when you perform the Knee-to-Chest Rock. Exercise experts call this movement *flexion*. Hospital studies have shown that flexion exercises work quickly and effectively to increase the mobility of the lower back.

Another pro-back movement, called *extension*, works to lengthen the spine. You can experience this sensation when you stretch your lower back in executing the Pelvic Tilt.

None of our exercises requires you to hyperextend or arch your back. In both the Cat Stretch and the Head Roll, you have the opportunity to arch your neck, but the instructions tell you to omit this step if neck arching is even the slightest bit uncomfortable. Our exercise philosophy precludes exaggerated arching for two reasons: (1) arching the spine, we believe, puts too much pressure on the disks, and (2) arching the lower back stretches the abdominal muscles.

Regarding the latter, the abdominal muscles really don't require stretching; they have too great a tendency to stretch and sag by themselves. What we really want you to do with your abdominals is build their strength by performing exercises such as the Pelvic Tilt, the Bent-Knee Sit-up, and the Sit-Down.

Strengthening

The exercises that build strength in your muscles usually call for you to work against some resistance—to make the muscles work hard so they grow big and strong. It's tempting to think that you can accomplish this goal with aerobic exercise alone, but the fact is you also need specific exercises that call for a short burst of strength from muscle contraction.

Strengthening exercises may be *isotonic* or *isometric*. The isotonic ones involve motion against resistance. For example, in a Push-Off, you push the weight of your body about twelve inches in an effort to strengthen your shoulders and upper back. The isometric exercises involve no obvious movement, just force against resistance. For example, in the Side Press, you push against a wall to strengthen your arm. You may be working just as hard as you did in the Push-Off, but only you can tell how much effort you're expending—since the wall doesn't move.

Fitness enthusiasts who exercise in gyms build strength by lifting weights. We don't include any weight resistance work here, because we feel it's unnecessary for addressing the problem of back pain. Lifting and maneuvering the weight of your own body is sufficient, we feel, for the goals of this program.

Many exercise instructors believe that strengthening exercises should not be done every day. In your back-exercise routine, however, we want you to include them and perform them with the stretches—especially the Pelvic Tilt and Bent-Knee Sit-ups. Unlike weight-resistance exercises, our strengtheners won't tax your body and call for a day or more of rest for muscle repair and recovery between sessions.

Instead, these exercises will safeguard your posture and work to reduce your pain.

Sample Exercise Program

The following program is suitable for a person who is reasonably fit, occasionally laid up with back pain, but free of neck pain.

Aerobic activity

Walk for twenty to forty minutes, three times a week.

Stretching

The range of repetitions listed below represents the first day of doing the exercises (the first number) and a month later (the second number).

- Knee-to-Chest (three to six repetitions)
- Knees-to-Chest Rock (two to five repetitions)
- Knee Cross (two to five repetitions each side)
- Cat Stretch (three to six repetitions)
- Knee Spread (two to four repetitions)
- Hamstring Stretch (two to five repetitions each side)
- Thigh Pull (two to four repetitions each side)
- Runner's Stretch (two to four repetitions each side)

Strengthening

The range of repetitions listed below represents the first day of doing the exercises (the first number) and a month later (the second number).

- Pelvic Tilt (five to ten repetitions)
- Bent-Knee Sit-ups (five to ten repetitions)
- Sit-downs (one to five repetitions)

CHAPTER 4

A Special Message for People with Chronically Disabling Back Pain

Our exercise program constitutes a *cure* for 90 percent of people with back pain. But what about the other 10 percent? If you are one of them, please read on.

First, let us assure you that you are not alone. From what we can gather, at least 1.5 million Americans, and perhaps as many as 5 million, are severely disabled by back pain that has resisted every treatment brought to bear. Some of these individuals have what physicians call "Failed Back Syndrome." This is an unfortunate euphemism for a poor surgical outcome from diskectomy or other operation on the spine. The term makes it sound as though the patient's back were guilty of some kind of gross failure, when really it is the surgery or other treatments that failed to bring improvement to the person. The individual continues to suffer, but with less hope than before, and the hope diminishes as the realization grows that no help may be forthcoming from any source.

Even without surgery, some backache sufferers find themselves growing progressively worse, no matter what they do. We want to tell you about one of these people, a participant in our original Back Pain Survey, who suffered the kind of anguish you may be going through.

When he filled out his survey questionnaire, Bob had seen both orthopedists and chiropractors, as well as osteopaths, naturopaths, and numerous other conventional and alternative health practitioners. No two of his twelve diagnoses were the same, so he never knew what was wrong with his back. Still, he continued to read widely about back pain, to seek professional help, and try each new seemingly sound and rational remedy.

In a page he stapled onto the survey, Bob described his predicament:

> Some doctors who know about the chronicity of my problem won't even allow me to make an appointment to see them. If they do agree to examine me, they're all but itching to get me out the door. It is assumed that I have workmen's compensation or some other kind of insurance, which I don't, or that I'm a neurotic who enjoys the attention. Actually, I live alone, and nobody pays me any attention unless I'm up and about. Some people obviously think I'm a malingerer, even though I worked from age fourteen to forty. It's just been the past five years that I've not been able to be on my feet long enough to hold down a job. I am living off my savings, which are about depleted.

The questionnaire explained that the information people provided would be used in a book we were writing about back pain (*Backache Relief*, Times Books 1985, NAL/Signet 1986).

Bob was a little concerned about that. In a postscript he added, "I hope that your book won't leave out people like me. I hope it won't be another simplistic *Six Minutes a Day to Relief*, full of 'guaranteed safe' exercises I can't even do."

We did not leave Bob out of our first book, and we won't leave him—or you—out of this one, either.

If you are suffering from long-standing, seemingly intractable back problems, you may require special preparations or expert exercise guidance from a trained practitioner before you can make use of the exercises we describe in subsequent chapters. Bob, when we last heard from him, had started to find his way out of that prolonged disability, and to look forward to functioning normally once again.

What follows are some suggestions on fighting your way back from extreme disability over a long period of time.

Try seeing a physiatrist.
Even if you have a long list of professionals you've already consulted, you may do well to take your troubles to a doctor of physical medicine and rehabilitation, also known as a physiatrist. These practitioners are accustomed to treating debilitating conditions, from spinal cord injuries to strokes, and are not easily frightened off by pain that has a long history. They are not trained as surgeons, although they can spot problems that do require surgical treatment, and then make appropriate referrals. Physiatrists recognize the value of exercise, and have a thorough knowledge of exercise as a prescription drug. Of all the medical specialists, the physiatrist is the most likely to be able to create an individualized exercise program that promises gradual improvement.

Another thing a physiatrist will likely do for you is to recommend physical therapy. The physical therapist, acting under the doctor's orders, will work with you on the successful execution of your exercises, as well as give you treatments that could include heat, or massage, or both.

In the UK, we do not have an equivalent of the US physiatrist. Instead, the closest practitioner is likely to be a doctor who specializes in rehabilitating those who have suffered from debilitating pain and disease, including those with chronic back pain. You can talk to your GP about whether or not you could be referred for such specialist treatment. If your condition is suitable, your GP will also refer you for physiotherapy.

Make a plan for achieving progress slowly.
If your back pain has been growing worse over a period of years, you can't really expect to finally hit on one solution that will solve your problems and land you back on your feet overnight. Anyone who promises you that kind of outcome has to be lying.

Accept the fact that your recovery may take as long as a year, and promise yourself that by the end of the year you will have made substantial progress. And then set out to make that promise come true the way several of our survey participants did—gradually. *Very* gradually.

Perhaps you can be out of bed only a few minutes a day. Try to stop blaming yourself for being incapacitated. Instead of fixating on all the things you used to do that you can't do now, look on those daily minutes out of bed as an indication that you have made some progress and can make much more. Time yourself when you're out of bed so that you know exactly what you can do—the precise number of minutes and seconds that you are up and about. Tell yourself, "Tomorrow I can manage one minute more than that." Just one more minute. One more minute of standing or walking. When you reach that goal, enjoy your success, rather than belittling your achievement as small or insignificant. In just one month, one minute a day translates into half an hour more per day—and thirty more successes. In two months you've gained an hour, and by year's end, six hours. Long before the year is out, you'll be ready for the pre-exercise positions in chapter 6, and then for a simple program of gentle movements to start a lifelong program of regular exercise.

Try to reduce the stress of incapacitation.
Being out of work, out of the swim, breeds its own stress. Being in pain is stressful. But stress, in turn, can often aggravate pain, setting up a vicious circle of emotional and physical anguish. If you have neck pain, you may be especially vulnerable to aggravation of pain by stress. Knowing the role stress can play for someone with long-standing backache, please consider the stress-reduction strategies in chapter 13 as being of particular importance for you.

Make your environment work for you.
You may feel "trapped" by your disability, and rail against the four walls. But there may be many small changes you can make in your surroundings that will collectively contribute to an improvement in your condition. To take the most obvious example, namely the bed you're lying in, ask yourself if the mattress is really firm and comfortable. Are you supporting your body with pillows to your best advantage? If you're watching television, is the set positioned so that you can see the screen without straining your neck or body alignment? Even if you're not carrying out your normal daily activities now, check the suggestions in chapters 14, 15, and 16 to discover ideas about back-safe strategies for doing a variety of everyday tasks. If you follow these suggestions as you make progress, you can avoid further injury.

Remember that your attitude about your body is the basis for improvement.
By celebrating each small success and making your environment as pleasant as possible, you are respecting and nurturing your body. In time, your pain will lessen and you will be able

to do many more things. Believe it or not, you have an advantage over many other backache sufferers, and that is that you will never take your recovery for granted. Once you regain your ability to move, you will take such joy in movement that no one will ever have to nag you to exercise. No doubt you will look forward to that fifteen or twenty minutes a day spent exercising as quality time when you are alone, quiet, in touch with yourself, meditative, knowing that you are doing something good for yourself. And because you have that attitude, you can look forward to keeping yourself well.

PART
TWO

The Motivation

> *Once people accept exercise as medicine, the hardest thing is to get them to take that medicine regularly.*

CHAPTER 5

How to Work Exercise into Your Life

Exercise is a life-transforming tool for back sufferers that will make more of a difference in your sense of well-being than anything else—including the best food, the greatest sex, the most exhilarating fun. The only catch is that you have to do it to reap the benefits.

If you're like most busy people, you already have too much to do. There isn't room in your day for even fifteen minutes of stretching and strengthening exercises, let alone the forty-five minutes to an hour, three times a week, that would satisfy the aerobic exercise requirement of our program.

We're going to help you find the time—somehow— because, again, we are confident that exercise will prove more beneficial to you in the long run than any other approach you can try.

Let's start with the argument that you just don't have any time. Well, then, you certainly don't have time to spend three days in bed, do you? What if we told you that the relatively small time commitment to exercise could buy you an insurance policy against the next time you might have to call in sick to work because "My back has gone out again"?

If time is money, then the time you invest in exercise, which costs you nothing, saves you whatever amount of money you could conceivably spend on chiropractic adjustments, X rays, or prescription medications your family doctor prescribes—the next time your back muscles seize up and lay you low.

What's that? You say you're already running so flat-out that you can't give yourself enough sleep at night, and so you're tired all day? That's no excuse, either. As you'll see, exercise, especially regular aerobic exercise, will change the way you feel, every minute of the day. Instead of depleting your energy, as you might suppose, exercise actually gives you more energy. Even though it burns up calories and cuts through fat on your body, it doesn't make you tired. On the contrary, exercise makes you feel more alert and alive—and because you tend to sleep better when you exercise, you're likely to find that you feel more rested even when you spend fewer hours in bed.

Maybe these arguments sound too pat. We set up a straw man, then knock it down, but meanwhile, you really are too busy to exercise. Let's try another approach. Let's look at your day and see if there's someplace, any place, that we can squeeze in the requisite amount of exercise. Maybe you can do your exercises while you're watching your children or warming food in the microwave. If you can allow for three five-minute mini-exercise sessions spread over the course of the day, you'll benefit from even that much, we promise. So ask yourself the following questions, and maybe you'll find the answer to the problem of not having time to exercise.

If you work at a regular job . . .
Can you walk to work instead of driving or taking public transportation?

Do you have time to walk on your lunch hour?

Is there a health club or a pool near your workplace where you can swim during your lunch hour?

If you work in a building that has several floors, can you climb the steps instead of riding the elevator?

Can you interest your employer in starting a "back school" to help your co-workers learn exercise and back-friendly work habits on the job?

Honestly, if while sitting at your desk, you went through the whole series of neck-stretching exercises, from Left-Right to Head Pull, would anyone think you were doing anything so terribly strange?

Couldn't you also get away with performing most of the neck-strengthening exercises, as well as the routine for the shoulders and upper back?

If you need to talk to a colleague in the building, would you consider walking there for a face-to-face conference instead of dialing his or her extension on the telephone?

If you work at home . . .
Isn't it possible to lie down on the floor and stretch your back while you're taking a respite shorter than a coffee break?

Since no one's around to watch you, can you do your neck exercises while you're on the telephone? (That way, you'll avoid doing something to hurt your neck, such as cradling the phone between your ear and your shoulder for too many minutes at a time.)

When it's time to check the mailbox or go to the post office, can you walk for twenty minutes?

If you are caring for young children . . .
Wouldn't the baby love to go for a long walk in the stroller?

Can the baby play or nap on a quilt on the floor while you do your routine lying down nearby?

Why not make your exercises a family activity? Or a game like "Simon Says"?

Can you walk briskly along with your older children while they ride their bikes?

If you are doing housework . . .
Can you find opportunities to make every chore a stretch? (This may involve putting aside some of your labor-saving devices in favor of doing things the old-fashioned way, such as hanging laundry on a line.)

If your house has more than one level, would you mind making several trips up and down for the laundry? (Taking the steps more frequently would probably be better for your back than struggling to carry a heavy load either up or down.)

If you own your own home . . .
Can you turn fall leaf-raking, winter snow-shoveling, and summer lawn care and gardening into aerobic activities? (If so, be sure to approach these activities safely, following the tips in chapter 15.)

If you enjoy soaking in the tub every evening . . .
Can you execute a Pelvic Tilt underwater?

How about a Bent-Knee Sit-up?

Would you believe that exercising in a warm tub can be especially soothing?

If all else fails . . .
Would you consider carrying out your neck, upper back, and standing back exercises in the shower?

Can you find five minutes, three times a day, to lie down on the floor and stretch your muscles? (Watch for opportunities, such as when you're waiting for some family member to get out of the bathroom, or for the stove timer to tell you that dinner is ready, or for your favorite television program to begin.)

Can you find a friend who also needs to exercise, and who'll visit with you while you both walk aerobically?

With the above possibilities in mind, can you create your own opportunities to give yourself the benefit of regular exercise?

You can. Of course you can.

CHAPTER 6

How to Assess Your Exercise Readiness and Assemble Your Tailor-Made Program

Now that you're motivated to exercise—aware of all the pain-relieving, mobility-increasing benefits a program of regular exercise can bring you—you're ready to begin selecting the elements of your individually tailored exercise routine.

In this chapter, we want to help you determine your level of exercise ability, based on factors such as your age, your assessment of your own general fitness, and the duration of your back pain. Then we can make specific exercise suggestions. An "off-the-rack" exercise program cannot possibly suit you as well as a program designed with your needs in mind.

The nature of your back problem also guides you in identifying the ideal exercises for you. As we've said earlier, few people can give a specific name or diagnosis to their back pain. Nevertheless, certain identifiable conditions, including sciatica and osteoarthritis-induced back pain, call for particular precautions.

Let's begin with a simple self-test that will match your level of back pain and limitation with a reasonable set of exercise goals.

SELF-TEST OF EXERCISE READINESS

Please circle the number that best completes each of the following statements:

Most days, I am . . .
  (1) inactive because of pain or chronic disability
  (2) inactive by choice—a "couch potato"
  (3) moderately active
  (4) very active

When I get up in the morning, I feel . . .
  (1) severe pain that never seems to go away completely
  (2) pain that warns me to be careful
  (3) pain on some days, no pain on others
  (4) hardly any pain at all

As I go through the day, I find that I . . .
  (1) need most things done for me
  (2) need help to do some things
  (3) manage well on my own, if I'm careful of my back
  (4) can keep up a normal pace of activity, at work and/or at home, with comfort

My back pain stems from . . .
- (1) osteoarthritis, or herniated disk, or sciatica
- (2) an accident that injured my back some time ago
- (3) muscle spasms
- (4) some unknown cause

Because of my back pain . . .
- (1) I've had surgery at least once
- (2) I've been confined to bed several times, and am somewhat limited in the things I can do
- (3) I've had to stay in bed on occasion, but between episodes of pain I get along fine
- (4) I may think twice before I try some new activity, but I can pretty much do what I want

My experience with exercise in general and back exercise in particular is . . .
- (1) nonexistent
- (2) limited
- (3) moderate
- (4) extensive

My age is . . .
- (1) over sixty-five
- (2) mid-fifties to early sixties
- (3) early forties to mid-fifties
- (4) forty or younger

Now we'd like you to classify yourself in one of four categories, based on your responses to the above questionnaire items. If you circled all ones, for example, or mostly ones, then you are in the "Basic Preparation" category. If your answers included more twos than ones, consider yourself in the "Proceed With Caution" group. If you found the threes to be most descriptive of your condition, please put yourself in the "Gentle Exercise" category. If you scored fours consistently, you are no doubt ready for the "Regular Exercise" category.

Over time, as you make progress and change your level of flexibility and strength, you may move on through the categories at whatever pace seems right for you. There is nothing to stop a person who begins in the Basic Preparation Category from becoming a Regular Exerciser. Indeed, by preparing for exercise and then proceeding with caution at first, you can *expect* to progress to Gentle Exercise and finally to Regular Exercise. And you needn't stop there.

Basic Preparation
(Category 1)

If you suffer from a case of chronically debilitating back pain, please see the special message in chapter 4 before you read on. We have every confidence that you will be able to use the exercises in this book, but first we want to prepare you to perform them safely.

If you are just now recuperating from an acute episode of debilitating back pain, you can try the following pre-exercise positions as soon as your contracted muscles have eased enough for you to move around in bed—or be up and about for just a few minutes at a time. These are such conservative movements that they are safe to attempt *before* your pain lessens enough to permit other exercises. Give yourself a week or two of assuming these positions, in bed, as meaningful first steps toward full activity.

Start slowly and hopefully. There's no need to do all of the positions in one session, or even all in one day at the outset. If you can be comfortable in the Basic Exercise Position for five minutes the first time you try it, move on to the Pelvic Lift later in the day or the next morning. Once you master the Pelvic Lift, and can assume that position for ten minutes at a time, twice a day, you may attempt the Knee Clasp.

BASIC EXERCISE POSITION

If you have been in severe pain, the muscles and ligaments in your lower back have no doubt contracted, creating an exaggerated "S" curve there. Holding the Basic Exercise Position for several minutes will begin to correct that painful swayback, or lordosis. You can gauge the amount of correction each time you slip your hand under the small of your back.

Starting position: Assume the fetal position, lying on your side with both knees bent. *a*

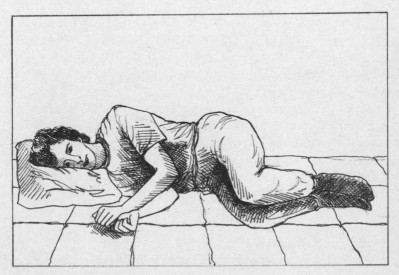

a

Steps:

1. Roll onto your back, and place your arms at your sides. ***b***

2. Position your feet flat on the mattress, with your heels about six to eighteen inches from your buttocks.

3. Hold this position for about two minutes.

4. Slip one hand, palm down, between the small of your back and your mattress. ***c***

5. Remove your hand, and lie in the Basic Exercise Position another two or three more minutes.

6. Repeat Step 4. You'll likely find there's a bit less room for your hand, now that you've been lying flat a longer time.

7. Return to the starting position.

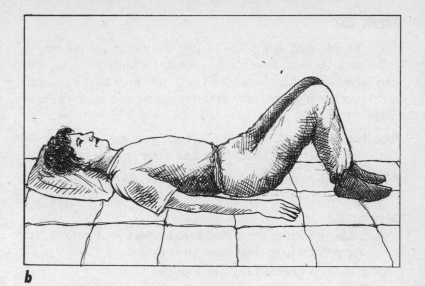

b

c

PELVIC LIFT

Most people find this position just the ticket for relaxing a tired back. As soon as you are comfortable with this pose, you can increase the time you spend in it, one minute per session, until you reach ten minutes in the morning and another ten at night.

Starting position: The Basic Exercise Position—lying flat on your back with your knees bent and your arms at your sides.

Materials: A bath towel, folded just once, so that it is not too bulky.

Steps:
1. Slide an inch of the folded towel under your buttocks, at the point where they meet your thighs.
2. Hold this position for two minutes.
3. Remove the towel.
4. Later in the day, repeat Steps 1–3.

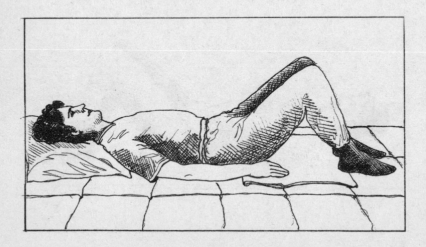

KNEE CLASP

These maneuvers are starting to feel like bona fide exercises. Please remember that the point of this stretch is to let you relax in a comfortably flexed position—and not to challenge you to draw your knees toward your chest as far as you possibly can.

Starting position: The Pelvic Lift Position—lying flat on your back with knees bent, arms at your sides, and a folded towel just under your buttocks. *a*

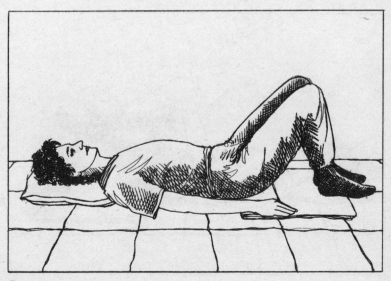

a

Steps:

1. Bring one knee up toward your chest and hold it there with your hand. **b**
2. Bring the other knee up. **c**
3. Clasp your hands together, holding your knees just below the kneecaps.
4. As gently as you can, pull your knees a few inches toward your chest. **d**
5. Hold this position for a count of six.
6. Return to the starting position.
7. Repeat Steps 1–6 six times.

b

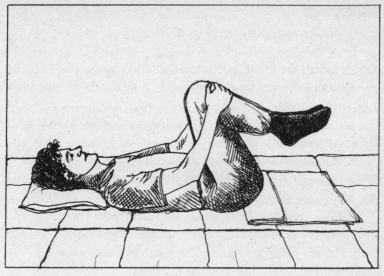

c

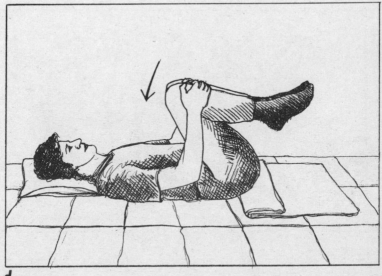

d

LEG SUPPORT

Even though this exercise calls for you to get down and then up from the floor, which may be difficult, we expect you will find it worth the trouble. The combination of the position and the leg support can be relaxing and should help reduce pain.

Starting position: Lie on a carpeted floor (or a gym mat, or a couple of folded blankets) near a sofa or a chair, in the Basic Exercise Position—flat on your back with knees bent and arms at your sides. Support your neck with a folded towel, or put a small pillow under your head and neck. *a*

Steps:
1. Raise one leg with knee bent and rest your calf and foot—but not your thigh—on the sofa or chair. *b*
2. Put the other leg up on the sofa the same way. *c*
3. Hold this position for five minutes.
4. One leg at a time, return to the starting position.

a

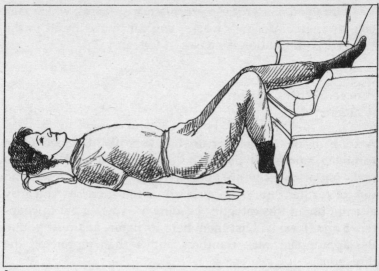

b

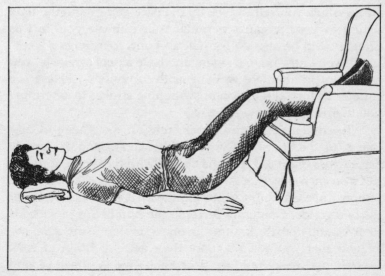

c

Once you master these preparatory exercises, which may take a minimum of two weeks, you can move ahead to the Proceed With Caution exercises in Category 2.

Proceed With Caution
(Category 2)

A long history of back pain has kept you inactive for a troubling amount of time. The exercises that will help you make important gains are necessarily gentle ones that carry no risk of further injury. Because all of the exercises you may attempt under this category heading are spelled out in chapters 8 and 9, we will list them here by name, and refer you to the appropriate page numbers, rather than reprint all the directions.

For your aerobic activity, try walking. Begin slowly, and for a maximum of twenty minutes at a time, three times a week. Allow yourself to pick up the pace and extend the time period as your progress permits. Your ultimate goal in this category will be to walk for half an hour, four times a week.

If you know how to swim, and have a pool available, you may want to alternate walking with swimming. (Please see chapter 10 for a discussion of swimming strokes to determine one that is appropriate for you.)

To stretch your lower back, rely on the Knee-to-Chest (page 76), the Knees-to-Chest Rock (page 74), and the Simple Knee Cross (page 82). You may begin with three repetitions— three on each side, that is—of both the Knee-to-Chest and the Simple Knee Cross. Try to sustain the Knees-to-Chest Rock for thirty seconds. Gradually increase the number of repetitions to five, and the Rock time to one minute. To be safe, we suggest that you add no more than one repetition of each exercise per week. Build up your Rock time in fifteen-second increments. In other words, it may well take you two weeks or longer to go from three to five repetitions, from thirty seconds to one minute.

To strengthen your abdominal muscles, practice five repetitions of the Pelvic Tilt (page 91). As you gain strength, you may build up to ten repetitions. The same holds true for the Standing Pelvic Tilt (page 93). Also attempt the Bent-Knee Sit-ups (page 96), starting with three repetitions a day, and gradually building to ten.

For your buttocks, hips, and legs, rely on The Squeeze (page 98), the Knee Spread (page 98), and the Hip Hikers (page 103), starting with three repetitions of each one every day and building gradually to five.

If you need to stretch the muscles of your neck, try doing the Left-Right (page 113), the Yes-No (page 114), and the Neck Tilt (page 120). It's safe to begin with three repetitions of each, then build to five. To strengthen the muscles of your neck, we recommend the Bed Head (page 121), beginning with three repetitions and moving up to five.

Stretch your shoulders and upper back with the Prone Shoulder Stretch (page 124) and the Shoulder Shrug (page 125). Start at three repetitions and progress to five at the usual pace. Strengthen the upper back area with the Side Press (page 133).

As you gain flexibility in this stage of your program, keep reminding yourself of the good progress you're making. It has taken you a long time to lose and then regain your sense of well-being, so we urge you to let yourself enjoy every aspect of improvement.

After several weeks of slow and steady progress have brought you to the completion of the Category 2 goals, you need not rush ahead to the next level. By all means, let your own assessment of your condition be your guide. You may want to approach Category 3 by taking just a few new exercises and incorporating them into the routine you're following now. On the other hand, you may switch to the

Category 3 exercises, holding on to those elements of Category 2 that seem particularly helpful to you.

Proceed With Caution

> Knee-to-Chest (page 76)
> Total Body Relaxation (page 158)
> Knees-to-Chest Rock (page 74)
> Simple Knee Cross (page 82)
> Pelvic Tilt (page 91)
> Standing Pelvic Tilt (page 93)
> Bent-Knee Sit-ups (page 96)
> The Squeeze (page 98)
> Knee Spread (page 98)
> Hip Hikers (page 103)
> Left-Right (page 113)
> Yes-No (page 114)
> Neck Tilt (page 120)
> Bed Head (page 121)
> Prone Shoulder Stretch (page 124)
> Shoulder Shrug (page 125)
> Side Press (page 133)

Gentle Exercise
(Category 3)

Because you are already fairly active and relatively pain-free, you can attempt a variety of movements. We encourage you to walk for fitness, or alternate swimming with walking, so that you give yourself a forty-minute aerobic workout at least four times a week. If time allows, and as your sense of yourself dictates, you can work up to six sessions per week of aerobic activity, each session lasting as long as an hour. We'd like you to set the pace of this activity at a comfortable level. In other words, when you walk, walk with purpose and direction as though you have somewhere to go—but *not* as though you have to rush because you're late for an appointment.

Work on stretching your lower back with five repetitions of the following six exercises: Knee-to-Chest (page 76), Double Knee-to-Chest (page 78), Knee Drops (page 79), Knee Cross (page 84), Flexibility Twist (page 162) and Twists and Tilts (page 89). If you are comfortable with these movements, you may increase the number of repetitions, one at a time, every three or four days, until you reach ten.

Strengthen your abdominal muscles with five repetitions each of the Pelvic Tilt (page 91), the Standing Pelvic Tilt (page 93), and the Bent-Knee Sit-ups (page 96). At the same pace as you increase your repetitions of stretching exercises, add repetitions of these movements, too, up to ten.

Work your buttocks, hips, and legs by attempting five repetitions of these four exercises: Knee Spread (page 98), Hamstring Stretch (page 100), Thigh Pull (page 104), and Runner's Stretch (page 108). Here, too, slowly work your way up to ten repetitions.

If you have tight neck muscles, loosen them with five daily repetitions of these three exercises: Left-Right Plus (page 114), Neck Bob (page 116), and Head Pull (page 119). Progressing gradually along with the rest of the regimen, you can increase the number of repetitions to ten.

Try to strengthen your neck with three repetitions each of the Neck Push (page 122) and Side Neck Push (page 123). Work up to five repetitions of each.

For stretching your shoulders and upper back, rely on the Shoulder Shrug (page 125), Shoulder Roll (page 126), and Airplane (page 130). Try beginning with three repetitions of each, then working up to five. For stretching these same areas, begin with three repetitions each of the Push-offs (page 132) and the Side Press (page 133), then gradually work toward five repetitions.

By the time you arrive at the full recommended number of repetitions in this category, you will be enjoying a greater range of motion, and probably less anxiety about suffering a relapse of back pain. At this point, you're ready for "Regular Exercise," which has a little more oomph.

Gentle Exercise

> Total Body Relaxation (page 158)
> Knee-to-Chest (page 76)
> Double Knee-to-Chest (page 78)
> Knee Drops (page 79)
> Knee Cross (page 84)
> Flexibility Twist (page 162)
> Twists and Tilts (page 89)
> Pelvic Tilt (page 91)
> Standing Pelvic Tilt (page 93)
> Bent-Knee Sit-ups (page 96)
> Knee Spread (page 98)
> Hamstring Stretch (page 100)
> Thigh Pull (page 104)
> Runner's Stretch (page 108)
> Left-Right Plus (page 114)
> Neck Bob (page 116)
> Head Pull (page 119)
> Neck Push (page 122)
> Side Neck Push (page 123)
> Shoulder Shrug (page 125)
> Shoulder Roll (page 126)
> Airplane (page 130)
> Push-offs (page 132)
> Side Press (page 133)

Regular Exercise
(Category 4)

Since you are on your feet and free of pain most of the time, you probably perform exercises as insurance against future episodes of back pain. Good for you! Indeed, from your active vantage point, some of these exercises may look too simple. But please don't scoff at them. They serve the important function of focusing on the very muscles and movements that ward off back troubles. Remember, you never outgrow your need for the Pelvic Tilt!

If you crave action, start pulling out the stops in your aerobic exercise. When you walk, go quickly. Swing your arms. You can even pump them to push up your heart rate and pep up your pace. Swim if you like. And try an exercise bike or ride a bike outdoors for an aerobic alternative.

In stretching your lower back, you may use any or all of the exercises in chapter 8. Begin with five repetitions of six of them: Knee-to-Chest (page 76), Knees-to-Chest Rock (page 74), Knee Cross (page 84), Cat Stretch (page 86), Flexibility Twist (page 162), and Twists and Tilts (page 89). Increase the number of repetitions every three or four days, until you are doing ten of each.

For abdominal strengthening, go for the Pelvic Tilt (page 91), Standing Pelvic Tilt (page 93), Bent-Knee Sit-ups (page 96), and Sit-downs (page 94). Here, too, start with five repetitions of each and work up to ten.

Stretch and strengthen your buttocks, hips, and legs with the Knee Spread (page 98), Hamstring Stretch (page 100), Hip Hikers (page 103), Standing Thigh Pull (page 106) and Runner's Stretch (page 108). Try five repetitions of each for starters, then work up to ten.

Neck-stretching exercises for you could include five repetitions each of Left-Right Plus (page 114), Neck Bob (page 116), Head Roll (page 117), and Head Pull (page 119). Work up to ten of each of these over time.

Strengthen your neck with the Bed Head (page 121), Neck Push (page 122), and Side Neck Push (page 123), beginning with three and working up to five repetitions of each.

To stretch your shoulders and upper back, start out with three repetitions each of the Shoulder Roll (page 126), Roller

Blades (page 128), Square Shoulder Stretch (page 129), Airplane (page 130), and Windmill (page 131). As you gain proficiency with these, increase the number of repetitions to five. Strengthen these areas with five Push-offs (page 132) and three Side Presses (page 133), gradually increasing to ten repetitions and five repetitions respectively. For your hamstrings, try the Sitting Spine Stretch (page 159).

Regular Exercise

Total Body Relaxation (page 158)
Knee-to-Chest (page 76)
Knees-to-Chest Rock (page 74)
Knee Cross (page 84)
Cat Stretch (page 86)
Flexibility Twist (page 162)
Twists and Tilts (page 89)
Pelvic Tilt (page 91)
Standing Pelvic Tilt (page 93)
Bent-Knee Sit-ups (page 96)
Sit-downs (page 94)
Knee Spread (page 98)
Hamstring Stretch (page 100)
Hip Hikers (page 103)
Standing Thigh Pull (page 106)
Runner's Stretch (page 108)
Left-Right Plus (page 114)
Neck Bob (page 116)
Head Roll (page 117)
Head Pull (page 119)
Bed Head (page 121)
Neck Push (page 122)
Side Neck Push (page 123)
Shoulder Roll (page 126)
Roller Blades (page 128)

Square Shoulder Stretch (page 129)
Airplane (page 130)
Windmill (page 131)
Push-offs (page 132)
Side Press (page 133)
Sitting Spine Stretch (page 159)

That's all you have to do, really, to safeguard your back through exercise. Except that you need to keep doing your exercises. And please don't forget to go about your normal activities in a back-friendly frame of mind—even when your back forgets to remind you. You're getting to the point at which you can tell people that your back *used to be* a problem.

You can use the following form to record your own exercise plan, and then keep track of additions and changes. This is a good way to mark your progress and to troubleshoot for the causes of later soreness, but if it seems like too much paperwork for you, by all means just move on to the next chapter.

BACK EXERCISE PROGRESS CHART

Week #   Day #

Aerobic activity _____   Length of time _____

Stretching and Strengthening Exercises

Exercise	Repetitions	Notes
_____	_____	_____
_____	_____	_____
_____	_____	_____
_____	_____	_____
_____	_____	_____
_____	_____	_____
_____	_____	_____
_____	_____	_____
_____	_____	_____
_____	_____	_____
_____	_____	_____
_____	_____	_____
_____	_____	_____
_____	_____	_____

CHAPTER 7

How to Sustain Your Motivation to Exercise

You are your own best judge of the strategies that will work to keep your motivation and your body primed to exercise. After all, who knows you better? Are you the persevering sort who feels duty-bound to stick with every new resolution? Or are you in danger of losing interest in this exercise endeavor during the several weeks it may take for you to see gratifying results? Are you a loner who will eagerly set out for an early-morning walk before going to work? Or do you prefer a social setting in which to exercise—walking with a group of friends, perhaps, or working out at a gym?

Pain and disability may be the chief motivating factors right now, but your attention to exercise is likely to relieve pain and help you become active again. Then what? Numerous studies in hospitals have shown that even when people get back on their feet because of exercise, they tend to drop the program within a few months, perhaps out of a sense of false security. They don't think they could wind up in bed in pain again. But, unfortunately, statistics prove them wrong. Dropping the exercise that made them well turns out to be an invitation for pain and spasm to return. And it often returns with a vengeance.

If our program of exercise is to be of any lasting benefit, we have to give you ways to sustain it indefinitely. We have to persuade you to stick with your exercise regimen through good times and bad—through family crises, during illness, on vacations, while traveling for business, and regardless of any other situation that tempts you to forget about exercise for a while.

How to Reinforce Your Plan to Exercise Every Day

• Keep a log of your exercise progress—*and* the improvements in your condition, including increased mobility and decreased pain. That way, you'll have a written reminder of the reasons to stay with the program.

• Set aside a place for performing your exercise routine. Keep everything you need handy—a towel, a mat, a special warm-up suit, or whatever else you've decided you need. Then you can get right to work during your allotted time. If you live in cramped quarters and can't create a designated exercise area, then put all the items into a shopping bag and stow it close to your favorite workout spot.

• Schedule a time of day that you regularly devote to exercise. Treat that time like a business meeting or a family outing. In other words, it's important time, and other things can't be allowed to interfere with it. (On those rare occasions when you can't stick to your set time, it's much better to find another time rather than lose that day of exercise. But if you have to miss a day because of illness, it won't set back your progress.)

• Sit down and write yourself a letter in which you explain all your exercise goals and hopes for improvement. Put the letter away in a safe place. You may never need to look at it again, but if you find yourself looking for excuses to avoid exercise, take out the letter and read it.

How to Keep Your Exercise Period Free of Distractions

• Choose a time of day when you're least likely to be disturbed.
• Ignore the telephone if it rings.
• Put a note on your door telling people that you will be right back, and that they should not bother ringing the bell.
• Play some pleasing music that will cover any extraneous, distracting sounds. The music may also help you keep count where you need to count, and move gracefully in time to the music.

How to Get Others to Help You Stick to Your Program

• Arrange to exercise regularly with a friend or two. This puts your exercise in a social context, which may make the activity more pleasant for you. What's more, when you're tempted to skip a day, you won't want to back out and disappoint your friends, will you?
• Ask your doctor to compile a list of your vital statistics. This should include your weight, pulse, blood pressure, and

cholesterol level, including the percentage of high- and low-density lipoproteins. Ask your doctor to recheck the measurements periodically, say every three or four months. You'll see documented evidence that you're shedding extra pounds, that your resting pulse may be slowing down the way an athlete's does, that your blood pressure is within normal limits, and that your cholesterol level stays in the low range.

• Enlist your children's cooperation, if they are old enough to understand, by explaining that your exercise time is important to your health, and that you want them to keep themselves occupied while you work out. If they're too young for such tactics, you can try to schedule your exercise period during the times when your infant naps or after your toddler has gone to bed. Another possibility is to let your youngsters join your activity: While you stretch and strengthen, they can work their bodies, too—practicing somersaults or other gymnastics.

How to Take Your Exercise Program on the Road

• When you plan to visit an out-of-town hotel, whether for vacation or a business trip, inquire about exercise facilities. Many hotels and motels now have equipment rooms with treadmills for walking and exercise bikes for riding. The swimming pool, assuming there is one, may give you an opportunity you don't usually have to work in some swimming. Some hotels offer walking/jogging maps of the neighborhood.

• Since your back-stretching and strengthening exercises require no special equipment, you can do those in your room at your convenience. Try to give yourself this important attention first thing in the morning, before other demands make themselves felt.

• Long plane flights make an ideal setting for a limited exercise routine—and a sorely needed one, too, if you are to avoid feeling cramped and stiff from too much sitting. Walk the aisles whenever the cabin crew allows. Try a few neck stretches in your seat.

• If you make long road trips in your car, do stop frequently to stretch and walk. These preventive measures can keep you from arriving at your destination in pain.

How to Modify Your Exercise Program During Illness

• Bad colds and flus will most likely ground you from your aerobic exercise. But you may be able to carry on with at least some of your stretching and strengthening in bed. And you may need to—if lying still for long periods of time leaves you stiff and uncomfortable.

• You may well find that stopping your aerobic exercise for any reason, for any period of time, actually leaves you feeling depressed. You've grown accustomed to the pleasant natural high you get when your heart and lungs are functioning at their peak performance, your muscles moving smoothly, and your brain releasing the body's own opiates, the endorphins. Promise yourself that you'll get back to regular walking or swimming as soon as your fever breaks.

P A R T
T H R E E

The Exercises

> All the step-by-step instructions
> are spelled out here, accompanied
> by line drawings to further clarify
> each exercise movement.

CHAPTER 8

Exercises for Low-Back Pain

The exercises in this chapter focus on the site of most people's back pain. The word "low" is almost superfluous, because nearly everyone who has a backache has pain in the lower back. Right at the spot where you can reach around and place a comforting hand on your back at waist height—that's where the pain often starts.

The remedy is on the other side, in the muscles that run from the ribs to the pelvis—up and down, around, and through your torso. These abdominal muscles, which consist of several layers of interacting fibers, control your posture and body alignment. Weakness or injury in these muscles usually translates into back pain. It stands to reason, then, that strengthening the abdominal muscles (and thereby protecting them from injury) can help prevent acute episodes of low-back pain. It's also true that gentle stretching of the lower back and strengthening of the abdominals can constitute a pain-relieving treatment for chronic low-back problems.

All of these exercises have been judged safe and effective for most people by the participants in our Back Pain Survey and by physician exercise specialists at The New York Hospital–Cornell University Medical Center. As with any exercise program, be sure to check with your doctor in case you have special restrictions. The exercises are grouped according to the important exercise goals of this chapter: stretching the lower back, strengthening the abdominal muscles, and stretching and strengthening the muscles of the buttocks, hips, and legs.

As you begin to exercise, listen to your body. You risk injury by pushing yourself through pain. The bodybuilder's adage, "No pain, no gain," simply doesn't apply here. In back exercise, the only important goal is normal function in every-day life. There's no one competing with you, so please don't push yourself too hard.

Start out with a maximum of three repetitions of each exercise you attempt. Advance slowly. Give yourself at least a week at each repetition level before you try to add more repetitions. And there's no point, really, in going beyond ten repetitions of any one exercise. Once you are strong and limber enough to work through ten repetitions of all the exercises in your program with ease, you can spend that much more time out walking or investigating other activities that bring you pleasure.

To Stretch the Lower Back

KNEES-TO-CHEST ROCK

This soft rocking motion takes advantage of the built-in relaxation of the knees-to-chest position. You will be giving yourself a slight lower-back massage in the process!

Starting position: Lie on your back, knees bent and feet flat on the floor, with your arms at your sides.

Steps:
1. Pull both knees to your chest, one at a time. (If you prefer, you may bring both knees up simultaneously.)
2. Hold your knees in this position. (For greatest ease, hold the backs of your thighs. If you are slightly more limber, hold your knees. To get the maximum stretch, clasp your arms around and just under both knees.)
3. Curl your head and shoulders forward, and gently rock to and fro, and from side to side in this position.

Note: Some people feel a strain in the neck while doing this exercise. If you feel just a slight strain with no pain afterward, there should be no reason to skip this one. But if it makes you genuinely uncomfortable, ease off until you have strengthened your neck with the exercises recommended for that purpose.

KNEE-TO-CHEST

As you lift your knee to your chest in this gentle stretch, you will feel the curve in your lower back flatten out.

Starting position: Lie on your back, knees bent and feet flat on the floor, arms relaxed at your sides.

Steps:
1. Lift your right knee toward your chest as far as you can. (For extra stretch, try pulling your knee a bit closer to your chest with your hands.) *a*
2. Lower that same knee to and through the starting position, so that your right leg is extended straight. *b*
3. Wobble your leg to relax your muscles. *c*
4. Return to the starting position.
5. Repeat steps 1–4 with your left leg.

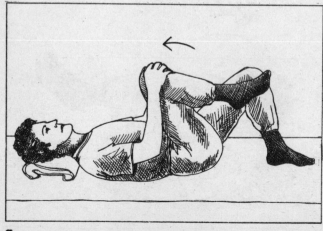

a

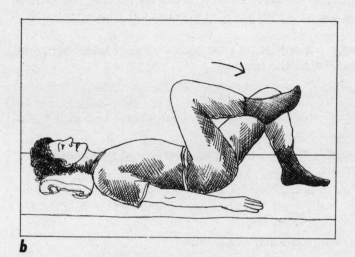

b

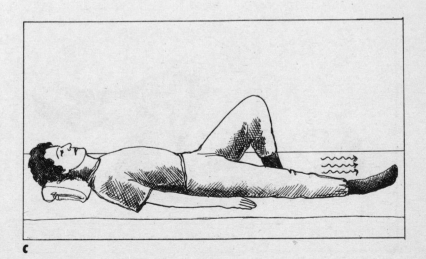

c

DOUBLE KNEE-TO-CHEST

The easiest way to perform this exercise is by keeping your knees together as you pull them to your chest. With experience, and for a greater stretch, you can try holding your knees about shoulder-width apart as you raise and lower them.

Starting position: Lie on your back with your knees bent and your feet flat on the floor.

Steps:
1. Clasp your hands around your knees and pull them toward your chest.
2. Pause if you feel resistance, then try to pull gently a bit farther.
3. Hold this position for a few seconds. (For added stretch, gradually work your way up to holding this position for twenty-five seconds.)
4. Return to the starting position.

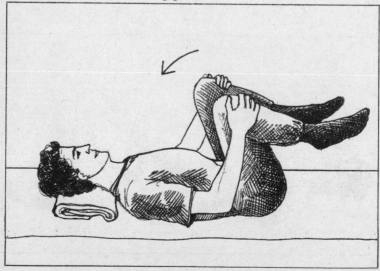

KNEE DROPS

Don't worry if you can't get your knees very far down when you first attempt this maneuver. You'll build up your ability in time.

Starting position: Lie on your back with your knees bent and your feet flat on the floor. *a*

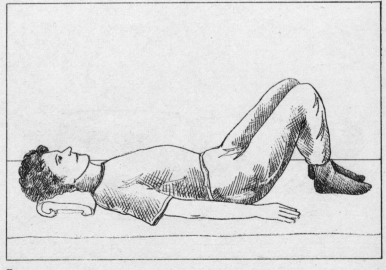

a

Steps:

1. Keeping your knees together, drop them both to the right as far as you can. (Your left hip and buttock will necessarily rise off the bed or floor as your knees drop to the right, but try to keep both your shoulders on the flat surface.) **b**

2. Return to the starting position. **c**

3. Drop both knees to the left. **d**

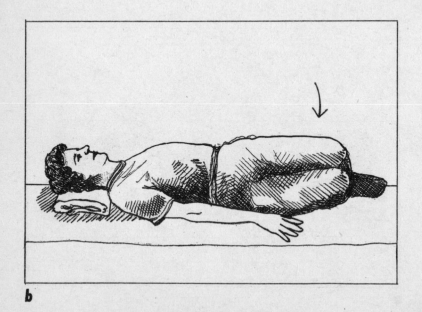

b

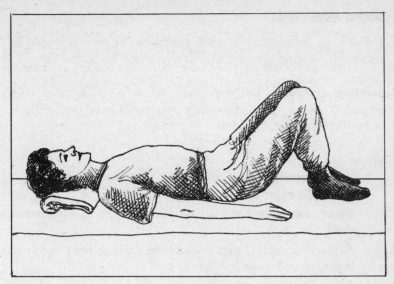

c

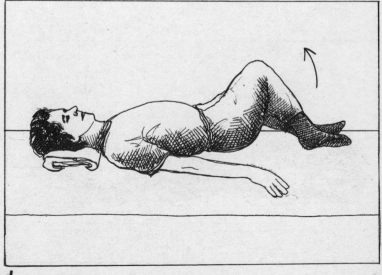

d

SIMPLE KNEE CROSS

These knee movements, which resemble the slow flapping of a butterfly's wing, gently stretch the lower back and hips.

Starting position: Lie on your left side, with your legs extended. You may want to place your right hand on the floor in front of you for support.

Steps:
1. Bend your right knee and pull it up toward your body so that your right foot is near your left knee. **a**
2. Press your right knee across your left leg, down toward the floor. **b**
3. Raise your right knee toward the ceiling, keeping your right foot on your left knee. **c**
4. Return to the starting position.
5. Turn onto your right side and repeat steps 1–4 with your left leg.

a

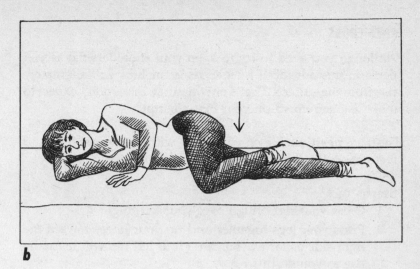

b

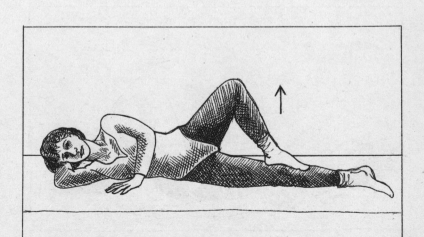

c

KNEE CROSS

Although you need to try to keep your shoulders flat as you perform this advanced knee cross, your hips will alternately rise from the surface. That's only natural. Also, don't expect to make a touch-down on your first attempt.

Starting position: Lie on your back, with your knees bent and feet flat on the floor, arms relaxed at your sides.

Steps:
1. Cross your right thigh over your left thigh. *a*
2. Press your legs together and tip your knees toward the right side as far as you can. (Your left hip will naturally rise as you do this.) *b*
3. Raise your knees and return to the starting position.
4. Repeat steps 1–3 on the other side, crossing your left thigh over the right, and tipping toward the left. *c*

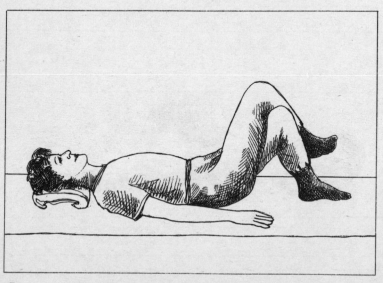

a

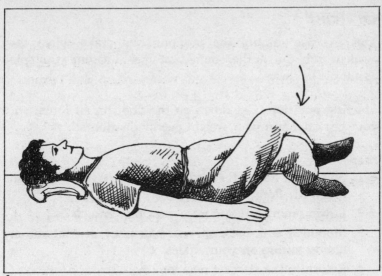

b

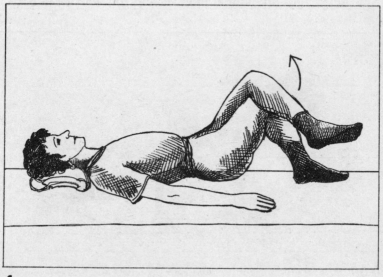

c

CAT STRETCH

This exercise mimics the motions cats make when they awaken from one of their famed cat naps. Imagine your spine as supple as theirs.

Starting position: Get down on the floor on all fours, with your back flat and your weight evenly distributed. *a*

Steps:
1. Slide your hands forward, letting your elbows bend and touch the floor.
2. Lower your head and raise your rear end. *b*
3. Smoothly sink back on your haunches, so that you are almost sitting on your ankles. *c*
4. Return to the starting position. *d*
5. Drop your head and pull in your abdominals to curve your back like a Halloween cat. *e*
6. Relax your abdominal muscles and roll your head back.

a

b

c

d

e

TWISTS AND TILTS

Give yourself a maximum sideways stretch as you twist and turn. Fight the urge to lean forward or backward, or to move your lower body.

Starting position: Stand with your hands on your hips.

Steps:
1. Lean the top of your body to the right. Resist the temptation to lean forward or backward as you bend sideways. Also try to keep your feet, legs, and hips steady. *a*
2. Straighten up slowly.
3. Repeat these motions to the left. *b*

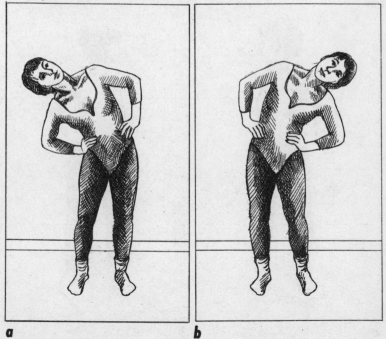

a   b

4. Twist the upper half of your body around to the left, as though you were trying to see behind you. **c**
5. Return to face front.
6. Repeat these motions to the right. **d**

c   d

To Strengthen the Abdominal Muscles

PELVIC TILT

This most basic strengthening exercise will flatten both your abdomen and the curve in your lower back.

Starting position: Lie on your back with your knees bent and your feet flat on the floor, arms relaxed at your sides. *a*

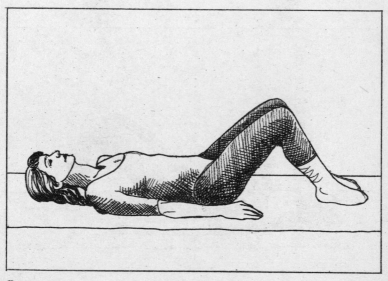

a

Steps:

1. Tighten your buttocks and pull in your abdominal muscles, so that your hips roll upward. Exhale as you do this. (Strive to work your buttocks and abdominal muscles, and resist the temptation to simply push off from the floor with your feet or hips.) *b*

2. Hold the position, but not your breath, for a few seconds.

3. Relax your muscles as you inhale and return to the starting position.

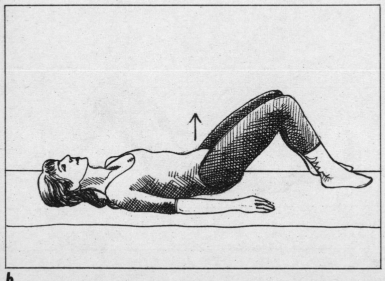

b

STANDING PELVIC TILT

A wall takes the place of bed or floor in this upright version of the basic Pelvic Tilt.

Starting position: Stand with your back against a wall, your feet a few inches out from the wall's base. *a*

Steps:
1. Exhaling, squeeze your buttocks together and pull in your gut, so that you can feel the curve in the small of your back flatten against the wall. Keep your shoulders relaxed as you do this. *b*
2. Hold the position for a few seconds as you breathe in and out normally.
3. Inhaling, relax and return to the starting position.

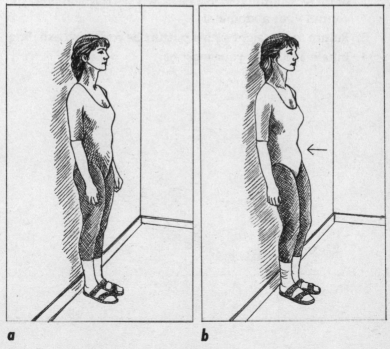

a   *b*

SIT-DOWNS

These reverse sit-ups are a bit more challenging, so please don't attempt them until you've built up your abdominal strength. Remember that the distance you move is secondary to the effort you put into strengthening your abdominal muscles.

Starting position: Sit on a bed or a bench that allows you room to lean back. Fold your arms across your chest. **a**

Steps:
1. Use your abdominal muscles to lean your body backward several inches—about as far as you would lift up for a sit-up. Exhale as you go. **b**
2. Hold the position, but don't hold your breath, for a count of three. Continue to exhale slowly, as this will help you control your abdominals.
3. Return to a straight sitting posture as you finish exhaling.
4. Inhale and relax your muscles.

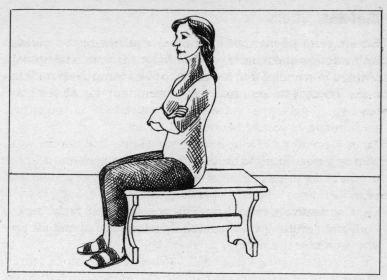

a

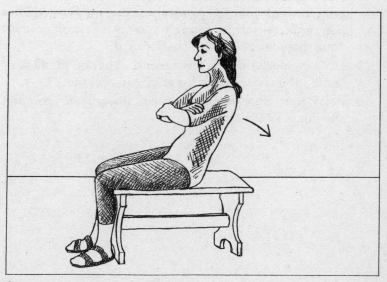

b

BENT-KNEE SIT-UPS

Sit-ups from a bent-knee position give just as good a workout to the abdominal muscles as the old straight-knee sit-ups you learned in school. More important, they are much safer for the back. Though steady breathing is important during any exercise, you'll get a real boost here if you exhale as you sit up, then inhale as you lie back down.

Starting position: Lie on your back, knees bent and feet flat on the floor, arms relaxed at your sides **(a)**. Most people lead with their arms when they perform this exercise, but you work your abdominals even harder if you fold your arms across your chest. Putting your hands behind your head can just give you a pain in the neck.

Steps:
1. Pull in your abdominals and raise the upper part of your body toward your knees as you exhale. (You need not rise very far—just far enough to see your navel, or to lift your shoulder blades off the floor.) **b**
2. Hold the position for a few seconds, but don't hold your breath. (Be conscious of breathing in and out.)
3. Relax your muscles slowly as you lower your head and shoulders while you inhale.

a

b

To Stretch and Strengthen
the Buttocks, Hips, and Leg Muscles

THE SQUEEZE

Good support for the lower back rests, literally, on strong buttocks, which can be built up with this isometric exercise; nothing appears to move, but the effects can be felt.

Starting position: You may perform this exercise lying down, sitting, or standing.

Steps:
1. Squeeze your buttocks together as tightly as you can.
2. Hold for a moment, then release, and relax.

KNEE SPREAD

Spreading your knees this way stretches the muscles of your hips, groin, and buttocks—and you don't have to strive to get your knees to the floor to accomplish your goal.

Starting position: Lie on your back with your knees bent and your feet flat on the floor. *a*

Steps:
1. Without expending any effort, allow your knees to spread apart by the weight of your legs. *b*
2. When you feel resistance, hold your legs still for a few seconds.
3. Return to the starting position.

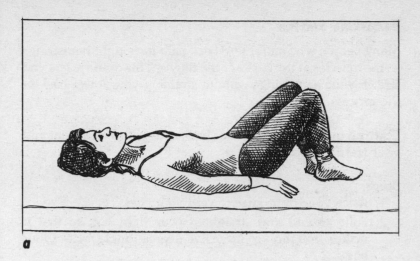

a

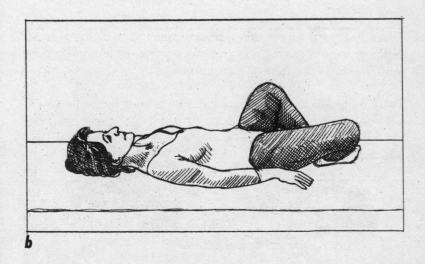

b

HAMSTRING STRETCH

Many people who suffer low-back pain have tight hamstrings —the muscles at the backs of the thighs. This exercise lets you stretch your hamstrings without straining your lower back in the process.

Starting position: Lie on your back with your knees bent and your feet flat on the floor. *a*

Steps:
1. Raise your right knee toward your chest. *b*
2. Fully extend and straighten your right leg, so that it makes roughly a forty-five-degree angle with your body. *c*

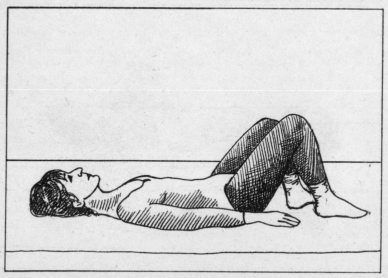

a

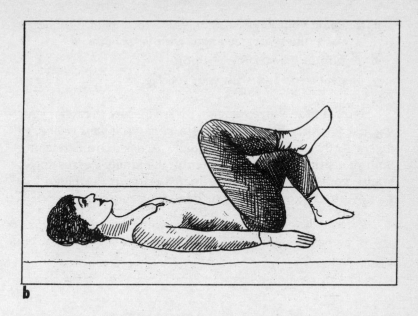

b

c

3. Keeping your knee straight, try to raise your right leg to make a ninety-degree angle with your body. **d**
4. Return to the starting position.
5. Repeat steps 1–4 with your left leg.

Note: In the above exercise, please be sure to extend your leg first at a forty-five-degree angle, *even if you think you can go higher*. At this angle, there is virtually no risk of overstretching your hamstrings. Before you attempt the ninety-degree angle, assure yourself that you have increased your flexibility, lest you overstretch or "pop" your hamstring muscle.

d

HIP HIKERS

Keeping full range of motion in your hips (a goal of this exercise) safeguards both your posture and your walking gait.

Starting position: Lie on your right side, with your knees straight and your right arm under your head. Prop your left hand on the floor in front of your body for support.

Steps:
1. Slowly lift your left leg as high as you can, keeping the knee straight.
2. Hold this extension for several seconds, feeling the stretch in your hip and thigh.
3. Gently lower your leg.
4. Repeat steps 1–3 twice. (This counts as three repetitions.)
5. Turn over and repeat the exercise, raising your right leg.

THIGH PULL

The flip side of the hamstrings are the quadriceps muscles at the front of the thighs. This exercise emphasizes body alignment as it stretches the area from hip to knee.

Starting position: Lie on your right side, your head resting on your right arm, and your left leg bent at the knee. Think of your body making a straight line from your head down the fronts of your thighs.

Steps:
1. With your left hand, grasp your left ankle. *a*
2. Keeping the knee bent, pull your left leg back and toward your buttocks as far as you comfortably can. Resist the temptation to arch your back.

a

3. Hold this position for a few moments, feeling the stretch along the front of your thigh.
4. Return to the starting position.
5. Repeat steps 1–4 twice. **b**
6. Turn onto your left side, and repeat the exercise with your right leg.

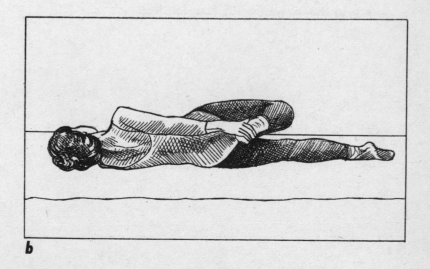

b

STANDING THIGH PULL

Holding your body in a Standing Pelvic Tilt while you do the following exercise will keep you properly aligned and help you avoid arching your back.

Starting position: Stand alongside a chair or other sturdy support that you can hold for balance.

Steps:
1. With your left hand on the support, bend your right knee and grasp your right ankle. *a*
2. Pull your right leg back and toward your buttocks, but not so far as to make you arch your back. *b*
3. Hold this position, feeling the stretch along the front of your thigh.
4. Release your ankle and slowly straighten your knee to return to the starting position.
5. Repeat steps 1–4 twice.
6. Turn to grip your support with your right hand, and repeat the exercise with your left leg.

a

b

RUNNER'S STRETCH

Fully stretching your lower legs can improve your standing posture and smooth out your walking gait—two important factors in warding off back pain.

Starting position: Stand facing a wall, with your hands on the wall at about shoulder height, and your feet about twelve inches away from the wall's base.

Steps:
1. Extend your left leg about twelve inches behind you, keeping your left knee straight, your toes on the floor, and your heel raised slightly off the floor. You may bend the knee of your standing (right) leg. *a*
2. Try to lower your left heel to the floor, or as far as you can, feeling the stretch in your Achilles' tendon. *b*
3. Hold the full stretch for a few moments.
4. Return to the starting position.
5. Repeat steps 1–4, stretching your right leg.

a

b

CHAPTER 9

Exercises for Upper-Back and Neck Pain

Although many doctors view upper-back and neck pain as "low-back pain that has migrated upward," different treatments and exercises apply.

In our original Back Pain Survey, less than half of the participants with neck pain were even aware that exercise could add strength and flexibility to their neck muscles. The other half—the participants with neck pain who did perform exercises to relieve that pain—saw improvement in their symptoms. The truth is, the results from neck exercise were not as dramatic as the results of exercise for low-back pain. But, based on our survey reports, we believe you can greatly improve your chances of getting a dramatic benefit from neck exercise by following a few simple guidelines:

• *Combine the neck exercises in this chapter with the low-back exercises in chapter 8.* Most of those survey participants with neck pain *also* had some pain or discomfort in the lower back. Performing both sets of exercises in a regular routine brought the most significant improvement.

• *Perform neck exercises frequently throughout the day.* Most of the movements described below can serve to relieve on-the-spot tension—as well as to build strength and flexibility. In other words, these exercises are "first aid" for neck pain. Any time you feel stress and discomfort accumulating in your neck, whether you are at work or at home, you may try alleviating the tension with a few neck exercises. Here, slight discomfort is expected while exercising. Remember, though, to drop any exercise that—*for you*—turns mild discomfort to pain.

• *Maintain good posture through your neck.* A mention of posture usually makes people suck in their abdominal muscles and throw their shoulders back. Since the spine begins in the neck, good posture also means keeping the head well aligned, as though it were a golden eagle on the top of a flagpole. To correct your neck posture, stretch your neck and head skyward momentarily—go straight up, as though your neck had grown longer—then relax and tuck in your chin, instead of letting it jut or droop. (See chapters 14 and 15 for more suggestions on maintaining proper alignment and avoiding neck pain during everyday activities such as reading or talking on the telephone.)

To Stretch the Neck

LEFT-RIGHT

These slow head turns to left and right help untie the knots of tension in the neck.

Starting position: You can do this exercise lying on your back in bed, or sitting or standing, with your arms at your sides.

Steps:

1. Keeping your head level, turn it to the right as far as you can, as though to stare across your right shoulder. *a*
2. Return your head and your gaze to center. *b*
3. Turn your head the other way to look as far left as you can.
4. Return to the starting position.

a   *b*

YES-NO

Nodding "yes" or shaking your head "no," the neck gets a workout by moving the head about.

Starting position: You may sit or stand virtually anywhere.

Steps:
1. Nod your head up and down slowly, several times.
2. Turn your head from side to side, as though making a slow, exaggerated "no" gesture.

LEFT-RIGHT PLUS

The extra chin-to-shoulder dip brings an added dimension to the side-to-side neck stretch.

Starting position: As above, you may lie on your back, or sit or stand with your arms at your sides. *a*

Steps:
1. Turn your head to the right as far as you can. *b*
2. From the right-facing position, tilt your head down, as though trying to touch your chin to your shoulder. *c*
3. Raise your head and return to center.
4. Repeat steps 1–3 in the opposite direction, turning to the left.

a

b

c

NECK BOB

This exercise may make you feel like a turtle poking its head out of its shell for a look-see, but it should also help relax your neck through a gentle stretch.

Starting position: Do this exercise while sitting or standing.

Steps:

1. Lower your chin toward your chest until you feel some resistance. **a**
2. Crane your head and neck forward as far as you can, without bending or moving your torso.
3. Hold the craned-forward position for a few seconds. **b**
4. Return to the starting position.

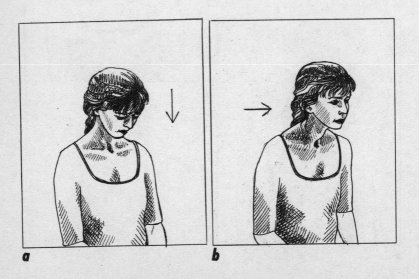

a   b

HEAD ROLL

This slow, continuous roll of the head gently stretches the neck muscles. You can make the side-to-side motions part of an in-bed exercise routine if you like. Remember, you get more of a stretch if you hold your shoulders still—and don't bring them up to meet your ears.

Starting position: Sit in a chair or stand at ease as you hold your head high and look straight ahead.

Steps:
1. Tilt your head to the left as though you were trying to put your ear on your shoulder. Stop when you've stretched your neck as far as you can. Don't try to bring your shoulder up to meet your ear. *a*
2. Roll your head forward and down, as though trying to touch your chin to your chest. *b*

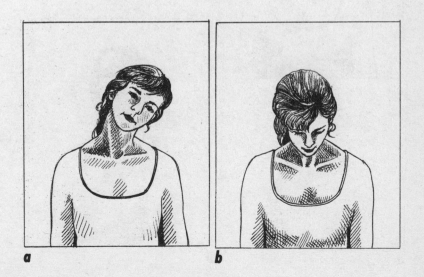

a   b

3. Continue the roll toward the right, as though trying to place your right ear on your right shoulder. **c**

4. Come full circle by tilting your head back, but not too far. (Feel free to omit this step, with its tilt backward, if arching is a problem for your upper spine.) **d**

5. Return to the starting position.

6. Repeat steps 1–5 in the opposite direction, circling your head to the left this time.

c

d

HEAD PULL

You may be able to get the most stretch in your neck by pulling your head with your hands.

Starting position: Sit in a chair with your back straight and your hands clasped behind your head. *a*

Steps:
1. Gently pull your head forward and down to stretch the back of your neck. *b*
2. Hold, feeling the stretch.
3. Return to the starting position.

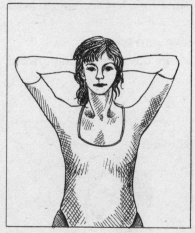

a

b

NECK TILT

Instead of a continuous rolling motion, this sideways neck stretch calls to mind the motions of an attentive bird, cocking its head first one way, then the other.

Starting position: Sit or stand comfortably, facing straight ahead.

Steps:
1. Tilt your head to the left, as though trying to touch your ear to your shoulder. Don't try to bring your shoulder up to your ear. *a*
2. When you feel resistance, pause for a few seconds to hold the position.
3. Return to the starting position and relax.
4. Repeat steps 1–3 in the opposite direction, tilting toward the right. *b*

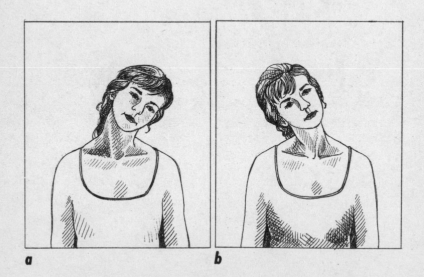

a   b

To Strengthen the Neck

BED HEAD

Your head makes a handy weight for your neck to press and push in this strengthening exercise.

Starting position: Lie on your back in bed or on the floor.

Steps:
1. Press your head straight back into your pillow or mat.
2. Hold for a moment, then release the pressure.
3. Lift your head above your pillow or mat as high as you can, without lifting your shoulders.
4. Hold, feeling the effort in your neck, then release.

NECK PUSH

This isometric exercise can strengthen your neck by making it work against the pressure of your own arm strength. You can also try doing it by pressing your forehead against a wall!

Starting position: Sit or stand comfortably, arms at your sides.

Steps:
1. Press the palm of one hand against your forehead, and your forehead against the palm of your hand.
2. Hold for a moment, keeping the pressure on your hand and head without moving either one.
3. Relax and return to the starting position.

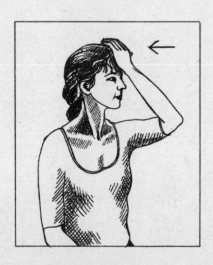

SIDE NECK PUSH

The hand-on-head stance called for here may imitate a look of anguish, but the results should bring relief instead.

Starting position: Do this exercise sitting, standing, or even lying down, arms at your sides.

Steps:
1. Press your left hand against the left side of your head, and simultaneously press your head against your hand.
2. Hold the position, hand and head pushing against each other.
3. Relax and return to the starting position.
4. Repeat steps 1–3, raising your right hand to the right side of your head.

To Stretch the Shoulders and Upper Back

PRONE SHOULDER STRETCH

Try not to raise your shoulders in this exercise, but just let the flowing motion of your arm stretch the neck and shoulder muscles.

Starting position: Lie on your back with your knees bent and feet flat, arms at your sides.

Steps:
1. Raise your right arm straight up to a ninety-degree angle, and keep moving it through a half-circle until it is extended behind you, palm up.
2. Relax for a moment, and then reverse movement and return to the starting position.
3. Repeat steps 1 and 2 with your left arm.

SHOULDER SHRUG

Even though your shoulders do the work by shrugging, your neck will appear to shrink and grow—and feel the positive effects over time.

Starting position: You can do this exercise lying in bed or sitting or standing, with your arms at your sides.

Steps:
1. Slowly and steadily raise your shoulders to a shrug. *a*
2. Hold for a moment, feeling the effect on your neck muscles.
3. Keeping your head still, gently press your shoulders as far down as you can. *b*
4. Hold, feeling the stretch in your neck.

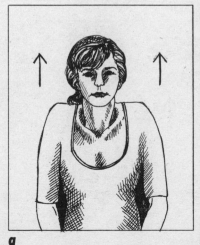 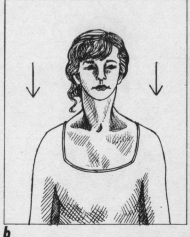

a   b

SHOULDER ROLL

Try to roll your shoulders through a full circle in one fluid motion. Even though each step is numbered separately, keep moving slowly from one to the next without stopping.

Starting position: Sit or stand with your shoulders relaxed. *a*

Steps:
1. Raise your shoulders. *b*
2. Bring your shoulders forward. *c*
3. Push your shoulders down. *d*
4. Pull your shoulders back. *e*
5. Return to the starting position. *f*
6. Circle your shoulders in the opposite direction, reversing the order of steps 1–5.

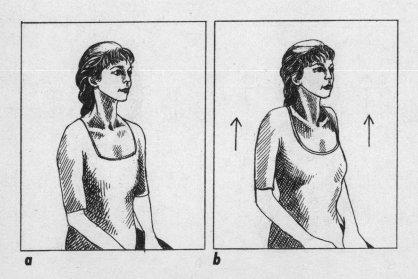

a　　　　*b*

c

d

e

f

ROLLER BLADES

This rolling movement of the shoulder blades feels like a sideways shrug. It will make your chest appear to swell with pride.

Starting position: Stand at ease, or sit on the edge of a chair. You can even do the first two steps lying down.

Steps:
1. Squeeze your shoulders together for a few seconds in an effort to make your shoulder blades meet in the middle of your back. *a*
2. Relax.
3. Try to make your shoulder blades meet again, this time by pushing your elbows together behind you. *b*

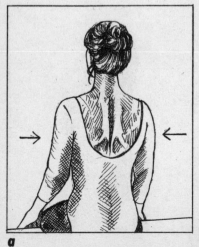

a　　　　　　　　　　　　　*b*

SQUARE SHOULDER STRETCH

Try to keep your neck relaxed as one arm pulls the other to stretch the deltoid muscles of your shoulders and upper arms.

Starting position: Sit on a straight-backed chair or stool. Cross your arms in front of you, left over right, so that each hand holds the opposite elbow, raise your arms over your head in this way, and then let your left hand hang free. *a*

Steps:
1. With your right hand, pull your left elbow toward and behind your head. *b*
2. Hold this stretch for several seconds, feeling the stretch in your shoulder and upper arm.
3. Relax and return to the starting position, and switch your grip to hold your right elbow in your left hand.
4. Repeat steps 1–3, using your left hand to pull your right elbow.

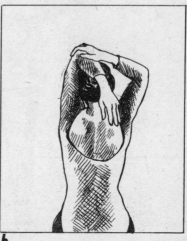

a   *b*

AIRPLANE

Try to keep your neck relaxed and your posture aligned as you make these motions of a child imitating an airplane.

Starting position: Stand with your arms straight out to the sides at shoulder height, palms down.

Steps:
1. Make several small forward circles with your arms, keeping your elbows straight.
2. Circle your arms in reverse.

WINDMILL

Picture your arms as the blades of a windmill as you perform this exercise—but don't try to go as fast!

Starting position: Stand at ease, arms at your sides.

Steps:
1. Keeping your right arm straight, describe several huge circles in the air in a forward motion. *a b*
2. Without stopping, circle your right arm in the opposite direction, going through a full range of motion.
3. Repeat steps 1–3 with your left arm.

a   b

To Strengthen the Shoulders and Upper Back

PUSH-OFFS

These standing push-ups are easier than the military kind. They increase in difficulty as you increase the distance between yourself and the wall to as far as two feet.

Starting position: Stand facing a wall, with your feet apart and about twelve inches away from the wall, with your palms resting on the wall at shoulder height. *a*

Steps:
1. Lean in toward the wall as far as possible, keeping your legs and back straight. *b*
2. Push yourself back to the starting position.

a　　　　　　　　　　*b*

SIDE PRESS

Stubbornly pushing against a wall is a sound isometric approach to increasing shoulder strength.

Starting position: Stand near a wall, with the left side of your body about six inches away from it.

Steps:
1. Extend your left arm out sideways until your forearm is pressing against the wall. *a*
2. Continue to push for several seconds, feeling the exertion in your shoulder.

a

3. Relax and return to the starting position.
4. Repeat steps 1–3 twice. *b*
5. Turn, and repeat the exercise with your right arm.

b

CHAPTER 10

Exercises for General Fitness

Fitness has become such a popular national pursuit that you can barely walk down the street these days without encountering joggers, cyclists, and rollerbladers out in force. But if you are walking down the street, you are already engaged in the all-time best activity for building cardiovascular fitness and keeping your back limber.

In this chapter we'll be discussing the four most popular fitness exercises for people with back pain—walking, swimming, cycling, and dancing.

Walking

Walking is the oldest and best of the weight-bearing exercises for people with back pain. Walking proved helpful in the long run for 98 percent of the participants in our Back Pain Survey who made this activity a regular part of their routine. They reported that walking not only increased the flexibility of their backs, but also improved their overall strength and muscle tone. Another important advantage was that walking at least thirty minutes a day, four times a week, greatly reduced stress and tension for these people. Even the twenty-six participants who couldn't lead normal lives because of back pain *all* improved in the long run by following their practitioners' advice to walk (or swim) regularly.

Hospital studies show that walkers accrue the same cardiovascular benefits that runners do, and with far fewer injuries. It makes an ideal back exercise because it is low-impact yet high-endurance—that is, once you have built up to taking relatively long walks several times a week. Because most people can walk for a longer time than they can run or play tennis, for example, walking tends to build muscular endurance while it burns calories.

Walking is easy, accessible, effective, and enjoyable. It can be geared to any level of fitness, and pursued by people of all ages. No exercise could be more convenient than walking. You need no special equipment and no special clothing, other than comfortable shoes. You don't have to travel to the gym or the pool; you just get up and go. For these reasons, you're far less likely to quit your walking regimen than any other exercise you might try.

Most people can easily fit walking into their daily activities if they try. You may even find that you can combine your daily activities—your errands, some light shopping—with your walk when you are pressed for time. Walking to work or to appointments is another way to fit exercise into the day's program. And although walking will quicken your heart rate and get your body into condition, it typically doesn't leave you perspiring so much that you require a shower or a change of clothing when you get where you're going.

If you are already in reasonably good shape, we recommend at least half an hour of brisk walking every other day. You may build up to walking three or four miles in an hour, five to seven days a week. What starts out as something you do to improve your back may well turn into the highlight of your day—the time you feel simultaneously relaxed and energized. At that point, you probably won't want to miss your daily walk.

Your walking pace is a measure of your fitness and freedom from pain. An ideal pace, according to Dr. James Rippe, director of the Exercise Physiology and Nutrition Laboratory at the University of Massachusetts School of Medicine, is to walk as though you have someplace to go. But Dr. John Duncan of the Cooper Institute for Aerobics Research in Dallas has shown in studies that even a slow pace can benefit your heart and lower your cholesterol level.

Most important, as far as your back is concerned, is to keep your posture alignment in check, with your abdominals holding your lower back in proper position. And walk with zest—with your hips and legs making great strides as you swing your arms and get the maximum enjoyment out of the activity.

At the risk of overstating the obvious, we would like to emphasize that the goal of walking is to move forward. Many people add extraneous motions to their walking gait. They may flop from side to side, or bounce up and down as they go. We want you to walk with your posture and purpose in mind. Try to imagine that you are being pulled forward by a string attached to the middle of your chest.

If you are just recuperating from an episode of incapacitating back pain, then you'll want to build up gradually to a fitness level of walking. You can begin by walking as much as you can around your house, as soon as you feel up to it. Even though you stay indoors, we urge you to wear good shoes as soon as you make the transition from being in bed most of the time to being up and about. A pair of walking or running shoes, or any comfortable shoes that offer good support, will help you through this recovery period. The best shoes are those you're already used to. If you do need to break in a new pair of shoes, we urge you to do it gradually, because any sudden change at this point could aggravate your back. (Even after you're up and about, we recommend wearing new shoes just half an hour the first time, then an additional half hour each succeeding day.)

When you venture outside the first few times, try to avoid steep grades and uneven ground, as walking up or down hills causes more of a strain on the muscles of the lower back. What's more, rocky ground or broken sidewalks can make it difficult for you to relax and stride comfortably, with your head held high and your gaze out to the world.

Swimming

Swimming is an ideal aerobic exercise for general fitness because it makes the arms and legs work hard to get the heart pumping. Some exercise experts, however, argue that swimming can't match up to walking or running as a weight-bearing exercise. Although it's true that the water provides a virtually stress-free environment, studies have shown that swimmers have thicker, stronger bones than people who perform no exercise at all. Swimming can indeed help you improve your muscle endurance and flexibility.

We didn't hear a single negative comment about swimming in our Back Pain Survey. We did, however, hear a few cautionary notes about which stroke to choose. A tiring, taxing stroke such as the butterfly, for example, which requires the arms to whirl like windmills while the lower back and legs mimic a leaping dolphin, is clearly too risky for anyone with back problems.

Some people with back pain find that the standard overhand crawl or "freestyle" puts too much of an arch in the lower back. Many prefer the sidestroke, with its froglike kicking motions, to the back-arching flutter-kick of the crawl. We consider the sidestroke to be the easiest on the back, and we recommend that you alternate sides so that you exercise your body evenly. The backstroke—not the back crawl, but the breaststroke flipped on its back—is the next easiest. Keep it simple by keeping your arms close to your sides as you cup your hands to push through the water, instead of reaching way up beyond your shoulder level for power strokes. You may add a frog-kick or a flutter-kick—whichever feels better to you.

You can experiment with different strokes to find the one that suits you best. You may find you like to combine a variety of strokes to add interest to your time in the water. By alternating between difficult and simple strokes, you can pace yourself—getting a good workout while avoiding rapid fatigue.

One advantage of swimming over other fitness activities is that water makes exercise a virtually no-sweat proposition. The reason? Water is four times more efficient than air at dissipating heat. This keeps your body from getting overheated so quickly, and enables you to continue feeling comfortable even though you may be working out very hard in hot weather.

If you have a pool near you and can swim regularly, try to build up to fifteen minutes of nonstop swimming, three times a week. You may find that swimming is more beneficial to you than anything else, even walking, depending on your particular condition. (See chapter 11 for a full discussion of exercises for various back ailments.)

Bicycling

A bicycle may be your best friend or your worst enemy, depending on the way it requires you to sit, position your hands, and extend your neck. The racing bike, which asks the rider to assume a near-fetal position and then crane his or her neck up to see straight ahead, has at last given way in popularity to the upright touring and all-terrain or "mountain" bikes. This trend is a real boon to back sufferers. You will be much more comfortable sitting straight up than hunching over for the sake of reducing air resistance on your body. After all, when your purpose in riding is to gain exercise and fresh air, as opposed to winning a race, sitting up is the position of choice.

Seat comfort is an all-important consideration. Whether you ride as an excuse to get out and about, or restrict your pedaling to an indoor exercise bike, you need to remain seated throughout your workout. Some people experience nothing more annoying than a mild soreness in their buttocks the first few days of getting used to a bicycle seat. Others find that the pain never goes away. This is especially important for people with sciatica pain, which typically runs through the buttocks. Obviously, if you can't get comfortable on a bicycle, then cycling is not for you. But before you give up the advantages of this sport, try experimenting with comfort solutions. You can, for example, add a padded seat cover, or change the seat altogether. Most people find the broad "saddle" style more comfortable than the small, hard racing seat.

Since we are recommending bicycle riding as a good fitness activity, we must add that biking requires certain safety precautions that have nothing to do with posture or seat selection. Now that the pattern of bicycle-related injuries has been well documented, we urge you to buy and wear a bike helmet. Even top pros who rarely fall off a bicycle avow that head protection is essential on every ride—not only on streets shared with auto traffic, but also on special bicycle paths in parks. If you're a night rider, you'll need reflectors on your bicycle as well as on your clothing and helmet, for safety's sake. It's also a good idea to equip your bicycle with a headlight and taillight.

Cycling can be enjoyed as an indoor sport with a stationary exercise bike. Many busy people like to work out with an exercise bike, rooted to the floor, because it allows them to pedal away while getting something else done—reading a book or a magazine, say, watching television, or even viewing a movie on videocassette.

We tend to think of cycling as legwork, and it is, but some stationary bikes include activities for the arms, too. As you pump the pedals with your feet on one of these, you can push and pull handles that exercise your upper body.

Dancing

Health experts consider dancing a reasonable alternative to other aerobic activities, including walking, swimming, and cycling. As the most social of all these outlets, dancing provides the combination of good movements and good times with others that puts you in the swing of things and makes you feel good to be alive.

Ballroom dancing and folk dancing may offer just the right activity level for you, as they need not be stressful exercises. If your back is basically strong, causing you only minor aches and pain, you may choose to investigate modern dance, jazz, or even ballet instruction.

When you and your partner dance to the music of a long song set, continuing until the music ends, you get great endurance exercise. What's more, the chance to be with other people in an active form of recreation makes dancing virtually boredom-proof. People may abandon their exercise bikes and find excuses to avoid the swimming pool on a chilly day, but dancing retains its appeal over the long haul. It's one of the most enjoyable ways to rediscover how much your body can do.

One of the chief benefits of dancing is the relaxed style of movement that comes from mastering steps to music. If you take up dancing, you may well find that as you become accustomed to rhythmically positioning your body in space, you develop dancelike ways of doing other activities. Your motions may become more fluid, so that you improve your walking gait, for example. Instead of striking a rigid pose while you stand at the kitchen counter or sit at your desk, you may bring the good body mechanics of dancing to bear by adding a little motion. Some dancers gently dip and shift their weight from one leg to the other while working standing up, or perform a rock-and-roll stretch of the lower back while typing at the computer keyboard.

Several participants in our Back Pain Survey learned exercise from dance instructors who taught modern dance and ballet. They went for instruction after a painful episode had ended, not in the throes of back pain. They enjoyed the idea of learning to dance and of practicing at least three times a week. Most found they experienced substantial improvement in their posture, abdominal strength, and overall flexibility, along with a substantial reduction of back pain.

Some Asian martial arts, such as t'ai chi ch'uan, offer a non-jarring, dancelike form of aerobic exercise that can be practiced daily, by oneself or in a group.

CHAPTER 11

Exercises for Specific Conditions

When we talk about tailoring a back-exercise program to your specific needs, we have in mind the specific condition—provided that one can be identified—that is the root cause of your back pain. Many, if not most, back problems elude specific diagnoses agreed on by different kinds of practitioners. Some conditions, however, are easily recognized. And according to the results of our Back Pain Survey, exercises that take these back problems into account offer the best chance of improvement. Whether or not you can name your condition, you may still be able to categorize your back problem according to the nature of your pain, the type of situation that may aggravate your pain, and the area of your back that hurts most.

Please don't feel at a disadvantage if you can't rattle off a bona fide medical term such as "herniated disk" or "scoliosis" that neatly pigeonholes your backache. Hardly anyone knows such things for certain. We found that more than half of our original survey respondents had received two or more different diagnoses from two or more practitioners. Most of these discrepancies represented major differences of opinion—not just variations in terminology.

The good news is that even if you never find out exactly what's wrong with your back, you can still get well. After all, you do know your own symptoms, and that knowledge will help you "categorize" your own pain, so long as serious medical conditions have been ruled out as the cause of your pain.

Following is a list of what we have found to be the seven most common categories of back pain (for obvious reasons, some of the names sound more specific than others):

- low back
- herniated (ruptured) and degenerative disk
- neck
- osteoarthritis
- sciatica
- scoliosis
- spondylolisthesis

You may be able to place yourself in one of the above categories, or you may feel that you belong in two or more of them. Indeed, if you have a herniated disk, you may well have sciatica as a result. Low-back and neck pain are frequent companions. And osteoarthritis may superimpose itself on one or more existing back problems.

The rest of this chapter will look at these categories one by one, and offer specific exercise suggestions. According to our survey results, for example, bicycling turns out to be an excellent workout for people with scoliosis. If your back pain falls into more than one category, you'll find more than one section of this chapter of value.

Low Back

This is the leading cause of disability among American adults under age forty-five. Only colds and sore throats top low-back pain as reasons for seeking medical attention.

Whether you have recently been laid up with an acute case of low-back pain, or have a chronic painful condition, you can begin to address your needs with the "Basic Preparation" exercises outlined in chapter 6. These will help you make the transition from bed rest to restored normal activity.

The part of your exercise routine that brings you the most pleasure will likely be the stretching exercises. By easing the tendency to muscle spasm in your lower back, you will also be helping yourself prevent future pain and disability by faithfully performing your low-back stretches.

As you recuperate, try to walk as much as you can. Although you may be tempted at first to switch your environment from your bed to a chair, you'll no doubt find that sitting puts much more strain on your back than lying down or standing up. Keep walking. Try to walk at least two miles a day. Other people may get in enough walking on their jobs, but this may not be enough to control your low-back pain. You will really benefit from daily periods spent in brisk, mind-clearing, arm-swinging, uninterrupted walking.

Herniated (Ruptured) and Degenerative Disk

While suffering the intense pain of a herniated disk, you may well need to spend several weeks in bed as an alternative to surgery. Or you may have an operation and go through a lengthy recovery period.

Results from our Back Pain Survey suggest that people with herniated disks need to be especially careful about exercise, since their rate of exercise-related injury is high. Among our participants, 15 percent of those who had disk problems incurred injury from exercise, while only 3 percent of the participants with low-back pain found exercise harmful. The point, however, is not to avoid back exercises, but to know which exercises to do and when to do them.

Some specialists and some exercise books offer dangerous exercise advice, such as telling individuals to stretch their hamstrings by bending over and touching their toes. We consider this a formula for disaster. Double leg raises probably should be outlawed because of the pressure they put on the disks. The same is true for straight-leg sit-ups.

For you, building strength, especially in your abdominal muscles, takes priority over all stretching exercises. As general fitness exercises, nothing can beat walking and swimming. Try to pursue them both, beginning as soon as possible after your acute pain ebbs. Indeed, we urge you to begin putting your fitness program into effect as soon as you're out of bed. This measure will help you beat the odds of remaining limited by disability.

The best professional treatment for chronic ruptured-disk pain, as revealed in our survey, is individualized back-exercise therapy. If you have not been able to perform back exercises because of pain, don't quit yet. Please show the program in this book to your doctor. It is probably sufficient to put you on the track toward wellness, but don't hesitate to seek the personal advice of a physiatrist, physical therapist, or other expert instructor in exercise as rehabilitation.

Neck

Although neck pain is often viewed as a back problem that just happened to land higher up on the spine, the causes and treatments differ substantially. For example, low-back pain usually benefits from a few days of bed rest; neck pain hardly ever does. Unless the neck pain stems from a serious accident involving a car crash or a bad fall, bed rest may make it worse. According to the results of our Back Pain Survey, neck pain was more likely than any other variety of back pain to benefit from chiropractic care.

Our survey participants found that no single approach was sufficient to provide long-term help. Chronic neck-pain sufferers who did away with disabling pain found the success lay in a combination of exercise, posture adjustment, and stress reduction (often achieved through exercise).

Rarely does a person with neck pain require exercise instruction from a professional. Neck-saving maneuvers can be learned in a matter of minutes. Unfortunately, many people with neck pain miss out on the benefits of exercise simply because they don't think to do it. They may see the value of exercising their arms and legs, but they seem to put their necks in a different category. The truth is, neck exercises offer proven help for pain and stiffness. We encourage you to incorporate the neck exercises outlined in chapter 9 in your daily routine.

The objective of neck exercise is to promote relaxation, to stretch the neck muscles so as to make them more flexible, and to strengthen them. Our survey participants found they tended to perform neck exercises more frequently when they were experiencing some discomfort. In other words, these particular movements seem to provide on-the-spot relief.

Osteoarthritis

Signs of osteoarthritis—pain and stiffness in the joints of the spine, bony growths or spurs that show up on X rays—seem to multiply with age. Other forms of arthritis, however, including rheumatoid arthritis and ankylosing spondylitis, are found just as often among young adults as among older ones, and follow a completely different course.

Osteoarthritis is often called a "wear and tear" condition because the cartilage that protects the ends of the bones flakes off, leaving rough edges that prevent the joints from functioning smoothly. One of the reasons that exercise figures so importantly in arthritis treatment is that it helps nourish the joints, to slow or reverse their destruction. Motion squeezes fluids in and out of the joint spaces, facilitating the delivery of nutrients to the cartilage, which has no blood supply of its own, and the removal of waste products.

Rest, which was long touted as the best treatment for arthritis of any kind, has proved to be a poor and even destructive substitute for activity.

Stretching exercises, which are often called "range of motion" maneuvers by arthritis specialists, actually preserve the motion of the various joints. Coupled with strengthening exercises, they help protect the joints from injury by building a strong support network in the surrounding muscles, tendons, and ligaments. All of the exercises in chapters 8 and 9 are suitable for people with back pain resulting from osteoarthritis.

You may find that exercise improves your function even

more than it relieves your pain, though it often serves both purposes equally well.

Walking and swimming were the two fitness exercises that gave the greatest help to the participants in our Back Pain Survey who suffered from osteoarthritis. (We also conducted a separate Arthritis Survey, to uncover useful information for people with osteoarthritis and rheumatoid arthritis—not solely in the back, but in all the joints of the body.)

Sciatica

Knifelike pain that runs along the sciatic nerve may result from disk problems, osteoarthritis, or other, perhaps unidentified, causes. Often compared to a bad toothache of the body, sciatica typically begins in the buttocks, near the spot where the sciatic nerve emerges from the spinal column, then courses through the thigh and calf, and on into the foot.

Participants in our Back Pain Survey who suffered from sciatica were typically treated with drugs and surgery, but the ones who fared best made progress through prescribed exercise taught to them by physiatrists, physical therapists, and, in some cases, chiropractors.

Some of the best movements for sciatica prove to be Pelvic Tilts, mild stretches of the lower back, and a fitness concentration on swimming or walking. We want you to proceed with more than usual caution, since the risk of exercise-related injury in sciatica is comparable to that associated with herniated disk. It is all too easy to feel worse instead of better.

The exercises in chapter 8 make up the kind of safe-not-sorry program that can lead you to meaningful improvement in a few months' time.

Scoliosis

Unlike other participants in our Back Pain Survey, people with the spine curvature called scoliosis had better luck exercising without professional input. What's more, they fared better with fitness exercises than with the traditional stretching and strengthening movements. This may be because the spine can become rigid in scoliosis. Thus, a low-back stretch may not achieve for you what it achieves for a person with low-back pain. It may even be painful or awkward for you to lie flat on the floor in basic exercise positions, if your curvature makes one side of your back protrude beyond the other. And yet you can benefit enormously from exercises that keep you in motion—especially bicycling, swimming, and walking.

Our participants with scoliosis had nothing but praise for yoga as an exercise technique. Practicing yoga with an instructor who selected appropriate positions brought dramatic pain relief and a heightened sense of well-being.

The best scenario for people with scoliosis was to pursue, actively and regularly, a combination of two fitness activities, such as yoga and swimming.

We advise you to try the exercises in chapters 8 and 9, as we feel they can do no harm. But the more important advice for you is contained in chapter 10.

Spondylolisthesis

Many people have never even heard of this condition, which involves an actual slippage of one or more of the vertebrae, most often the lowest lumbar vertebra. The term "slipped disk," as we mentioned earlier, is a misnomer, as disks do not slip. Unfortunately, vertebrae *can* slip, causing great strain on the back muscles, as well as nerve compression and sciatica.

Only ten of the participants in our Back Pain Survey had a diagnosis of spondylolisthesis. Seven of them attributed their improved functioning and their pain relief to exercise, and a few mentioned yoga specifically as the form of exercise they favored. Proper exercise can actually stop the progression of this condition.

If you have spondylolisthesis, you can use the exercises in chapter 8 to strengthen your abdominal muscles, as this is one of the most important remedies. Walking and swimming are the safest fitness activities to include in your regimen.

P A R T
F O U R

Mind-Body Work

> Mental exercises that promote
> stress reduction and relaxation can
> complement any physical exercise
> program.

CHAPTER 12

Yoga

With its traditional emphasis on the integration of spine, mind, and spirit, yoga provides an excellent format for backache relief. In fact, our Back Pain Survey revealed yoga instruction and practice to be among the most successful of all treatment modalities for people who were not incapacitated by their back pain. And those participants who were troubled by osteoarthritis, neck pain, and scoliosis found it particularly effective.

The word *yoga* means "unity" or "harmony." Yoga is a way of healing the body through exercises that combine postures, movements, and breathing techniques.

To the extent that stretching and strengthening your body is helpful—and we believe this beyond a doubt—yoga instruction can be an excellent way to rid yourself of back pain. To the extent that stress contributes to back pain—and *most* of our survey participants felt that it did—yoga instruction can bring significant relief. The yoga philosophy of never forcing or straining, and of moving in a fluid, meditative manner, makes excellent sense for people with back problems. But yoga philosophy also encompasses the harmony of mind, body, and spirit—a concept that is difficult for some back sufferers to grasp, or to take seriously. Although yoga traces its history to the Hindu culture of India, it is not a religion.

This chapter explains the relative values of self-taught yoga, compared to attending yoga classes or seeking individual instruction. It also includes a step-by-step illustrated guide to *modified* yoga positions that are safe for people with back problems.

A few of our Back Pain Survey participants learned yoga entirely on their own, from books and articles. But those who were helped the most got started with professional and personalized instruction. Not all yoga teachers have the experience or the desire to work effectively with people who report a history of back problems. Some of them, however, possess advanced degrees in exercise physiology and may be especially qualified to prescribe exercise. An important determinant of success is the instructor's willingness to modify the therapy to suit your needs.

If yoga instruction is available where you live, we encourage you to drop by the school or studio and speak with an instructor. You may get a chance to see the instructors in action, and determine whether you feel you'll get the kind of intelligent, individual attention that you were hoping to find.

Before we extol yoga any further, however, we must interject a note of caution: Many formal yoga positions are dangerous to attempt during any episode of pain. This is especially true for just-recovering back sufferers.

At least two regular yoga positions could actually cause considerable injury to your back if you tried to perform them while you were in pain, or before you had developed the necessary flexibility. One is the Cobra, which calls for you to lie on your stomach and arch your back by raising your head and chest. The other is the Plow, in which you lie on your back, then raise your straightened legs (ouch!) up and over your head, until you can touch your toes behind your head.

Here's one yoga exercise that you can perform anywhere, as it involves nothing more than deep breathing to help you relax and tone your abdominal muscles:

• Start by taking a deep breath from your abdomen. (Put your fingers on your belly to convince yourself that it—and not just your chest—is expanding.)
• Keep inhaling through your nose for six seconds.
• Hold the air inside your lungs for three seconds.
• Exhale through your mouth for seven seconds. As you do so, let yourself go limp.
• Repeat this series of steps a few times. Five minutes spent in this kind of deep, relaxed breathing can make you feel both invigorated and relaxed. Try it during your peak work hours, and judge the effect for yourself.

The following series of yoga postures constitutes a safe taste of this form of exercise—provided that you are not in pain when you attempt them. Any or all of these can be combined with the stretching and strengthening exercises in chapters 8 and 9 to individualize or vary your daily regimen.

You may find that you want to attempt the Total Body Relaxation exercise twice a day, for the sheer stress relief it brings. As for the other exercises in this section, we suggest that you begin with three repetitions of each. Once you are comfortable with that number, you can increase it by one repetition every other day until you are performing a total of ten repetitions.

TOTAL BODY RELAXATION

It may well take you several minutes to spread the feeling of relaxation throughout your body. There's no need to rush. Just enjoy the sensation of willing your body to relax. It will convince you that you can gain control over physical pain, as well as anxiety, stress, and fear.

Starting position: Lie on your back with a pillow under your knees, legs slightly apart, and arms at your sides.

Steps:
1. Let your body go limp, so that your neck, arms, and legs shift naturally into their most comfortable positions.
2. Think about relaxing your muscles, starting with your feet, ankles, and legs.
3. Concentrate on making the individual muscles and joints relax, working your way up your body to your neck and head.

Note: It may help you to tense some of your muscles slightly, prior to releasing and relaxing them. For example, first make a fist, and then let your hand go limp.

Some people find that doing this exercise in the dark is so relaxing that it actually helps them fall asleep!

SITTING SPINE STRETCH

Reaching over in this sitting posture, you will feel the stretch in your spine all the way down to your coccyx and sitting bones—and on into the hamstring muscles at the backs of your thighs. Please be careful not to push too far.

Starting position: Sit on the floor with your legs fully extended in front of you, your ankles touching each other. *a*

Steps:

1. Raise your arms in front of you to about shoulder height. *b*

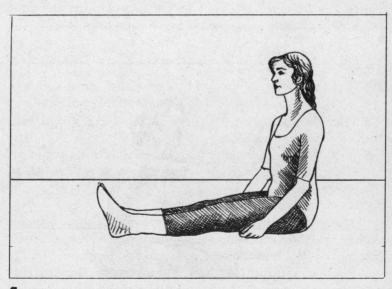

a

b

c

d

2. Slowly lean your upper body as far forward as you can *(c)*, while simultaneously lowering your hands to your knees. *d*
3. When you feel resistance, stop and hold the position for a count of ten.
4. Return to the starting position.

Note: This exercise is definitely not for anyone in pain. We cautioned you against this kind of movement in the note with the Hamstring Stretch in chapter 8. However, you might add it to your regimen after you have progressed beyond the pain-free stage and feel ready for more advanced stretching.

FLEXIBILITY TWIST

Let your arms lead your upper body from side to side, to put your back muscles through gentle paces.

Starting position: Stand with your feet close together, arms at your sides. *a*

Steps:

1. Raise your arms to shoulder level in front of you, and touch your hands together. *b*

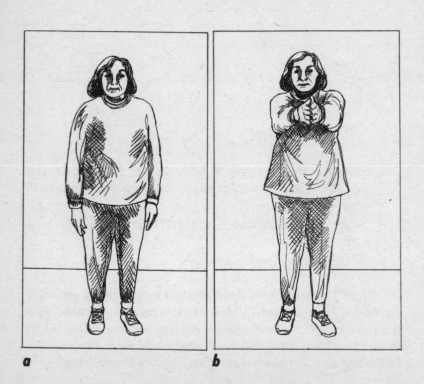

a   *b*

2. Slowly turn your upper body to the left. **c**

3. When you meet resistance, hold the stretch for ten seconds. (If you find it tough to keep your balance as you twist your upper body with your feet close together, widen your stance a bit.)

4. Return to the starting position, dropping your arms and relaxing for a few seconds.

5. Repeat steps 1–4, turning to the right this time. **d**

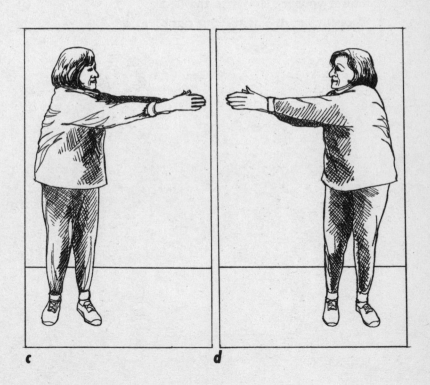

c   d

MODIFIED LOCUST

A strategically placed pillow under your abdomen keeps you from arching your back as you raise your legs in this modified locust position.

Starting position: Lie facedown, arms at your sides, with a pillow tucked under your abdomen for lower back support.

Steps:
1. Keeping your knee locked, raise your left leg about a foot off the floor. *a*
2. Hold your leg in this position for a count of six.
3. Lower your leg slowly to the floor.
4. Repeat steps 1–3 with your right leg. *b*

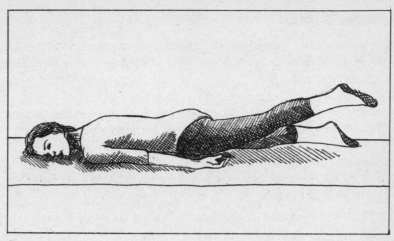

a

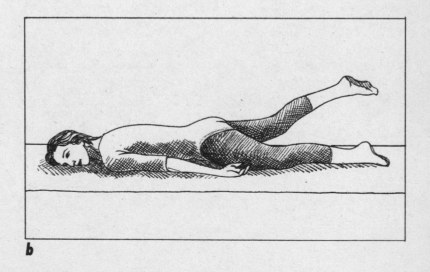

b

CHAPTER 13

Meditation, Imagery, and More

Although we don't believe that stress necessarily causes back pain, there is no doubt that incapacitating back pain causes stress. And stress, in turn, can readily magnify the pain you feel.

Certain kinds of back pain, according to reports from the participants in our Back Pain Survey, seem more susceptible to aggravation by stress than others. Neck pain, for example, tends to worsen noticeably in times of increased stress. More than 80 percent of survey participants who suffered from neck pain said their pain grew worse whenever they were under a lot of stress. A possible explanation is that stress and tension make you hunch or stiffen your shoulders, and this strain makes itself felt in the muscles of the neck.

If you have been making the rounds, seeing different practitioners over a long period of time, you may have heard the term "stress" used as though it were a diagnosis. When no obvious cause can be found for your pain, someone is bound to suggest that you are suffering from stress. Implicit in this suggestion are several negative messages, including the following:

"There's nothing really wrong with you."

"You've let stress get the upper hand in your life, and now you're paying the price."

"I can't do a thing to help you."

If stress is an element in your pain cycle, you deserve some sympathy, not blame. Doctors who understand the connection between pain and stress can help their patients greatly by explaining it—and by encouraging them to learn a few simple stress-reduction techniques that can serve as pain-blockers.

By "stress reduction" we mean reducing the negative effects of stress—the sensation that your heart is racing away, the knots in your stomach, the rapid breathing, the rising panic, the feeling of spasm in your back or neck. Whether or not you can actually reduce the stress in your life is another matter entirely. The most stressful events or situations may simply be beyond your power to control. Nevertheless, if you can control your reactions to them, you've accomplished a great deal.

Stress-reduction techniques—including deep breathing, visualization, and meditation—can be of great use in helping you feel calmer, reducing your pain, and preparing you for exercise. This chapter explains how to practice a few stress-reduction techniques to best advantage. Think of them as mental exercises, easy and pleasant to perform.

The truth is, any technique that provides a break from

stressful activities may turn out to help your back. Even something as simple as taking a "stretch break" every hour on the hour can be of tremendous benefit. Although we urge you to experiment with the proven effective strategies of deep breathing, meditation, visualization (or imagery), and progressive relaxation, we know of many people who can get their stress *and* pain levels down by taking a walk for twenty minutes.

Our survey participants, as a group, came up with no clear consensus on a favorite method, but individuals expressed strong preferences. Many vendors of relaxation tapes and stress-reduction gadgets may try to convince you that their approach is the best, but you are the best judge of what technique appeals to you most, and therefore what is most likely to work for you.

Practitioners of yoga know that deep breathing has tremendous powers of relaxation. Just as smiling can sometimes lift your spirits, breathing slowly and deeply can make your whole body feel calmer. Deep breathing figures in virtually every stress-reduction technique, so we'll begin with this basic approach.

Deep Breathing

Ordinarily, you don't have to think about breathing. Your body does it automatically. But when the automatic response is panting in response to some stress perceived as a threat, you can make yourself feel better by taking conscious control of the breathing process. Try it. Inhale through your nose for six seconds; hold your breath for one second; exhale through your mouth for seven seconds. Keep your eyes closed. Do you feel yourself getting a bit more relaxed with each exhalation?

Try to become conscious of the breath filling and leaving your lungs. Let your chest expand fully. Relax your shoulders as you inhale, since raising your shoulders does not help to fill the lungs with air. Concentrate instead on widening the girth of your chest, as though it were a balloon being inflated. Put your hand on your abdomen, to feel how it, too, is expanding, as your diaphragm drops down to increase the influx of air into your body.

Stay relaxed as you hold the air in for just a moment or two, and then slowly begin to let it out through your mouth. Exhale so fully that you actually squeeze the air out of your lungs by contracting your chest. Then picture physical tension leaving your body with the expelled breath.

Once you become accustomed to deep breathing, knowing that you can rely on it as an instant aid to relaxation, you may find that you use it periodically throughout the day, any time something unpleasant jars you. You may also use deep breathing at night as a way to relax before falling asleep, and again in the morning, to prepare yourself to meet the day.

Meditation

Heart specialists such as Dr. Herbert Benson of Harvard Medical School and Dr. Dean Ornish of the Preventive Medicine Research Institute in Sausalito, California, have made meditation a medical treatment. Back sufferers benefit from its stress-reducing effects, too. It was Dr. Benson who gave the name "relaxation response" to the altered state of well-being brought on by meditation. The relaxation response is a physiological state of deep rest while wide awake. It is said to be even more restful and restorative than sleep, because the profound relaxation leaves a lingering sense of calm refreshment. Indeed, a twenty-minute period of meditation may exert a positive effect on an entire day.

Many approaches to meditation can be used to good advantage, but we particularly like Dr. Benson's approach.

The basic outline here is drawn from his book called *Your Maximum Mind*:

• Choose a word or a phrase that will serve as your focus for the meditation exercise. You may choose a pleasant thought, such as "peace," or the opening words of a prayer, or even a soothing sound that has no particular meaning.

• Sit in a comfortable position. Close your eyes. Relax your muscles.

• Breathe deeply and, with each exhalation, repeat to yourself your focus word or phrase.

• Also use the repetition of your focus word to push away worries or extraneous thoughts that may come into your mind while you are meditating.

• Continue your focused breathing and repetition for ten to twenty minutes.

It sounds awfully simple, doesn't it? But please don't let the simplicity fool you into thinking that there's nothing much to it. Practice brings total concentration, and total concentration breeds relaxation that works to reduce stress and improve the quality of your life.

If possible, choose a special place for meditation. You might even keep a few items there—photos or memorabilia—that evoke positive feelings. Also try to choose a special time of day when you are least likely to be interrupted. Avoid distractions by taking your phone off the hook, or by asking family and friends not to call you at this time.

Visualization (Imagery)

The power of positive thinking makes it possible for you to soothe yourself with beautiful images that you conjure up and elaborate upon in your mind. These could be landscapes, works of art, or wonderful moments in your life. The idea of visualization is to create a safe haven in your mind where you can go to escape from pain or anxiety.

If this sounds farfetched, try to remember a time when you had the opposite experience—when thinking of a sad event left you feeling depressed, or when planning what you would say in an argument got you so worked up you could barely sit still. The brain and body seem to make little distinction between actual images and imagined ones. This is why you can create the sensation of peaceful relaxation by picturing an idyllic scene where you lie on warm sand, smelling the salt air of the ocean, and hearing the waves pounding on the shore.

Another positive image is to picture a soft glove or gentle hand touching the painful areas of your body with warmth and healing power.

Progressive Relaxation

Relaxing your body inch by inch, one small part at a time, gets you progressively relaxed until you reach the critical threshold where stress-reduction occurs.

Progressive Relaxation resembles the Total Body Relaxation described in chapter 12. The idea here is to get relaxed by first tensing the muscles and then releasing them, proceeding in an orderly fashion from one end of the body to the other. It doesn't really matter whether you go from head to toe or begin at your feet and work up.

Here is a plan of action:

- Lie in a comfortable position. Close your eyes.
- Move your body, wriggling your arms and legs, just to settle yourself comfortably.
- Lie still and breathe deeply for a few minutes.

- If you are starting from your head, make some very exaggerated movements with your face—sneer, grin, frown, yawn, raise your eyebrows and then knit them together in a scowl. Then let your face relax.
- Tense your neck by lifting your head, then lie back.
- One at a time, tighten each arm and raise it, then let it go limp at your side.
- Clench each fist, then let your hands relax.
- Tighten your abdomen and your buttocks, and let them go.
- Spread tension along the length of one leg by straightening the knee and lifting the leg slightly. Then relax that leg and let it slump back into place. Do the same with your other leg.
- Point your toes and arch your foot as sharply as you can, then let it flop free. Do the same with your other foot.
- Lie still and breathe deeply.

You may find that you want to experiment with the different approaches, or mix and match them. What's to stop you, for example, from using a favorite image as your meditation focus?

As you become adept at incorporating these stress-reduction techniques into your daily routines, people may ask you why you're smiling.

P A R T
F I V E

Lifestyle Changes

> *Small adjustments in performing everyday activities count among the most important steps toward achieving freedom from back pain.*

CHAPTER 14

Positioning Yourself

The chair you sit in, the mattress you sleep on, the posture you assume while sitting or standing—all these factors collectively influence the amount of back pain you suffer. Our Back Pain Survey participants found that they could increase their comfort throughout the day by choosing the best positions for all activities—and that includes inactivity, too.

The idea of this careful, close scrutiny may seem daunting at first. If you have to police yourself all the time, how can you ever relax and enjoy life? You can, because once you get the basic idea of keeping your back in a relaxed yet correct posture, you will begin to feel the benefits of doing so. You'll have less pain, and be able to do more. As practice becomes habit, you won't have to think continually about how you're standing or holding your head. By then, all these good measures will have become second nature to you.

In this chapter, we offer numerous suggestions that we hope will help you move through the day with the greatest of ease. Let's start first thing in the morning, with the moment you get out of bed.

Getting Out of Bed

Many people who wouldn't attempt a sit-up on a bet actually try to pull themselves out of bed with their abdominal muscles. We want you to exercise, of course, but only when you're warmed up and ready. Getting out of bed need not be an exercise challenge.

To make the process easy on yourself, ease your way over to the side of the bed, so that you are lying on your side with your knees bent, facing the edge. If you choose to lie on your left side, then you can place your right palm on the mattress next to your left shoulder. In one fluid motion, push down with your right palm and swing yourself upright, taking your legs off the bed and setting your feet on the floor. Now, keeping your back straight, stand up. If you like, you can use both hands to push yourself to a standing position.

Washing Up

When you brush your teeth or wash your face at the bathroom sink, you needn't stand at attention. Try keeping your back straight and bending your knees just a bit. This precaution takes the strain off your hamstrings when you lean forward to splash water on your face.

Standing

Try to pay constant attention to your posture. Keep your abdomen, buttocks, and chin tucked in, and the rest of your body will tend to follow suit and line up properly. Your abdominal muscles, which hold in your gut, give the all-important support to your lower back when they are in this tucked-in position. Tucking in your buttocks, which naturally fits with pulling in your abdominals, helps normalize the S-shaped curve in your lower back, and thereby ease pain. Tucking in your chin helps you maintain the proper curve in your neck, easing the strain on that part of your spine.

We simply can't overemphasize the importance of good posture as a way to hasten recovery from acute episodes of low-back pain, and to prevent future episodes from occurring.

Good posture does not require you to distribute your weight evenly on both legs at all times. If you need to stand in one place for a spell, as in a ticket line or a checkout line, for example, try shifting your weight from one foot to the other every few minutes. In other situations where you need to be on your feet for extended periods, the best way to pass the time may be to walk about instead of standing rooted to the spot.

Sitting

More important than the chair you sit in is the time you spend sitting. Since sitting offers more opportunity for back aggravation than either standing or lying down, you may need to limit your sitting time. Whenever possible, break up long sits by getting up to stretch. You can do this most easily at home, of course, but try to stretch at work, too. If you're driving on a long car trip, let yourself stop frequently for stretch breaks. On

179

long plane flights, too, look for times when you can move about in the aisles, and seize the opportunity.

Good sitting posture means planting yourself firmly on your bottom, with your abdominals pulled in to help keep your lower back straight. Common sitting habits that could cause you grief include slouching back in your chair, leaning too far forward, and crossing your legs. Instead, try resting your feet on a footstool, as a way to help you sit tall and keep pressure off the backs of your thighs. (At work, some of our survey participants said they liked to open a bottom desk drawer and prop their feet on it while typing, writing, or talking on the telephone.)

Your chair owes you a firm support, both under your bottom and behind your back. If your chair isn't up to the task, you can correct it with a firm bottom support or a back-support cushion, or both, so as to avoid any strain or discomfort. Many varieties of firm chair pads and backrests, including some models that combine both types of support, are sold in stores and by mail order. Try to experiment to find one that feels right for you—and is priced right, too.

If you love to attend outdoor concerts or sporting events where you're expected to sit on backless bleachers, you may want to invest in a stadium chair—a padded seat and back support that clamps right onto the bleachers.*

Holding Your Own

In general, we found that our survey participants did best when they held their postures by the strength of their own muscles, instead of relying on back braces and cervical collars. Although these devices seem designed to be helpful, they can actually keep you from developing the good habit of good

*Bleachers = benches

posture. What's more, immobilizing any part of your body is almost always a poor alternative to exercising it gently and moving it correctly.

Talking on the Telephone

You can easily talk yourself into a pain in the neck with a telephone. The temptation to free your hands by cradling the phone between your shoulder and your ear (and leaving it there indefinitely) is almost irresistible. Phone rests that encourage this behavior were definitely *not* designed for people who suffer from neck or back pain. If you must have your hands free while you carry on telephone conversations, by all means invest in a speakerphone or a headset that gives you mobility without muscle strain.

Working

Depending on the demands your job makes on your back, you may find that you need to make some adjustments at your workplace. A few offices and industries now offer on-the-job education programs aimed specifically at showing employees how to avoid back injuries. We applaud these efforts, and expect to see more of them.

If you have a regular office job, it may be possible for you to accomplish the same amount of work in a new position. Several of our survey participants, in fact, reported that they could work more effectively on their feet. A few of them were allowed to add height to their desks by setting up a crate or lectern on the desk surface, which allowed them to do their deskwork standing up.

If your job calls for a lot of typing into a computer, try to arrange your workstation so that you can comfortably read what you need to type. Copy holders that attach to the side of the computer monitor, at eye level, can help you avoid neck and back strain.

Taking Breaks

Even if you maintain ideal posture sitting and standing, you can go yourself one better by taking a few respites, of just five to ten minutes each, every day. During these breaks, try to put yourself in a completely different position. One of the most popular among our survey participants was lying on the floor with feet and calves propped up on a sofa or chair, for ten minutes at a time.

The strain-easing posture can also prove to be a break from stress if you spend this time engaged in deep breathing.

Reading and Watching Television

Try to catch up on your reading *before* bedtime, so you can hold a book at a comfortable eye level on a table or desk. If you like to sit in a special armchair that won't tuck under a table, then pile some pillows in your lap to help support the book, rather than tilting your neck down and straining to see it.

If you regularly read in bed by placing a couple of pillows under your head to help you see the book or magazine propped on your abdomen, you have probably noticed that this position soon produces neck strain or eyestrain or both. And if you hold your reading material over your head while you're lying down, you strain your shoulders, neck, and back. Indeed, most of our survey participants reported, with some remorse, that reading in bed was one pastime they had to learn to live without. They substituted reading just before retiring—sitting up in a good chair, or standing, with the book propped up on a box atop a kitchen counter.

Television viewing, too, is best done from a chair—if you want to keep your neck happy. But since you don't have to hold the television(!), it's easier to watch TV while lying down than to read in that position. Try to assume a position that would be comfortable for sleeping, such as lying on your side, with a pillow under your head and neck.

Driving

You'll probably find that sitting in a car can be made more manageable with a back support of some kind. Our survey participants particularly liked car seats or back cushions that aligned their backs at a right angle to their thighs, which provided maximum driving comfort.

Other positioning strategies that help are pulling the driver's seat as close as possible to the steering wheel. This closeness will enable you to sit with your knees slightly elevated, and to diminish the strain that often comes from overreaching to reach the wheel. You can also make use of the built-in armrest on the left-hand door for added arm support. And if you drive a car with bucket seats, you may have a divider or equipment box at your right that doubles as a second armrest.

When you get in or out of a car, try to eliminate awkward leg stretches and body twists. For example, on entering the vehicle, open the door and then turn your back to the seat, so you can sit straight down. Then bring in your legs, using your abdominal muscles for support, and turn to face forward. Similarly, when getting out of the car, move yourself to the very edge of the seat, turn sideways, and then put your feet on the ground and stand up.

Getting into Bed

Back up to your bed until you can feel it with the backs of your legs, so you won't be tempted to twist or turn around to see where you're going. Pull in your abdominal muscles to keep your back straight, and sit down. Then, reversing the fluid motion that got you out of bed this morning, and using your arms and hands to help support and guide your body, lie down on your side as you swing your legs onto the bed.

Now that you're in bed, and given the fact that you spend one-third of your life in it, how happy are you with your mattress? Most people with back pain find that even a firm mattress feels better if it's positioned on top of a three-quarter-inch-thick plywood bedboard. On the road, many of our survey participants carry folding bedboards that can fit into a suitcase, just in case the bed at the hotel or motel where they're heading doesn't stack up to the comfort of their own beds.

Positions for Lovemaking

Our survey participants spoke candidly about positions that enabled them to make love without making trouble for their backs. The most frequently recommended position called for both partners to lie on their sides, with knees bent, facing each other. Lying front to back, nested like spoons, with the man behind the woman, is another safe position for sexual intercourse. If you are comfortable lying on your back with your knees elevated—and if your partner is strong enough to keep most of his or her weight off you—then this modified missionary position is also a safe one.

We heard the three suggestions listed above repeatedly from survey participants who said they had an active sex life despite back pain. Others declined to mention specific positions, but stressed the importance of maintaining open communication with one's partner—and openness to sexual pleasures other than intercourse.

Sleeping

Most people with low-back pain find that the most comfortable way to sleep is on one's side, in a modified fetal position. Try it, keeping your pillow tucked under your head and neck only, and not under your shoulders. A relatively flat pillow seems to work better than a very fluffy one, because it won't raise your head so high as to strain your neck. To further reduce any strain on your spine, try putting a thin pillow between your knees.

If you have neck pain, you may find that your most comfortable sleep position is on your back, with one pillow under your head and neck, and another one or two pillows propped under your knees, to keep your back from arching.

Sleeping on the stomach (a position many people love) is, sad to say, the toughest on the back. If you cannot break this habit, no matter how hard you try, then at least try to do without a pillow under your head. Put the pillow under your tummy instead—to minimize the arching of your back.

CHAPTER 15

Accomplishing Tasks

Doing what needs to be done—that's just what people with back pain too often find they can't do. Or they're afraid to do those things, for fear of creating more back trouble. Yet a few simple precautions can help anyone perform everyday activities without pain or risk of injury, and many inventive gadgets can make any number of jobs easier to tackle. These kinds of moment-to-moment strategies, many of them drawn from our Back Pain Survey participants' experiences, add up to a back-friendly lifestyle.

In addition to our survey results on the importance of approaching tasks in ways that make good back sense, medical doctors have also endorsed such measures. The prestigious

Quebec Task Force, a group of doctors reviewing back treatments, found that the two most important means of improving back fitness are exercise and learning how to safeguard your back as you go about doing what you have to do—and doing what you love to do—at work, at home, and on the road.

This chapter takes the back into account while analyzing everyday activities from bathing to housework and yard work. It describes ways of doing chores, as well as techniques for lifting and carrying that can help you avoid painful backache.

Lifting

Every time you pick up an object from the floor, whether it's a pin or a bag of groceries, you have the opportunity to hurt your back—or help it. The participants in our Back Pain Survey waxed eloquent on the topic of lifting. In fact, they were downright adamant about bending at the knees—not at the waist—to pick up *anything*, whether it's as light as a tissue or as heavy as a potted plant. Bending at the knees allows you to keep your back straight as you stoop, and to take the weight of whatever you're lifting with your legs instead of your back.

If you find it difficult to squat in this fashion, or to stand up again after you do, you can try placing a chair or stepladder near you for support.

To further minimize any risk of injury, hold the item you're lifting close to your body. This is especially important with heavy items. And speaking of heavy items, always ask yourself first if you really need to lift them. Maybe you can slide them to their destination, or enlist someone else's aid.

Another approach to heavy lifting, although it sounds awkward, is to turn your back to the object and extend your arms *behind* you. When in doubt, ask for help.

Carrying

Less is preferable to more in this department. Try to lighten the load of your shoulder bag, pocketbook, or briefcase. You might even consider using a backpack instead. Although it looks less elegant, it distributes weight more evenly and often proves to be the most comfortable way to transport everyday items.

When you buy your groceries, pack them in two bags of equal weight, with carrying handles. It is much easier to carry groceries with your arms at your sides than to clutch bags to your chest or balance them on your hips. Lifting your arms while holding heavy packages puts more strain on the back, participants say. Better yet, consider buying a wheeled shopping cart for bringing home large orders—or see if your supermarket will deliver them.

Child Care

The least stressful way to carry an infant a long distance is on your back in a carrier. The hip carry, in comparison, caused pain for most of our survey participants who had young children.

If your baby and your back act up at the same time, try holding or comforting your child while you kneel at his or her level—or while both of you are lying down. Another favorite position is to sit in a rocking chair while feeding or lulling an infant to sleep.

Be advised that most of the furniture designed for babies —bassinets, playpens, even cribs—can play havoc with a parent's back. They all involve leaning at awkward angles, whether you are putting your child in them or taking him out. If your child is sleeping in a crib, drop the collapsible side before you reach in, so you can bend at your knees instead of leaning over the bars. Take the same approach to the child's playpen.

Some of our participants replaced the bassinet with a large wicker laundry basket, lined with soft blankets and set on the floor.

A notable exception in this back-straining category is the adjustable changing table, which can be raised to the right height for your back, allowing you to diaper and dress your baby in comfort.

Making Your Bed

As with any job that requires you to lower yourself, bend at your knees instead of at your waist. You can stay in a kneeling position as you work your way around the bed. Go slowly, and reposition yourself as often as necessary to avoid overstretching your back.

Unless your bed rolls easily, you'll do best to keep it at least a foot away from the wall, so that you can smooth the sheets and blankets from all sides with equal effort.

If you're in pain, let yourself off the hook and don't bother making the bed at all.

Getting Organized

Standing on tiptoe and reaching to retrieve boxes and jars from high shelves can aggravate back pain. Try to save yourself a certain amount of reaching high overhead and stooping to the floor by organizing your cupboards and closets with your back in mind. For example, instead of parking your shoes on the closet floor, hang them in a shoebag on the door.

In any storage area, try to put the things you use most

often at the most convenient height. For getting to those infrequently used items that live on high shelves, keep a sturdy stepladder handy.

Washing Dishes

Leaning over the sink to wash dishes may cause problems for your back. Automatic dishwashers don't necessarily solve these problems, since loading and unloading them may make even more demands on your back than washing the old-fashioned way.

You can ease the reach across to the faucets by turning sideways. It's usually easier to reach sideways than forward. Once the water is running, stand close to the sink for minimal strain. Belly up to it, in fact, and use a waterproof apron to keep yourself dry.

As you wash individual items, lift them out of the sink and hold them close, too. Shift your weight from one foot to the other on long stints. Or simply place one foot on a footstool to help keep your back relaxed. And do break up the task by letting pots and pans soak awhile. You can always go back to them later.

Vacuuming

Judging from comments offered by our survey participants, the people who suffer the most back pain from vacuuming are those who strive for perfection in this chore. The best advice seems to be to lower your standards a bit, and don't feel guilty about leaving some dust if that means sparing your back.

Maneuver the machine with one hand, and leave the other at your side. Fifteen minutes at a time makes a reasonable round of vacuuming. But by all means stop before that if you feel the fatigue in your back.

Please don't vacuum when you're in pain, no matter who is coming to dinner.

If you're in the market for a new vacuum cleaner, look for one that you can push with minimal exertion.

Other Household Chores

For mopping, choose a sponge mop that you can wring out from the far end of the handle, with no leaning over. These are readily available in supermarkets and hardware stores. You may find that you can stand up straighter if you hold the mop with one hand instead of two.

Whenever and wherever possible, extend your reach with long-handled gadgets that do the reaching for you, and enable you to keep your own arms and hands close to your sides. Shops and mail-order catalogs carry specially made items that will help you pick items from shelves or off the floor, scrub the bathtub without stretching across it, and wash windows from a safe vantage point. There's even a dustpan and brush with handles long enough to let you collect your sweepings while standing tall.

There are a number of organizations in the UK which supply equipment and back-friendly house cleaning tools for those who have difficulty in using 'ordinary' equivalents. A list of names and addresses, including companies that offer a mail order service, is given under 'Helpful Addresses' on page 201.

Painting

If you feel up to tackling a big chore like this one, good for you! Make it a safe-back activity by standing as close as you possibly can to whatever you're painting. This will allow you to strike the best posture and keep your arms close to your body for minimal back strain. Also try to position yourself so that you need not raise your arms higher than your chest or lower than past your waist.

Choose your weapon with an eye to getting the job done quickly and easily. Rollers work best because they are light and efficient. Paintbrushes take longer, and paint guns, though fast, are heavy to hold for any appreciable time.

Pace yourself, as you would on any big project. Remember that it makes no sense to finish the job the day you start it—if doing so threatens to finish you.

If you insist on painting the ceilings yourself, protect your neck by looking down frequently. Treat yourself to a one-minute break every five minutes and a ten-minute break every half hour. By all means, do the neck and shoulder exercises described in chapter 9.

Raking Leaves

Autumn leaves, like winter snows, probably cause several million Americans to seek professional treatment for back pain every year. Please keep yourself out of these grim statistics by approaching seasonal chores with extra caution.

The danger lies in excessive forward leaning and arm extension. These awkward, unsupported positions leave your back vulnerable to injury.

When you rake, keep your knees in the unlocked, or slightly bent, position. When it's time to pick up the leaves you've raked into piles, kneel or squat rather than stooping. To carry bags of leaves safely, take two small bags of equal weight at a time, with your arms at your sides. Holding a large bag out in front of your body can readily harm your back.

Many special tools can make this job easier, including a rake with a bend in the handle that allows you to stand up straighter as you work, shifting a greater share of the effort from your back to your arms. Another back-saver is a large-wheeled garden cart (not a wheelbarrow) that lets you wheel your leaves to the curb.

Shoveling Snow

Do dress yourself in layers before tackling this task, so you can keep your back warm throughout, but shed clothing as the effort of shoveling heats your body.

When hefting the shovel, remember to bend your legs and not your back. Keep the shovel as close to your body as you can, and keep the size of each shovelful modest. Wet snow makes for heavy lifting.

Gardening

Although it is theoretically possible to work in your garden without bending at the waist or working your back into a state of fatigue, few people do. They'd just as soon try to keep their hands clean while working the soil. The effort seems to come between them and the basic joy of gardening. A solution offered by one of our survey participants was to lie down on her side to pull weeds.

When people ask you what gifts you'd like for your birthday or other occasion, give them the names of garden tools designed for people with back problems. These include tongs that scoop up piles of leaves and weeds, long-handled tools, lightweight hoses on retractable reels, and connectors that allow easy access to hard-to-reach outdoor spigots.

CHAPTER 16

Enjoying Life

As you stretch and strengthen your back with the helpful exercises you've learned, you will grow increasingly more flexible and resistant to future back injury. This is a great gift that you are giving yourself—one that will enable you to enjoy life more fully.

When we reviewed the comments of survey participants who had resolved years or even decades of chronic back pain, we noticed another "gift" of theirs. It was nothing as tangible as an exercise program or a set of strategies for completing chores. It was their attitude.

They had promised themselves that they would get well. They had made up their minds to put an end to back pain.

And they had put themselves in charge of that task, giving it top priority in their lives. They had stopped asking "Why me?" They had come to accept their back problem, and that acceptance was the key to finding a solution.

Realizing that they knew more about their own bodies than anyone else possibly could, they listened to the experts without awe. They sought professional care when they needed to, but they did not expect any practitioner to have "the answer" or to "cure" them. They acted as partners in their treatment. Even though they were suffering, they did not see themselves as helpless victims waiting to be rescued by someone else.

Exercise can help you develop this attitude of mastery. Exercise is a powerful, effective treatment that you dispense to yourself on a daily basis. In a relatively short time, you can see it working as promised, building your body and your confidence at the same time.

As you improve your ability to enjoy life by treating your body with exercise, you will be disproving some long-standing myths about back pain. Maybe you've heard some of these myths, or believed in them yourself:

• *Back pain is inevitable. It's just the price we pay for walking upright.* Pain is not the natural condition of the body. If anything, back pain results from not walking upright enough. Although back pain is extremely common in the United States, where it affects an estimated 80 percent of all adults, statistics from other countries indicate a much lower incidence. Back pain, therefore, is not an essential part of the human condition, but a reflection of lifestyle trends. We in the United States have adopted an excessively sedentary lifestyle. But that can be changed at will. Exercise, coupled with attention to posture and care in performing daily tasks, will convince your body that there is nothing inevitable about back pain.

- *Back pain is a normal aspect of aging.* Again, pain is neither natural nor normal. Aging does not hurt, unless it is accompanied by illness or neglect of one's health. Analyses of national medical records show that back pain is *not* correlated with advanced age. In fact, the reverse is true: The vast majority of backache sufferers are younger than forty-five. As you grow older, treating your body well, you have every reason to expect that your back pain will continue to diminish until it disappears altogether.

- *There's nothing really wrong with you.* Even if nothing shows up on the X rays or other diagnostic tests, even if the doctor cannot imagine why you are in pain, there *is* something really wrong with you if you are in pain.

- *Any exercise program will help banish back pain.* This is only half true. You know, if you've tried exercise before, that not all routines work for all people. Some noninjurious exercise is better than no exercise, but an individually prescribed program, or the tailored program you have now assembled from the ingredients offered here, can do much more for you than can an "off-the-rack" exercise regimen. (Indeed, we remind you that strenuous, arching forms of exercise can wreck backs.)

- *Back practitioners routinely offer exercise advice, but back sufferers are too lazy to follow it.* You know from your own experience just how much exercise advice you were offered. Maybe it was an encouraging word, with a few specific suggestions, but more likely you came to the exercise conclusion yourself. You've turned to this book for detailed instructions about assembling and implementing an exercise program. And now you're going to stick to that program because you want to improve your own condition. You are taking action, and you will succeed.

Many of the participants in our Back Pain Survey expressed the opinion that their *approach* to back exercise—and by that they meant their attitude and preparation for exercise —was at least as important as the mechanical components of the exercise therapy itself. Here are some points to remember as you implement your exercise program over the coming weeks:

• Exercise therapy is more beneficial for your back than anything you can put into or onto your body.

• Although your exercise movements may be slow and gradual now, they will result in dramatic improvements over time. You can expect small but noticeable gains within a few weeks.

• If exercise is something you've never looked forward to before, open your mind to enjoying it now. The time you spend exercising truly is quality time.

As you become used to exercising, you may wonder how you ever got along without it. When you miss a few days of walking or swimming or cycling, you'll miss the relaxation and clear thinking that those activities convey. You'll miss the reassuring physical sensation of tiredness followed by renewed energy. These are the positive additions to your life that exercise has brought. You will be eager to get back to exercising to experience again these pleasant feelings. Exercise, which you once may have viewed as a duty, is now a delight for you—an indulgence of body and mind that you enjoy thoroughly.

To add to your enjoyment of exercise and your new feeling of vitality, try some of the following physical rewards as treats for your body:

• *Massage.* Like exercise, massage offers you another drug-free muscle relaxant that will help your muscles unwind. You can perform self-massage on some areas of your body, but you will probably get the most pleasure out of a full-body massage from a professional—or even from a willing partner. You may need to tell your inexperienced masseur to use a light oil and a fairly light touch, so as to avoid putting too much pressure on your lower back. Also tell your partner to concentrate on your legs, back, and neck, massaging toward the heart, and using either a long, gliding motion with the palms, or a circular motion with the fingertips and palms.

• *Good food.* Feeding your body well is part of pampering yourself. Try to eat more fruits, vegetables, and whole grains, and to cut down on junk foods, processed foods, fats, caffeine, sugar, and alcohol. Also, avoid constipation (a real hardship for back sufferers) by drinking enough water and including generous portions of fiber in your diet. You may notice a positive change in the appearance of your body, brought on by your commitment to exercise and good posture. Taking care to eat only good foods will help you keep your weight in the ideal range for your height, so that you look even better.

• *Sleep.* Promise yourself the amount of sleep you need to feel comfortable and to maintain good spirits and good posture throughout the day. Try not to think of time spent sleeping as lost or wasted. It isn't. It's crucial time spent restoring your mental and physical energy.

• *Hydrotherapy.* Turn your tub into a relaxing hydrotherapy center where you can enjoy luxurious warm baths. You may want to purchase a waterproof pillow or a mat that covers the full length of your tub. A less expensive alternative is to pad the tub bottom with a thick bath mat, and roll a towel into a neck support or a lumbar support. Our survey participants consider twenty minutes the ideal length for a bath, as longer can make you feel tired. They also prefer warm water to hot, since very hot water can sometimes put muscles in spasm. Experiment to find the most comfortable position. A safe one is to lean your back against one end of the tub, and bend your knees so you can keep your feet flat on the bottom of the tub. If you feel stiff after maintaining one position for several minutes, prop your feet on the sides of the tub for a change. You can even execute a few exercises in the tub, such as shoulder shrugs and knee-to-chest stretches.

• *Join a health club.* Although you can perform all your exercises perfectly well right at home, you may still benefit from joining a local health club. If, for example, the club has a swimming pool and a whirlpool that you can use, these facilities may be worth the price of membership. You can take advantage of the swimming pool for aerobic fitness, and the whirlpool for relaxation and stress reduction. Membership in a health club also puts you in touch with other people who are trying to keep their bodies in the best possible shape, just as you are.

You are about to join the ranks of back sufferers who have beaten the rap—who have endured the pain and gotten past it. You have decided what you need to do to get well, and you are putting that plan into effect right now.

We salute you in your efforts.

HELPFUL
ADDRESSES

The following list of addresses includes some self-help organizations for those in the UK who suffer from back pain, as well as a number of complementary and alternative practitioners' associations from whom you can get a list of registered therapists in your area. This list also contains some Internet sites where it is possible to view and in some cases purchase back-care products online, a potential boon if you do not live near a specialist shop or if your local shop stocks only a limited range of goods. Many house and garden companies, DIY centres and some Internet sites offer useful implements like E-Z Reach long-handled grippers or window washers and long-reach gardening tools.

Arthritis and Rheumatism Council
    17 Cleland Park South, Bangor, Country Down, Northern Ireland BT20 3EW. Tel: 01247 463109
The Back Shop
    24 New Cavendish Street, London W1M 7LH. Tel: 0171 935 9148
Backsaver.com
    Internet: www.backsaver.com. US-based Internet site with the best chairs available. Plus magnet therapy products, massage equipment, and sound-sleep accessories.
British Institute of Muscularskeletal Medicine
    27 Green Lane, Middlesex, HA6 2PX. Tel: 01923 820110
British Osteopathic Association
    Langham House East, Luton, Bedfordshire LU1 2NA. Tel: 01582 488455. Internet: www.osteopathy.org
The Chartered Society of Physiotherapy
    14 Bedford Row, London WC1R 4ED. Tel: 0171 242 1941
The Chattanooga Group, Inc
    Internet: www.chattanoogagroup.com. A corporate site, but with much helpful information and retail links on hydrocollators and other healthcare equipment.
Disability Net
    Internet: www.disabilitynet.co.uk. UK Internet-based news and information site for those with a disability.
The FeelGood Catalog
    Internet: www.feelgoodcatalog.com. US company and website offering handy tools for ADL functions (activities of daily living)

Intelihealth.com
  Internet: www.intelihealth.com. US-based Internet site with a special section on managing pain and stress and healthy backs. Everything from knee supports to a steam bath or cardiovascular equipment.
National Ankylosing Spondylitis Society
  PO Box 197, Mayfield, East Sussex TN20 6ZL. Tel: 01435 873527. Internet: web.ukonline.co.uk/members/nass/
National Back Pain Association
  16 Elmtree Road, Teddington, Middlesex TW11 8ST. Tel: 0181 977 5474.
National Osteoporosis Society
  PO Box 10, Radstock, Bath BA3 3YB. Tel: 01761 471771. Internet: www.nos.org.uk
Royal Association for Disability and Rehabilitation (RADAR)
  Unit 12, City Forum, 250 City Road, London EC1V 8AF. Tel: 0171 250 3222. Internet: www.radar.org.uk. (Remap, which you can contact through RADAR, designs and makes equipment for disabled people to help them in employment.)
Scoliosis Association UK
  2 Iverbury Court, 325 Latimer Road, London W10 6RA
Scottish Chiropractic Association
  16 Jenny Moores Road, St Boswells, Melrose, Roxburghshire TD6 0AL. Tel: 01835 823645